Realignment

Realignment

The Theory That Changed the Way We Think About American Politics

Theodore Rosenof

ROWMAN & LITTLEFIELD PUBLISHERS, INC.
Lanham • Boulder • New York • Oxford

ROWMAN & LITTLEFIELD PUBLISHERS, INC.

A Member of the Rowman & Littlefield Publishing Group
4501 Forbes Boulevard, Suite 200, Lanham, Maryland 20706
www.rowmanlittlefield.com

PO Box 317
Oxford
OX2 9RU, UK

British Library Cataloguing in Publication Information Available

Library of Congress Cataloging-in-Publication Data

Rosenof, Theodore.
Realignment: the theory that changed the way we think about American
   politics / Theodore Rosenof.
      p. cm.
   Includes bibliographical references and index.
   ISBN 0-7425-3104-X (hardcover: alk. paper) — ISBN 0-7425-3105-8
   (pbk.: alk. paper)
   1. Voting—United States. 2. Elections—United States. 3. Political
   science—United States. I. Title.
JK1967 .R66 2003
324.973'001—dc21   2002153094

Printed in the United States of America

∞ ™ The paper used in this publication meets the minimum requirements of American
National Standard for Information Sciences—Permanence of Paper for Printed Library
Materials, ANSI/NISO Z39.48-1992.

To Josephine Schmitt Rosenof
To the memory of Max Rosenof
To the memory of Hugh Francis Byrnes

Contents

Acknowledgments

I wish to thank the Mercy College Faculty Development Committee for funding major expenses, the Committee on Personnel, Promotion, and Tenure for its approval of a semester sabbatical leave, and my division chair, Ann Grow, for counsel and support. Interlibrary loan specialists Heather Blenkinsopp and Madge Muckenhaupt provided indispensable assistance in obtaining books and articles. Arthur M. Schlesinger, Jr. graciously granted permission to research his father's papers at Harvard's Pusey Library. The Schlesinger, Arthur N. Holcombe, and the portion of the V. O. Key Papers in the Pusey Library are cited courtesy of the Harvard University Archives. The Angus Campbell, Philip Converse, and James Pollock Papers in the Bentley Historical Library are cited with the permission of the University of Michigan Library. I am grateful to the University of Chicago's Regenstein Library archival staff for allowing me to research the newly accessed Harold F. Gosnell Papers, to the archival staff at the University of Connecticut's Dodd Research Center for granting me access to the unprocessed Samuel Lubell Papers, and to the archival staff of Wesleyan University's Olin Library for making available the newly opened E. E. Schattschneider Papers. (I note that the Schattschneider Papers were reorganized following my research and hence my references are to an earlier format.) A grant from the John F. Kennedy Library Foundation facilitated research in the V. O. Key collection at the John F. Kennedy Library; Alan Lawson kindly wrote to the Foundation on my behalf. The archival staff of the Franklin D. Roosevelt Library, as always, aided me efficiently and courteously. I am grateful to history editor Mary Carpenter, editorial assistant Laura Roberts, production editor Lori Pierelli, and the editorial committee of Rowman & Littlefield for considering, accepting, and preparing

my manuscript for publication and to two anonymous readers for assessments and helpful suggestions. My wife Pat, son Chuck, and daughter Liza
provided essential tolerance and support. Pat further assisted during research in the V. O. Key collection at the Pusey Library, and Liza came to
my rescue in all matters relating to computer function and malfunction.

Introduction

When political science emerged as an academic discipline in the late nineteenth century, its emphasis was on the formal institutions, structures, and organizations of government and politics. Hence, early political scientists wrote about the nature and framework of the American constitutional system of government, dwelling on the factual makeup of the different branches of government and their constitutional relationships with one another. In American politics, the key institution was the political party, and stress was likewise placed on its organizational makeup and (a subject of much attention a century ago) the central role of "bosses" and the "spoils system" in the party structure. Beginning in the 1920s, this traditional institutional emphasis underwent modification. To be sure, the nature of institutions remained a basic and integral part of the study of American government and politics. But a clear shift in emphasis was underway, and what became known as the "behavioral" approach to government and politics emerged. In the realm of politics this new emphasis focused on electoral patterns and voting behavior. This approach evidenced a growing concern with process and movement, stressed dynamics over stasis, relied upon quantifiably verifiable generalizations, and in time culminated in realignment theory.

Further, insofar as elections were traditionally viewed as discrete events, outcomes were seen to pivot on matters of the moment: campaigns, issues, personalities, chance remarks. Thus, it was said that the infelicitous observation of a supporter cost Republican candidate James G. Blaine the presidency in the exceedingly close contest of 1884 and that a perceived snub did in Grand Old Party (GOP) nominee Charles Evans Hughes in his narrow loss of 1916. In more recent decades, note the brouhaha over Richard Nixon's physical appearance in his first televised TV debate with John F. Kennedy in 1960 or Gerald Ford's premature "liberation" of Poland from Soviet control in a

1976 debate with Jimmy Carter. And one need look only to 2000 for additional instances: Al Gore's audible sighs in the first debate with George W. Bush and the butterfly design of the ballot in a Florida county, which misled enough voters to tip the balance for the nation. In a narrowly decided contest virtually anything could be said to have made the difference. The point to make about realignment theory in this regard is not that it eschews such ephemeral matters, but that it relates them to a larger context.

What, for example, made the elections of 1960, 1976, or 2000 so close that pancake makeup, a slip of the tongue, or a rolling of the eyes could have been deemed decisive? Why were other elections runaways, so that nothing said or done over the course of a campaign would have made a significant difference? Realignment theory endeavors to provide a coherent answer by placing immediate events in long-term perspective. To be sure, historical connections were not ignored prior to the emergence of realignment theory in the mid-twentieth century. An awareness of such connections forms the background of its development. But the new theory provided a more systematic and usable historical perspective than the looser observations evinced earlier. It stressed the long-term electoral underpinnings of parties; it held that individual elections had to be understood, in part, as episodes along a historical continuum; and, very importantly, it posited that certain "critical" contests could usher in partisan dominance for decades to come. Henceforth, strategists and analysts would plot not only to win or understand the immediate election, but also to shape or project the course of power and influence well into the future.

The history of realignment theory simultaneously deals with the history of the analysis of electoral change. Indeed, the two subjects are wholly intertwined, with the behavioral tools of analysis dating to the 1920s providing the means through which realignment theory was fashioned in the wake of the election of 1948. Realignment theory then dominated the analysis of change into the 1970s and has been widely influential (as well as increasingly criticized) ever since. This said, my basic purpose is twofold. First, it is to explain the historical background, origins, and development of realignment theory as analysts responded to elections. Second, it is to show how a highly useful and insightful theory necessarily based (as originally conceived) on retrospective analysis was also misused to provide quick appraisals of the realignment potential of current elections. While analyses of elections over time led to the forging of realignment theory, and that theory, properly applied, illuminated the meaning of sequential elections, misapplication served to undermine the credibility of the theory itself.

Prior to the impact of the Great Depression and the New Deal, it was commonly assumed that the Republicans were the dominant political party. The Democrats were commonly deemed a permanent minority destined for power only in the event of a Republican split or exceptional circumstances. The upheaval of the 1930s brought this traditional assumption into question. Some analysts persisted in the belief that Democratic dominance under Franklin D. Roosevelt was but a temporary departure from the Republican norm. Others fashioned notions of cyclical partisan alternation in place of the concept of long-term or secular Republican hegemony. Still others—notably the political scientist Harold F. Gosnell—played with the striking thought that historic Republican control had given way to a new era of Democratic power.

But this notion of a new Democratic epoch remained highly tentative and normally subordinate to concepts of eventual Republican restoration or continuing cyclical alternation. Thoughts of a big Democratic secular breakthrough were strong following Roosevelt's landslide reelection of 1936. In the wake of Republican gains in 1938, however, there was a tendency to see a Republican resurgence underway or an inclination to view electoral trends in cyclical terms. Roosevelt's 1940 and 1944 reelections were explained in terms of foreign policy crisis and personal appeal. Once Roosevelt passed from the scene or World War II ended, the refrain ran, traditional patterns— or a full swing of the cycle—would be forthcoming. The sweeping Republican victory of 1946, which restored Congress to the party's control for the first time since the onset of the Depression, provided all the assurance most analysts needed that 1948 would bring a complete Republican restoration or cyclical swing with the party's retaking of the White House.

The 1948 election remains extraordinary in the annals of American electoral history. Harry Truman's upset victory over Thomas Dewey was anticipated by virtually no one. The shock of the election result was vital to the emergence of realignment theory. An outcome so far removed from common and expert expectations forced political analysts back to the drawing boards to develop an explanation that could account for this astounding victory. And an explanation for so striking an event appeared to require something more than reference to the vagaries of the 1948 campaign itself: Truman's strategy, Dewey's complacency. Surely a more in-depth analysis was essential, an analysis delving back into what had then come to be viewed as the enduring changes wrought by the 1930s. It is no overstatement to assert that a single election, 1948, set in motion the full development of a theory that shaped electoral analysis for years to come.

The initial breakthrough for realignment theory came from Samuel Lubell, a political journalist rather than an academic analyst, in his 1952 *The Future of American Politics*. Partly this breakthrough was simply fortuitous, reflective of Lubell's gifts and insight. But partly it was no accident. After all, the interpretation of election outcomes was never the domain of academics alone; it was also very much within the realm of journalists. Lubell added knowledge of political scientists' contributions and the longer-run perspective of historians to the journalist's flair. (It is no accident that historians played a role as well, given the retrospective nature of realignment theory.) In any event, Lubell in *The Future of American Politics* explicitly rejected as invalid the traditional notion of secular Republican dominance and the fashionable 1940s notion of cyclical alternation. What had actually occurred, he contended, was realignment from Republican to Democratic dominance—realignment confirmed by Truman's 1948 victory.

In the wake of 1948, the most influential academic student of American politics of his time, V. O. Key, also engaged in an intensive rethinking of earlier concepts. Key gradually emerged with what proved to be the most influential statement and development of realignment theory: his concept of critical elections. Key had been much influenced by cyclical notions of American politics, and the 1948 election result jolted him no less than it did others. His initial effort at a secular formulation paralleled that of Lubell, but less comprehensively, as Key acknowledged. Now, however, Key set forth his idea that electoral contests in times of great stress—the Civil War, the crisis of the 1890s, and the Great Depression—cut so deeply that people continued to vote the way they had been driven to do in a time of great emotion. Here was a notion to explain not only 1948 in the wake of the 1930s, but also the lasting electoral impacts of the 1860s and of the 1890s. The passage of time, Key concluded, demonstrated whether dramatic electoral departures endured—the test of realignment.

If Key, following Lubell, provided a "macro" version of realignment theory, Angus Campbell provided the "micro" underpinnings of the theory. Campbell was a social psychologist, rather than a political scientist, but one whose work came to focus on the motivations of the individual voter. Campbell originated the concept of "party identification," the notion that individual voters developed and normally maintained a strong sense of allegiance to one party. They might deviate from that loyalty in any given election due to temporary exigencies, but only major upheaval would lead them to break permanently with their partisan allegiance. Such upheavals inaugurated eras of electoral realignment. Key and Campbell influenced one another's work, and Campbell went on to meld Key's macro and his own micro contributions into an overall framework of election classification. Campbell's work was based on surveys of voters. In Campbell's formulation, such surveys demonstrated whether departures at the polls reflected temporary phenomena or changes in more deeply rooted party identifications.

With Lubell's breakthrough, Key's refinement, and Campbell's contribution, realignment theory was in place. But it was no sooner formed than added ingredients complicated its course. Realignment theory was built upon the rejection of earlier cyclical theories; founding statements of the theory posited historical realignment instances as discrete, sharing the common characteristics that made them realigning, but not appearing as manifestations of a cyclically recurring pattern. Realignment was seen as secular and discontinuous, not cyclical and emergent at regular intervals. Indeed, Lubell, Key, and Campbell all explicitly rejected prerealignment cyclical concepts. But notions of cycles made their way into realignment theory through the back door. As scholars applied realignment theory to past elections, a cyclical pattern was discerned. Critical elections appeared forthcoming every twenty-eight to thirty-six years: 1800, 1828, 1860, 1896, and 1932.

As the impact of realignment theory developed in full force, especially via the tumultuous elections of 1964 and 1968, the cyclical expectation came to the fore. A new critical election was now deemed "due." Electoral analysts followed the election returns, eagerly looking for a "critical" break in patterns, while making judgments about current elections too quickly in terms of a valid retrospective application of realignment theory (a tendency facilitated by the instant "elections" made possible by voter surveys). Hence, in the wake of Lyndon Johnson's 1964 landslide over Barry Goldwater came proclamations of existent or impending "realignment" further strengthening the reigning Democratic majority. Then, in 1968 with Richard Nixon's narrow victory over Hubert Humphrey, in a race featuring a strong showing by independent George Wallace running to the right of Nixon, came proclamations, in the words of the one of the era's most influential analysts, Kevin Phillips, of an "emerging Republican majority." The expectation that the Wallace turnout of 1968 would provide a way station to Republican voting appeared to be confirmed by Nixon's massive landslide over the Democrats' hapless George McGovern in 1972.

But a complication in terms of realignment theory became evident. Realignment theory suggested an overall shift in partisan dominance. Republicans, for example, had dominated both branches of Congress, as well as the presidency most of the time between 1896 and 1932. The same was true of the Democrats between 1932 and 1968. But the Democrats retained control of Congress in 1970 and did so even in the midst of Nixon's presidential landslide in 1972. Jimmy Carter's Democratic victory in 1976 seemed to many to call into question whether 1968–1972 involved realignment at all or only a deviation due to temporary factors, making the Nixon era comparable to Dwight D. Eisenhower's 1952 and 1956 Republican presidential victories. The explosive election of 1980, however, revived realignment theory: It brought not only the Republican Ronald Reagan's decisive presidential victory, but also the Republican takeover of the Senate. But, despite Reagan's massive landslide reelection of 1984, the Democrats continued to hold the House of Representatives throughout and retook the Senate in 1986. The election of Reagan's vice president,

George Bush, to the White House in 1988 reinforced the idea of Republican presidential dominance, but continuing Democratic control of Congress called into question the overall applicability of realignment theory.

Indeed, dating back to the 1970s, criticisms of realignment theory emerged and blossomed even as efforts were made to revise the theory in order to adapt it to new contingencies. Increasingly, critics focused on short-term factors as determinants of voting behavior. Stress on realignment gave way to stress on what was dubbed "dealignment"—the notion that party loyalty had frayed in the wake of the 1960s as increasingly independent voters picked and chose from election to election, free of significant attachments to party. Phillips moved to this position, and the most influential academic student of realignment at the time, Walter Dean Burnham, appeared to sway between the idea that dealignment had brought an end to realignments and the idea that dealignment constituted the latest version of realignment. The vagaries of the 1990s— Bill Clinton's election in 1992, the Republican takeover of Congress in 1994, Clinton's reelection in 1996, the Republicans' tenuous hold on Congress in 1998—at times provided renewed attention to realignment theory (as in 1994). But often the apparent confusion of the decade—topped off by the disputed election of 2000—lent itself to a focus on short-term voting determinants and discussion of the electoral underpinnings of "divided government."

Nonetheless, assertions of the continued validity of realignment theory were also heard. Notably, it was widely held in the 1990s that realignment had occurred in the 1960s, even if not in the form anticipated. In my view, realignment theory remains useful, but has too often been misapplied. A theory born in revolt against cyclical notions was subsequently encumbered with cycles. A theory maintaining that realignment could be ascertained only in the fullness of time became a tool for instant analysis. Here the theory carried over into a speculative venture for which it was unintended and ill suited. Realignment theory was properly geared to retrospective judgment rather than to quick prognostication. It was designed to provide the in-depth analysis made possible by a long-term perspective. Election-year excitement over what appeared to be incipient realignment too often had the opposite of the theory's intended effect: Realignment theory was subordinated to and distorted by the short-run perspective of the latest election returns (or subsequent survey results). In terms of its original intent, however, realignment theory yet retains a capacity to illuminate.

Chapter One

The Study of Behavior

The study of American electoral behavior in a time-related focus had origins, appropriately enough, in the work of leading historians, as well as political scientists. Frederick Jackson Turner, whose work on the role of the frontier in American history dated from the 1890s, was also the developer of the concept of sectionalism as an important influence in American history. In his own work, in the work of his students, and in work inspired by his, such as that of the political scientist Arthur N. Holcombe, formulations were set forth stressing the underlying sectional patterns of American electoral behavior across time. Analyses were made in terms of political maps based on aggregate voting statistics. Correlations were provided between voting and demographic data. Highly influential in its time and with reverberations throughout twentieth-century electoral analysis, the Turner method also had its limits. It tended to be static, reflecting historical traditions—important as baselines for change, but lacking explanations of dramatic upheaval.[1]

A second source of early electoral—particularly political party—analysis, often intertwined with Turnerian influences, was that emanating from Charles A. Beard, a historian, as well as a political scientist. Well known for his stress on economic factors in history and politics, Beard posited a view of American political history based on the notion of essential continuity. In his concept, while party names changed from the late eighteenth to the mid-nineteenth centuries, essential patterns remained intact and endured indeed into his own time, the early to mid-twentieth century. One pattern, dating to the Federalists and continuing via the Republican Party, largely reflected urban business interests. The other, going back to Thomas Jefferson and continuing with the modern Democratic Party, reflected the concerns of farmers and workers. Beard's concept, however, like Turner's, downplayed instances of and lacked the power to explain major political upheavals.[2]

1

Modern electoral analysis in a truly substantive and systematic fashion dates from the 1920s in terms of the emergence of an approach within political science. However, there were social-science precursors, as well as influences traceable to historians. A major source of this approach derived from Franklin H. Giddings, a Columbia University sociologist, who influenced the work of such students of quantitative electoral analysis as William F. Ogburn and Stuart A. Rice.[3] Rice, in particular, emerged as an important figure in the 1920s. He was remarkable not only for his pioneering use of quantitative data in electoral analysis, but also for his conceptual anticipations of what became major approaches to electoral change only a quarter-century and more later. Working under Giddings, Rice earned his doctorate in sociology from Columbia. He received accolades both at the time and subsequently for his quantitative investigations into electoral behavior.[4] It was "amazing," wrote Seymour Martin Lipset in 1959, "how many of the main lines" of inquiry in the field "were laid out, defended in sophisticated theoretical and methodological terms, and actually given flesh by concrete research examples by Rice."[5]

Rice, in outlining his approach, called it "behavioralistic." Too often, he maintained, political science had been concerned with particulars. But through the analysis of aggregate voting data across time, sequences and patterns could be discerned; secular trends and cycles would be revealed. Quantitative data allowed for a precision not available in traditional scholarly approaches. The subject, he declared, was "virgin."[6] Moving from techniques to concepts, Rice, in his 1924 book, *Farmers and Workers in American Politics*, included a chapter on "Realignment of Forces in American Politics." Here, in embryonic form, he touched on notions later developed by V. O. Key and others. A new political alignment, Rice wrote, may result from "an unforeseen and harrowing experience," or "a new issue," cutting across established "lines of party division," may trigger realignment as old issues lose "their vitality." Anticipating the later approach of Angus Campbell and the Michigan School, Rice in a 1924 article linked party loyalty to realignment—precisely what Campbell and Key did in a more developed and systematic fashion over three decades later. So powerful was "party loyalty itself as an . . . influence," wrote Rice, that it would endure "until . . . broken by some new and disturbing question . . . resulting in a new party cleavage."[7]

Charles Merriam was another very important figure of the 1920s, although Merriam's great influence was less intellectual and substantive than institutional and personal. Merriam had a strong interest in the use of quantitative data in political science and in applying insights from other social-science disciplines, notably psychology, to political analysis. Although he was a prolific writer, Merriam's work in that regard, as in others, was most important for the inspiration it provided to his students and other scholars. As head of the University of Chicago's Department of Political Science, Merriam was able to gain the influence and funds needed to advance his vision. Out of his entrepreneurial efforts came the Chicago School of political and electoral analysis, a precursor, if not actually the parent, of the post–World War II "behaviorial school" in which major patterns of mid-century electoral analysis evolved. In the long run, the most important product of the Chicago School in terms of electoral analysis was V. O. Key; in the shorter run, the figure of great importance was another Merriam student and subsequently a faculty colleague and coauthor, Harold F. Gosnell.[8]

Gosnell developed very much within the fertile context nurtured by Merriam, but there were other Chicago influences as well. James Field, of the economics department, aided Gosnell in the area of statistical techniques. William F. Ogburn, who moved from Columbia to Chicago in 1927, was also of assistance. Gosnell had met Ogburn in Europe in 1925, occupied an adjoining office in Chicago, and acknowledged Ogburn's example in the application of statistics to political research.[9] Like Merriam, Gosnell was interested in the application of psychological as well as statistical tools to political analysis; he also believed that political scientists could learn from economists. In understanding cycles and trends, Gosnell wrote, economists had advanced well beyond political scientists, who now had to catch up. Quantitative data, as compared with historical narrative, allowed for greater precision and less subjectivity. The past was vital to understanding the present, but statistical data analyzed over time could provide surer insights than traditional historical and political methodology; a "statistical politics" could be based on the wealth of electoral data available in almanacs and yearbooks. The end result, Gosnell anticipated, would be a science of electoral politics based not on "mechanical relationships," but rather on an understanding geared to "tendencies" and "trends."[10]

In 1924 Merriam and Gosnell coauthored *Non-Voting*, widely considered a pioneering work not only for its use of quantitative data per se, but also for its employment of survey data in particular. In this work, largely written by Gosnell, Chicago nonvoters were surveyed and compared with voters, thus presaging the widespread use of survey data after World War II by the Michigan School. Indeed, leaders of the Michigan School such as Angus Campbell and Philip Converse explicitly acknowledged the pioneering status of *Non-Voting* in terms of its use of survey techniques and the way those techniques allowed access to the individual not available through aggregate data. *Non-Voting* thus presented a premier example of how a general approach tendered by Merriam was systemically developed and followed through upon by his student Gosnell.[11] Their goal, Merriam and Gosnell wrote, was not again simply to decry low voter turnout, but to ascertain reasons for it through a compilation of material throwing light on the nature of the electoral process and thus providing a more in-depth understanding of "one of the least explored of the fields of politics." Political science had provided much scholarship on theory and on the mechanics of the law, "but practically nothing on the motives that animate the voter"; hence, the need for the "study of the voter's psychology."[12] Here, too, in the linking of survey data to the individual and thus to the psychology of voting, Merriam and Gosnell anticipated the social-psychological emphases, as well as the survey techniques, of Angus Campbell and his associates.

Gosnell followed up the 1924 study with his 1927 *Getting out the Vote*, again based on the use of survey techniques. Among other works, he produced *Why Europe Votes* in 1930 and *Machine Politics* in 1937, characterizing the latter as an analysis "of the social and economic background of voting behavior" in Chicago.[13] *Grass Roots Politics* appeared in 1942. As is often the case with pioneers, Gosnell was heralded for his breakthroughs, but also noted for his limitations as compared with those who followed. Despite his pioneering use of survey data, most of his work was based on election statistics, which Gosnell then correlated with economic and demographic data.[14] Hence, most evaluations of Gosnell were based on his studies which employed aggregate data; but here, too, he was widely viewed as a breakthrough scholar in the use of statistical data and correlational techniques.[15] Herbert Tingsten, for example, in his own 1937 study, *Political Behavior,* drew upon and paid tribute to Gosnell's contributions to the field.[16] Thus, what is often referred to as a pioneer work was itself based in part upon Gosnell's even earlier work. V. O. Key, noting that "the correlation analysis of electoral data was developed around 1930," acknowledged that "a good deal of work" was that of Gosnell.[17] Key, seldom given to fulsome praise, declared in 1956 that "among political scientists the grand-daddy of the whole business is Harold F. Gosnell whose books and articles of twenty years or so ago introduced us to the art of correlation of election returns with social characteristics."[18] Political historian Richard Jensen in 1969 summed up the case. Gosnell's work included "dazzling statistical displays," wrote Jensen; Gosnell "revolutionized election analysis" through the use of statistical techniques in their historical settings across time.[19]

In the 1930s, David Truman later recalled, Gosnell's interests were not yet common in universities throughout the country; indeed, much of what Gosnell did was considered by peers to be outside the domain of political science and, in Truman's words, "very screwy stuff."[20] Years later it was suggested that Gosnell had approached "a generalized model of American voting behavior."[21] No one, of course, would now call Gosnell's work "screwy," but neither did he approach a "generalized model." Neither his techniques, largely based on aggregate data, nor his goals appeared to be geared to that end. Gosnell was particularly interested in accounting for shifts in the patterns of electoral behavior and in correlations between voting behavior and demographic categories; election and other statistics could facilitate the uncovering of basic developments and relationships along these lines. Gosnell appeared less interested in drawing conclusions that might be deemed applicable across timelines.[22] Here, in studies largely geared to the 1920s and 1930s, but done in the 1950s, V. O. Key attempted to go beyond Gosnell by moving from studies of shifts to the development of such concepts as "critical elections" and "secular realignment" to be applied to electoral analysis across time. Samuel J. Eldersveld, who began his career as Gosnell's own career as an electoral analyst peaked, in particular stressed the limits of the Gosnell approach in this regard. That approach, Eldersveld concluded, was of value in that it provided much information about particulars; but that was also its weakness. It was "particularlistic," failing to generate hypotheses and provide the integration of material needed to add significantly to a general theory of voting behavior.[23]

Students of voting behavior and electoral trends in the 1920s and 1930s were conscious that they were breaking with, or at least deviating from, the hitherto predominant institutional bias of political science. They stressed that they were focused on "process" as distinct from "structure," and that they believed that through the use and analysis of quantitative data, new knowledge and understanding could be gained as to the actual functioning of election mechanics. This in turn would provide new tools and information to assess and understand the nature of electoral and political change, providing a dynamic, rather than a static, approach to the subject and making apparent the "patterns" across time that eluded both institutional and particularistic historical accounts.[24] These early students were also at times aware of their limits; they realized they were pathfinders, and they noted that while they often were able to discern facts and patterns through statistical analysis of aggregate data, the psychology of voting, the underlying reasons and motivations for voting change not related through aggregate data, would have to await further investigation employing psychological techniques.[25] As the young Samuel Eldersveld himself put it in 1942, writing with senior coauthor James Pollock, their study of Michigan politics in the 1930s evolved out of a field that remained "rudimentary." Citing the work of Harold Gosnell, Eldersveld and Pollock stressed the need for the accumulation of statistical data that would illuminate the nature of Michigan politics over the course of a turbulent decade. They were content with generalizations that would apply to time and place rather than with the establishment of general rules of voting behavior. The uncovering of patterns and tendencies, rather than strict rules, constituted their present objective. Hence, while "conceived as behavioralistic," their study did "not have an atomistic psychological conception of behavioralism." As such, theirs was a "preliminary" and "exploratory study."[26]

The forays of the 1920s and 1930s may be considered preliminary to the extended investigations into electoral behavior in post–World War II America. Emanating especially, although not exclusively, out of Chicago, an embryonic behavioral revolution occurred before the war heralding the comprehensive revolution that reshaped political science thereafter.[27] As with the later revolution, the first also centered especially on electoral and voting behavior, a field of investigation most given to quantitative data and techniques. As the analysts of the 1920s and 1930s pioneered approaches and techniques, so, too, did they—at least tentatively—advance key concepts more fully articulated, developed, and applied by others after World War II. Along with traditional discussions of sections and class in American politics, and with a greater emphasis on the latter over the course of the 1930s, early students paid considerable attention to the role of party loyalty in relation to electoral stability and change. Much was made of the strong tendency of voters continuously to favor one party or the other. Debate occurred as to whether campaigns had any significant affect on outcomes in terms of changing the intentions of significant numbers of voters, or whether party loyalties were simply reinforced over the course of campaigns with partisans charged up to go out and exercise their franchise. All this was viewed in turn as facilitating electoral regularity and stability.[28] On the other hand, attention was drawn to greater swings in the vote from election to election as evidence of possible nationalizing forces on the electorate.[29] The trick, as two students of the 1928 election put it, was to weigh the relative importance of elements of party loyalty against the impact of newer issues, candidates, and economic, social, and demographic changes in order to gain insight into the current state of electoral evolution.[30] In all these respects, then, writers of the 1920s and 1930s, however embryonically, at least broached concepts later developed by such major figures of the postwar era as V. O. Key and Angus Campbell.

Chapter Two

Discerning Patterns

To pre–Great Depression analysts, a basic lodestone of American politics was Republican Party dominance. This was essentially recognition of a fact, rather than a point of departure for a more general theory of electoral politics. The Republicans were sometimes referred to as the "majority party" and the Democrats as the "minority" or "opposition party," but such terms were shorthand and lacked the conceptual development later given to them by Samuel Lubell, with whom the terms "majority" and "minority" party have since been associated. These earlier writers often noted that during the first twenty years after Reconstruction, the two parties had essentially been evenly divided in terms of electoral support, but that since 1896 the Republicans had normally held sway. Only one Democrat had been elected president since 1896, they emphasized, and Woodrow Wilson's victories could be seen as what a later generation of political scientists deemed "deviating," that is, as departures from a Republican norm. They were due to the exceptional circumstances of the Republican split of 1912 and the exigencies of 1916. Some analysts, with a more sweeping vision, divided virtually all of American political history up into two broad epochs: an era of Democratic dominance before the Civil War and of Republican dominance thereafter. Whatever the precise delineations, however, political analysis assumed, before the full impact of the Great Depression hit, that the Republicans were normally the majority party, while the Democrats were a ragtag and ill-fitting coalition of outsiders, based above all on the backwater white South, destined to govern only rarely, confined otherwise to cantankerous opposition, and always in danger of possible ultimate extinction.[1] As one commentator put it in 1925, the political history of the country since 1896 provided "irrefutable proof" of the hopelessness of the Democratic Party's "reestablishment as a virile national force"; the party's "progressive disintegration" was "almost assured."[2]

The Democratic Party, of course, in the wake of the Great Depression, won a huge victory in 1932. But no one knew then what it portended. Indeed, a memorandum prepared in January 1933 by Democratic Party analyst Emil Hurja for Louis McHenry Howe, President-Elect Franklin Roosevelt's close adviser, reflected the continuing concern over the historic secular strength of the GOP since 1896. The memorandum sketched a view of contemporary politics not too unlike that associated with the idea of a Republican "electoral lock" on the presidency fashionable in the 1980s. Hurja divided the country into historically strong Democratic states, states carried by Hoover in 1932, and thirteen states he saw as keys to victory or defeat in the near future. These thirteen states, he emphasized, had been normally Republican in the whole era between 1896 and 1932. On only two occasions, both in 1916, had states from among the vital thirteen reached a level of Democratic strength in a presidential election equal to that gained nationally by Roosevelt in 1932.[3] This sort of analysis could be viewed as demonstrative of the extraordinary nature of 1932, but it could not foretell whether that extraordinary election marked an enduring departure or merely a deviation from the era of normal Republican majority status.

Certainly many observers at the time, including Republican Party leaders, looked at the 1932 Democratic victory as a temporary setback due to hard times, a deviation from the norm of secular Republican dominance. As the Republican Party had quickly recovered from the debacle of 1912, so, too, could it recover from the avalanche of 1932. In this scenario Franklin Roosevelt would prove no more than a latter-day Woodrow Wilson, interrupting but not ending Republican rule.[4] The course of the 1930s and most of the 1940s seemed to some to validate this essential proposition. To be sure, Roosevelt won an even greater landslide victory in 1936 than in 1932, and this followed virtually unprecedented Democratic congressional gains in the off-year election of 1934. But big GOP gains in 1938, in the wake of recession, seemed to many to portend a Republican presidential victory and restoration of a Republican governing norm in 1940. Republican defeat in 1940 was explained away by the extraordinary power of Roosevelt's personality, plus the sense of crisis engendered by the outbreak and course of World War II in Europe. Even still, Roosevelt's victory margin that year was narrower than in both 1932 and 1936. Big Republican gains in the congressional races of 1942 again seemed to point toward a GOP presidential victory in 1944. But, again, Roosevelt and reluctance to change leadership in the midst of the war were widely viewed as the reasons for the Democratic victory that year, postponing the eventual GOP return to power. The Republican takeover of Congress in the 1946 election finally appeared to validate the long-standing analysis: With Roosevelt gone and the war over, surely 1948 would be the year of Republican restoration.[5]

A distinct, yet related, concept was also employed in the 1930s and 1940s to foretell a Republican comeback. This was the theory of the pendulum of political cycles. The notion here was that political momentum shifted back and forth at roughly regular intervals; having swung one way, it would, pendulum like, start back the other; and once it was heading back, there would be no significant contrary movement. This, like the expected swing back to a Republican norm after 1932 and 1936, suggested that with the shift toward the GOP in 1938, the not too distant outcome would be a period of Republican rule. Thus, apart from issues, personalities, campaigns, and events, there was an underlying "rhythm" to the inexorable and predictable shifting of partisan control in politics. In this respect, too, the Roosevelt era would be an updated version of the Wilson phase of the political cycle, leading not to enduring rearrangement, but merely functioning as part of an alternating cycle.[6] Frank R. Kent, a veteran political journalist and analyst, writing in April 1940, for example, maintained that political life was basically governed by political "tides" and that having started in one direction, as with the shift toward the Republicans in 1938, they were not known suddenly to reverse course. The Democratic tide of 1930–1936 had now become the Republican tide dating from 1938.[7] Similarly, the journalist Raymond Clapper, writing in 1943, saw American politics as characterized by the cyclical movements of the pendulum, now on a Republican upswing with the Democrats living on "borrowed time."[8] Political scientists Peter H. Odegard and E. Allen Helms, writing in 1947, interpreted presidential elections since 1916 in terms of the oscillations of the "political pendulum." The swing back to the Republicans began in 1940, was speeded by the off-year election of 1946, and appeared "to portend a Republican victory in 1948."[9]

While popular during the late 1930s and 1940s, and given particular expression by historian Arthur M. Schlesinger and economist-turned-political-analyst Louis Bean, the focus on cycles was, of course, nothing new in social science, as evidenced by the role of cycles in economic theory. The idea was applied to political life by A. Lawrence Lowell in his famous 1898 essay, "Oscillations in Politics." While presenting the idea of oscillations or pendulum swings as an underlying characteristic of American politics since the 1830s, Lowell was careful to note that other factors were also at work in determining electoral outcomes. Further, foreshadowing the notion of critical elections and realignment, Lowell cautioned that "oscillations that might occur with regularity in ordinary times will, of course, be entirely interrupted whenever some overmastering issue arises, like that which culminated . . . in the Civil War." Applying the idea to British politics, Lowell held that fluctuations of party strength there were due—rather as Arthur M. Schlesinger later suggested in an American context—to the waxing and waning of new ideas, while in America they were attributable to reactions against the party in power.[10] William Bennett Munro in 1928 set forth "The Law of the Pendulum." In terms very similar to those to be employed by Schlesinger, Munro held that a "psychological" process was at work in politics. Eager for change and activism, as in the Wilson years, people eventually tired of the ferment and lapsed into the comforts of conservatism. To be sure, Munro acknowledged, cyclical alternations were somewhat irregular; extraordinary leadership or dramatic events could play into the timing, but underlying patterns nonetheless persisted. Nor, Munro allowed, was the pendulum metaphor altogether appropriate. The base of the pendulum could move, leading the alternating patterns to end at different points, more reformist or more conservative, from where they began.[11]

There were also analysts who viewed the period from the late 1920s through the 1940s in terms of substantive, secular, and permanent change. Particularly important here was the perception that politics was moving from sectionally based alignments to alignments geared more to class, economics, and urban status. In this view, the Democratic Party, which once had as its bastion the rural white South, was now increasingly attuned to the urban and working-class areas of the North, shifting in fundamental ways the political patterns that had existed before the Great Depression and New Deal.[12] Over time, and especially after the surprising 1948 election, the perception of significant change led to the development of realignment theory. But notions of realignment before the 1950s were loose, particularistic, and unsystematic. Certainly there was wide recognition that the era of the Civil War and Reconstruction had led to enormous and lasting upheaval in party politics and voting patterns; and there was also some awareness of the role of the 1896 election in establishing long-term Republican hegemony. F. Stuart Chapin in 1912 and Stuart A. Rice in 1924 noted wider swings in presidential-election voting patterns, contributing, Rice observed, to the idea that change in party alignments was "imminent."[13] Charles Merriam in 1922 held that while habitual party voting was deeply entrenched, allegiance could be shaken by "revolutions" convulsing the political world. In 1896, 1912, and 1920, he wrote, great masses of voters "transferred their allegiance either temporarily or permanently"; thus, "habits of party allegiance" could be altered by changed circumstances.[14] At a time when Democratic Party prospects seemed notably bleak, an occasional observer foresaw at least the possibility of dramatic change along the lines of what was actually to occur. Howard R. Bruce in 1927, pinpointing three sources of Democratic revival that were actually forthcoming, held that it would "require a great leader, an issue of transcending importance, or an overpowering national emergency to bring into being again a strong, united party."[15] Frank R. Kent prophesied in 1928 that with the nation's problems more and more geared to industry, conservatism would give way to the Democratic Party's "more progressive tradition."[16]

Some political analysts from the 1920s to the 1940s, aware of elections such as those of 1860 and 1896, which upset old allegiances and inaugurated new ones, examined each new election that deviated sharply from earlier ones for signs of such epochal contests. (Analysts from the 1960s on similarly scrutinized elections for signs of impending realignment following the full development of the concept.) Both 1932 and 1936 were viewed as sharp deviations from historic patterns and as having possibly inaugurated new configurations.[17] Charles and Mary Beard, for example, characterized the 1932 election in terms of a "crack" in party alignments and the "staggering" defeat of the GOP in the 1936 election as comparable not to 1912, but as something new— no "repetition of any episode in history."[18] Ralph and Mildred Fletcher in 1936 contended that "certain elections" constituted "periods of great change in . . . party allegiance" and that 1932 had wrought "the greatest change of all" among elections since 1896.[19] Roosevelt speechwriter Stanley High in April 1936, in a memorandum for the president, looked at the forthcoming election in long-run terms. The issue of the election was one of "direction"; the voters would decide not on whether to proceed with specific policies, but rather on whether or not the "New Deal tendency" would set the nation's course for the next half-century.[20] Roy V. Peel and Thomas C. Donnelly noted in their book on the 1928 campaign that the Democrats under Alfred E. Smith had targeted the East and made inroads among "normally Republican Italians and Jews."[21] In their follow-up book on the 1932 election, they observed that Roosevelt had carried "normally Republican" states and voters and that ethnic groups and urban areas attracted to Smith in 1928 went for Roosevelt four years later. Roosevelt thus "shattered traditions" in the "revolutionary" election of 1932. Peel and Donnelly concluded that "a realignment of forces took place during the years 1929–1933 which may, or may not, prove to be permanent. Much depends on the success of the New Deal."[22]

Wilfred E. Binkley was the author of the standard history of American political parties in the 1940s and 1950s. *American Political Parties: Their Natural History* first appeared in 1943 and was regularly updated and reissued thereafter. It was written in a thoroughly Beardian tradition. Indeed, as Binkley happily noted to a fellow political scientist in late 1942, Beard himself had "read 'every word of it'" for the publisher. The manuscript, as returned by Beard, had "the penciled marginal criticisms, questions, and suggestions of the master," giving Binkley "an advantage" he "could not have hoped for."[23] In 1947, in the second edition of the book, Binkley held that the Great Depression had had the most profound impact on politics of any event since the Civil War; that four successive presidential defeats had rendered hollow

1920s claims of normal Republican dominance; that Republicans should not facilely assume that Roosevelt's death insured a GOP return to power; and that while a majority of voters doubtless were Republican before the Depression, by 1945 a majority "doubtless considered themselves Democrats."[24] But, as Gerald Gamm has noted, Binkley, despite his insights, did not develop his analytical observations into a systematic theory of political realignment.[25] This was true generally of pre-1948 analysts, however much they may have stressed the impact of the changes wrought in the 1930s.

Perhaps the most remarkable of all the pre-1948 analyses, save Samuel Lubell's 1941 article, which presaged his seminal *The Future of American Politics*, appeared in *Michigan Politics in Transition* by Samuel J. Eldersveld and James K. Pollock, published in 1942. Pollock, the senior author, had written an unremarkable case study of voting behavior in 1939.[26] Even as the book was published, it fell to Pollock, as Eldersveld's dissertation adviser, to give his young graduate student coauthor bad news: Doctoral committee members had found Eldersveld's thesis as submitted unacceptable. The devastated Eldersveld, in uniform during the war, continued to ruminate over his plight and to plot his thesis revisions.[27] *Michigan Politics in Transition*, while limited to one state, rivals Lubell's 1941 article as an analytical breakthrough in terms of its argument that the 1930s did not constitute a deviation from a Republican norm or a cyclical alternation, but rather a Democratic surge of an enduring kind. This was reflected in the book's language, as well as in its urban and ethnic emphases. Perhaps because the book was a state study and because it was published during the war, it appears not to have had a wide impact on the development of a secularly geared theory of electoral change, which had yet to await the shock of 1948, Lubell's *The Future of American Politics*, and V. O. Key's seminal articles of the 1950s. The book was nonetheless a remarkable forerunner conceptually and the young Eldersveld may rank here as a pioneer akin to the older Harold F. Gosnell—whose work was cited early on in *Michigan Politics in Transition*. Eldersveld, however, like Gosnell, did not turn his particular insights into a more general theory: That awaited Lubell and Key.

Eldersveld and Pollock, despite caveats pertaining to GOP gains in and after 1938, definitely put themselves down on the side of historic change. Their operative argument was that "a major shift" had transformed "party allegiance." The crucial decade of the 1930s, they maintained, could no longer be considered merely "transitional"; with the appearance of "new patterns of electoral behavior" historic "voting tendencies" had faded; the "change in party allegiance" had "brought about a clearly distinguishable realignment" and with it a "tidal surge of Democratic votes" intruding "itself in precedent-shattering fashion." Further, the authors wrote, the Democratic surge was based not only upon switching by formerly Republican voters. It also reflected an increase in participation by previously inactive citizens, what a later generation of scholars referred to as a new alignment based on "mobilization" as distinct from or in addition to "conversion." Additionally, the huge Democratic gains reflected a new outpouring of strength in the big cities; the pro-Democratic realignment was distinctly a massive urban phenomenon. And the Democratic vote was augmented significantly by an outpouring of support among the "foreign-born," that is, among what later scholars would call the newer ethnic groups, immigrants and children of immigrants from southern and eastern Europe. This urban dimension of the Democratic upsweep, Eldersveld and Pollock concluded, citing the work of Arthur N. Holcombe, validated "the hypothesis . . . that the new party politics is class politics and urban." In all these respects, the authors added, the present study could "be only a suggestive prelude"; dealing comprehensively with the issues of increased voter participation, the economic basis of the "electoral shift," and the impact of "urban voting behavior" would constitute "a magnum opus."[28] Eldersveld at the end of the decade did contribute a major article on urban voting trends, which Samuel Lubell was to draw upon in *The Future of American Politics*. The magnum opus on the subject, however, was not to be Eldersveld's; it was Lubell who in 1952 produced precisely what Eldersveld had alluded to a decade earlier.

The 1948 election produced the critical shock that led to the development of a realignment theory based on the upheaval of the 1930s. Harry Truman's famous upset victory in 1948 demonstrated, as the scholarly and journalistic postmortems acknowledged, that the realignments of the 1930s had stuck, that even without the charismatic Roosevelt, the Democrats were now what Lubell was to call the new "majority party." James Reston of the *New York Times* recalled in his memoirs decades later the sense of shame he felt over his newspaper's coverage of the election and how he wrote a "letter of apology" for it, which the *Times* printed. In that letter Reston observed, as did innumerable others thereafter, that not "enough weight" had been given to the "influence of the Roosevelt era on the thinking of the nation," and "consequently we were wrong, not only on the election, but . . . on the whole political direction of our time."[29] The young Austin Ranney after the election wrote to fellow political scientist E. E. Schattschneider that however pleased they were about the electoral result as Democrats, "as political scientists we should be downright depressed." The outcome indicated "that we just don't know as much about the nature of American politics and public opinion as we may have thought we did on November 1st. Not that we are any worse than any other kind of 'experts'; but it's humiliating all the same."[30]

The older Schattschneider was to make important contributions to realignment theory. But he also provides an example of an insightful analyst of the developments of the 1930s and 1940s, who was acutely aware of basic trends and their implications, but who was not quite able to make the conceptual leaps and breakthroughs that came with Lubell and Key. In a circa-1945 prospectus for a proposed book, Schattschneider wrote about how the Democratic Party, based on the upsurge in strength in the northern states, was now able to win the presidency without the South. The major industrial states of the North now seemed "to dominate national politics to an unprecedented degree." Further, youth appeared to be disproportionately Democratic in its inclinations and this suggested an even further intensification of the pro-Democratic trend.[31] In a circa-1947 memorandum, Schattschneider held that "something like a revolution in the party system" had occurred. Developments since 1930 had "so changed party alignments . . . that a reexamination of the party system as a whole" was now needed "to bring scholarship into contact with reality."[32] The 1948 results confirmed Schattschneider's earlier emphases. In notes written shortly after the election, Schattschneider maintained that it was "impossible to understand" the 1948 election without the realization that a "peaceful revolution" had been underway since 1932. The 1948 outcome demonstrated that the "revolution" was "real and permanent, not something created out of the magic of a Roosevelt." The 1948 election upset was surprising only "because we underestimated the proportions and the durability of the political revolution of the last sixteen years."[33] About two years later Schattschneider noted that the "policy revolution of 1932" had "not yet been followed by a sufficient number of comprehensive reappraisals of the party system to establish a generally accepted description of the present status of the system. Professor Holcombe's *Our More Perfect Union* is in fact the first major attempt to make this kind of appraisal."[34] Schattschneider was on the mark in that no seminal reappraisal had appeared. That came in 1952 with Lubell's *The Future of American Politics*, the kind of book that Schattschneider and other academics had anticipated and called for, but which actually arrived via a journalist from outside the disciplinary guild. Arthur N. Holcombe's book was a worthy finale to a long and distinguished career as a student of American politics, but it was hardly a seminal analysis of the upheavals of the 1930s. The older generation of analysts with pre-Depression roots nonetheless grappled impressively with the political and electoral changes wrought by the Depression and New Deal. They served as pathfinders and precursors as they sought to make sense of the changes that underlay the future of political analysis.

Chapter Three

Evaluators of Transition

Among the most significant contemporary analysts of the political changes of the 1930s and 1940s were Arthur N. Holcombe, Arthur M. Schlesinger, Louis Bean, and Harold F. Gosnell. Holcombe's career antedated the Great Depression in important ways; he was the preeminent proponent of a sectionally based interpretation of American politics in the 1920s. But in the 1930s he gave first importance to the impact of class and urban influences on voting trends as he undertook to assess the altered configurations of politics under the impact of the Great Depression and New Deal. Arthur M. Schlesinger and Louis Bean advanced influential cyclical theories of political change, differing in important ways, but similar in their basic character and in the fact that each contained a secular component within its cyclical framework. Harold F. Gosnell, in some respects the most impressive of all prewar figures, came closest to making a breakthrough to the kind of analysis that came to prevail after 1948.

Arthur N. Holcombe was born in Winchester, Massachusetts, in 1884 and seldom strayed far from home. A self-described "Connecticut Yankee," he understated when he noted that the great part of his academic life had occurred "within the limits of New England." Indeed, following his graduation from Harvard in 1906, postgraduate study in Berlin and London, and the acquisition of a Harvard Ph.D. in 1909, he remained at Harvard for the duration of his academic career, formally retiring in 1955.[1]

Students recalled Holcombe as well-organized, open, and welcoming. As one related, Holcombe had a "kind of father-like attitude" toward graduate students. His office "door was always open, and you could walk up, tap on the door, and he'd say, 'Come in,' turn around from his typewriter and talk to you, and before you got down the hall when you were leaving, you would hear the typewriter clicking again." The specialist in southern politics R. Taylor Cole recalled that "Holcombe offered me my first job at Harvard under rather unusual circumstances. He asked me . . . what I would do if I had a Negro in class, and I said I'd . . . teach him. The next day I was offered an instructorship."[2] Holcombe was also a supporter of the New Deal at a time when political conservatism reigned in academic circles. He noted early in 1936 that among his colleagues there was an increasing intensity of opposition to the New Deal, and he found himself "growing more conspicuously a member of a minority in sticking" with the Roosevelt administration.[3] He wrote *Government in a Planned Democracy* "under the impulse of the New Deal atmosphere," he noted.[4] And in 1934 he expressed the thought that "the political philosophy of the New Deal" was bringing "the theory" of his 1933 book, *The New Party Politics*, "to practice."[5]

Holcombe's first major foray into political analysis came in his highly influential and impressive 1924 book, *The Political Parties of To-Day*. The book reflected Holcombe's sectionally oriented interpretation of American politics, which also focused upon the major economic components of each section. Within that framework, he attempted an overall political analysis, which, with different emphases, anticipated the later work of Samuel Lubell. As late as 1951, one scholar held that the book constituted the "first" and, at that time, the "only attempt at a political ecology of the entire United States."[6] Holcombe also attempted to trace and analyze historic electoral patterns and prospects, anticipating, without systematically developing, later concepts of V. O. Key. Political patterns, wrote Holcombe, were "like rivers . . . pursuing courses which the flowing waters" could not "greatly alter"; traditions and interests formed "the banks of the stream" and guided "its current in the channels." But while typically "proceeding serenely in the channels which habit . . . fixed," catastrophe and upheaval at times smashed "the old" and built "anew." Surveying American political history, Holcombe divided it into two major components: Democratic dominance before the Civil War and Republican dominance thereafter. Within those categories, Holcombe also discerned lesser divisions; for example, in the twenty years after Reconstruction there was a rough balance between the major parties within the larger time frame of Republican hegemony. A period of "unchecked Republican supremacy" dated from the 1896 election, interrupted only by the Wilson victories of 1912 and 1916 and a period of "temporary supremacy" for the Democrats. The GOP victory of 1920 marked a return to "normal" in the national alignment of parties, including a "position of inferiority" for the Democrats and the "final failure of the Wilsonian strategy" to create a Democratic electoral majority. "Despite the political stresses and strains" of the 1910s, Holcombe concluded, "the partisan alignment established in 1896 continued to hold fast."[7]

Holcombe thus anticipated some of the breaks and periods in party history later associated with realignment theory. He also offered some notions, reflective at this point of his sectional perspective, as to how and why those breaks occurred. "There must be a direct clash of sectional interests to produce a realignment of parties in American politics," he contended. The "exceptional" election involving a "head-on collision between vital sectional interests as in 1860 and 1896" was "almost certain to produce a substantial readjustment in the partisan alignment." It also created an opportunity for one party to dominate political life "as consistently as the Jacksonian Democrats" before 1860 and "the Conservative Republicans" after 1896. In more general terms, Holcombe held that any "issue on which . . . a realignment of parties might take place" would have to "make a powerful appeal," bring forth "strong opposition," and "vitally affect large masses of people." In addition, since a "realignment of parties" constituted "a gigantic undertaking," it required for "its consummation either a fortuitous combination of circumstances or extraordinarily forceful and spirited leadership."[8]

With the 1930s Holcombe moved from a sectionally to a class- and urban-oriented interpretation of American politics. Consistent with his emphasis on economics within sectionalism, Holcombe contended that the new urban politics, while including ethnic and religious dimensions, likewise focused on economic issues. This reflected their intrinsic importance, augmented by the onset of the Great Depression, and also demonstrated the basic "rationality" of voters. Interests, as distinct from principles, he believed, divided the two major parties; and urban and industrial development required a larger role for public policy and government. Holcombe viewed the Al Smith campaign of 1928, with its unprecedented Democratic appeal to city voters, as a foreshadowing of the new urban politics. The huge 1936 Democratic landslide provided further strong evidence of class-based politics in the urban areas of the country. A realignment of politics along more modern lines, he added, would include the advantage of bringing "the final elimination of obsolete issues growing out of the Civil War."[9] While his views were often cited in analyses of the rise of working-class voters in the Democratic electoral coalition, Holcombe himself, as he made particularly clear in private correspondence, looked toward the urban middle class to avoid political extremes by playing a moderating and balancing role in politics, comparable to that of nineteenth-century Midwestern farmers.[10]

Holcombe's view of the prospects of enduring realignment arising out of the 1930s tended to reflect the ebb and flow of events (much as elections from the 1960s onward were assessed contemporaneously in the wake of the advent of realignment theory). Thus, in 1931 Holcombe confidently prophesied that any Democrat would defeat any Republican in 1932 if the Depression continued. However, he added, "a return to normal in business" would mean "a return to normal also in politics," and victory for the Republicans as the dominant party since 1896. Franklin Roosevelt, he opined shortly after the 1932 election, possessed "exceptionally good political sense"; hence, he anticipated the developments of 1933 "with more interest than anything in . . . American politics" since World War I.[11] During the 1936 campaign Holcombe could, in the same month, anticipate a close electoral result and a Republican disaster as bad as the Democratic showing in the election of 1904. The end result he viewed as "a magnificent expression of public confidence in the President."[12] Still, he added, in a postelection analysis, while the election "resulted in a Democratic victory of unprecedented magnitude," Roosevelt's margin of victory was not much larger than the Republican Warren Harding's in 1920, while the losing Republican Alf Landon had actually polled better than had the Democratic nominees in 1920 and 1924.[13] Later in the decade, Holcombe saw "the pattern of voting strength" evidenced by the 1938 election as "very similar to that prevailing before the New Deal began," although he cautioned that a 1940 GOP victory was not to be assumed. The Democrats had made "a real dent" in traditional Republican strength only among northern African Americans and among coal miners. These groups would have to be recaptured, or inroads made elsewhere, for the Republican Party to recover the strength it had in the 1920s.[14]

In his 1940 book, *The Middle Classes in American Politics*, Holcombe allowed that the Democratic campaign of 1932, like the election of 1896, appeared to have brought about some permanent partisan change. But he apparently remained sufficiently ambivalent about enduring realignment that he actually included passages in that book first written for publication prior to the 1936 election. He wrote, on the one hand, that Roosevelt's assault against the Republicans seemed to constitute "a greater threat to the old order in national politics than any . . . since the present party alignment was first established." On the other hand, he concluded with question marks, would the Republicans "recover their former authority after an interlude of Democratic ascendancy?" Or did the 1930s "presage a permanent change in the relations between the two great parties" amounting to a "realignment"?[15] In 1946 Holcombe noted that, as a historical fact, loss of congressional control in midterm elections by the party in the White House had invariably led to the loss of the presidency in the following election.[16] In his 1950 *Our More Perfect Union,* Holcombe performed his final balancing act, but with an appropriate post-1948 conclusion. As Samuel Lubell was shortly to stress in his *The Future of American Politics*, Holcombe reiterated his view that much of American political history reflected periods of domination by one major party or the other. He still asked whether the Roosevelt era would be seen as a Democratic interlude like that of Wilson or whether it would transform the Democrats from an "opposition" into an "administration party." But now he had his answer. Under Roosevelt, the Democrats had made "serious inroads upon the Republican sources of strength," he concluded, and the 1948 election "finally demonstrated that the Democratic Party had succeeded under the New Deal in exchanging roles with their Republican opponents."[17]

Arthur M. Schlesinger was born in Xenia, Ohio, in 1888, and attended Ohio State University, graduating in 1910. He pursued graduate work at Columbia University where Charles Beard influenced him as to the relations between economics and politics. At Columbia he also took a course with the sociologist Franklin H. Giddings. Schlesinger taught at Ohio State from 1912 to 1919 before moving to the University of Iowa and in 1924 to Harvard. He became known in particular for his infusion of social and cultural subjects into the writing and teaching of American history; his *New Viewpoints in American History*, published in 1922, became a landmark volume in that respect.[18] *New Viewpoints* also contained early speculations about the nature of American politics. Like other contemporary commentators on political history, he divided it into two basic epochs, one of Democratic dominance prior to the Civil War and of Republican hegemony thereafter. He further contended that "the present era" of party history began "about 1896 or 1900." But he also set forth the nub of his cyclical theory, contending that politics operated in terms of an "alternating order," although the basic movement had been "from conservatism to radicalism"—he later spoke of liberalism and reform—in terms of "the trend of public policy."[19] In a 1924 lecture he advanced a cyclical theory holding that conservatism would continue to hold sway until about 1932. Here, he recalled in his autobiography, he first publicly articulated the concept more fully developed in his 1939 *Yale Review* article, "Tides of American Politics."[20]

Schlesinger had been intrigued by the use of cyclical theory in economics and undertook to test whether such analysis could make sense in the context of American political history. He was, he noted, "immensely interested in . . . business cycles," and while he lacked "technical competence" in economics, he wanted to apply "such rich analysis to the mass swings" between conservatism and liberalism. He agreed that the "swings" could not "be reduced to exact mathematics." But he "thought it . . . more challenging to put the matter in mathematical terms," by which he meant calculating the time duration of conservative and liberal eras. His basic interest lay in "the explanation of the fundamental shifts."[21] In the *Yale Review* piece Schlesinger was at pains to explain what he was and was not doing. He was not dealing with political-party or electoral shifts, although his approach certainly overlapped with and impinged on them; rather, he was primarily interested in discerning shifting political and ideological moods as reflected in public policy that affected both major parties. Throughout American history, he contended, dating back to the republic's origins, there had been swings between conservative and reform eras, each typically lasting about sixteen and a half years, although following the intense transformation of the Civil War era, a longer, compensating era of conservatism followed. These eras, Schlesinger stressed, might be associated with economic traumas at times, but economic swings were not basically responsible for the conservative and reform swings; they were due to "deeper" causes, reflective of an underlying "rhythm," essentially psychological in nature. As problems piled up, people were stimulated through reform to resolve them; as people tired of the ferment of change, they lapsed for a time again into conservative repose. His theory, Schlesinger added, was predictive; reform and conservative eras would alternate in the future as in the past. A return of conservatism in the late 1940s, he predicted, would be followed by a renewal of liberal reform in the early 1960s.[22]

Schlesinger noted at the time that he had been told that President Roosevelt had read his "Tides" essay "with much interest," and in his autobiography he suggested that the notion of liberalism would continue to hold sway until the late 1940s played a role in FDR's decision to seek a third term in 1940.[23] That reflected a cyclical theory's predictive nature; sentiment would swing back and forth. But Schlesinger's cyclical theory also had a secular element, here presaging developments in political analysis of the 1950s, even as his notion of recurrent shifts between two continuing tendencies throughout American history suggested a Beardian perspective. The appropriate metaphor for his theory, he held, was not a pendulum, but rather a spiral. Schlesinger associated periods of reform with governmental activism and periods of conservatism with lassitude. Liberals would energize public policy; conservatives would lapse into inaction. Thus, over time, liberalism would become "more liberal and conservatism less conservative." The swings would occur on an ascending spiral of liberal reform accomplishment; conservative eras in that sense would essentially be pauses in the story of continuing, if intermittent, liberal reform triumph, a conclusion that neatly fit Schlesinger's own New Deal ideological and policy preferences.[24]

Schlesinger's stress on ideology and policy differentiated his theory from the party and electoral emphases of most other political analysts. The distinguished political scientist Harold D. Lasswell in 1940 urged the historian to undertake a book dealing with the role "played by public opinion" in American history, holding that it was "extremely difficult to think of anyone" else for the task.[25] Schlesinger's emphasis on such matters anticipated the efforts to add policy components to the electoral skeleton of later realignment theory. His notion that both major parties in one way or another partook of the dominant mood of a time anticipated also Samuel Lubell's theory of a politics in which a minority party operated within and reflected the dominant parameters of policy and ideology set by the majority party. But these aspects of Schlesinger's theory also put him on the defensive in the context of 1948. Moods are more slippery than electoral counts; assessments of the liberal or conservative nature of policy are less definitive than knowing which party carried an election and by how much. Schlesinger noted in his 1939 "Tides" essay that his expectation that the reform era would continue for several more years did not assume that the Democratic Party would remain in power, only that the New Deal "political mood" would continue to guide the "conduct of the government." In 1946 he believed that the country had entered "a time of drift and disillusion."[26] Arthur Schlesinger, Jr. that same year, applying his father's theory, wrote of the "exhaustion" of the New Deal's "reform impulse." Time was now operating "against the New Deal," which "had probably run its course" in terms of favorable public opinion.[27] The election of 1946, with its GOP takeover of Congress, made it seem that the elder Schlesinger was right on the mark in his prediction of a coming conservative era.

Then came the shock of 1948. Schlesinger certainly did not remotely foresee Harry Truman's upset victory. Like virtually everyone else he had assumed a Republican win. Indeed, in a September 1948 letter to the publisher of his forthcoming book of essays, *Paths to the Present*, which included a revised and updated version of the "Tides" article, Schlesinger urged reconsideration of the plan not to publish the book until the spring of 1949. "There is a special reason why it should appear before President Truman steps out of office," he explained, obviously expecting a Truman departure on January 20, 1949, "for the three chapters on the presidency all state that . . . his record is as yet incomplete."[28] The election outcome made Schlesinger seem as off-base in 1948 as he had appeared prescient in 1946. Yet the openness of his concept allowed for wiggle room. The 1946 election, he insisted, had indeed inaugurated a conservative era, which Truman's victory did not halt.[29] As he wrote to Samuel Lubell in 1952 "regarding the present conservative swing," his essay on "Tides" included in *Paths to the Present* had been "widely misunderstood by reviewers when the book appeared shortly after the 1948 election. Unlike Louis Bean, I was not engaged . . . in charting the party turnover at the polls, but the deeper trends determining the course of legislation regardless of the party in power."[30]

As suggested by Schlesinger's letter to Lubell, Louis Bean was both a fellow cyclical theorist and something of a rival in the development and application of cyclical theory. Bean was born in Russian Lithuania in 1896, arrived in the United States in 1906, grew up in New Hampshire, graduated from the University of Rochester, and earned a master's degree in business administration from Harvard. He entered government service in the Department of Agriculture in 1923 and remained continuously in public service until 1953. He spent the last twenty years as a policy adviser to major figures of the Roosevelt and Truman administrations, dispensing political strategy suggestions as well, once his expertise in that field developed. Trained as a statistician, Bean traced his interest in quantitative political analysis to a 1936 *World Almanac* compilation of presidential election returns since 1896 and proceeded thereafter to write *Ballot Behavior* and other books and articles outlining his approach to the subject.[31] He undertook to apply his training and skills in economic analysis, including knowledge of business cycles and long-term economic trends, to the study of politics. His goal was to uncover "the basic characteristics of American political behavior" and in a "quantitative way" to account for the "factors . . . responsible for shifts in the balance between the major parties."[32]

Developing analyses based on his statistical study of voting returns since the 1850s, Bean concluded that "cycles" or "tides" had characterized American political history, creating a pattern of partisan alternation. These recurrent cycles were somewhat irregular in duration, but on average lasted about two decades. Bean acknowledged the existence of voting patterns based on ethnicity and religion, but he considered economic factors most important in explaining the swings of the political pendulum. Economic downturns in 1857, 1873, 1893, and 1908 all presaged changes in partisan predominance; the economic debacle of 1929 underlay the Democratic dominance of the 1930s.[33] Similar to Schlesinger's theory in terms of duration of tides, Bean considered the historian's concept insufficiently quantitative. Bean's theory also did not include an underlying psychological element. Like Schlesinger's, however, Bean's theory contained a secular element. He held that in addition to the cyclical movements, there was an upward secular Democratic trend due to the growth of cities and the Democrats' support among urban voters, making Bean's analysis somewhat congruent with Holcombe's in this respect.[34]

In applying his analyses to the late 1930s and the 1940s, Bean deviated from some common assumptions of the time. He did not believe, for example, that the 1938 GOP election surge necessarily presaged a 1940 presidential victory. Nor did he think that the strong Republican gains in 1942, which he attributed to a low turnout, foretold a Republican triumph in 1944.[35] Indeed, Bean's reflections on the discrepancies between the off-year elections of 1938 and 1942 and the presidential elections of 1940 and 1944 led him to develop a two-tiered electoral theory, which held that off-year and presidential-year elections proceeded at different levels due in part to turnout; thus, an off-year surge by the party out of the White House did not necessarily presage an impending return.[36] Applying this analysis to the GOP triumph of 1946, Bean, unlike so many others, rejected the notion of a more or less preordained forthcoming Republican presidential victory. He concluded that 1946, on the contrary, largely reflected the voters' ephemeral aggravation over problems of postwar readjustment, rather than anything of a more fundamental nature. There had been no significant shift in voters' party allegiances; nor was 1946 a vote for conservative policies. Instead of a new Republican cycle, Bean speculated that the 1946 election might reflect only the end of the "New Deal tide," that is, the decline of a particular Democratic cycle. It did not automatically mean a new Republican cycle; it might even be a trough pending a new upward Democratic cycle. Given the Democratic secular trend, 1946 might only represent the low point from which a Democratic resurgence might begin.[37]

Bean's name remains forever associated with the 1948 election and Truman's upset victory. For the remainder of his life, which lasted almost another half-century, Bean was celebrated as the "prophet" who alone "predicted" Truman's triumph. The truth, as revealed by Bean's private correspondence, was somewhat more complicated. In his 1948 book, *How to Predict Elections*, Bean certainly suggested, contrary to nearly everyone else, that Truman could win. This was enough to cause the author to stand out in a year when few gave Truman any chance at all. His analysis of the direction of the political tide likewise suggested that elements conducive to a Democratic victory were in place. Many voters disapproved of the policies of the Republican Congress elected in 1946, he wrote. With an anticipated higher turnout, the 1948 Democratic nominee could be expected to do about as well as Roosevelt had in 1940 and 1944; thus, the GOP victory of 1946 might prove short-lived.[38] His own campaign advice called for the Democrats to promote turnout and to provide a "very extensive dramatization" of economic issues designed to appeal to farmers, workers, and consumers.[39] But Bean was torn throughout the course of the 1948 campaign between his analysis, which pointed one way, and the persuasiveness of the polls and the unanimity of opinion, which pointed the other. In the end he was swayed by the polls even as, shortly thereafter, he was celebrated as the prophet of the Truman miracle.[40]

The 1948 election outcome appeared to support Bean's analysis of the political trend, whatever the shakiness of his legendary prediction. Indeed, Bean suggested that, rather than Schlesinger's anticipated conservative cycle, 1948 might mark the beginning of a new upward Democratic surge and a reform era stretching into the 1950s.[41] Thus, the 1948 victory, he concluded, "was no ordinary one." It "resembled a tidal movement like the . . . change in political direction in 1930." It possibly marked "the beginning of a new long-time swing of the political pendulum" in the Democrats' favor.[42] Bean's language characterizing the 1948 contest suggested an approach to the later theory of "critical elections." But 1948 proved to be no harbinger of a new political era, even as it did prove critical to the development of realignment theory. In this respect, 1948 was ironic in terms of Bean's career and influence as a political analyst. It made Bean's reputation as a prophet, but it set in motion an intellectual ferment that eclipsed his analytical impact. By triggering the development of the secular analyses of political and electoral behavior of Samuel

Lubell and V. O. Key, the 1948 election left the cyclical theories of Bean and Schlesinger (although the latter benefited from the prodigious and prolific efforts of his historian and publicist son) in the dust. Bean and Schlesinger provided essentially cyclical theories albeit with secular components; Lubell and Key were to provide essentially secular theories into which, however, some of their followers were to incorporate cyclical components.

Harold F. Gosnell was born in Lockport in the far western reaches of New York State between Buffalo and Rochester in 1896 and was educated at the University of Rochester. He took his graduate training at the University of Chicago, where he was a student and then a colleague of Charles Merriam and where he remained until 1942.[43] Gosnell's industriousness was noted at an early date. Under his name in the 1918 University of Rochester yearbook appeared an apt characterization: "Did somebody mention work? Well, Harold has got Webster busy looking up a new definition. . . . He's an animated perpetual motion machine."[44] Despite an immense outpouring of publications since the 1920s, however, Gosnell left Chicago under unpleasant circumstances. The university president, Robert Maynard Hutchins, was hostile to modern social-science approaches and not inclined to bestow benefits upon their practitioners.[45] As he departed, Gosnell made clear his feeling that he had been treated unfairly.[46] To Gosnell, Hutchins's "battle against social science research" smacked of a "medievalism" and "neoscholasticism" of which he wanted no part.[47] The function of college deans under Hutchins, Gosnell later wrote, was to carry out the president's "orders for executions."[48] During the remainder of his career, Gosnell worked in the federal government, including stints in the Office of Price Administration, the Bureau of the Budget, the State Department, and the Central Intelligence Agency. He also continued to teach, at American University and Howard, and to write, although now largely in the area of political biography, leaving behind the innovative work he had done in voting-behavior and electoral analysis during his Chicago years.[49] His departure from Chicago thus marked not only a disruption in the pattern of an academic career, but also a break in Gosnell's work as an academic political analyst. Although not yet fifty years old at the end of World War II, he would remain a prewar figure in the postwar history of the rapidly growing and developing field to which he had so significantly contributed.

Gosnell was later characterized by Gabriel A. Almond as "a very shy and gentle soul" who was "quite undervalued" at Chicago. Almond noted that after departing Chicago, Gosnell would send Christmas cards—Gosnell had talent as a cartoonist—"that were extraordinarily revealing of a much livelier . . . more imaginative kind of personality than we had associated him with." At Chicago, however, Almond recalled, Gosnell's preoccupation "with quantitative analysis was viewed as a purely technical kind of accomplishment." He was "solidly productive . . . just one book after another . . . but he wasn't really taken seriously . . . as a figure of creative and seminal importance." It was a "tragedy," Almond concluded, that so "ingenious and . . . creative" a scholar was not more appreciated.[50] Along with his work on electoral behavior, Gosnell was also a pioneer analyst of African-American politics and employed black assistants.[51] A young black graduate student recalled that he had gone to Chicago for study because Gosnell was "the only teacher-scholar in the United States who had expressed long-term interest in black politics." Robert Martin remembered Gosnell as "a fine teacher, though not a very exciting lecturer." He would never forget, Martin added, how Gosnell "would come to class at times . . . and proceed to draw angles . . . to illustrate his discussion. I doubt that more than half of the class was able to follow him and fully comprehend his points."[52] A 1941 Gosnell exam question on voting behavior included reference to "standard deviations" and "regression equations."[53]

Gosnell, in his analyses of American politics from the 1920s to the early 1940s, demonstrated a breadth of scope and analysis. He focused, among other things, on the existence of what V. O. Key was later to call "critical elections," that is, elections that led to sharp and durable changes in voting patterns. As Gosnell put it in 1935, throughout American political history there had occurred, "at irregular intervals . . . certain crucial presidential elections" which appeared to "set the party alignments for several decades." The 1896 election, for example, undid an era of relatively even party balance nationally and led to an era of Republican dominance. It ushered in a party system in which different sections of the nation were geared so heavily to one party or the other that lack of competitiveness had resulted in declining rates of voter participation. Such elections broke through the crust of "habitual" voting and "old party traditions." Within the chronological limits of what later became known as the "system of '96," Gosnell noted, the Democrats had triumphed in presidential elections only under Wilson. Those triumphs were made possible, he held, by Republican division in 1912 and by a "personal" rather than "party" appeal in 1916; hence, they were triumphs that in no basic way undermined the existence of a party alignment characterized by Republican hegemony.[54]

Over the course of the 1930s, Gosnell sought to apply his concepts through a series of case studies of electoral patterns under the general rubric of "the effect of the Depression upon voting behavior," gauging the changes wrought during a decade of crisis and upheaval.[55] His language and conclusions were at times dramatic and far-reaching. "A new era in American politics was definitely started by the election of 1932," he wrote in 1935, ending the long period of Republican dominance.[56] There was "no question," he reiterated in 1937, that 1932 had ended long time Republican control of the national government and had inaugurated a new period of political history.[57] "We have just witnessed . . . a peaceful American revolution," he declared following the 1936 election. The time of the 1920s style GOP was "simply gone."[58] In Wisconsin, he held in 1940, the 1932 election had constituted "a political revolution."[59] In 1940 Gosnell characterized the transformation of historically Republican Pennsylvania, which Hoover had carried in 1932, into a state supportive of the New Deal as "a revolution in the politics of industrial America."[60] In Iowa, he wrote in 1941, the 1932 election overcame "the inertia of 70 years of Republicanism"; the Roosevelt votes of 1932 and 1936 thus "were little short of revolutionary."[61] How lasting were the realignments of the 1930s? The politics of Pennsylvania, he concluded in 1940, had "been fundamentally altered during the past ten years" and would "probably never revert" to its earlier character. The Democratic losses in the 1938 election were "not likely to be as lasting as Democratic defeats in preceding decades."[62] The Democratic victories nationally of 1932, 1936, and 1940, he concluded in 1942, had wrought "a general shift in party alignments." Roosevelt's victories did not rely upon the same base of support as those of Wilson. With enhanced northern support, the Democrats were no longer as reliant on the South as in Wilson's time.[63]

In tracing the roots and nature of the 1930s realignments in the North, Gosnell stressed economics. While acknowledging that sectional, religious, and ethnic influences played an important role in determining party identities, he held that economic factors had become increasingly important. The upheavals of the 1930s, accordingly, building upon the 1928 Democratic appeal to workers, had created a political configuration increasingly based on "income groupings." The 1932 election had been characterized by a general reaction against Hoover and the Republicans, but thereafter the division had been more reflective of economic categories, interests, and conditions. Moreover, Gosnell added, the 1930s had brought a mobilization of new voters—often urban, foreign-born, Catholic, working-class, unionized—into the Democratic fold, "a huge army" of the "formerly . . . indifferent," as he put it in a Pennsylvania context. Among African Americans in northern cities, Gosnell observed, the impact of economics on working-class voters had led them to the Democrats, while the better off maintained their traditional Republican allegiance. This kind of economically based voting behavior was not wholly new, Gosnell concluded; it resembled 1896 in some respects and to a degree the contests of 1924 and 1928. But it was undoing Republican gains among lower-income voters dating back to the turn of the century, and together with increased mobilization of new voters, it was creating a new national political alignment.[64] These conclusions bore similarities to Holcombe's, although Gosnell added more of a labor-oriented, working-class twist to his analysis and was more inclined to see epochal changes. Indeed, he saw evidence of "an increasing class conflict in American politics" in contrast to Holcombe's "thesis" that "the role of the middle classes" was to soften "class conflicts."[65]

Gosnell coauthored the 1929, 1940, and 1949 editions of Charles Merriam's *The American Party System*. In 1929, in reviewing American political history, he and Merriam outlined four broad eras of party division, the last dating from shortly after Reconstruction.[66] In the 1940 edition, in a chapter for which Gosnell was responsible, a fifth period was added, that since 1929, a point reiterated in the 1949 edition.[67] This schema proposed the era of the Great Depression and New Deal as a discrete historical turning point. On the other hand, Gosnell was also impressed by the strength of partisan tradition and the slowness with which voting habits changed. He seemed at times to have had difficulty in weighing and synthesizing the relative strength of continuity and change. Hence, for example, he could write in 1935 that while an economic downturn produced "a reaction against the party in power," voting habits of individuals changed slowly, reflecting the "distinct lag in the adjustment of political attitudes to changing material conditions."[68] This suggested gradual, rather than sudden, change. In 1941, however, he alluded to the recent phenomenon of greater sudden swings from one election to another, as, for example, between 1928 and 1932.[69] Gosnell brought the differing strands together most effectively in his case study of Chicago electoral patterns. The most important factors in 1930s Chicago voting, he held, antedated the Depression and New Deal and reflected long-standing electoral traditions. Working-class, foreign-born, and Catholic voters had been attracted to the Democrats prior to 1929 or 1932. But, Gosnell added, the New Deal's policies had the effect of intensifying their party loyalty, commitment, and vote.[70]

As he ended his studies of electoral patterns at the beginning of the 1940s, Gosnell was most swayed by prevailing cyclical theories. He drew explicit attention in his 1942 book, *Grass Roots Politics*, to Schlesinger's "Tides" essay and to Bean's *Ballot Behavior*. In 1940 articles on Pennsylvania and Wisconsin, he remarked how Democratic reverses in the 1938 election had reflected the swing of the "political pendulum." In a 1942 article, he held that the United States was now in the midst of a fifth historical "political cycle" of alternating party rule, with Democratic strength probably peaking in 1936. In *Grass Roots Politics* Gosnell concluded that "changes in American politics are usually not abrupt," reflecting "a gradual shift from one phase of the political cycle to another." A party in power gradually lost appeal, giving way to the rival, which then repeated the process, the time frame running from sixteen to twenty-four years historically.[71] (Gosnell had known Louis Bean as a fellow student at Rochester, and they became reacquainted after Bean undertook his electoral studies.)[72] Thus, an analyst who appeared on the verge of a breakthrough toward a secularly based analysis ended with an emphasis on cycles, pendulums, and recurrent patterns, rather than on sharp turning points and historically discrete periods. After World War II Gosnell went on to more traditional biographical accounts of the political career of Franklin Delano Roosevelt (FDR) and of the presidency of Harry Truman, demonstrating a talent for sprightly writing, as well as for quantitative methodological analysis.

In those accounts he continued to write of the cyclical nature of American politics and of the periodic swings of the political pendulum. But in his 1952 book, *Champion Campaigner: Franklin D. Roosevelt*, Gosnell reiterated his earlier points about the 1928 election's reorientation of the Democratic Party and about the "electoral upheaval" of 1932. Like others, he also took account of the defining quality of the election of 1948. The Democratic victory that year, Gosnell concluded, showed that the Roosevelt era, unlike the Wilson era, was not just an interlude in a long run of Republican domination. There proved, in the end, to be no real parallel between the Republican victories of 1918 and 1946. Wilson's victories were ephemeral, but 1948 showed that Roosevelt's were not based on personality alone. Instead, 1948 demonstrated that "Roosevelt had laid a firm foundation for the future of his party" and that "a majority of . . . American voters were still Democratic."[73]

Gosnell departed from the field of quantitative electoral analysis on the very eve of its post–World War II blossoming. Insights from Gosnell and others afterward gave way to what were deemed the more generally applicable and certainly extraordinarily influential "critical election" and "secular realignment" theories of V. O. Key. Gosnell in a sense had come too soon. In another sense, ironically, he had perhaps continued too long. The crucial year in the breakthrough toward secular theory came in 1948, and Gosnell by then had moved in other, albeit related, scholarly directions. On the other hand, he expressed secular perspectives in the wake of 1932 and 1936 only to turn later to cyclical theory. Had he ended sooner, his earlier forays might have seemed more impressive in the light of subsequent intellectual development. In the end it remained for younger figures, coming of age in the Roosevelt era, to make the explanatory breakthroughs that Gosnell and others approached, but could not quite pin down. Holcombe, Schlesinger, Bean, and Gosnell were all born in the late nineteenth century. Samuel Lubell, on the other hand, was born in 1911 and V. O. Key in 1908. They came to 1948 and its aftermath without the longer time frames of their predecessors; they could bring the fresher perspective conducive to seminal analytical breakthroughs. Gosnell, now on the periphery, rather than at the center, of electoral analysis, nonetheless remained abreast of postwar developments and figures. He groused about how the study of voting behavior was increasingly dominated by sociologists and social psychologists, rather than political scientists. He contrasted the low expenditures made for his 1920s Chicago studies with the much larger funds available for postwar surveys done by sociologists and social psychologists, which made him feel like "Rip Van Winkle."[74] But Gosnell had taught Key at Chicago and remained an admirer. Key, Gosnell recalled, had "a magic typewriter." His former student "could pick up the latest research, assimilate it, and grind out superb copy" faster than anyone else Gosnell knew.[75] Gosnell declared Samuel Lubell "a one man survey team," who defied traditional "canons" and to whom electoral study was "an art."[76] Key made the important analytical refinements, but Lubell's accomplishment from outside the guild was in some ways even more impressive. It took the election of 1948 to comprehensively formulate and drive home the points Lubell was to make in *The Future of American Politics*. But, remarkably, the kernel of Lubell's contribution was set forth as early as 1941.

Chapter Four

The Breakthrough of Samuel Lubell

Samuel Lubell was one of a kind. Born Samuel Lubelsky in 1911 in a village on the Russian-German border in what became Poland, the last in a family of nine children, Lubell never knew his exact birth date. Believing he was born in November, and already intrigued by politics, at the age of six he picked November 3, election day, as his official birthday. Four years earlier, his family had arrived in the United States in steerage. Lubell grew up in New York City, attended the City College of New York (CCNY) as an evening student from 1927 to 1931, and then transferred to the Columbia University School of Journalism, from which he graduated in 1933. In the summer of 1930, with a CCNY classmate, Lubell, who "had never been west of the Hudson River," for ten weeks hitchhiked across various parts of North America, at a total cost, he noted, of $10.38. The summer of 1933 brought a similar trip, now including some writing. The award of a Pulitzer Traveling Scholarship from Columbia in 1934 allowed Lubell to visit England, France, Italy, Austria, Germany, Poland, and Russia. Back in the United States, the fledgling, but well-traveled, journalist wrote for the *Long Island Daily Press*, followed by the *Washington Post*, the *Richmond Times-Dispatch*, and the *Washington Herald*. In 1938 he left the newspaper grind for a try at freelance magazine writing, and in 1941 he married Helen Spotot with whom he had two sons.[1]

But the young journalist was not only a journalist. He also dabbled in politics and worked in government. And he made powerful connections. Beginning in December 1941, Lubell worked as a writer for the Office of Facts and Figures, later the Office of War Information. He furthered served as an assistant to James F. Byrnes, director of the Office of Economic Stabilization, and former senator and Supreme Court justice. Most significantly and lastingly, he became a valued aide to the elder statesman and Wall Street speculator turned Washington political operative Bernard Baruch. A central figure in the

31

government's economic mobilization for World War I, Baruch was still highly active during World War II. Lubell did his part in highlighting and enhancing Baruch's role and reputation. The wartime Baruch-Hancock Report on rubber was set forth, Jordan Schwarz, Baruch's biographer writes, "in the best publicist language Samuel Lubell could" muster. Placed on Baruch's payroll, Lubell became the researcher and ghostwriter of most of Baruch's public pronouncements. Lubell also drafted Baruch's memoir, *My Own Story*. In a follow-up book, Baruch quite appropriately characterized Lubell as possessing an "infinite" capacity for work and praised him as "a loyal and tireless aide." When Lubell's opus, *The Future of American Politics*, was published in 1952, Baruch returned the favor. Walter Winchell, the nationally syndicated news and gossip columnist, wrote in May 4, 1952, "Bernard Baruch's book-of-the-week is *The Future of American Politics* by Samuel Lubell."[2]

Meanwhile, Lubell's journalistic career also proceeded apace. Between 1944 and 1946 he worked as a foreign correspondent in Europe and Asia. With his postwar focus on domestic politics, he traveled throughout the United States, interviewing voters using what became his trademark technique. By 1952 his reports were published in fifty newspapers, including those of the Scripps-Howard chain. *Time* reported in 1956 that the inveterate doorbell ringer Lubell had "been bitten by three dogs, taken for a masher by housewives, a salesman by husbands," and on at least one occasion as a spy for the Congress of Industrial Organizations.[3] An aide to the mighty shortly after he turned thirty, author of a highly acclaimed book just after he turned forty, Lubell combined humble origins with deep pride in his accomplishments. In a 1960 letter to a student newspaper inquiry from his old high school, Lubell recalled that as a student at James Monroe High School in the Bronx, he "was rather brash and awkward . . . the shortest boy in class" and "with a front tooth missing!" Despite the pain, he wrote, given ability, "it probably helps to be awkward when you're young," because "when you are awkward, you keep trying." When you "get pushed down—the recoil is all the higher."[4] In 1952 Lubell pronounced himself "the best person in the country to undertake" an in-depth coverage of that year's election, not, he quickly added, because he had any "personal magic as a reporter," but because of the intensive work he had done leading to *The Future of American Politics*.[5] In a 1955 letter to the publisher of his follow-up book, *The Revolt of Moderates*, Lubell allowed that it was important to stress the readability of the volume, but he did not want that to obscure the book's "'landmark' quality" as "a quite important and even profound analysis of the American political character."[6] In 1967, when historian John Braeman asked permission to reprint Lubell's 1941 *Saturday Evening Post* article on FDR's third-term election in a book of readings on political history, Lubell suggested in response that in addition to the usual credit, Braeman "might want to add something more provocative. You could make the point that 'this article states for the first time many of the findings which were developed later by Mr. Lubell in *The Future of American Politics*.'"[7] At fifty-six, Lubell might still have been brash, but he also could not have been more accurate.

Students of American politics were quick to recognize the breakthrough quality of Lubell's work when *The Future of American Politics* appeared. But in Lubell's case, the story indeed began not with the 1948 election, but with the article of 1941. In that article, in clear if embryonic form, appeared many of the basic points of the later book. Lubell pointed to labor, immigrants and their children, African Americans, and big-city residents as the mainstays of the coalition that reelected FDR. He stressed the role of class in voting behavior, holding that the New Deal had "drawn a class line across the face of American politics." He rejected the notion of a mechanical political pendulum swaying back and forth between the parties and heading again toward the GOP. Instead, he stressed long-term factors such as the birth rates among late-nineteenth- and early-twentieth-century immigrants, as well as the impact of the Great Depression and New Deal. And he declared that the upheaval of the 1930s constituted a break with the past and the possible ushering in of a Democratic Party era. Thus, 1940 "was not just another election," and the victory was not just due to Roosevelt's magic touch. Once Roosevelt left the scene, Lubell contended, the electoral pattern would "not slip back automatically into its former slots." If the Democratic Party held together, he observed somewhat tentatively at this point, it could "become the normal majority party, with the Republicans occupying the unenviable position of the Democrats after the Civil War."[8]

In preparing for and in writing *The Future of American Politics*, Lubell noted that the original "inspiration" for the book dated from the 1941 article as augmented by a 1949 piece on Truman's surprise victory. Thus, the book involved "something like twelve years of thinking" in addition to the shorter period of intensive effort.[9] It also involved giving thought to the merit of competing titles. Before settling on the final choice, Lubell considered *All FDR's Children* and *The Hidden Revolution in American Politics*, the latter to be resurrected almost two decades later in slightly altered form.[10] The background of the book, Lubell related, further included the perusal of "every study of voting behavior" he "could find," of which he deemed "particularly stimulating" or "revealing" works by Eldersveld, Bean, Gosnell, Key, Rice, Holcombe, and Schattschneider, among others.[11] Preparation for the book also included the composition of a detailed prospectus in December 1949 in which Lubell outlined his approach, as well as his thesis. His forthcoming book would reflect his belief that elections across time provided portrayals not just of politics, but of the social, economic, and cultural patterns and climate of the nation. Hence, he would deal not only with the origins and course of Roosevelt's coalition, with the significance of Truman's upset win, and with the implications of the Democrats' association with government-fostered prosperity and the Republicans' with the Depression. He would also discuss the rise of the city, ethnicity and religion, race relations, and cultural conflict as components of the transformation of the United States "from a 'normally Republican' to a 'normally Democratic' country."[12]

In time, Lubell's approach became famous and was celebrated for and imitated in terms of its patented combination of journalistic sweep and flair with scholarly perspective and knowledge. Lubell himself noted that he tried to bring together "the crafts of both historian and reporter," and others similarly alluded to his ability to link journalism and political science, infusing political reporting with novel techniques and bringing the fresh observations of an outsider to a formal academic discipline.[13] His approach involved the study of election returns combined with interviews of voters in areas selected on the basis of historical voting patterns. In this way, he and others believed, he successfully moved the study of American politics from a focus on the candidates to an effort better to understand and appreciate the motivations and concerns of the voters themselves.[14] In Lubell's terms, elections and election statistics reflected not only reactions to the issues and candidates of the day; they also reflected history. Each presidential election constituted "a self-portrait of America" in its historical setting. Elections embodied traditions, experiences, and conflicts that had shaped the outlooks of the various groups that made up the American voting population. They carried the economic, class, sectional, cultural, ethnic, religious, and generational streams and influences that permeated American society. Voters, then, in a given election, were not simply responding to the stimuli of the campaign; in voting they were influenced by their histories and the histories of the segments of the population with which they identified; they were voting in part in response to "subconscious" feelings and emotions shared within each group.[15] He was impressed by the degree to which the past, in the form of "the stream of voting consciousness," persisted in shaping electoral patterns.[16] His focus, therefore, was on "enduring interrelationships" that illustrated "how strongly stratified the bases of American voting" were.[17] Election statistics, in Lubell's formulation, were not "one body of water," but rather constituted "many rivers"; his "key concept" was that Americans had "always voted less as individuals than as part of a particular voting stream, with its own marked flow."[18]

Occasionally a critic would suggest that Lubell was none too precise in his approach. Political scientist Richard Neustadt, for example, in reviewing Lubell's *Revolt of the Moderates*, duly alluded to the author's "remarkable first book," *The Future of American Politics*. But following a description of Lubell's "raw materials," he remarked that readers had "no independent check upon the author's own interpretations of his own material," a problem "compounded by the wide latitude Lubell sometimes gives himself in drawing illustrations from his data file."[19] Political scientist Oliver Garceau similarly remarked that Lubell's "research method" had produced "valuable" and successful results, but that "systematic research" was "a social activity, not an individual one," and it was not clear to Garceau "just what" Lubell did.[20] Decades later, political scientist Everett Carll Ladd contended that Lubell's "methodology" was not as thoroughgoing or systematic as Lubell had claimed.[21] Lubell, for his part, insisted that he did not "decry" the quantitative approach of scholarly political scientists; he himself, he pointed out, relied heavily on election statistics. Yet in 1960 he did decry "too heavy—and too limiting—an emphasis on hypotheses susceptible of 'proof' only in quantitative terms." Too full a reliance on "numerical yardsticks" risked ignoring or foreclosing "more fruitful avenues to understanding."[22] A few years later Lubell again demonstrated the outlook of what V. O. Key in 1957 termed "this lone-wolf operator."[23] Polls, Lubell held in 1964, were at best efforts to be "scientific," since there was "no 'scientific' way of polling public opinion." And he was unimpressed with the introduction of computers into election-night analysis. "A machine is no better than the person who programs it," he declaimed, "and if the programmer knows what he is doing he doesn't need the machine." Further, he added, "if you can keep the information in your head there's really not much advantage in putting it into a machine."[24]

Whatever the contemporary or subsequent caveats as to his approach, Lubell's *The Future of American Politics* appeared on stage to great applause, an author's dream come true. The "most exciting and enlightening book we have seen on American politics," declared one enthusiastic reviewer, "an extremely wise and stimulating work, attractive to novices and experts alike," in which Lubell explained "the political weather better than the 'political scientists.'"[25] To Arthur M. Schlesinger, Jr., Lubell's book was "the most suggestive and challenging . . . about the American party system . . . in some time." It "broke new paths," resulting in "a striking new portrait of American politics," and establishing Lubell "as the preeminent diagnostician of our contemporary politics."[26] Nathan Glazer hailed Lubell's book as "the best . . . yet written on American politics of the last twenty years; and if a better one should appear, it is hard to see how it could be anything but a further development of the basic pattern laid down by Lubell."[27] Arthur Holcombe called the book "penetrating," and Sidney Hyman declared it "in a class by itself."[28] University of Chicago historian Daniel Boorstin wrote to Lubell, noting "how widely and favorably received was your *Future of American Politics* in academic as well as nonacademic circles," and urging him to contribute a book on World War I and the 1920s to a series Boorstin was editing—what later became William Leuchtenburg's *Perils of Prosperity*.[29] *The Revolt of the Moderates* had some of the problems of a sequel; the initial shock of a new stimulus was gone. But Seymour Martin Lipset, in a letter to Lubell, called it "clearly the best single study written about American electoral and political behavior." Lipset added that he felt embarrassment for himself and his "academic colleagues" because in all "the reams of paper we have written, none of us have come as close as you to imaginatively grasping what American politics are all about, as well as to really empirically documenting the hypotheses."[30] Political scientist Peter Odegard summed up Lubell's skill in setting forth a thesis, writing that this outsider had "an extraordinary knack for saying clearly what many of the more sophisticated scholars obscure in a mass of gobbledygook."[31]

In *The Future of American Politics* Lubell certainly drove home his central thesis of political and electoral discontinuity. Pendulums and cycles were discarded, as was the customary stress on continuity and duality—interpreting American political history in terms of two opposing forces or tendencies or parties in opposition throughout the republic's more than a century and a half under the Constitution. Lubell was struck by how different the contemporary era was from anything that had gone before. Republicans had long believed that it was Roosevelt who had kept them at bay; once Roosevelt was gone, all would return to "normal," that is Republican ascendancy; or it was the shock of the Depression or the interruption of World War II. Lubell's point was that it went far deeper into the underlying currents of history. What was "normal" had changed. What was "distinctive" about "the political revolution . . . Roosevelt began and Truman inherited" lay not in any similarity to previous political struggles "but in its abrupt break with the continuity of the past." The analogy lay with the explosive divide of the Civil War. If the Civil War constituted a "'Second American Revolution,' then the toppling of the dominance held by the Republicans for nearly three fourths of a century can be considered as the Third American Revolution." This was his central story, "the transformation of the United States from a nation with a traditional Republican majority to one with a normal Democratic majority."[32] And his "main theme" and purpose was to explain the "forces" that lay behind this historic political transformation.[33]

The 1936 election crystallized the new dominant Democratic coalition, according to Lubell. The 1940 election demonstrated its continuity, while 1948 drove home its durability and dominance. The 1932 election, despite the voters' big swing to the Democrats in reaction to the Great Depression, "still mirrored the orbit . . . of the old Republican order." The states Roosevelt lost were all in the East. The 1936 election conveyed not just gratitude for movement out of depression; it was "also the year of realignment in which the

Democrats became the nation's normal majority party," ending the long reign of Republican dominance and establishing "a new era in American politics." In the big cities "the political allegiances that had grown out of the Civil War were uprooted for good" to be replaced by new ones rooted in the contemporary era. The Democratic dominance established in 1936 proved decisive in Roosevelt's third-term victory in 1940. The full restoration of prosperity during the war solidified the support of Democratic voters.[34] The election of 1948 confirmed it. Not that Lubell demonstrated the prescience of Louis Bean before the fact. Indeed, he had deemed Truman's election chances "hopeless" and made a bet at ten-to-one odds that Thomas Dewey would win. Truman's victory did not prove the winning bettor's "political sagacity"—he insisted in paying off the wager—but merely shrewdness in grasping at the "sucker odds."[35] Lubell quickly assayed the election results in terms of his own forthcoming analysis. In a December 1948 letter, he announced that he had "no hesitation in saying that the Truman election marks . . . a political revolution" and "the crumbling of what remained of the post Civil War political lineup."[36] In that sense, Truman's election confirmed not only the durability of the Democratic coalition as shaped by Roosevelt, but also the political sagacity of Lubell's own 1941 article on FDR's third-term win.

In January 1949 Lubell set forth his analysis of the meaning of Truman's victory in another *Saturday Evening Post* article. That win, he held, should end all talk of political pendulums. "The great Republican mistake" lay in the assumption that the alleged pendulum swing that had led to GOP control of Congress in 1946 would automatically result in a White House victory in 1948. But the emergence of a Democratic majority based on the big cities dashed hopes of a "natural pendulum swing" to the GOP. The notion of a Republican revival made sense only in the context of the "normally Republican majority" of earlier times, reflecting legacies of the Civil War. Truman's win "resulted from factors which have been remaking our political life for at least a generation," and in terms of those forces, Republicans appeared "weaker today than during Roosevelt's dazzling victories." Truman's triumph revealed that the Republicans had now been "relegated . . . to the minority status long held by the Democrats. Henceforth political dopesters must think of the United States as 'normally Democratic' or have their predictions boomerang."[37] The 1949 analysis was fleshed out in *The Future of American Politics*. Truman's win, wrote Lubell, shattered the Republicans' "alibi" that their losses through 1944 had all been due to the "devilishly clever" Roosevelt. The 1948 victory reflected Democratic allegiances forged in the crucible of the 1930s and the new "orbit" established by a normal Democratic majority. And it illustrated how the Democrats had replaced the Republicans in the role the latter party had held since the 1890s—as the party of prosperity.[38]

Lubell, of course, always considered himself more than an election analyst narrowly conceived. Hence, it was not enough for him just to isolate the importance of 1936 or simply to highlight the drama of 1948. He believed elections reflected underlying currents of American history; hence, he was driven to discover the roots of electoral manifestations of change, those of the 1930s, but also those antedating the Depression decade. Out of the 1930s, contended Lubell, came economic- and class-based voting. Among urban dwellers in particular, voting in the wake of the Depression broke sharply along class lines. The strength of low-income and working-class support for the Democrats in big cities constituted a "nationalizing force" overcoming previous sectionally based politics and suppressing politics based on religious and racial division. The key to the forging of a Democratic majority lay in this mobilization of large masses of urban voters and in the finessing of cultural conflicts. The continued success of the Democrats lay in successfully stressing the common purpose of an economically united coalition and in sidestepping potentially divisive crosscutting issues. Further, this new generation of working-class urban voters, Lubell stressed, had no Republican heritage or tradition to go back to, which negated any hopes of a Republican revival— there was nothing to revive.[39] In terms of his emphasis on class and economic factors growing out of the 1930s, Lubell obviously shared much in common with Holcombe and Gosnell. But he did not, in chronological terms, start his story of the new Democratic majority in the 1930s. He went back before the Depression, and in so doing, he added complexity to his analysis and became an originator of what came to be known as the "ethnocultural" interpretation of American politics.

Famously, Lubell in *The Future of American Politics* wrote of how the "Al Smith Revolution" preceded the "Roosevelt Revolution," thus beginning an extended debate over the relative impact of cultural and economic influences on—and over 1920s versus 1930s origins of—the new Democratic majority. "It was Smith who first slashed through the traditional alignments that had held so firmly since the Civil War," declared Lubell, "clearing the way for the more comprehensive realignment" wrought by Roosevelt. As historians and political scientists have pointed out, Lubell here appeared to assume that what Smith had begun, Roosevelt continued, that the one voting trend flowed into the other. This, it has been held, confused the very different sources of what occurred in 1928 with what took place in the 1930s. Had there been no Great Depression, there was no reason to assume that the Smith voting patterns of 1928 would have endured.[40] Lubell undertook, however, to demonstrate how the two sources were in fact essentially fused together. Based on his study of election returns since the Civil War, he held that ethnicity had always been "almost as important a voting force" as sectionalism and economic factors.[41]

Ethnic characteristics and conflicts were historically important in the way that they merged with economic status and divisiveness to produce "distinctive voting streams."[42] In a letter to the elder Arthur M. Schlesinger, Lubell went so far as to suggest, albeit in fairly vague terms, that "even if . . . there had been no [D]epression, the political balance in the country would have changed in the 1930–1940 decade" due to the political impact of the birthrates of the pre-1920 period.[43] He thus believed it to be a "mistake to regard the Roosevelt coalition as strictly a product of the [D]epression" since the Democratic vote in the big cities was on the rise in the 1920s. That growing "urban revolt" drew its strength from the high birthrate that Lubell alluded to in his letter to Schlesinger—the high birthrate among the immigrants from southern and eastern Europe. Their children, as they came of age and voted, would encompass numbers large enough to shift any existing political balance. They responded to the urban and Catholic Al Smith in 1928. And, as it turned out, "the [D]epression—striking when most of them had barely entered the adult world—sharpened" their sense of the need for a New Deal and formed them into "the chief carriers of the Roosevelt Revolution." It was "the big-city masses" who "furnished the votes which re-elected Roosevelt again and again—and, in the process, ended the traditional Republican majority." The ethnic minorities in this way constituted the core of the new Democratic majority.[44]

If Lubell pushed the origins of the Democratic coalition backward to a degree, he also pushed the crystallization of that coalition forward. It was, after all, the 1936 election that he designated as the decisive moment: 1932 had been a reaction against Hoover and the Republicans; 1936 was a fervent endorsement of Roosevelt and the New Deal. As he put it in a 1951 letter, the prevailing belief was "that the [D]epression caused the political realignment" which made the Democrats the new "majority party." In fact, Lubell contended, "the [D]epression did not realign the parties; that . . . realignment took place after Roosevelt came to office and centered around what he did."[45] This made 1936, not 1932, the defining election year, and here Lubell anticipated what some later scholars considered an important aspect of realignment theory. A vote against a dominant party provided only an opportunity for the newly victorious party to make a single triumph into a longer period of domination; an enduring political success required the perception of significant accomplishment once in office. In accounting for the nature of realignment, Lubell pointed to both long-range and short-run factors. In terms of what V. O. Key was later to term "secular realignment," Lubell focused on demography. On previous occasions in American history, Lubell wrote, when new majority parties emerged, migration provided an important underlying basis, as in the westward movement of the Jacksonian era and the population growth of the Midwest preceding the emergence of the

Republican Party. The analog for the New Deal era was provided by the surge in the urban population and the birthrates of the immigrants.[46] In explaining the short-run factors, Lubell again looked to history. Only twice in American history, he wrote, had a new majority coalition arisen to replace an old one, first in the Civil War era and then during the New Deal. Both cases demonstrated "that a major realignment requires the rise of new issues powerful enough to dissolve old chains of political loyalty." The 1890s provided an additional example. From the end of Reconstruction into the early 1890s, the two parties were roughly equal in strength. It took the depression beginning in 1893, with the Democrats in the White House, for the Republicans to emerge as the undisputed majority party.[47]

Drawing further conclusions, Lubell again stressed the importance of gradual change as well as the importance of critical turning points. He held that "the tenacious strength of political loyalties" following realignments was not to be "underestimated." Once people became emotionally attached to a party, he contended, foreshadowing conclusions that were to come out of the melding of the work of V. O. Key and Angus Campbell, it took "an almost catastrophic event" to bring about significant change. But Lubell also believed that the emergence of "a whole new generation, free of . . . old memories," could weaken old loyalties among the electorate. A "preliminary period" could in this fashion pave the way for decisive realignments, which then occurred in an atmosphere of passion. "Bitter conflict," Lubell held, had "accompanied every decisive realignment" in American history: the rise of the Republicans with the Civil War, the undisputed Republican supremacy arising out of the 1890s, and the overturning of Republican supremacy with the New Deal. It took "the heat of red-hot conflict" to "melt" remaining strong partisan loyalties. With such realignments, "fierce partisan passions" were created and the political outlooks of multitudes of voters were "virtually frozen," awaiting a new period of gradual weakening and a new critical period of realignment.[48] Although Lubell himself sharply disavowed cyclical theory, later students were to add cyclical notions to his recurring historical pattern. Beyond this, Lubell set forth—to be sure less systematically and elegantly than did V. O. Key—much of the framework of the debate over realignment theory for decades to come. Scholars were to argue over the relative importance of ethnocultural and economic change in realignment and over the relative strength of gradual change and quick upheavals. In all of this, Lubell set the rough parameters.

Nor was that all. His "definitive study," as he called it, "not only of the Roosevelt-Truman elections," but of all presidential elections since 1892, led him to devise "a new theory of the nature of American political parties."[49] The new theory was, he hastened to add in a letter, not the central point of *The Future of American Politics*, but rather "an incidental secondary sidelight to the main theme," which was the creation of the new Democratic majority of the 1930s.[50] Thus, Lubell's overall concept of American political parties and history derived from his intensive study of the Roosevelt era. As political scientist Oliver Garceau put it, the "really interesting new idea" of the book lay in this general concept. As Garceau summarized it, "one party was always in the ascendancy, . . . the major conflicts of the period were worked out within that one party," and "major social trauma was necessary to reduce the dominance of that major party" given its rootedness "in identifications of people with their party."[51] As Lubell himself traced the idea historically, through most periods one party or the other held the upper hand; only rarely, as in the period from Reconstruction to the 1890s, were the two parties essentially evenly divided.[52] His basic idea was not that the "majority party" would win all elections, but rather that it created the "orbit" in which both parties moved. The dominant party was the "sun," and the minority party was the "moon," which reflected the power of the sun. The major issues, debates, and conflicts of an era were played out above all within the dominant party; and the orbit shaped by the dominant party would continue to provide the parameters of politics until new issues and controversies arose powerful enough to replace those which had held sway. Each time one dominant party gave way to another, historical continuity was "shattered" and the "drama of American politics" was "transformed." The new majority party brought "its own orbit of conflict," and over time would slowly lose or consolidate its power.[53]

It is not too hard to see how this general theory reflected the particularities of the Roosevelt era. In a way, the concept, and even Lubell's "majority" and "minority" party terminology, seemed a return to the idea of normal Republican hegemony prior to 1929, now with the Democrats replacing the Republicans. But that earlier notion was essentially a recognition of a fact; it was Lubell who took that fact—combined with the fact of five successive Democratic presidential victories—and turned the evidence into a concept encompassing the overall pattern of American political history. While Lubell decisively rejected cyclical theories, his concept also bore some resemblance to Arthur M. Schlesinger's notion of a spiral. In Schlesinger's terms, conservatives over time accepted reform advances; in that sense, they could be viewed as operating within Lubell's "orbit." Indeed, Lubell wrote to the elder Schlesinger in March 1952, while it appeared that Truman's 1948 victory contradicted the historian's prediction of a coming conservative era, in reality this conclusion merely reflected the tendency to think of the Republicans as the conservative party and the Democrats as the liberal party. A "conservative swing" had in fact occurred, Lubell suggested, within the Democratic coalition itself. Hence, Schlesinger's theory was "not disproved" by the 1948 electoral verdict; rather, it could be given renewed validity through Lubell's analysis.[54]

As contemporary analysts pointed to Lubell's significance as an interpreter of American politics, so, too, have his contributions been recognized by later generations of scholars.[55] Times, to be sure, changed, and as Everett Carll Ladd pointed out in 1990, Lubell's notion of a normal majority party, while it made sense from 1896 to 1965, did not apply equally well to much of the rest of American political history—although Lubell did point out historical periods of relative balance and, of course, lacked Ladd's perspective.[56] In his own time, along with his wide impact on both the scholarly and journalistic worlds, Lubell developed a connection with the political scientist who was to parlay ideas of realignment into an enormously influential theory. This was the most important academic analyst of American politics of his generation, V. O. Key. Together, each in his work and way, Key and Lubell shaped the future of electoral and political analysis. Allan J. Lichtman, in his book on the 1928 election, wrote of Key in 1955, "echoing language" earlier used by Lubell regarding the importance of 1928 to the politics of the Roosevelt era.[57] But that was just one aspect of the larger picture. Peter Natchez wrote that "the notation of a critical election" was "first discussed by Samuel Lubell."[58] The actual terminology, however, was Key's. Arthur Schlesinger, Jr. contended that the "realignment model" of American politics was "first launched by Samuel Lubell" and later "elaborated" on by academic political scientists, "notably V. O. Key." Schlesinger, however, deemed "the theory of periodic party realignment" to be "an alternative cyclical interpretation of American political history" as distinct from his father's and his.[59] But the idea of a "realignment cycle," while in a sense implicit in the earlier work, was essentially added and elaborated upon by later scholars and belied Lubell's and Key's sharp break with the cyclical theories of the late 1930s and 1940s. Nathan Glazer, in his review of *The Future of American Politics*, held that later work would be an elaboration of Lubell's analysis.[60] While Key was developing similar ideas at the same time, this perhaps best captures the impact of Lubell on Key—Lubell's insights helped Key to crystallize notions already underway. Lubell's idea of a "majority party" and Key's notions of "critical elections" and "secular realignment" all entered the field of electoral and political analysis in a powerful and enduring way, both substantively and terminologically. Key's concepts were in a sense an effort to explain more systematically how majority-party status was attained.

V. O. Key was not one to grant praise easily; hence, his reaction to *The Future of American Politics* was all the more impressive. Key's review of the book appeared in the April 12, 1952, issue of the *Saturday Review*, seven years to the day after Roosevelt's death. In a cover letter to the magazine accompanying the review, Key allowed that his evaluation "sounds as if I had gone off the deep end, but it is my guess that the book will be uniformly well received."[61] In the review itself, Key wrote that *The Future of American Politics* "by a wide margin" constituted "the most perceptive general analysis of American politics of the Roosevelt Revolution and the Fair Deal." He drew particular attention to the book's "detailed analysis" of the elements making up the new Democratic majority, notably "the great urban minorities," whose quest for political recognition coincided with the impact of an economic crisis that "burned into them Democratic loyalties."[62] Before the review appeared, Key drafted two versions of a letter to be sent directly to Lubell, one dated March 23 and one March 24. Most of the language of each draft was the same. In both versions Key complimented Lubell on his "remarkably good job" in writing *The Future of American Politics*, and in each Key alluded to his current *Virginia Quarterly Review* article, "which managed to hit some of the points you make, but . . . failed to spot a considerable number of them." In the March 23 draft, Key gave Lubell's effort perhaps the greatest compliment he could offer: "It's the sort of book that I should have liked to do myself." The March 24 draft was less personal: "All students of American politics will owe you a very real debt." The March 24 draft concluded with an invitation to meet Key at Harvard: "If you are ever in the neighborhood here, I hope that you would find it convenient to drop by my office. I should like very much to meet you."[63] In a follow-up letter to Lubell of March 28, Key wrote that he was "not very proud" of his review, but that it would have "two or three sentences that might be usable by your publishers." He added his office and home telephone numbers and concluded: "If I do not hear from you I shall try to get in touch with you in New York sometime."[64] For a professor whose graduate student recommendations were known for their sparing nature, this was going off the deep end indeed.

Key alluded to Lubell's work as an example for aspiring students of a quantitative approach to politics in his 1954 book, *A Primer of Statistics for Political Scientists*. Electoral statistics collected by others, he cautioned, might not give a sense of their "meaning" to those not doing the collecting. Further, "until one checks on the ground," a scholar could not know whether an explanation derived from statistical data alone had "a wisp of a foundation." But despite such limitations associated with aggregate statistics, "with a little leg work and some ingenuity, a student" might still "do pretty well," as evidenced by the "basic technique of Samuel Lubell's *The Future of American Politics*."[65] Lubell in turn was happy to call on Key's expertise. In a letter to Key of early 1956, he asked the scholar's advice in connection with the forthcoming *Revolt of the Moderates*. He particularly inquired about academic political scientists whose work might relate to Lubell's own, as well as asking Key's help in spotting "any serious blunder I am about to let drop on my neck."[66] In response, Key briefed Lubell on historical and contemporary developments in electoral and political analysis in the academic world.[67] Lubell also called upon Key to write on his behalf for foundation backing for new projects. In support of Lubell's application to the Guggenheim Foundation (which had already helped back the work for *The Future of American Politics*), Key wrote in 1953 that Lubell dealt with "questions of great importance." Key's "only reservation" was whether Lubell's project as proposed was too "ambitious," but added that this was not a cause for "worry" because Lubell had already laid so much of the basis for the new undertaking.[68] In support of Lubell's quest for a Ford Foundation grant in 1956, Key wrote that while Lubell's work lacked, "of course, the earmarks of system and technique of the professional scholar," it had "qualities of imagination, of freshness, and of reality that the academics often lack. In fact, he hides away in his presentations a fairly systematic approach and has more of the technique of the scholar about him than he is willing to admit."[69] And in a 1957 letter to the Pulitzer Advisory Board, Key again alluded to Lubell's "remarkable" work and "original thoughts and new insights and interpretations." Lubell, Key wrote, had "had widespread influence among academic students of politics," and it would be "quite difficult to name another . . . whose impact has been quite so great or so widespread in recent years."[70] But many academic political scientists would not have found the task so difficult: They would have named V. O. Key himself.

Chapter Five

The Advent of V. O. Key

Valdimer Orlando Key, Jr. was born in Austin, Texas, in 1908 and reared in the west Texas town of Lamesa, about sixty miles south of Lubbock. His father, a lawyer and landowner of southern family origins, had populist-progressive political leanings. Key, always known to colleagues as "V. O.," was an avid reader as a youngster. In response to his father's insistence on chores, he reportedly said of west Texas, "If I ever leave this country, I'm never coming back." Told by the local school superintendent that V. O. by age sixteen knew more than his teachers, his father sent the young Key to McMurry Academy in Abilene for his last two years of high school and first year of higher education. Key then transferred to the University of Texas at Austin from which he graduated in 1929 and from which he received a master's degree in political science in 1930. Fellow political scientist R. Taylor Cole recalled an "extraordinarily stimulating" political science "atmosphere" at the university in the 1920s, where young faculty from major institutions, free from the constraints of "local mores," encouraged students to proceed in "novel" directions. One of those instructors, Roscoe C. Martin, who much later was to be instrumental in persuading Key to undertake *Southern Politics*, encouraged him to head to the University of Chicago. There he studied under Charles Merriam, receiving his doctorate in 1934. He married a fellow political scientist, Luella Gettys, that year, and after teaching briefly at the University of California at Los Angeles, moved to Washington, D.C., in 1936, where he worked first for the Social Science Research Council and then for the National Resources Planning Board. In 1938 he joined the Johns Hopkins University faculty and during World War II worked in the Bureau of the Budget. Government service, in Key's as in the cases of many other social scientists, exposed scholars in a very direct way to the world about which they wrote. After the war, Key returned to

Johns Hopkins, left for Yale in 1949 and for Harvard in 1951, where he remained for the duration of his career and life.[1]

The University of Chicago was formative in V. O. Key's intellectual development. There, Key absorbed an approach to the study of politics that focused
on processes and behavior as distinct from the description of institutions. At
Chicago, where Key was, Gabriel Almond recalls, "Merriam's favorite," the
young Texan also studied with Harold Gosnell and developed a life-long interest in the use of electoral data in political analysis. Like other products of
the Chicago School, Key emerged in the 1940s as a leader in the development
of American political science in the post–World War II era.[2] In a 1957 memorandum on "Research in Political Science," which he termed "more autobio-
graphical than I would care to admit," Key discussed how out of Chicago in
the 1920s and 1930s there developed "the most thoroughgoing and influential
redrawing of the boundaries of disciplinary subdivisions," with "new fields"
cutting across traditional categories, including studies of "political parties and
electoral problems," concerned "with the functioning of parties and 'political
activity' everywhere." Such "redefinition of areas of interest within political
science," Key added, "had a far greater intellectual significance than may appear at first glance." For the investigation "of phenomena from a new stance
almost invariably" resulted in "new insights." When areas of examination previously analyzed "independently by different persons" were "brought into jux-
taposition in the same mind," the likelihood of "new findings" increased.[3] This
observation, based on Chicago, neatly summed up much of Key's own career
in terms of method, insights, contributions, and impact.

Key's first big influence on his field came in 1942 with the publication and
favorable reception of his text *Politics, Parties, and Pressure Groups*. In that
book, Key departed from the institutional analysis of American politics to
concentrate instead on the analysis of power and behavior. David Truman,
then a young instructor, recalled writing Key "a fan letter" after reading the
first edition of the text "because that book was like a breath of fresh air."[4]
From Harold Gosnell, who had coauthored the last three editions of Charles
Merriam's text in the field, came a letter of congratulations to Key in 1959 on
the latest edition of Key's "parties book," which, wrote Gosnell, "deserves to
be first in the field!"[5] Alexander Heard, who worked with Key on *Southern
Politics*, later wrote of *Politics, Parties, and Pressure Groups* that the "widely
used, much quoted" text was "sometimes cited as if it were a technical mono-
graph instead of a textbook."[6] The text, as well as *Southern Politics*, has
sometimes been alluded to in terms of the "behavioral revolution" that swept
through the discipline of political science after World War II and of which
Key himself has sometimes been termed a leader. Key, however, shied away
from the terminology, and while he certainly utilized the tools of quantitative

analysis for their precision, he was also always cognizant that quantitative data required qualitative analysis. It was both in terms of the use of quantitative data and in the power of his qualitative analysis that Key was so greatly to influence the study of politics, and not only among political scientists. Samuel P. Hays was one among a number of "new political historians" also inspired by this political scientist with a "historical bent."[7]

Key was not considered among colleagues as possessed of a scintillating personality. Heinz Eulau called him "a very nice man, his sourpuss demeanor notwithstanding."[8] Alexander Heard characterized him as "mild-mannered."[9] Key was known for his lack of effusiveness in his graduate student recommendations.[10] But he also wrote letters of encouragement to newcomers with whose work he was impressed—Samuel Lubell was not alone in this regard. David Truman recalled that after he had published an early article, Key, in "a very characteristic V. O. gesture," sent him "a little note, saying, 'I enjoyed your article. I hope perhaps we can get together for lunch sometime.'"[11] Austin Ranney recalled that as a young scholar, he "very timidly wrote to V. O." asking advice on whether he should proceed on a particular project and "back almost by return mail came a five-page single-spaced letter pecked out. . . . You hadn't lived unless you had a letter from V. O., and he typed all his own letters . . . on a typewriter that must have been made around 1890." Ranney "had rarely had treatment like that from any senior scholar," much less one he had not previously known.[12] A fellow Ph.D. in political science, Luella Gettys Key, and her husband collaborated on some early work, but by the time Alexander Heard joined with Key on *Southern Politics* in the years just after World War II, Key's wife's contribution was limited, Heard recalled, to indexing, occasionally commenting on a draft manuscript, housework, and cooking. Another student of Key's career has suggested that Luella Key's contributions to her husband's work were "probably underestimated." But both agree that Key, who had no children, was consumed by his scholarship, working "all the time," Heard remembered. He would spend some time with his wife before dinner, but after dinner it was "back to work." Key made the charts and maps for *Southern Politics*, wrote Heard. "He said it relaxed him."[13]

Key was very much a man of his discipline, and the members of his discipline reciprocated his regard. When Lubell's *The Future of American Politics*, which Key so much admired, received a professional award, Key found it "satisfactory, given the prevailing ground rules." However, he allowed that he felt "some pedagogical annoyance that they go so often to people not members of the guild." Still, he feared, to make such awards available only to members of a professional association might make his fellow political scientists appear "parochial."[14] Key was also a student of particular subfields within his discipline and could grouse a bit in that regard as well. In commenting on a book on Texas politics, for example, Key held that "a major American state and its politics appear significant alongside many of the political orders to which students of comparative government devote lavish attention."[15] Following Key's early death in 1963, Angus Campbell, with whom he had often worked closely, wrote that Key

> uniquely in his generation of political scientists . . . combined a profound knowledge of the institutional structure of American politics with a sure grasp of quantitative methods and a sophisticated interest in the developing promise of "behavioral" research. As a respected elder statesman in a field largely populated by younger men, he filled a role which no one has inherited from him.[16]

Still later, James Sundquist wrote of the "universal reverence" political scientists felt for Key.[17] And William C. Havard characterized Key as "a sort of institutional embodiment of American political science from the 1930s on."[18]

Alexander Heard believed that Key's magnum opus, *Southern Politics*, had its deepest roots in Key's own upbringing. Key's father had dabbled in local politics, and, Heard recounted, "young Key spent much time around the courthouse square." Key himself told Heard that "sensitivities" developed in west Texas underlay his later capacity for political analysis, and Heard concluded that Key's "unusual interpretative instincts were bred in those early experiences in Texas."[19] Whatever its origins, there was widespread agreement among political analysts as to Key's extraordinarily gifted capacity for hypothesis and creative insight. One colleague pronounced himself "amazed at the meaning" that Key could "extract from . . . statistics."[20] Walter Dean Burnham, more than anyone else Key's successor as the premier scholarly analyst of American politics, wrote that Key moved "from data point to data point, using his unparalleled capacity for intuitive integration" to develop penetrating analyses.[21] E. E. Schattschneider, no slouch himself, declared Key's "hunches" in a preliminary draft of *Southern Politics* "wonderfully stimulating" and Key's "hypotheses" no less than "brilliant."[22] The Schattschneider-led committee on more responsible party government called in its 1950 report for just the kind of scholarly effort Key set forth in his seminal articles later in the decade: studies of American politics based on "a combination of creative hypotheses and realistic investigations."[23] Key was further able to draw upon raw materials gathered and concepts originated by others as a basis for additional refinement and insight and as a means to develop innovative analytical syntheses.[24] Indeed, Key's greatest gift may have been as a creative synthesizer whose original thoughts about notions advanced by others resulted in something distinctive and new as a final product. Like other scholars, in economics or history, for example, Key took existing strands of thought, added his own powerful analysis, and came up with a more systematic, inclusive, refined, and insightful generalization than had gone before. In this sense the contributions of a Holcombe or Gosnell or even Lubell provided grist for Key's mill.

Various comments by Key himself suggested he was well aware of this talent and its possibilities and importance for political analysis. As he put it, he often began "with some vaguely defined problem" and then shaped "it up more sharply" as he dug into the data.[25] And he believed that bold ideas could be set forth in brief compass. One "fresh idea briefly put may enlarge our understanding far more than many . . . books," he held.[26] He had "a hunch" that many "'landmark' studies" appeared in article form; "any idea of . . . importance" could be stated "succinctly" to fit the format. Evidence of seminal importance would come with further studies elaborating upon the landmark piece.[27] In this way "the insights" of one individual "may color an entire discipline for decades."[28] Certainly these observations were to apply to Key's "Critical Elections" and "Secular Realignment" articles for decades after they appeared. Key went beyond the empirical observations and case-study-based generalizations of predecessors; yet, he stopped short of any operative belief that "laws" could be "discovered" that would be deemed behaviorally valid. He developed generalizations, as in his 1950s articles, that endeavored to encompass many case studies, but that remained within certain historic chronological and national institutional parameters. He used the term "theory" in his article "Critical Elections," but, as has been noted, he proceeded "almost wholly descriptively."[29] Key himself claimed that "the rivalry between the Great Thinkers and the Industrious Data Collectors" was "an empty one" since "imaginative interpretation" and realistic grounding were both essential to successful analysis.[30] As with any highly influential piece, Key's articles of the 1950s, briefly setting forth interpretations of American political and electoral behavior across time, were contemporaneously and subsequently subject to differing emphases and understandings. Some commentators wrote of Key's tendency to "bury important points in footnotes" or to hide "important conceptual distinctions" in spare sentences.[31] Political historian J. Morgan Kousser was impressed by Key's "'humanistic' penchant for ambiguity and complexity."[32] But William C. Havard viewed Key's "parsimonious" approach as providing the most simple and direct route to the conclusions he wished to offer.[33] Perhaps Alexander Heard penetrated most deeply into what Key was about. In recalling how he tried to bring a "poetic" Key passage in a draft of *Southern Politics* down to earth, and how Key rejected his suggestions, Heard concluded that "Key was trying to communicate more than simple rational prose would convey. He was trying to convey a spirit, something beyond factual information."[34]

In the wake of the 1948 election, Key himself underwent something of a secular realignment, moving gradually from a perspective on American politics based on continuity and cycles to one geared to discontinuity and enduring change. Key's seminal articles of the 1950s in this critical respect departed significantly from much of his 1940s analysis. In an article appearing just after the 1940 election, for example, Key wrote in a vein quite similar to other commentators at the time, although in sharp contrast to what Samuel Lubell contended in his 1941 *Saturday Evening Post* piece on the same subject. Key believed that the 1940 election did not indicate that lower-income voters had been "wedded" to the Democratic Party. Class-based "political attitudes were by no means rigidly stratified." Rather, the 1940 verdict was a "personal victory" for President Roosevelt, and it was not certain whether a successor could maintain the unity of the Democratic electoral coalition. Further, many voters opted for the president because of the outbreak of war in Europe, and insofar as foreign policy was electorally important, Republicans could "take heart." The conclusion to be drawn was that the New Deal had "not irrevocably cemented a majority to the Democratic cause."[35] Similarly, in the first edition of his *Politics, Parties, and Pressure Groups*, published in 1942, Key, citing Arthur Holcombe, de-emphasized any epochal significance pertaining to the Democratic victories of 1932 and 1936. The Democrats had been able to "wean away" many western farmers and northern workers from the Republicans, but the basic sources of each party's strength remained essentially as before.[36]

In a 1946 article Key explicitly set forth a cyclical theory of American politics. Key wrote in a letter the following year that he knew "Louis Bean very well," and that Bean knew "a great deal more about statistics than about politics" (a judgment similar to that made later by Key of survey-based studies of voting behavior).[37] Nonetheless, in the 1946 article, Key held that Bean and others had "shown the existence of great cycles in our national politics." Hence, the Democrats reached a low in 1904, a peak in 1912, another low in 1924, a new peak in 1936, and suffered erosion of strength in 1940 and 1944. Conversely, the GOP peaked in 1904, reached a low in 1912, peaked again in 1924, and once again went into the trough in 1936. Writing just before the 1946 off-year election, Key suggested that the Democrats were now in much the same position as in 1918 and as the Republicans were in 1910 and 1930— "approaching the end of a cycle of power." The war had slowed the ending of the Democratic cycle, but, Key concluded, "the cyclical pattern of our politics since 1896" suggested a Republican takeover of the House of Representatives in 1946 and a Republican retaking of the presidency in 1948 or 1952.[38] In the 1947 edition of his parties text, Key again discussed the existence and role of cycles in American politics. He also alluded to the special importance of certain elections. The year 1896 "marked a turning point at which the party battle began to take its modern form," and 1932 "marked another great turning point in American party history." But such observations went undeveloped at this point. Rather, emphasis was placed on cyclical patterns, and discussion ensued of the Bean and Schlesinger versions. Key did allow that the pattern of cyclical alternation of party control might not be "a permanent feature of American politics." The decades after the Civil War suggested a deviation from the pattern. Yet Key was content to assume "for the sake of discussion" that the cyclical pattern "of party strength since 1888" reflected "a more or less fixed pattern of American politics." One conclusion of this assumption was that cyclical movements rendered campaigning less effective; the best campaign running against the tide could not undo it; "once the tide starts running against one party, it will run until it is reversed."[39]

Key continued at times to use the language of political "cycles" and "tides" well into the 1950s.[40] But after 1948 Key was engaged in a process of gradual rethinking. It took a number of years for his new perspectives to jell. But it does appear that the 1948 election supplied the initial jolt. And Key, like virtually everyone else, was jolted by Truman's surprise victory. Key was a reader for the publisher of Louis Bean's 1948 book, *How to Predict Elections*, which supplied the basis for Bean's claim as the "prophet" of Truman's victory. Key, in his letter to the publisher, wrote warmly of Bean's "fascinating application of arithmetic to politics," but added a note of caution. Bean, Key suggested, should tone down allusions to any high Truman standing in public esteem since it seemed unlikely that the allusions would be accurate when the book appeared.[41] Just after the election Key allowed in his characteristically understated way that "Bean certainly was not so bad." As to himself, Key fessed up: "I would have lost my shirt had I been a betting man."[42] He remained "still a little disorganized after the outcome of the great plebiscite." He had been right about North Carolina and Texas. "Beyond that I was about as bad as Dr. Gallup."[43] Key was further concerned about the polls in relation to the study of politics. He believed that given their commercial interest, the pollsters' emphasis on predicting outcomes diverted attention from more important electoral analysis. He thought that some of the Gallup error lay in the difficulty in sampling lower-income voters, but "God knows where the rest of the error came from."[44]

The confusion sown by 1948 led Key along secular paths. In 1950, for example, in a letter to fellow political scientist Malcolm Moos, Key noted the power of the post–Civil War Republican Party and wondered now whether "the Republicans might not get back in during" the present generation. "Maybe the Demos have grabbed the wave of the future by the tail, as did the Republicans in the '70's, and won't be beat until they kill themselves."[45] More systematic rethinking became evident in 1952. In one article, Key associated long-run augmentation of one party's strength with its ability to attract new voters in an expanding electorate. He considered this true of the Republicans in 1896 and

1920 and of the Democrats moving from 1924 to 1932.[46] Here was an emphasis on secular change, although the inclusion of 1920 suggested a lingering whiff of cyclical theory. In the 1952 edition of *Politics, Parties, and Pressure Groups* Key again suggested that significant leaps in one party's strength might be due less to the conversion of voters than to that party's greater success in attracting young and other new voters. He further suggested that "decisive and fundamental electoral realignments" occurred "at rather widely spaced intervals." Quadrennial campaigns, rather than being decisive, were merely occasions when the "dominant party" defended itself—usually successfully, but occasionally giving way to the opposition "for a short period." A durable party coalition reigned for an extended period of time, eventually breaking down, to be replaced by a new durable party coalition. Applying the concept to party history, Key held that the Republicans were normally dominant from the Civil War to the Great Depression, with an occasional Democratic interlude, albeit one during which the Democrats were never able to develop policies diverging "markedly from the prevailing pattern." In 1932 the Democrats forged a new dominant coalition that they hoped would make the country as "'normally' Democratic" as it had previously been Republican. That coalition, Key added, was in part based on Democratic urban, Catholic, working-class voter additions of the Al Smith campaign of 1928, and on the party's subsequent appeal to younger voters. Cycles of the Louis Bean type, Key now held, were shorter movements within these larger chronological configurations, as in an allusion to the 1920 swing of the "pendulum." Conceptually and terminologically, Key's discussion seemed to reflect somewhat the perspectives of Lubell's *The Future of American Politics*. Lubell was not cited in the discussion of secular political change, although reference was made elsewhere in the 1952 edition of Key's text to Lubell's book.[47]

The most noted and celebrated of Key's early secular efforts came in his 1952 *Virginia Quarterly Review* article, which, as he noted to Lubell at the time, made some, but not all, of the points brought out by the latter's book. For almost a century, Key held, catastrophe had "fixed the grand outlines of the partisan division among American voters." To be sure, he allowed, so sweeping a pronouncement ignored "episodic variations" and issues, yet it revealed a fundamental point. The Civil War had bred patterns of party loyalty into voters that had largely endured until 1932 and in some respects beyond. The result was a country that long was "'normally' Republican." It took the "second catastrophe" of the Great Depression again to shake party alignments. The 1932 election, Key now held, was not a "routine victory"; rather, the Democratic triumph greatly "weakened . . . the coalition that had ruled the country" for the great part of seven decades. Further, it took the 1936 election to bring home "the full import of the New Deal" for partisan alignments. The election of 1932 reflected a nationwide reaction against the association of Re-

publican rule with economic disaster. The election of 1936, "however, represented something new," the creation of a Democratic majority coalition.
Whatever the vicissitudes of a given election, the nation had become "'normally' Democratic instead of 'normally' Republican." Key added a caveat,
however, suggesting that the new Democratic coalition would most likely not
have the extraordinarily extended staying power of the old Republican one.
The conditions of urban life, he felt, were less conducive to that end "than
was the old rural sectionalism."[48]

The year 1953 brought additional Key rethinking. In a coauthored article
completed that year, he suggested that "a series of 'peculiar' elections"
might "have cumulative effects productive of a secular growth of one
party."[49] In a letter to Angus Campbell, he speculated that in certain turbulent elections a greater voter turnout might accrue to the benefit of one party,
but not of the other, whereas voter alignments seemed not to change much
when turnout remained steady. He added that he was not sure that there was
"anything epoch making" in this observation, "except that there are elections
and elections."[50] In a 1953 review Key held that despite the tenacity of
"party identification," there were occasions when "fairly rapid party realignments" had occurred in American history.[51] The year 1954 brought forth
from Key an explicit rejection of the cyclical theory of politics as espoused
"notably by Louis Bean." Key now found it "most hazardous" to try "to develop a general cyclical theory." The "ups and downs" of politics might simply reflect "unique incidents," rather than "a cyclical pattern of behavior."[52]
More significantly, 1954 witnessed the circulation among fellow political
analysts of the draft of the Key piece that was to be the most influential he
ever penned: his theory of critical elections. And comments made about the
circulated draft by his colleagues, along with Key's responses, revealed an
array of viewpoints, criticisms, and even exegeses foretelling the decades of
discussion to come.

M. Brewster Smith suggested to Key that the critical election category could
be subdivided. Key's discussion of the 1896 and 1928 elections, Smith believed, indicated that these "two specimens" might justify creating different
"species within the same genus." The term "realignment" seemed to Smith to
fit the case of 1928 more than that of 1896. Such distinctions, Smith concluded, should be sharpened, rather than minimized, under the common rubric
of a critical election. Smith further noted that what Key provided was not so
much a "theory," but rather a "concept" illustrated by data. And, reflecting a
point highly relevant to the decades to come, Smith considered it an "important question" as to whether the "earmarks of a critical election . . . could be
determined contemporaneously, rather than in the light of subsequent developments."[53] Countless analysts of future elections would conclude that only
subsequent elections and developments would conclusively reveal whether the

election at hand was a critical one, even as they feverishly speculated in its immediate wake as to each election's likely ultimate significance. Robert Lane
also contended that Key's critical election category could be further subdivided and suggested the addition of "divisive" and "consensual" characteristics. For example, Lane suggested, the 1928 election was both "critical" and
"divisive" in that it brought forth patterns that were "sharp and durable," but
also reflected conflict between urban Catholic and rural Protestant voters. The
1896 election, while "critical" in the sense of creating "sharp and durable" patterns, was also "consensual" in that in New England "a kind of classless
union" of voters was created. Lane further held that there were examples of
elections that brought "sharp" but "ephemeral" change; hence, the "typology"
of elections could be extended, and "the possibilities for expanding the theory"
seemed worthy of further exploration. Lane concluded that "noncritical" elections were of interest as well, those that evidenced gradual change; indeed,
Lane contended, "every election" held out some examples of realignment.[54]
On this last point Key agreed, acknowledging that in some measure realignment occurred "at every or perhaps most elections."[55]

Key's good friend Oliver Garceau weighed in with comments that anticipated the later "conversion versus mobilization" debate concerning the origins of the new Democratic majority coming out of the Roosevelt era. The
upsurge of the Democratic vote among low-income, urban Catholics in New
England in 1928, Garceau contended, clearly reflected the "activation" of a
group already inclined toward the Democrats, rather than the "conversion" of
one that previously had Republican leanings. The election of 1896, on the
other hand, seemed to Garceau to be more a matter of "conversion." Garceau
also wondered about the possibility of using a "sudden expansion of the vote
as a test" for a critical election. Finally, Garceau maintained that the 1932
election, as contrasted with that of 1928, brought about a voting shift "for
more substantial reasons" and thus 1932 appeared to be more like a "critical
election than 1928 even in New England." Additionally, 1928 should not be
overemphasized since it lay in a line of increased Democratic polling among
the voters at issue from 1920 into the 1930s.[56] Key, in responding, agreed
"that 1928 was more a matter of activation than conversion," although he was
not clear how to tell for sure. A sudden expansion of the vote, Key believed,
at times seemed to be associated with a critical election, as in 1928, but it was
not a necessary condition for an election to be critical, a conclusion linked to
"the classification of 1896 as critical." As to the relative importance of the
1928 and 1932 elections, Key continued to emphasize the former since so
many of the 1932 Democratic voters "had already been taken into camp in
1928." Garceau's last comment raised in Key the issue of what he was to term
"secular realignment." The notion that 1928 was "a step in a progression be-

ginning earlier" had "considerable merit," Key held. It pertained, for example, to demographic trends—such as the gradual movement of immigrants
into the Democratic Party.[57]

"A Theory of Critical Elections" was published in 1955 in *The Journal of
Politics*. In it Key noted that "the argument" had been "stated unencumbered by
supporting data" in his 1952 *Virginia Quarterly Review* piece. He also cited
Lubell's *The Future of American Politics* in his discussion of the 1928 election.
Key was circumspect and cautious with regard to his theoretic contribution
(more so than many of his followers were to be). A difficulty in proposing an
election category, he averred, was "that no single actual case" exactly fit its
"specifications," while including a "greater . . . number of differentiating criteria" only accentuated that problem. The need was to group together elections
that shared the essential characteristics of the type while recognizing the existence of differing "peripheral characteristics." In introductory fashion, Key held
that elections occurred "in a stream of connected antecedent and subsequent behavior." Proceeding to his definition of what constituted a critical election, he
contended that it was one "in which the decisive results of the voting" revealed
"a sharp alteration of the preexisting cleavage within the electorate." Further,
and this Key called "perhaps . . . the truly differentiating characteristic of this
sort of election," the "realignment" reflected in the voting returns of a critical
election would persist for a number of following elections. In this latter respect,
a critical election differed from one that brought sharp, but ephemeral, voting
pattern changes. Moreover, while all elections involved some realignment, a
critical instance involved realignment "radically different in extent." Key allowed for differentiation within the category. Thus, the election of 1896 led to
GOP gains across demographic groups, while that of 1928 saw Democratic
gains among specific demographic groups. The election of 1896 apparently involved considerable conversion of Democratic voters into Republicans,
whereas that of 1928 witnessed Democratic gains based "in considerable measure" on the entrance "of new voters into the active electorate." Further, Key allowed that, in and of themselves, the changes wrought in 1928 would not likely
have persisted for a quarter-century. It took the 1932 election "to reinforce and
to maintain the 1928 cleavage," and the new groupings apparent in 1928 would
in any case have been forthcoming in 1932 due to the Depression. Key ad-
dressed several other points more briefly, but pregnantly, given the abundance
of later discussion. Reflecting, perhaps, the draft comments of Robert Lane and
anticipating certainly the work of Angus Campbell on the issue, Key suggested
the utility of a further development of an "electoral typology." He also, very importantly in terms of his overall outlook, undertook, however tentatively, to link
critical elections to the broader political and governmental system. How, he
asked, was a new electoral coalition to be maintained once formed? What were

the consequences for "the legislative process" of electoral upheavals? Did an electorate stable and "quiescent" over an extended time frame reflect a satisfaction with existing public policy? Exploration of such questions proceeding from his critical election formulation, Key contended, "could provide a means for better integrating the study of electoral behavior with the analysis of political systems."[58] Or, as he expressed it in his letter to his friend Garceau, "the real reason" he "put together the whole business" was as "a sort of continuation of my argument with the electoral behavior boys that the stuff they do has to be tied into matters of 'political relevance' one way or another if it is to amount to anything more than an interesting exercise."[59] Here Key reflected both the overlap and the gap between himself and those he viewed as excessively narrowly focused students of voting behavior—an overlap he sought to develop and a gap he undertook to bridge.

Key's essential achievement in his "Critical Elections" piece, it is generally agreed, lay in his ability to provide a clear, systematic, and insightful analysis and historical exposition of a type of electoral behavior, melding together looser observations into a more coherent formulation.[60] A second highly influential article came four years later with the *Journal of Politics* publication of "Secular Realignment and the Party System." While having considerable impact, this piece did not have the extraordinary effect of that of 1955. In part, it may have had less impact precisely because of that extraordinary effect: The focus on sharp, dramatic breaks took attention away from the less exciting and more gradual changes discussed in the 1959 article. However, a basic point is that Key saw two paths to political realignment: a sudden one, as discussed via critical elections, but also a more gradual one—that involving long-run developments. The distinction was sometimes obscured as analysts began speaking of a series of critical elections constituting a realigning period.[61] In his "Secular Realignment" article, Key again held that elections could best be understood not in terms of "static models," but in a "time dimension," and that understanding required focus on electoral patterns and shifts as distinct from the assumption that voters reached "more or less rational" decisions in response to "issues of the moment" or to "skillful campaigners." A historical approach regarded election returns as "periodic readings of . . . streams . . . that are undergoing steady expansion or contraction" and elections as "steps in a more or less continuous creation of new loyalties and decay of old." Secular realignment in Key's formulation involved major shifts in electoral alignments that resulted from the cumulative effect of long-run, gradual changes, "secular" trends that could be discerned beneath the shorter-run oscillations. Key differentiated such trends from the impact of critical elections resulting from turbulent events or intense issues; here the emphasis was on changes that occurred over decades resulting "in a more or less continuous creation of new" voting patterns and "decay of old" ones. Such changes operated "inexorably, and almost imperceptibly, election after election" to fashion new electoral patterns.[62] While the "Critical Elections" article was inspired by the changes wrought in the Roosevelt era culminating in the election of 1948 even as Key sought to apply this analysis more extensively to American political history, the "Secular Realignment" article appeared more nearly to come out of the relatively stable electoral atmosphere of the 1950s, with perhaps special applicability to the part of the country that Key knew best, namely, the South. While long of lesser impact, the secular realignment piece was to emerge with greater influence as the 1960s, 1970s, and 1980s failed to produce any generally agreed upon "critical election," and it was to reemerge with particular relevance to the political transformation of the South.

The 1958 edition of Key's text reflected how secular analysis had replaced a cyclical perspective in his understanding of American politics, although a trace of cyclical terminology survived in his secular framework. His historical account stressed long-term Republican control after the Civil War and until 1932, buttressed by the 1896 election and only briefly interrupted by Democratic rule. The elections of 1896 and 1928 were discussed in terms of the applicability of the critical election concept. Key found agreeable the notion that a single election did not create a durable new coalition, but rather that it gave a different party an "opportunity" to create a durable coalition.[63] In the 1964 edition, published shortly after his death, Key reiterated his secular points, and alluded to the idea of a "critical period" as distinct from a single critical election, as in "the period 1928–1936" when "a new cleavage was driven through the electorate and the country became normally Democratic." Such elections and periods constituted, Key added, driving home a process and point of considerable import to him, "the most striking instances of electoral interposition in the governing process," for they cleared "the way for a broad new direction in the course of public policy."[64] In his posthumously published book, *The Responsible Electorate*, Key displayed particular interest in this relation between electoral change and public policy. Maintaining a durable new coalition, Key held, required public policies attractive to its member groups, but public policies attractive to some groups necessarily antagonized others, and thus a majority coalition did "not hold together like a ball of sticky popcorn"; rather, it no sooner formed than it began to "crumble." Elections thus became improvisational efforts to satisfy as much of the coalition as possible, while replacing dissatisfied elements with new recruits. The Democratic victories of the 1930s and 1940s occurred against just such a backdrop "of marked and abrupt innovations in governmental policy." The minority party, in its turn, had to depend upon the recruitment of dissatisfied elements of the existing majority coalition. The misfortune of the Republicans in the 1930s and 1940s was that no issue emerged that would allow them to wean away a sufficient number of erstwhile Democrats to prevail. This revealed, Key concluded, much as Lubell had argued in *The Future of American Politics*, "how completely the minority party is a captive of the majority—and of the situation."[65]

In the 1958 edition of *Politics, Parties, and Pressure Groups*, Key quite explicitly rejected the notion of a cyclical theory of politics.[66] He had replaced that earlier perspective with his systematically fashioned secular interpretive framework. One of the ironies of the history of electoral analysis, however, was that Key did not permanently drive a stake through cyclical theory and that cyclical theory rose again to enter—and to shape—secular analysis. Key, in rejecting cyclical theory, held that changes in party strength were "not characterized by a neat periodicity."[67] And insofar as striking changes were produced by external or "exogenous" events—such as a Civil War or a Great Depression—the changes had to be irregular and hence could not be cyclical. Much the same point could be made in regard to the demographic and other factors that underlay secular realignment; these were trends as distinct from cycles. But notions of the "weakening" or "decay" of new coalitions across time, including Lubell's introduction of generational factors, contributed in time to a reintroduction of cycles into electoral analysis and indeed into the very heart of realignment theory. Hence, a perspective built on the rejection of cyclical theory in the end opened a door to cyclical theory's pivotal reemergence. The historical application of realignment theory led to the conclusion that realignments occurred regularly or cyclically every thirty-two or so years. Hence, if the last critical election was deemed to be that of 1932 or 1936, analysts were on the lookout for 1964 or 1968.

Key's greatest single area of expertise, of course, lay in the politics of the South. He did not come out of the South, of course, in the same way that Lubell came out of the urban, immigrant heartland of the Northeast. Lubell was himself an urban immigrant, albeit a very young one. Key, hailing from west Texas, came at most from the peripheral South. Reflecting common-enough analytical trends of the time, Key discussed "the erosion of sectionalism" and the emergence of a more class- and economic-based politics. He did so, however, carefully and with qualification, given what he felt was the lack of rigid class traditions in the country. The centrality of such political appeals, he felt, varied with economic conditions and the impact of public economic policies.[68] Whatever his caveats, however, economics played a crucial role in Key's analysis of the prospects of southern politics. The book *Southern Politics* itself, published in 1949, was award winning, established the benchmark from which later studies of the subject proceeded, and both enhanced and cemented the reputation that Key had already developed through his popular text.[69]

Recruiting Key to undertake the study was a story in itself. The idea of the project originated with Roscoe C. Martin, an instructor at the University of Texas during Key's undergraduate days, and in the 1940s a professor and administrator at the University of Alabama. According to Alexander Heard, who worked with Key on the project, Martin believed that Key was not only the best person to do the job, but "the only one."[70] It took quite an effort, however, for Martin to haul Key in. In a letter of 1945, Key wrote to Martin inquiring whether the latter had "succeeded yet in lining up anybody for the study of Southern Politics," noting that E. E. Schattschneider was "planning to cover some of the territory in a study . . . now . . . under way."[71] In a 1946 letter to Martin, Key viewed "with alarm and with sympathy your problems in lining up somebody to do the Southern politics study. It is a hot potato, but it would be an extraordinarily good way for a young guy with some imagination to become a national figure." Maybe, Key added, in reference to the recent publication of *An American Dilemma* by Gunnar Myrdal, Martin could "import a Swede . . . to do the job."[72] But Martin, according to Heard's account, was "tenacious" in going after a reluctant Key. Key had to devote himself to his work at Johns Hopkins? The president of the university wrote to Key of the importance of the project to their institution. Key still had duties as a consultant to the Bureau of the Budget? Forthcoming was a letter from the director of the bureau advising Key that his work as a consultant should not stand in the way. Topping it off came a letter from the president of the United States urging Key on.[73]

E. E. Schattschneider served as a consultant for the project and read Key's drafts. He had no doubt as to the importance of Key's ongoing accomplishment. He was, he wrote to Key, "aware of the historical significance of your book," judging it "incomparably the best job of political research" he had "ever seen." He felt "confident" that the book would "produce a revolution in the study of politics, not merely in the South, but everywhere."[74] Schattschneider also, of course, served as a critic. He wondered, for example, if Key had taken sufficient note of the impact of the election of 1948 in terms of the erosion of Democratic strength in the South.[75] The election of 1948, after all, was not just the year of Truman's triumph. In the southern context, what was most noteworthy was the breakaway States Rights Democratic Party (or "Dixiecrats"). Led by presidential candidate J. Strom Thurmond, the Dixiecrats protested the national Democratic Party's pro–civil rights stance, capturing the electoral votes of four states of the Deep South. The Dixiecrats failed, however, in toppling Truman or in spreading beyond the southern heartland. Key, in responding to Schattschneider, expressed doubt that the election had changed the validity of his "conclusions in any material way." He did, however, believe that "the fundamental situation" in the more peripheral South, in states such as Texas and Florida with fewer African Americans and an emerging upscale class of whites, augured "well for the Republicans in the long run," which Key defined as twenty to twenty-five years.[76]

As the southern political past pivoted on race, Key believed in the late 1940s that the southern political future would increasingly pivot on economics. Here, for all of the historical rootedness of his analysis of southern politics on the race issue, Key felt that the prevailing national forces and trends that evolved out of the 1930s would in time reshape southern politics over increasingly national lines. As he saw it, the economic modernization of the South—the spread of industrialization—would facilitate the evolution in the South of a more economic and class-based politics such as had developed in the North. Whites at the lower end of the social scale, combined with African Americans who characteristically sided with liberal political forces, would discern a common interest. The ferocity of racial divisions would thereby be lessened. Similarly, business-minded and better-off white southerners would find common cause with business-minded and better-off northern Republicans. In such an atmosphere, too, discrimination against African Americans, including widespread denial of the right to vote, would become less pronounced. Crosscutting economic issues would thus help undermine and defuse the historically central racial issue and divide. In this mood, Key could hold that the 1948 "Dixiecrat 'rebellion' was pretty farcical," that it might even constitute "the dying gasp of the Old South." He added, however, in 1949 that the "hard core of resistance" among southern whites on the race issue, in areas of heavy African-American population, had "yet to be cracked," and it remained unclear as to whether a "workable solution" could be developed in that regard.[77]

Key, his major work on the South complete, continued into the 1950s to glimpse the prospects of change in southern politics, especially the likelihood of the emergence of sufficient Republican strength to create a genuine two-party system. Following the 1952 election, when the appeal of the Republican candidate, General Dwight D. Eisenhower, led to major Republican gains in the presidential vote in that region, Key prophesied that, whatever the lag in GOP state-by-state organizational strength, the South would be "contested territory" in future presidential elections. Further, he held, party reconfigurations in the South would "ultimately determine realignment of the national Democratic and Republican parties." He added, however, that in the Deep South the "race question" would still "have the greatest significance in molding whatever kind of party alignment eventually" developed.[78] In 1953 he speculated about the possibility that the 1948 Dixiecrats might have provided a "third party . . . bridge" for Democrats on their way to becoming Republicans.[79] In 1955 he suggested that the Republican gains of 1952 marked a culmination of a gradual buildup in sentiment. Southerners who were similar to northern Republicans were now voting Republican at the presidential level. Key further held that it was incorrect to expect Republican strength in the South to increase smoothly and at an even pace; rather, it was likely to require "jolts that from time to time" would "jar the Southern system from its ancient mold."[80] This seemed to suggest "critical" jerks within a "secular" realignment. In 1956 Key again indicated that he believed the process would be secular. He felt a "bearishness" about "short-run prospects" for southern Republicanism; but the "long, long-run" might be "something else again."[81]

Later analysts of southern politics, for all their reverence for Key, took him to task for what they saw as his excessive optimism about the evolution of economically-based politics and about a gradual defusing of the race issue. The developments arising out of the later 1950s and the 1960s, they contended, demonstrated the continuing power of a racially based southern politics, contrary to Key's hopes and expectations. The Dixiecrats, from that perspective, were less a "dying gasp" than an early harbinger of what was to come.[82] Key, however, his massive work on southern politics over, devoted himself after midcentury to other, at times overlapping, concerns. These centered, of course, on his development of secular perspectives on politics. In that regard, Key's efforts were augmented by scholars more narrowly focused on voting behavior. Key believed that such scholars were often focused too narrowly, that voting behavior needed to be integrated into a broader political analysis. Through his endeavors, those of the Michigan School led by Angus Campbell, and those of others, major efforts were undertaken to develop such unifying and synthesizing approaches. These efforts bore fruit in the full and highly influential development of a comprehensive theory of realignment.

Chapter Six

Origins of the Michigan School

The significance of Angus Campbell and the Michigan School of voter-behavior analysis pivoted on the use of surveys as distinct from electoral data. The survey method—with its opportunity to pose questions—proved vastly important in the postwar era in providing a different tool for measurement and in adding to aggregate election returns a focus on the individual voter. As Claude Robinson put it in 1941, addressing the rudiments, accuracy in "appraising election trends and assigning causes" was more likely to be achieved through sampling than from study of elections per se, for sampling provided "'elections' at the will of the investigator." Or, as V. O. Key himself noted in his "Critical Elections" piece, tentative conclusions he drew as regards voter behavior had "to be read with the caution invariably applicable to inferences about individual behavior from aggregate statistics." More precise interpretation of such "behavior . . . would need a voting history of individual voters over a period of several elections, a body of data not readily available." But, Key added, a 1952 Michigan survey did provide "findings" that were "parallel" to his.[1]

The survey approach reached to the "micro" level of the individual voter and thus facilitated probing of motivation, overcoming a basic limit of electoral data. The survey method became by 1960 a tool as central (to Campbell, more central) to the determination of whether realignment had occurred than the actual election returns. The development of scientific polling in the 1930s provided a basis for what became this most favored tool of the post–World War II vogue of behavioral analysis. Pollsters' individual interviews across demographic groups (along with the even earlier work of Gosnell) attracted later academic practitioners. Operating at the micro level offered greater reliability than the more cumbersome and unwieldy attempt to extricate and infer demographic voting patterns from electoral data units. Still, to academics the pollsters' methods sometimes seemed too slapdash, too commercially oriented, and too geared to horserace predictions. This uneasiness was brought home in the wake of the pollsters' erroneous and much ridiculed forecasts of the 1948 election results, the same event that gave Michigan its initial boost. Surveys in the hands of scholars, they believed, could be more careful, more probing, more systematic, and more precise.[2]

The scholarly survey became associated after 1948 above all with Angus Campbell and the Michigan School. It was Michigan that became known for its penetrating probing of the attitudes of individuals from diverse demographic groups and, vitally, for conducting national surveys in successive electoral periods—eventually facilitating generalizations across elections and time frames. Importantly, however, in the history of survey-based voter analysis, Paul Lazarsfeld and the Columbia School preceded Campbell and Michigan. If survey research reached its culmination at Michigan in the 1950s and 1960s, the Columbia effort of the 1940s and early 1950s constituted at the very least an important precursor, especially methodologically, but also conceptually. The Columbia surveys were limited, however, to panels in a particular community in a particular election year. And the Columbia approach also included other ingredients that undermined its ability to keep traction even as it paved the way for the enormously influential Michigan analysis.

Paul Lazarsfeld was born in Austria, studied at the Psychological Institute of the University of Vienna, and settled in the United States in the 1930s, bringing with him great talent as an academic entrepreneur and an analytic perspective that American students of politics sometimes characterized as "European."[3] Having established an affiliation with Columbia University and assembled a staff and financing, Lazarsfeld set out to undertake research in his new geographical environment. Lazarsfeld, for the purpose of his study of the 1940 campaign, settled on Erie County, Ohio, for an intensive investigation of voters' decision-making processes as revealed in successive panel interviews. Expecting to witness and document how the campaign and media influenced that decision-making process, Lazarsfeld and his associates were surprised by how little change in viewpoint and voting intention was expressed by members of the panel in their interviews. They concluded, in one of their two most distinctive and important judgments, that an underlying electoral stability characterized voter behavior over the course of the 1940 campaign. Voters did not make a choice based on the persuasiveness of the campaign or the influence of the media; both campaign and media appeared to make little difference in voters' determination of how to cast their ballots.[4] This notion of an underlying base of stability, over time and via Michigan, became highly important as a baseline against which to measure lasting change. This basic point of the Lazarsfeld study was publicized as early as November 1940 by *Life*, which helped support the undertaking. The "first great discovery" of the study, *Life* proclaimed, was that a majority of Erie County voters, as reflected in the panel members, "preserved their voting intentions unchanged throughout" the campaign.[5]

A second judgment dealt with why this was so, for, as *Life* put it, the purpose of the study was to discover not just how voters would vote but also why voters voted the way they did.[6] The conclusion here, as expressed in *The People's Choice* in 1944, became one of the most famous and most criticized lines in the history of electoral analysis, namely, "a person thinks, politically, as he is, socially. Social characteristics determine political preference."[7] This conclusion, critics held, ignored politics; it made voter choice simply a matter of class or occupational background; it involved simplistic social determinism; it reflected the European analytical background of its main expounder.[8] Further, the emphasis on a continuity rooted in "sociological" factors could not explain dramatic electoral change.[9] Combining both criticisms, a veteran of the Gallup polling organization, observing in 1998 the fiftieth anniversary of the pollsters' 1948 debacle, still placed the blame on Lazarsfeld. "The real villain of 1948 was Paul Lazarsfeld," he concluded, since the pollsters, relying on Lazarsfeld's analysis, concluded that given underlying social factors, the course of the campaign would make little difference and so decided not to do late polling.[10]

Try as they might in later years, Lazarsfeld and his associates could not undo the damage done by the "social characteristics" line, and the Columbia voting studies came to an end by the mid-1950s.[11] They undertook to defend themselves and to deflect criticism in basically two ways: first, to acknowledge terminological imprecision, and, second, to move in the same direction as some of the critics. Both Lazarsfeld and his associate, Bernard Berelson, agreed that the "social characteristics" language had been unfortunate. "We certainly have been guilty of using loose language" on the matter of social characteristics, Lazarsfeld allowed. On this issue he and his colleagues were "caught . . . 'with our pants down'"; the entire concept needed "considerably more careful presentation and analysis."[12] Berelson agreed that "the shorthand phrase" about social characteristics was too vague and seemingly too all-encompassing and for that "we have to take the complete blame . . . in not being sufficiently precise." The Columbia team ought to have been "a good deal more careful in our use of language." The point actually being driven home by the shorthand, however, Berelson contended, was that voters did not consciously and rationally make decisions based on the issues of the campaign; underlying factors were highly influential. Social characteristics affected "perception of political realities" and determined "the values and criteria by which political judgments" were made. In that sense, the voter was "a hitchhiker" on his "social characteristics."[13] Berelson here, in a sense, was turning social characteristics into the prism through which political matters were viewed, a metaphor the Michigan School was in the process of applying to the concept of party identification.

In other respects as well, Lazarsfeld and Berleson seemed to be moving toward Michigan—and toward the increasingly secular perspectives of V. O. Key. In a 1953 response to an article by Key, Lazarsfeld alluded to the existence of "long-term changes," as well as to eras of stability and short-run change in American political history.[14] In their 1954 study, *Voting*, based on Elmira, New York, the Columbia team alluded to "the long-lasting nature of . . . political loyalties" based originally on ethnic, religious, sectional, and economic divisions. "The vote," in that sense, they contended, was "a kind of 'moving average' of reactions to the political past." Many campaigns—not, they allowed, that of 1952—reinforced long-held electoral patterns and predispositions.[15] This was not too unlike contemporaneous work of the emerging Michigan School. Similarly, Berelson, in a letter to Key, called for ending the "bad distinction" between "sociological" and "political" factors, agreeing that "social characteristics" were "articulated in terms of political issues" and noting how the social and the political melded historically to produce such phenomena as the "religious vote."[16] In his 1968 introduction to a reissue of *The People's Choice*, Lazarsfeld seemed to move even more decisively in Michigan's direction with an emphasis on the importance of "party loyalty."[17] Still, Lazarsfeld remained at pains to establish at least Columbia's chronological and methodological precedence in relation to Michigan. On that "relation between Columbia and Michigan," he wrote to Key in 1962, the "priorities" were Columbia's, and as far as "research instruments" and "ideas" went, "the flow" proceeded "from Columbia to Michigan."[18]

The nature and import of the relation between Columbia and Michigan has been a matter of discussion for decades. Some analysts have emphasized conflict between the two and others similarities. There were, to be sure, differences. The Columbia studies sampled selected communities; Michigan used national surveys. Columbia did focus on social characteristics, Michigan on individual party identification. Columbia's approach was "sociological," Michigan's "social psychological." Of particular importance, Michigan gradually developed a time dimension—comparing behavior across succeeding elections. Basic commonalities between the two schools, however, were profound. Both focused on the underlying stability of the electorate; both downplayed decision making among voters based on issues; both utilized the idea of a prism through which voters viewed and thereby simplified choices in politics; both sought to establish generalizations about the nature of voter behavior. Perhaps the most vital point of difference was in practical outcome, namely, that Columbia gave way to Michigan as a force in the academic world. Hence, whatever Columbia's importance in paving the way, it was Michigan's formulations that became highly influential, dominating analysis of voting behavior in the 1960s, and—joined with Key's secular concepts— fleshing out the theory of realignment.[19]

Angus Campbell, the leader of the Michigan School, was born in Indiana in 1910, the son of an educator father, and reared in Oregon. He studied psychology at the University of Oregon and at Stanford; as a newly minted Ph.D. he worked at Northwestern where he was much influenced by the anthropologist Melville J. Hershkovits. During World War II, Campbell worked in the federal government in the Division of Program Surveys of the Bureau of Agricultural Economics. In 1946 he and others established the Survey Research Center (SRC) at the University of Michigan. A skilled academic entrepreneur and scholar, Campbell headed the SRC from 1948 to 1970.[20] Although the SRC became extraordinarily influential, it was, Heinz Eulau recalled from a 1954 seminar, housed in an "old, run-down . . . monstrosity, once a hospital."[21] Campbell himself referred to SRC headquarters as "the worst fire trap on campus."[22] As a personality and colleague, Campbell was considered solid, reliable, practical, cautious, and judicious. At a distance, his personal reserve and sometimes dour aura could seem standoffish.[23] He did not, however, lack imagination. One of his collaborators, Warren Miller, recalled that Campbell had hoped to use video film in conducting survey interviews to capture not just the words, but the accents of the respondents and also the interiors of their houses to provide a sense of cultural and ethnic flavor.[24] Nor did he lack scope of ambition. In an article written in the early phase of the Michigan undertaking, Campbell noted the "inadequacies" of the present state of knowledge of voting behavior and called for the development of the field by "imaginative people in the social sciences." Only "a long-term research program" could do the job, he concluded.[25] This, in fact, was precisely what Campbell was in the process of organizing and carrying out. In a 1952 letter to E. E. Schattschneider, who was coming to Michigan to teach during the summer, Campbell suggested consideration of his new coauthored *The People Elect a President* for supplementary course reading. He happily characterized the book as "one of the pioneer studies of American political behavior through the techniques of survey research."[26]

Campbell, a social psychologist by training, was critical of what he considered academic political scientists' focus on leaders and institutions at the expense of voters. Writing to V. O. Key in 1951, Campbell observed that there seemed "to be a much greater interest in the reactions of the general public among psychologists than among political scientists." He had the impression from the latter that they considered "political party organization . . . the proper item for study in the area of politics, not the people."[27] In referring to the "people" or "general public"—the terms used are themselves worthy of note as reflective of the American liberal that Campbell was—he had in mind not the social groups of Lazarsfeld, but rather individuals. The focus was on the psychology, personality, and perceptions of the individual as distinct from the social characteristics of the group, and Campbell widened the focus of his surveys accordingly to encompass individual beliefs and values.[28] Of particular importance, Campbell was impressed by the relative lack of class feeling in the United States as compared with the European experience. American party followings, he wrote, were more "heterogeneous" and less class-oriented than those in a country such as Norway. In the absence of strong class identities and class-oriented politics, the parties themselves in the United States served to guide voters.[29]

Survey methodology as distinct from a reliance on aggregate electoral data was absolutely central to Campbell's approach. Only the survey, by providing direct and immediate access to the individual, could elicit the rich array of information conducive to understanding the voter's psychology and outlook. Only the survey could probe the motivations and beliefs that the Michigan School considered intermediary between a voter's objective circumstances and the subjective casting of the ballot.[30] As Campbell put it in 1952, studies based on aggregate data could not "give more than a limited insight into the dynamics of the vote" since individual behavior could not be discerned and determined. Survey techniques thus "opened the way for a new . . . approach to the study of national elections."[31] The origin of that study, going back to 1948, was based on a good bit of serendipity. Here, again, Harry Truman's surprise victory proved determinative in the history of electoral analysis. In 1948 the SRC was conducting a series of interviews under the general rubric of public affairs. In a survey of foreign policy attitudes in October 1948, two questions were included as measures of political concern. Respondents were asked if they intended to vote and for what party they planned to cast their ballot in the coming election. The sample of 610 was exceedingly small, but unlike the pollsters, who had called the race for the Republican nominee, Thomas Dewey, the SRC result went down to the wire, neck and neck, with about a fifth of prospective voters declaring themselves still undecided. The interest in the survey result following the November upset led the Social Science Research Council to provide the SRC with a grant for follow-up study. Had the professional pollsters not erred in 1948, Heinz Eulau notes, the opening would not have been there for the Michigan group to ride through. The subsequent story was one of abundant financing and a steady climb to academic influence and fame.[32]

Campbell and his associates made due acknowledgment of those who had gone before and had contributed to their own analysis. In *The People Elect a*

President Campbell alluded to *The People's Choice* as the "first" demonstration of the value of the survey method to the study of political behavior. That "remarkable project," although limited to one community, "set the stage for the application of the survey method to a national" election study.[33] In 1954's *The Voter Decides* Campbell noted V. O. Key's emphasis on the durability of partisan attachments.[34] But while the connection with Key blossomed despite some differences, the Michigan group undertook to sharpen its own analysis by contrasting it with that of Lazarsfeld and his colleagues. In some good measure, Michigan defined itself in terms of its divergence from Columbia. As Campbell wryly put it in a letter to a writer on voting behavior who had scrambled the title of the 1954 book, "you have changed the title of our book from the good psychological . . . 'The Voter Decides' to a . . . sociological . . . 'The Voters Decide.'"[35] The Michigan critique of Columbia had an immediate focus and also a more general one. Campbell, writing to Key in December 1952, the month following the election of Dwight D. Eisenhower to the presidency on the Republican ticket, allowed that there was merit to the Lazarsfeld analysis in that "group anchoring" did exercise "an influence on political behavior." Hence, added Campbell, something was needed to keep Lazarsfeld from "slipping off" the "hook." The answer—"the trick"—wrote Campbell, was "to find variations in political behavior that cannot be derived from . . . social characteristics."[36] The 1952 election became the "variation" Campbell and Michigan used as a weapon to pummel Lazarsfeld and Columbia. Surely, Campbell and his associates argued, whatever the congruence of the Lazarsfeld approach with the New Deal–oriented election of 1948, the 1952 contest, with its vast vote swing, could not be attributed to "social characteristics." Such characteristics were relatively stable and hence lacked explanatory power for so massive an electoral shift.[37]

In a manuscript tellingly entitled "Social Determinism and Political Preference," which Campbell enclosed with his December 1952 letter to Key, the Michigan group let loose at Columbia in a more general way. "The Lazarsfeld formulation regarding social characteristics" the Michiganders declared "a very incomplete and rather misleading explanation of electoral behavior." A "psychological model," including individual, as well as group dynamics, provided a more inclusive and powerful tool for understanding voter behavior than Columbia's "sociological analysis." They further noted the absence of "party loyalty" in the competing formulation, holding that while such loyalty might have partial class or religious origin, it could also have other "historical sources" and therefore "should be treated as an independent variable."[38] Here lay the psychological and political key to understanding voter behavior, Campbell believed. It resided in the strong attachment many voters felt for a political party—the concept of party identification. That identification was not a simple product of social or economic circumstances. An Irish Catholic of the nineteenth century might have voted Democratic, for example, because of the relative friendliness of that party toward Irish Catholic immigrants. But present-day Irish Catholics identified with the Democratic Party, Campbell held, not because they were Irish Catholics, but because they were Democrats. Political identification thus had an autonomous existence.[39] To the Michigan School it was the single most important factor in an evolving and broadening analysis.

Most of Campbell's publications were coauthored, but Philip E. Converse, one of the four authors of the preeminent and classic Michigan production, *The American Voter*, declared that "Angus Campbell . . . originated the concept . . . of party identification."[40] The concept was first publicly broached in a coauthored 1951–1952 *Public Opinion Quarterly* article. Here Campbell suggested that party identification was something of an "independent variable" and that it, not social characteristics, underlay voters' policy attitudes. Voters used their attachment to party as a kind of "reference point" to reach foreign policy positions; that is, Democratic or Republican identifiers tended to accept views of foreign-policy issues associated with each party's leaders.[41] In *The People Elect a President*, characterized by the authors as a "pilot study" and "largely descriptive in character," the idea of party identification as an "independent influence" was set forth as an example of a concept to develop as "the core of subsequent research."[42] In *The Voter Decides* of 1954, the concept of party identification was placed in the comparative historical context provided by two recent elections, those of 1952 and 1948, and it was further related to both the long- and the short-term. Based on surveys, Campbell and his coauthors concluded that party identification did "not change easily" and that voters held on to their party identity with "tenacity," even when crossing over to vote for the candidate of another party. They did not know "how long" it took for conversion from one party to another to occur; this appeared to have happened during the Roosevelt era, but it had not yet occurred during the Eisenhower years. The election of 1948 was one in which party loyalty strongly determined the actual vote; that of 1952 was one in which "the more variable factors of issues and candidates" seemed to assume "unusual importance."[43] As Warren E. Miller, a coauthor of both *The Voter Decides* and later *The American Voter*, subsequently put it, issue and candidate orientations were "short-term evaluations," whereas "party identification . . . was a basic enduring commitment."[44] In *Group Differences in Attitudes and Votes*, published in 1956, party identification was declared to have "greater ability to order political data" than any competing concept. It facilitated differentiation between underlying sources of voter psychology and the casting of a ballot, for example, between partisan "conversions" as distinct from "defections" in a given election such as that of 1952. And it implied "a personal sense of belonging" to a party strong enough to impact a voter's stand on issues, as well as electoral behavior.[45]

Thus, even before the publication of *The American Voter* in 1960, Campbell and his associates had set forth their basic idea of party identification. They turned the notion of being a Republican or a Democrat from a matter of voting or registering to a matter of psychological attachment. They used the concept of party identification to give their analysis a temporal dimension; that is, by studying voter interview responses across elections, they could assess the relationship between party identity and actual voting. They could then weigh the relative importance of long-run considerations, such as party loyalty, and short-run factors, such as issues and candidates, in given elections. Thus, while party identification was deemed the single most reliable predictor of the actual vote, short-term factors provided an analytical means to account for deviations between identification and voting.[46] Donald E. Stokes, the fourth *American Voter* coauthor, noted that the Michigan surveys of voters across elections threw "light on the problem of change." The Columbia studies by contrast were static, confined to a single community during one election. Further, wrote Stokes, the misfortune of Columbia was compounded by the fact that its initial effort dealt with the 1940 election, one whose patterns "differed little from those of preceding elections." He had "often wondered whether the static social determinism of *The People's Choice* would have emerged from a campaign in which the tides of short-term change were more nearly at flood." Had Lazarsfeld and his associates proceeded from an election such as that of 1952, it was "entirely unlikely" that they would have reached similarly static conclusions.[47] Michigan, by contrast, could have its cake and eat it too. The concept of party identification, analogous to Columbia's social characteristics, posited a stable base, but by differentiating between identification and actual voting, and by conducting surveys across elections, Campbell and company developed an analysis encompassing both long- and short-term factors.

Stokes also put his finger on another key Michigan accomplishment. Focused on individual psychology via surveys, Michigan "developed a special interest in the aggregation of individual" data to help "explain the electorate's collective decision," in other words, to interpret the meaning of elections.[48] As Campbell himself put it, he was much interested in "explaining macropolitical movements through the use of micropolitical data," in bringing "together the depth of history with the contemporaneity of survey research"— which became increasingly viable as surveys were undertaken in successive elections.[49] The integration of the insights of the study of voting behavior with larger political and governmental processes was also a continuing preoccupation of V. O. Key's as he simultaneously encouraged, helped shape, and yet remained to a degree critical of the Michigan approach. As Michigan's influence mounted, Heinz Eulau recalled, "all roads traveled by social scientists seemed to lead to Ann Arbor, Michigan, and the university's enterprising . . . Survey Research Center."[50] Key traveled that road, but it had been and continued to be very much a two-way street. In 1947, just before Michigan's star began its ascent, Key noted the "striking" lack of work done in the United States on "the careful analysis of voting behavior."[51] Key subsequently used his influence as a member of the Social Science Research Council's Committee on Political Behavior to encourage and facilitate funding for the fledgling Michigan studies.[52] Key contributed the foreword to *The Voter Decides,* which he later described as a "classic."[53] In 1955 Key recommended his "good friend" Angus Campbell as a potential contributor to the *Virginia Quarterly Review*.[54] In May 1959 he looked forward to spending the coming academic year at the SRC—"Angus Campbell's shop trying to learn one end of a punch card from another and also to hobnob with the social psychologists to see what I can learn from them."[55] The ongoing interaction of Campbell and Key constituted a classic case of scholarly synergy.

Chapter Seven

The Crystallization of Theory

Angus Campbell's appeal to V. O. Key lay in part in Michigan's possibilities as an alternative to Columbia. Key was quite critical of the latter, disputing the notion that social characteristics determined political outcomes. Such an approach, Key held, failed to explain sharp breaks in electoral continuity and failed to take into account historical traditions that persisted in ways that cut across class and other social categories.[1] To Paul Lazarsfeld himself, Key wrote that the Columbia approach would be more fruitful if it branched out in additional directions; there was not "only one road to salvation."[2] To Lazarsfeld's associate, Bernard Berelson, Key contended in 1951 that by providing more of a historical and political context, sketching out "the impact of culture and history," their "entire analysis" could be placed in "perspective." This could help explain why people of different classes voted similarly, perhaps a more important electoral dimension to overall understanding than why people of the same class voted the same way. Berelson might find useful, Key added, work done by Angus Campbell on partisan attitudes. Nor should "survey people" ignore what a political scientist such as Key knew: "that there are . . . social 'entities' called parties which have an existence through time and which possess considerable stability."[3] In a 1952 letter to Berelson, Key held that class-based voter categories were valid only when class or economic issues predominated. Different cleavages developed over different issues. Further, given the limited time span of survey research, generalizations about campaigns and elections were exceedingly perilous. Key did not recall the authors of *The People's Choice*, based on the 1940 campaign, shouting

> from the housetops that we had to remember that a factor common to 1936 and 1940 was a fellow called FDR. . . . When we woke up with a hangover after election day 1948, some of us felt like the nearsighted fellow who had been

peering at a lattice and swore that it was a solid board fence. We opined that maybe we hadn't been alert enough to limit the finding of vote-intention stability to specified conditions. The addition of a second case permitted a modification of a set of generalizations that had been read into one case.[4]

Writing to others, Key was somewhat more caustic. In a 1952 letter to Angus Campbell, Key wrote of the phrase "social characteristics determine political preference" that "no more impressive half truth" was ever uttered. It ignored both the political continuity of historical traditions and the potential impact of election campaigns.[5] He lived, he declared in a 1953 letter, "in mortal terror of what I have denominated the Lazarsfeldian lacuna, viz., that some variable so big that it escapes observation accounts for something."[6] To Samuel Lubell, Key in 1956 recommended Angus Campbell as "the chief of a non-Lazarsfeldian crowd," and noted how "in 1940 Lazarsfeld more or less forgot that FDR was running and that everybody had more or less made up their minds about him. He then deduced as a general proposition that election campaigns did not change very many votes."[7] In a 1958 letter, Key held that "had we stopped with . . . Lazarsfeld's study of 1940 we would have a most erroneous notion of the place of class in the political order." The role of class in politics in fact changed with changing circumstances.[8] In 1960 Key undertook to defend Warren Miller, who he feared had "been caught in the crossfire" between the Michigan School of which Miller was a member and "a sociological-determinist crowd." Key held that there could "be no denying that as election after election" occurred and new information accumulated "the sociologically oriented crowd" became "less persuasive."[9] In 1963 Key viewed Columbia's importance essentially as a spur to Michigan's rise. *The People's Choice*, Key wrote, did not "hold a lot of validity . . . but it . . . set in motion" subsequent studies of greater sophistication.[10]

A central and persistent concern of Key's was that the findings of voting behavior studies be integrated into the broader political and governmental process. The need, he held, was to bridge the gap between "microanalysis and macroanalysis," to use the individual data made available by surveys to understand the electorate as a whole and the nature of elections better, and to harness the enhanced understanding of voting behavior to illuminate the workings of political and governmental institutions and elites.[11] Campbell and his colleagues learned from Key and went a long way in his direction. They built on Key's concept of partisan attachments and of the voter's "standing decision" to favor one party or the other.[12] In 1952 Key suggested to Campbell that asking interviewees whether they were "intensely, moderately, or only slightly loyal" to a party might provide a "better predictor than . . . other attributes."[13] And Key was called upon to provide assistance as the finishing touches were put on *The American Voter*.[14] Asked by the editor of *Public Opinion Quarterly* to contribute an article, Key requested that he be allowed to do a "longish" review of the forthcoming book, using "the review as a springboard" to discuss the "weaknesses" of survey research from the political scientist's standpoint and also the "advances" made by the present study. He allowed "that the review would be loaded in the sense" that he had already read the manuscript and believed it "a pretty good book."[15] In the actual review article, Key reiterated his general concern about the need to relate individual survey research to the larger political and governmental process, but then added that this was very much what *The American Voter* had accomplished. The book's "great merit" lay in the way it took "steps in the adaptation of survey analysis to the study of problems that really bear on the political system." Further, the use of survey materials across time had "permitted the examination of electoral behavior" and "changes through time."[16] Following the book's publication, Key wrote to his friend Campbell to ward off the latter's anxieties. "You should be of more optimistic cheer about your treatise," Key advised encouragingly. "It takes about five to ten years for a book to percolate around and affect the course of thought. But give you five, six, or seven years, you will meet your ideas floating around in the books that you read."[17] Once again, even in an effort at providing cheer, Key engaged in what turned out to be quite an understatement.

Key wrote in 1958 that survey research was not without flaws and that one of his "favorite pastimes" had "been in quibbling with the SRC staff, but," he added, he had "gained far more than" he had "given them in these exchanges." Survey research had given him "clues" that he as a "lone-wolf worker" could never have procured himself. "A Gallup poll," he concluded, related "to an SRC survey about as a two-bit magnifying glass" did "to an electron microscope."[18] He later found SRC information very illuminating in exploring the dimensions of the religious factor in the 1960 election. Here, ironically, just following publication of *The American Voter* and its fuller construction of an analysis based on the concept of party identification, which in turn built upon some of his own observations, Key sprouted doubts. For in the wake of the 1960 election, he speculated that "a decline" might be underway "in some of the ancient anchorages, e.g., partisan loyalty."[19] But as the Michigan team after 1960 continued to add to its analysis, Key continued to play a supportive role. Philip E. Converse, in developing his concept of the "normal vote" as an elaboration on party identification, responded to Key's reading of his manuscript for *The American Political Science Review* with "a hasty mea culpa for the hard time" Key had had in making his way through the Converse effort. However, Converse added, "there was a certain poetic justice in it, since it was your original query . . . ('Is this "normal vote" something you boys pull out of the air?') which made" him undertake the full project. The answer to Key's original question, Converse added, was no. Key in reply urged Converse to follow through on his effort to explain the concept.[20]

The American Voter was the culmination of the Michigan research and conceptual effort. It was launched with a May 1960 news story in the *New York Times* headlined "12-Year Voter Study Indicates Democratic Victory in the Fall," based on the book's notion that 1952 and 1956 were "deviating elections" from a Democratic Party norm.[21] Campbell wrote to Key in July of that year that while many considered the volume "an infallible protection against insomnia," he was "confident" that it would become a "substantial" addition "to every political science library in the United States."[22] Like Key's, Campbell's characterization proved too modest. *The American Voter* proved enormously influential. An early commentator had it right, for the book provided the gateway to "valuable studies of the politics of mid-twentieth-century America."[23] Already in 1964, with the impending appearance of an abridged paper edition, coauthor Donald Stokes urged his colleagues to retain the original title in order "to respect the historical identity of *The American Voter*" as the "landmark of research . . . known by its present title."[24] A 1967 correspondent dubbed Campbell and company "the Michigan jet set" as the Ann Arbor scholars traveled abroad to interact with European students of electoral behavior.[25] Gerald M. Pomper, a later critic, acknowledged that *The American Voter* was a "seminal" work that set "the boundaries and standards for subsequent research."[26] Two other later writers contended that through the success of the Michigan team, "Ann Arbor became Mecca to a generation of scholars."[27] *The American Voter* was both a culmination and a beginning. It effectively summed up and developed a dozen years of Michigan scholarship, benefiting from data cutting now across several elections. It demonstrated the value of survey research and rode the crest of the wave of the "behavioral revolution." Connecting with Key's secular concepts, it broadened the study of voter behavior into a study of the electorate and of elections across time that led to a more comprehensive theory of realignment.[28]

In *The American Voter* and in subsequent publications of the early and mid-1960s Campbell, Converse, Miller, and Stokes presented the Michigan analysis in its fullest, most systematic, and most developed form. Class, they held, did not hold the same political importance in the United States as in Europe, due in part to the historic strength of sectionalism in America; sharp economic downturns, on the other hand, as in the 1890s and 1930s, had had major political repercussions. Partisan identification, Michigan's key concept, they stressed, was sharply differentiated from the vote; party identification was a "durable attachment," while short-term factors could sway voters temporarily to the opposition party.[29] Constituting an element of psychological stability, party identification also contributed to political stability, guarding against the disarray associated with demagogic appeals.[30] The Michigan team further held that party identification provided a prism through which voters formed opinions as to issues; partisan attachment geared them to one or the other party's positions on matters of policy. The strength of party identification also usually made elections something other than judgments on policies or administrations. Rather than making "periodic reviews of governmental conduct," voters most characteristically reflected their underlying party attachments in their electoral behavior. Thus, the roots of the voters' responses were to be found not merely in the interval since the previous election, but also in the further reaches of historical time. And while the initial roots of party loyalty may have been related to factors such as ethnicity, religion, and class, party loyalty was then "maintained long after its nonpolitical sources . . . faded."[31] Later commentators pointed out that the period during which *The American Voter* took shape was one characterized by issues largely inherited from the New Deal, lacking in current intensity, and thus accounting for the stress on party strength versus issues. But as they and members of the Michigan team themselves pointed out, the strength of party loyalty was reflective of the earlier strength of issues; that is, party loyalties of the 1950s were forged in part in the intense issues environment of the 1930s.[32]

A key part of the mature Michigan analysis lay in the differentiation between the short-term factors of a given election and the long-term influence of party identification. In any given election, the Michiganders wrote, the issues, candidates, and events of the moment may cause voters to cast ballots contrary to their party identification. In 1952, for example, the circumstances of that election year led millions of Democrats to vote Republican for president. In 1960, similarly, many Protestant Democrats could not bring themselves to vote for the Democratic and Catholic candidate for president. Except in the rare circumstances of partisan realignment, however, the Michigan team held, such temporary departures from party loyalty due to the exigencies of a given election did not change underlying party identification. The latter was powerful enough to draw party identifiers back to their party vote as the exigencies faded. The "normal vote," as Philip Converse called it, based on party identification or "standing strength," constituted the baseline against which the impact of short-term forces could be weighed. Thus, the Michigan team developed an analysis that provided for a basic element of stability via party identification while also accounting for elections during which the hold of party identification temporarily weakened. All this, it is not too hard to see, reflected patterns of the 1950s and of 1960. A huge Republican presidential vote in 1952 and 1956 did not increase the proportion of Republican party identifiers. The Democrats, having narrowly lost control of Congress in 1952, regained it in 1954, held it in 1956, and sharply increased their margins of control in 1958. John F. Kennedy recaptured the White House for the Democrats in 1960, but in the Michigan analysis, did so with less than the normal Democratic vote because of the short-term factor of religion in the election.[33]

In linking the Michigan analysis to Key's concepts of secular change, Angus Campbell rejected a competing theory of political change—the cyclical concept of Arthur M. Schlesinger. The election of 1952, for example, Campbell held, did not represent a conservative swing, but rather frustration over "specific grievances" and therefore lacked the "highly charged" atmosphere and historical importance of such elections as "1856–60, 1896, and 1932–36."[34] In applying their notion of party identification to the concept of realignment, the authors of *The American Voter* cautioned against focusing on any one election; rather than a "realigning election," they suggested the idea of a "realigning electoral era."[35] They held that the Democratic upsurge of the 1930s probably reflected the impact of new voters, as well as the conversion of party identifiers.[36] They related realignment to performance and policy. A negative reaction against a party in power provided an opportunity; the success of a party newly chosen gave that party a chance to deepen and consolidate its electoral grip.[37] Of overwhelmingly greatest importance, however, was the Michigan merging of party identification with the concept of realignment. In his original article on critical elections, V. O. Key had used electoral data; he had discussed realignment in terms of durable shifts in party strength as reflected in voting returns. Campbell and his associates, employing survey data, used party identification as the determinant of realignment. Realignment meant a significant and lasting shift in party identification among the electorate.[38] In a sense this alteration could be seen as a strengthening of Key's concept in that it provided a differentiation between changed voting returns and party strength as defined in deeper psychological terms. But it also provided a source of confusion and frustration when in future elections voting returns shifted and to a fair degree endured at the presidential level, even as surveys indicated that underlying party identifications remained unchanged or were changing only glacially.

The capstone of the Michigan team's synthesis of their analysis with Key's secular concepts came with Angus Campbell's scheme of election classification. That classification, which Campbell acknowledged constituted "an extension of V. O. Key's theory of critical elections," involved a division of elections into categories designated realigning, deviating, and maintaining.[39] A "realigning" election, or period, was one in which major and durable shifts occurred in party identification. A "deviating" election was one, such as 1952 and 1956, in which short-term factors caused the minority party to prevail over the identification advantage of the majority party. A "maintaining" election—the term "coined" by Campbell, according to Converse, based on Key's "prior suggestions"—was one in which the majority party with its party-identification predominance prevailed electorally. This classification system proved enormously influential and was widely considered to constitute, along with other aspects of the Michigan analysis, a successful joining together of the "micro" research results of surveys with the "macro" electoral concerns of traditional political scientists. That is, data from individuals was now successfully developed and integrated into a theory encompassing and characterizing national elections.[40] As Heinz Eulau put it in his review of *The American Voter*, the charge that survey research could not "capture the dynamics of . . . change . . . in the electoral process" was belied by the book's success in undertaking an analysis with "longitudinal depth."[41] Eulau, Philip Converse, and Warren Miller recalled that while the "Michigan model" and Key's secular studies were independently undertaken, "they occurred at about the same time and the fit between the . . . micro and macro observations was elegant. . . . Thus a microlevel model developed from . . . survey data" provided explanatory assistance in understanding "the character of . . . processes underlying major political changes."[42]

Eulau, Converse, and Miller were right. In theory and in terms of what appeared to be the realities of American politics through the 1950s and the election of 1960, the fit between Michigan and the secular Key was indeed "elegant." The concept of party identification and the normal vote provided the baseline against which to judge both short- and long-term shifts. For a deviating election to occur, for example, required some measure against which deviation could be calculated. Party identification and the normal vote constituted that measure. For a realigning election or era to be gauged, similarly, a benchmark was needed. In the Michigan analysis, party identification and the normal vote provided that benchmark. A deviating election did not bring lasting changes in party loyalty; a realigning process did. On the other side of the coin, it took the fire and intensity of a realignment to burn into voters the kind of strong party loyalty that followed the Civil War and the depressions of the 1890s and 1930s. The concept of party identification also provided a formula to help characterize and understand the periods of stability and short-run interruptions between realigning elections. These were periods when stable party identity competed with the exigencies of particular elections. While the theoretical fit was elegant, so was the chronological fit. As numerous commentators have noted since, *The American Voter* marvelously reflected the patterns of the decade of its gestation: the underlying predominance of Democratic Party identifiers, Republican presidential victories in 1952 and 1956 under a popular war hero, and resurgence of the underlying Democratic advantage in the elections of 1958 and 1960. In that sense, just as the election of 1948 was critical for the development of the secular concepts of Key and Samuel Lubell, the elections of 1952 through 1958 provided the electoral patterns that appeared to shape the ultimate Michigan product in *The American Voter*.

Michigan shaped voting-behavior analysis and, combined with Key's concepts, secular analysis in a way that dominated the discipline into the 1960s.

But there were other influences as well, notably that provided by E. E. Schattschneider. Schattschneider in a sense reflected the continuing force of the 1930s and 1940s on analyses made during the 1950s and 1960s and also provided a bridge to the issue-oriented criticisms of the Michigan School, which began to appear by the late 1960s and into the 1970s. Schattschneider, born in Minnesota in 1892, was considerably older than Key and Campbell, but his actual academic career essentially paralleled theirs chronologically. He received his bachelor's degree from the University of Wisconsin in 1915; his doctorate from Columbia, however, was not earned until 1935. From 1919 to 1927 he taught high school in Butler, Pennsylvania. He worked at the college level beginning in 1927, and in 1930 settled in at Wesleyan University where he remained for the rest of his career.[43] His was a colorful personality. Heinz Eulau recalled that no one was better at jokes and storytelling than "Schatt." Harold Lasswell, Eulau related, "roared with laughter at Schatt's priceless jokes or stories. He rarely told a joke or story himself but he knew when he met a master."[44] Austin Ranney characterized Schattschneider as "an enthusiast," akin to "cool, clear, spring water to a man who'd felt like he'd come out of a desert."[45] In his first book, *Politics, Pressures, and the Tariff*, a study of the Smoot-Hawley tariff act of 1930, Schattschneider noted that the 1930 legislation was a revision of that passed in 1922 "at or near the peak of a great era of Republican supremacy." In that book he also evinced an interest in both institutional structures and dynamic processes—an interest that would continue to characterize his work thereafter.[46]

Following 1948, and from the perspective of the 1950s, Schattschneider was impressed by the degree of upheaval wrought by the 1930s and undertook to compare it with similar occasions in American political history. Sectionalism, he held, over recent elections had given way to the "nationalization" of American politics everywhere outside the South. The changes of the 1930s had undone the great era of a sectionally based Republican supremacy extending from 1896 to 1932. The election of 1896 had produced a party alignment that proved "remarkably stable, maintaining itself almost without modification for thirty-six years" with an almost permanent GOP hold on power. The contest of 1932 similarly was "no ordinary election," no "ordinary" switch in party control. It displaced and replaced what was later called "the system of '96" with its own particular characteristics, including a Democratic hegemony not reliant on the South. The 1948 election confirmed it, and the Republican presidential takeover thereafter did not alter the basic characteristics of what had been put in place in the 1930s.[47] To Schattschneider, the nationalization of politics coming out of the system created in the 1930s meant an issue-oriented politics. The new political alignment meant a new "agenda" of issues and public policies; the sectionally oriented agenda

of 1896–1932 now, except for the South, had given way to a nationally oriented agenda reflecting economic divisions. Realignment, in the
Schattschneider mode, pivoted on the ability of crossover issues to overcome
the established issues of an existing alignment.[48] Further, Schattschneider
contended that electoral politics had to be related to institutional politics, or,
put differently, what happened among voters had to be connected to what was
happening in government. There was, he held, "a very serious misconception
involved in an examination of electoral behavior standing by itself. Politics,"
to Schattschneider, was "least meaningful at the grass roots." To understand
politics, voters and elections had to be linked to what government was actually doing in terms of policy.[49] Moreover, Schattschneider passionately believed this was as it should be. Politics should be about issues, policies, and
programs. He was chair of the discipline's committee on responsible party
government and he advocated a party system in which each party took clear
national stands on issues so that voters knew with some certainty which party
as a unit favored which set of policies and would cast their ballots accordingly.[50] He was critical of analysts such as Arthur Holcombe who interpreted
politics in terms of divisions among sectional and economic groups. Holcombe, he held, never seemed "to have imagined that differences of principle
about the broad outlines of public policy" might be an appropriate "basis of
party politics." In fact, contended Schattschneider, contemporary politics
could only be understood in terms of divisions over public policy.[51] To study
electoral behavior "as if it were . . . a mere reflection of economic geography"
ignored what was to Schattschneider the central point that voting meant
power and power meant an ability to shape a dominant agenda. A focus on
"political ecology," that is, on "detailed studies of the geographical distribution of the party vote," making "voting behavior a subordinate appendage of
economic geography," belied the importance of politics in terms of national
policies. "Recent history" supported the belief that an issue-oriented politics
could "transform the political map of the country almost beyond recognition
in a remarkably short period of time." Only by examining "the behavior of
the parties in the government" would the meaning of "election statistics
become intelligible."[52] From this perspective, wrote Schattschneider, "the
breakup of the Solid South" was a positive development. A section of the
country still outside the new nationalization of politics, insofar as it began to
conform to divisions elsewhere, would increase the possibility of a system
composed of two parties presenting distinctive national policy agendas.[53]

In the 1950 report of the committee on more responsible party government,
the electorate was divided between those who voted regularly along party lines
and those who based "their electoral choice upon the political performance of the
two parties." It was the latter group, the committee headed by Schattschneider

speculated, that might lead the way toward more responsible party government.[54] The impact of *The American Voter* was such that the standard view of electoral behavior came very much to pivot on the party identifier. But the second type of voter was taken up in V. O. Key's posthumously published *The Responsible Electorate*. Together with Schattschneider's emphasis on the issues agenda and public policy, Key's analysis of what became known as "retrospective voting" paved the way for revisionist analyses of electoral behavior. Key, to be sure, had been an important, sometimes critical, supporter of the Michigan School as it developed and extended its analysis. *The Responsible Electorate* appeared to have one foot in the Michigan camp, even as it moved beyond it. Even before that book, Key in his 1961 *Public Opinion and American Democracy* both echoed the Michigan perspective that voters tended to use party identity as a shortcut to reach issues stands and introduced the notion that some voters judged parties based on evaluations of short-run past performance. Additionally, Key contended, voting did include a "policy component," and voters' views of policy innovations were in part shaped by the skill with which political leaders presented them.[55] Key's developing analysis was not wholly congruent with Schattschneider's call for "prospective" voting, that is, for voting explicitly geared to policy alternatives, but it did represent a shift at the very least in emphasis from the prevailing Michigan model. In *The Responsible Electorate* itself, Key divided the electorate into "standpatters" who tended to adhere to party regularity and "switchers" who shifted parties from one election to the next. The latter group, he held, was larger than generally supposed; it tended to vote retrospectively, for example against a party in power with whose performance it was dissatisfied, as in 1952; and it was not devoid of policy concerns and judgments. It was this group, as distinct from those psychologically geared to party, whose voting behavior best explained shifting patterns between elections.[56]

The degree to which *The Responsible Electorate* marked a departure by Key away from Michigan has been a subject of discussion and some dispute since its publication. Some have held that Key basically retained much of the Michigan outlook, but was simply extending a particular line of analysis, while others have seen it as a more basic departure.[57] Angus Campbell, in a review of his friend's book, noted how Key reminded analysts that issues did play a role in politics, but understandably Campbell emphasized the degree to which the book did not depart from Michigan. Key, Campbell concluded, "recognized the profound effect on all political perceptions . . . of the individual citizen's commitment to his party."[58] Philip Converse, in his review, similarly denied that Key's work was "sharply discontinuous from past work in the area."[59] And Milton Cummings, who prepared the unfinished book for publication following Key's death, agreed with Converse.[60] Key himself noted in *The Responsible Elec-*

torate that in the 1960 election—the last presidential contest he lived to see—party and other group identifications remained important because the policy differences between the two candidates were not large. But, he concluded, the role of "policy preferences would have been considerably greater if Barry Goldwater, not Richard Nixon, had been the Republican presidential nominee in 1960."[61] Ironically, in later years retrospective voting would be viewed as an alternative to realignment theory, although both in good measure were spawned by the singular individual V. O. Key. Key's effort was all the more impressive because it was undertaken before the electoral events of 1964–1972 brought the Michigan model into some disrepair and disrepute. The retrospective analysis did not immediately take hold. It took some wild electoral gyrations and a perceived decline in party identification for that to occur.

Key, in developing his original secular analyses, reacted against his previous adherence, especially to Bean's cyclical theory, and Campbell explicitly rejected Schlesinger's cyclical concept. Yet the idea of cycles reappeared to become in some versions a central element of realignment theory and simultaneously a source, arguably, of a degree of obfuscation and a dose of determinism as political analysts set out to understand the nature and significance of elections from 1964 on. Even as the theory of realignment jelled, forays into history resulted in identifications of elections or electoral eras comparable to those of the Civil War, the 1890s, and the 1930s. Political historians discerned several partisan "systems" prior to those of 1896 and 1932. The "first" party system existed from the 1790s to circa 1828, the "second" from circa 1828 to the Civil War, the "third" from the war to the 1890s. The "fourth" was the "system of '96," and the "fifth" was the system of the New Deal. It was not hard to calculate, from this historical periodicity, that new systems appeared every thirty-two or thirty-six years, or what some referred to as every generation. With the idea of a party "system," notions developed of creation, course, and decline. A party system began with a critical election or realigning era; it proceeded over a long span of relative electoral stability; gradually it declined to be replaced by a new critical era with a new system.[62] Thus, William Nisbet Chambers could note the "roughly cyclic pattern" of American political history. Joel H. Silbey and Samuel T. McSeveney could point to the "strikingly cyclical quality" of American electoral patterns. And Thomas Jahnige could contend in 1971 that the country was "now at the end of another thirty-six year cycle."[63]

Two of the earliest efforts to combine cyclical with secular analysis as applied across historical time occurred in the 1950s. Paul T. David in 1956 wrote of "turning points in political history" occurring approximately every twenty-eight years and requiring "about a generation each" to be fully worked out. In his schema the periods were 1832–1860, 1864–1892, and 1896–1924, and he speculated that another turning point possibly was on the horizon.[64] Avery Leiserson in 1958 contended that "critical elections" appeared to have occurred in 1800, 1828, 1860, 1896, and 1932, giving American electoral history "a distinctly cyclical character."[65] At least implicitly cyclical notions appeared elsewhere as well. Lubell's realignment concept groped toward an explanation of the origins, course, and decline of a dominant party coalition, focusing on the gradual decline of partisan fervor as the developments that had originally fired it receded over time. Eventually, newer voters (or a new generation) would be ripe for a possible new alignment. Such notions could help explain the cyclical periodicity some commentators discerned. (It would take a later academic analyst, Walter Dean Burnham, to expand upon and fortify this notion of recurring historical cycles with an explanation focused on the nation's cumbersome constitutional and governmental system.) The vicissitudes of 1952–1960 — the Republican challenge to long-term Democratic rule — led Lubell and other analysts to endeavor to weigh the forces of coalitional change and continuity in the 1950s and early 1960s. That analytical effort, in turn, proved to be but a prelude to what followed from 1964 into the 1970s when realignment theory was applied, tested, and, in some views, found wanting, or at the very least in need of revision.

Chapter Eight

Assessing Coalitions

Decisive in the development of secular electoral analysis, the election of 1948 at a more practical level left the Republican Party reeling. Confident of victory under Dewey, Truman's win was enormously demoralizing to the GOP. Arthur Krock of the *New York Times* in 1949 wrote of the Republicans' doldrums and how they now viewed 1946 as an exception to the downturn of the party dating back to 1932. With the prospect of settling into "the role of a steadily shrinking minority" confronting them, Republican leaders were hoping that something would "turn up in the way of events" or that "a new national figure" would emerge to lead them with a "popular appeal" transcending Democratic issues.[1] Journalist Hedley Donovan in 1952 held that, if the nation had indeed become normally Democratic, then conceivably it would take an occurrence of the magnitude of "1929–32" to change course, and "no such upheaval" appeared "in sight."[2] Krock proved closer to the mark. Events intervened, notably the Korean War, and a national figure emerged, transcending Democratic issues, in the person of General Dwight D. Eisenhower. The question was how enduring the GOP triumph of 1952 would prove after Korea and after Eisenhower. Was the formerly dominant Republican Party on the way to resuming its pre-Roosevelt status? Or would the Eisenhower years merely constitute an interruption in an era of continuing Democratic dominance?

In looking for bases for a secular Republican advantage, analysts in the 1950s highlighted the extraordinary growth of suburbs in postwar America. The movement from the cities to the suburbs, the expansion of the middle class in a growing economy, the aura of prosperity and consumerism, all augured well, some argued, for shifts from the labor-oriented Democrats to the upscale Republicans.[3] Wrote William H. Whyte in *The Organization Man*, one of the famous books of the decade, city migrants to the suburbs converted to Republicanism "rather rapidly," for Democratic identification was "part of

an environment" they wished "to leave behind."[4] Political analyst and poll-
ster Louis Harris explored the question in his 1954 *Is There a Republican Majority?* in which he extended Samuel Lubell's demographic analysis and drew
the opposite partisan conclusion. Harris held that the GOP victory of 1952
was set in motion with the end of massive immigration in the 1920s, the drop
in the birthrate in the depressed 1930s, and the consequent halt to growth in
the big cities. Continuing the parallelism with Lubell, Harris held that
Thomas Dewey in 1948 was to Eisenhower in 1952 what the 1928 Al Smith
had been to the 1932 Roosevelt: a harbinger of things to come. As Smith foretold a Democratic upsurge based on the cities even in defeat, Dewey foretold
a Republican rise based on the suburbs even in the debacle of 1948. Further,
as the Depression made it possible for the Democrats to build upon Smith's
advances, the ascendancy of "foreign policy . . . over economic security" allowed the GOP to join favorable issues to demography. Economics provided
the only remaining Democratic appeal in 1952, and under the prevailing circumstances, it was not enough. And while Harris felt that the Democrats
would have won in 1952 without the negative foreign policy impact, he also
held that "the election of 1952 was . . . no fluke of temporary circumstances."
Barring a Republican depression, Harris considered it unlikely that the coalition built by Roosevelt could ever be restored to majority status. He considered it more likely, however, that a large group of unaffiliated voters would
hold the balance of power in the near future between two parties of roughly
equal strength than that the Republicans could consolidate a stable majority
based on 1952. The best long-run shot for the Republicans, Harris concluded,
lay in growing with the middle-class, white-collar suburbs.[5]

A second source of possible Republican secular growth often pointed to in
the 1950s lay in the South. Much of this speculation was based on a southern
version of the view that prosperous suburban voters would gravitate to the
Republicans. Here the argument was that the more economically based political divisions that arose nationally in the 1930s were spreading into the South
and that more prosperous and business-oriented white southerners would
gravitate toward the Republicans and away from their traditional Civil
War–based Democratic allegiance. In this analysis the Republicans could be
expected to fare best in the upper or outer South where economics could more
easily trump the traditional race issue that had historically bound most southern whites to the Democratic Party.[6] This projection was based on the kind of
analysis that V. O. Key provided in *Southern Politics* and appeared to be supported by the strong Eisenhower showing in middle-class southern white metropolitan areas. Others, however, were not so sure that the southern and
southern Republican future lay with an economically based politics. The Dixiecrat revolt of 1948 and the growing struggles of the 1950s over civil rights

suggested the continuing power of race-based politics. Theodore H. White in his classic *The Making of the President 1960*, published the year after the election, pointed to Republican strength in both the metropolitan and "Old South" and held that the GOP opportunity in the region was "permanent." That opportunity could be seized in turns of economics or race, he held, and would occupy and divide Republican strategists as they moved toward 1964.[7]

The Democratic retaking of Congress in 1954 and the party's congressional victory in 1956, even in the midst of the Republican presidential landslide, contributed to mid-1950s discussion of the virtually "unprecedented" existence of what later commentators called "divided government."[8] But with the big GOP setbacks in the congressional races of 1958, and with the loss of the White House in 1960, discussion along these lines receded, as did speculation about a rising GOP. The Democrats in 1960 held their own in the suburbs and blunted the Republican advance in the South. The tendency now was to view the Eisenhower victories as deviations from what remained a normal Democratic majority, although Theodore White, noting the narrowness of Kennedy's victory, demurred.[9] James Reston of the *New York Times* in November 1960 held that John F. Kennedy had based his campaign on the cyclical notion of "Arthur Schlesinger, the sage of Xenia, Ohio," an assertion that Schlesinger happily noted in his autobiography and one easy to believe with Arthur Schlesinger, Jr. serving on Kennedy's campaign staff.[10] E. E. Schattschneider, coming out of 1948 convinced as to the secular durability of the Democratic majority based in large measure on "new voters" of the 1920s and 1930s, assured the defeated Democratic presidential candidate, Adlai E. Stevenson, in November 1952 that the Democrats were "still the majority party in the country" and that he had "never felt so certain of anything in my life" than that the Democratic Party would return to power soon.[11] (Stevenson had shown an appeal of his own to many suburban professionals.) The breadth of the Eisenhower electoral showing, Schattschneider subsequently argued, demonstrated the continuation of the nationalization of politics that was a defining characteristic of the system that emerged in the 1930s.[12] The most influential analysis of enduring Democratic strength was that emanating from Ann Arbor, Michigan. In 1956 Angus Campbell appeared somewhat to buy into the thesis that the Republicans would be the prime beneficiaries of increased suburbanization.[13] But his and the overall Michigan analysis tended strongly to point in other directions. In 1954 and again in 1956 Campbell answered the question of whether there was "a gradual slippage of Democrats into the Republican ranks" negatively. There had been no change in the proportions of party identifiers between 1952 and 1954.[14] The point was fully brought home in 1960. In the *New York Times* story launching *The American Voter*, the Eisenhower victories were declared "deviating elections" from the

Democrats' continuing majority-party status, a fact that pointed "toward a Democratic victory" in 1960.[15] The Eisenhower era, the authors of *The American Voter* affirmed, had not undone the appeal of the Democratic Party.[16] V. O. Key's forays into interpreting the contemporary national scene were not dissimilar. The 1954 Democratic congressional victory, he wrote, demonstrated the "wide gap" between Eisenhower's personal popularity and the Republican Party's appeal.[17] In 1956 he suggested that the election of 1952 could be seen as a product of "a special set of circumstances," although he also saw a slow realignment underway in the South as part of an increasing pattern of competition between the parties throughout the nation.[18] Looking back on the 1950s from the vantage point of 1961, Key sounded a theme that would gain resonance in the period of "divided government" after 1968. The electorate of the Eisenhower era, he maintained, had consisted of "two non-congruent majorities." Satisfaction with Democratic domestic policies kept Congress after 1954 in that party's hands, whereas dissatisfaction with Democratic foreign policy by 1952 resulted in the Eisenhower presidency.[19] In *The Responsible Electorate* Key characterized the Eisenhower triumph of 1952 as "at bottom" one that "rested on a transient majority," which evaporated as the issues that created it faded, while on the major domestic economic issues, a "popular majority" remained opposed to Republican positions.[20]

The busiest analyst of 1950s political trends was one Samuel Lubell. His major project, following *The Future of American Politics*, was *The Revolt of the Moderates*, published in 1956. As the first book analyzed the forces that had resulted in the surprise Democratic victory of 1948, the sequel undertook to analyze what had happened since and to project the near-term consequences of the Republican victory of 1952. As he described the forthcoming book in 1954, he intended now "to do for the Republican Party what my earlier book did for the Democratic Party" and to bring the story of "the political picture in the country up to date."[21] He was confident that *The Revolt of the Moderates* forecast "the shape of American politics for the next five to ten years."[22] Key reviewed the book in a way that reflected his "own undemonstrative spirit" and noted privately to Lubell that the aspect of the book that both "worried" him the most and brought out his "greatest admiration" was the effort "to put all the pieces together and figure out . . . the plot of the whole play . . . before the first act was over." This was a "far more difficult" task than the undertaking in *The Future of American Politics* to explain the origins and nature of the Roosevelt coalition.[23]

That was the task that Lubell set for himself both in the book and in pieces published over the course of the decade. And Key was right; it was not easy, for Lubell on the spot had to try to disentangle what was fleeting from what was likely to prove more permanent, a task that was to bedevil analysts for years to come. He did believe firmly that the country was again in a process of realignment. But by this he did not mean, in the mid-century context, a sharp or sudden break with the past; he meant a much more gradual transformation, feeding in part off of growing and festering divisions in the Democratic Party. The famed Roosevelt coalition was "on the wane"; short-term issues like the Korean War shifted voters toward the GOP despite Democratic popularity on the economy; Eisenhower's 1952 victory swept across different voting groups. Still, Republicans had not yet put together a durable majority coalition of their own.[24] The result, Lubell believed, was a period of partisan balance. Oliver Garceau, in critiquing *The Revolt of the Moderates*, held that Lubell had not done a satisfactory job of explaining how the country had gotten from there to here. In *The Future of American Politics*, wrote Garceau, Lubell had developed the idea of a majority party and had contended that upheaval was needed to bring about the overthrow of that party's dominance. "But when we get to the *Moderates*, we have a two party balance. . . . No effort is made to square this with the preceding book. No explanation is offered for the disappearance, in a period of bland social relations, of the dominance of the Democrats."[25] But Lubell, along with his association of realignment with sharp departures, also wrote of the gradual weakening of a majority coalition prior to a decisive break with the past, and it was this scenario that he applied to the 1950s.

The decline of the Democrats and the 1952 victory of Eisenhower had created a period of relatively even party balance not unlike that between Reconstruction and the depression of the 1890s. This was, Lubell believed in terms of his thesis that American politics was most often characterized by majority and minority parties, an interim era. Eventually, a majority party would emerge. But for the time being, the country was experiencing the politics of stalemate. The very election of Eisenhower, not a Democrat but hardly a symbol of Republicanism either, reflected the stasis. A decisive movement toward majority status for either party was not likely to come, Lubell believed, until 1960 or 1964. Meanwhile, the country experienced divided government, with voters opting for a Republican president and after 1954 a Democratic Congress.[26] Briefly, in the first flush of Eisenhower's 1952 victory, Lubell had used stronger language. In a January 1953 article in the *Saturday Evening Post*, Lubell provided an analysis of Eisenhower's 1952 victory somewhat along the dramatic lines of his earlier analyses of Roosevelt's 1940 win and Truman's 1948 upset. Eisenhower's, Lubell contended, was not merely a "personal" victory. From the voting returns he discerned "an almost unbelievable fact," that of "little evidence of New Deal influence in the voting. From the Eisenhower electoral maps the proverbial visitor from Mars would never know that Franklin D. Roosevelt had lived!" The Eisenhower vote, he

added, reflected above all the power of frustration over the Korean War cutting across the different categories of voters, thus raising the question of
whether it was "a freakish political event" or "a political revolution, inaugu-
rating a new era." But his conclusion at least by implication went beyond anything that followed over the remainder of the decade. Not only did the Roosevelt coalition appear "like Humpty Dumpty after his fall, beyond being
pieced together again," but "a great many voters not only switched, they
changed their political allegiance."[27] In subsequent 1950s analyses, Lubell
would be more cautious.

The gist of his more durable analysis of the decade was that the dominance
of the Democrats as a majority party had given way to a system characterized
by increased competitiveness throughout the country, "real two-party politics
on a nationwide basis." There was no longer a "normal" majority vote on
which either party could depend. The departure of Eisenhower would not
change this reality based on lessened party loyalty among voters, which made
them less like rooted trees and "more like political tumbleweeds."[28] The attachments formed during the Roosevelt years had weakened; "the grip of
the past" was "being pried loose, finger by finger." The "mills of political
realignment . . . ground slowly," but "eventually the sands of stalemate"
would "run out and an effective majority" would "be recreated." Perhaps, he
speculated, a new generation lacking old loyalties would have to appear before a decisive realignment occurred.[29] Powerful new issues, cutting across
the economic divisions and issues inherited from the 1930s, would be required to advance and complete a realignment.[30] Additionally, a lot depended,
Lubell held, on how the Republicans governed. Economic disaster under a
Republican president obviously would only refire memories of Herbert
Hoover and the Depression; a positive performance would help overcome the
advantage of the Democrats' association with economic security.[31] The coming election, he pointed out in 1956, would be the first time since 1932 that
voters were judging an incumbent GOP administration. Hitherto they had cast
ballots for or against the Democrats; now the issue was whether four years of
Republicanism had altered views of Republicans or whether the party was
"still tagged with the symbols Roosevelt pinned on it." The election would
test the degree to which Eisenhower had "been successful in bringing together a new coalition capable of replacing the old Roosevelt coalition."[32]

Lubell wrote prior to the 1952 GOP victory, in *The Future of American Politics*, that the political strategy of a minority party such as the Republicans
necessarily revolved "around one question": What element of the majority
coalition could be "split off most readily"?[33] There were two major possibilities Lubell saw during the decade. The first included new middle-class voters. One of the most influential analyses Lubell ever set forth was his argument in *The Future of American Politics* that ethnic voters of working-class

background, fleeing the cities for the suburbs and experiencing upward mobility and prosperity, would not forsake their Democratic allegiance for Republicanism. These voters, Lubell held, were different from the old middle class, both in terms of religion and ethnicity and in the way they associated their good fortune with government programs and Democratic rule.[34] But there was actually more to Lubell's analysis in this area as he developed it across the decade. He emphasized the desire of voters to hold on to their social and economic gains, whether threatened by Republican programs perceived as harmful to prosperity and economic security or by Democrats as deliverers of inflation and high taxes.[35] The great challenge to the GOP, he held, lay in overcoming its association with economic hard times, an effort helped by the continuing prosperity following Eisenhower's 1952 victory.[36] And Lubell held that the strength of prosperity, the growth of the middle class, and the rise of suburbia were over most of the course of the 1950s all operating to enhance Republican electoral prospects. While a recession clearly hurt the GOP in the 1958 election, Lubell held that an economic rebound could cause a swaying electorate to move back in the Republican direction.[37] There was "little question," he contended, that in the "burgeoning middle class" lay the key to Republican "hopes for regaining ascendancy as the normal majority party."[38] Middle-class expansion had "solidified . . . Republican strength in the suburbs."[39] The "long-range trend of realignment was working in favor of the Republicans" in urban and suburban areas, Lubell wrote in 1959, until it was arrested by recession, reflecting "the rapid expansion of the nation's middle class since the end of World War II."[40]

Lubell also saw actual and prospective GOP gains at the Democrats' expense along lines related to region and race. Lubell wrote in *The Future of American Politics* that the rapidity with which "a nationwide political realignment" would come would likely pivot on what happened in the South.[41] Writing in 1961, he held that there had been a significant shift in "party loyalty" among southern whites toward the Republicans since 1948.[42] Lubell analyzed that shift in both economic and racial terms across the decade. In 1950 he pointed both to the spread of industrialization and the controversy over civil rights as ingredients in the movement from the Democratic Party to Republicanism. The inroads of realignment, he predicted, would come first in presidential voting, especially if Eisenhower—widely perceived as apart from party—were the Republican nominee in 1952 and gave many southern whites "the justification" they were "groping for to break with a Democratic allegiance."[43] A new southern middle class felt it had more in common economically with Republicans than with the national Democratic party.[44] But race also played a role. The spread of African-American voting in the South, Lubell cautioned in 1957, would likely bring an increased white racist turnout hammering "additional nails in the coffin of Southern liberalism."[45] Even earlier, in

1949, Lubell had presciently expressed disagreement with V. O. Key's characterization of the Dixiecrats as, in Lubell's paraphrase, "the last spasm of a dying order in the South." His "own feeling" was that there were still "a good many spasms left in the 'old South.'"[46]

Nor did Lubell confine his analysis of race to the South. Quite to the contrary. Some recent historians have stressed how northern white, urban, working-class, racial resentments, usually associated with the ferment of the 1960s, had earlier roots.[47] Whatever the overall merit of this perspective, Lubell was well aware of the actual and potential antagonisms within the northern wing of the Roosevelt coalition, although just how those resentments would be exploited by the opposition remained fluid at that time. To Lubell, a good part of the success of the Roosevelt coalition lay in the Democrats' ability to focus on the common economic interests of the coalition's component groups while playing down divisive racial and religious factors. However, with the spread of prosperity, economic anxieties were softened, and with the movement of African Americans north and the rise of the civil rights issue, racial antagonisms were becoming increasingly national, threatening the Democrats' northern, as well as its southern electoral base. The impinging of urban black neighborhoods on white ones Lubell singled out as an especially explosive ingredient in the North.[48] African Americans' attachment to the Democrats, Lubell wrote in *The Future of American Politics*, could lead Republicans to write them off and seek to form successful coalitions without them.[49] Tactically, he wrote in 1957, Republicans could push for just enough civil rights legislation to exacerbate tensions between northern and southern Democrats. And while Republicans did not yet have to choose between an appeal to white southerners and blacks, he speculated that the politically wiser decision might be to go for the latter as a way of striking "at the very core" of the Democratic coalition in the urban North.[50]

Prior to the 1960 election, Lubell raised the question as to whether the Democrats were "still the majority party." He believed that the country remained "in a twilight period," although the Democrats' strong vote in 1958 in the wake of recession suggested that their hold remained powerful, especially on economic issues.[51] Lubell was not pleased by the 1960 presidential debates, believing that they lessened political stability by de-emphasizing party and issues in favor of "personality, particularly on its theatrical side." If such debates became a permanent campaign feature, he speculated—quite presciently to the literal-minded from a 1980 perspective—it would "strengthen the trend toward actor-presidents."[52] More ominously, for Democrats, was a Lubell report featured in the November 8, 1963, issue of *Time*. President Kennedy's reelection drive, Lubell held, faced a far closer contest than had appeared to be the case only months before because of the rise of civil rights as the public's foremost concern. "Interviews in five Eastern states, where Kennedy should be at his strongest," *Time* quoted Lubell, "show him losing a tenth of his 1960 support—mainly because 'he gives in too much to the Negro.'"[53] Days later Kennedy was assassinated; a year later Lyndon Johnson won so huge a landslide victory that some analysts saw in it a realignment adding to Democratic strength. Subsequent developments, however, were such that Lubell's November 1963 comments could be read as a prologue to upheaval.

Chapter Nine

Weighing Upheaval

The upsurge of the civil rights struggle in the early 1960s, the increasing attention paid to racial strife in the North, as well as in the South, and the prospect that the Republican Party might nominate Senator Barry Goldwater for president in 1964 all raised the possibility of political upheaval.[1] A bitterly divisive set of issues and their nationalization, violent scenes of racial strife splashed across the nation's newspapers and its TV screens, and support for a GOP presidential candidate who would push the party toward an effort to capitalize on white resistance to full access to civil rights set journalists and scholars alike scurrying to assess the chances for realignment. The first presidential election to which a fully developed theory of realignment could be applied came in 1964. And it was applied both in terms of the short-run belief that the electoral results wrought a realignment that served to enhance the Democrats' majority-party status and in the long-run conclusion that Goldwater's vote was the first phase of a shift toward the Republicans, which culminated in the 1980s. Initially, that is before the 1964 nomination, it appeared to some that the GOP gamble on Goldwater, if carried through, might result, if not in an outright victory, in at least cutting deeply into traditional Democratic strength.[2] Two of what turned out to be the most insightful analyses actually appeared in 1963, one just before the assassination of President Kennedy and one just after. Political scientist Roger D. Masters, writing in early November, raised the possibility that a Goldwater defeat in 1964 nonetheless might lead to lasting GOP conquests in the South sufficient to provide a growing basis for Republican victory in 1968.[3] Political scientist Paul T. David, in support of that analysis, wrote in December that a Goldwater nomination might lead the country into a realignment comparable to those of the Civil War, 1890s, and New Deal eras, with Goldwater playing a role akin to that of Al Smith in 1928, leaving someone else to play the Republican FDR in 1968.[4]

The widespread conclusion, however, in the immediate aftermath of the huge 1964 Democratic victory, was that the election had affirmed and possibly added to the Democrats' strength as the majority and that the Republicans had grievously erred in nominating a candidate so out of sync with most of the electorate. Goldwater's inroads were largely confined to the Deep South states, which was little consolation, it seemed, in a national defeat of historic proportions. John Allswang, a young political historian working as an interviewer for Samuel Lubell in Chicago, suggested even before the ballots were in that the Republicans were possibly "in the process of relegating themselves to a permanent minority" with no realistic expectations of winning Congress or the presidency.[5] Paul Tillet, writing after the election, acknowledged the GOP gains in the Deep South, but noted that the party had lost ground in the upper South and had "cut itself off absolutely" from African-American voters. The Democrats, meanwhile, had "cast off" what Tillet called their "southern bond." The GOP, Tillet speculated, faced the possibility of floundering "in minority status" for "a generation or more."[6] Nelson Polsby in 1966, and together with Aaron Wildavsky in 1968, agreed. The "shrinking" Republican Party had grossly miscalculated in nominating Goldwater. The growing bloc of African-American voters had been lost while efforts to appeal to discontented whites had not brought significant success outside the Deep South. The Republicans appeared to have put themselves in a position where they could not expect "to return . . . to power for any lengthy period of time."[7]

Political scientist Gerald Pomper was quick to seize on 1964 as a possible critical election adding to Democratic strength as the majority party, even as the Republicans made less important gains in the Deep South. The contest of 1964, he wrote, bore "many of the hallmarks of a critical election" realigning "party loyalties." Final determination would have to await the elections of 1968 and 1972 as to whether the movements of 1964 were merely temporary deviations, but it would be "quite remarkable if such were the case."[8] Years later, Pomper allowed that the 1964 election was not as critical as he had earlier contended; the opportunity to create a stronger long-term Democratic majority, he believed, had been aborted by subsequent upheaval; the realigning potential of 1964 was not confirmed and developed by subsequent successful Democratic political leadership.[9] The cautious Angus Campbell, by now the respected doyen of analysts of electoral behavior, carefully qualified his conclusions as to the meaning of 1964, yet there was no mistaking his sense of "far-reaching" implications. The Michigan School, he noted, distinguished between wide electoral swings that merely reflected temporary phenomena and movements reflective of more deeply rooted factors. In the latter case, durable party identifications changed and an election would be deemed realigning. Civil rights, Campbell believed, in 1964 in some measure provided such a factor, moving different segments of the electorate in different directions. The question was whether a net shift toward the Democrats registered in surveys of party identification would prove durable. The Republican landslides of the 1950s had not brought comparable shifts in surveys of party identification—the basis for the Michigan concept of a "deviating" election. If the detected shift in party identification proved lasting, Campbell concluded, it would suggest the onset of a realignment era enhancing the Democrats' majority-party status.[10]

Samuel Lubell, as usual, was less cautiously excited. Indeed, he almost reflected the national mood swings the country experienced in 1963 and 1964. There was no hiding his concern as the civil rights struggle mounted that the issue of race was increasingly nationalizing—and potentially destabilizing— American politics. Continuing lines of thought he had developed much earlier, he speculated that racial division might tear the Democratic coalition apart, not only in terms of southern losses, but also in terms of driving a wedge through the very heart of the coalition's northern components.[11] Expressing such concerns in a letter written shortly before President Kennedy's death, Lubell speculated that "a new conservative coalition might swirl into being and actually sweep to victory or, if it did not capture the White House, would still change the shape of American politics from now on out." Thus, "the 1964 vote . . . could turn out to be the most far-reaching . . . election since Roosevelt's 1932 New Deal triumph."[12] Days later, with Lyndon Johnson of Texas as president, Lubell wrote that in the South, the picture had "reversed itself completely. Right now Johnson could lock up the whole south."[13] In June 1964 Lubell saw "racial conflict" as "perhaps the main issue of party realignment . . . likely to settle whether the Democrats" could retain their strength. Racial division threatened to divert portions of the northern Democratic white urban vote, and unless this threat was effectively met, the Roosevelt coalition would be "torn apart."[14] In August, Lubell saw major Goldwater inroads in the South, but in the North, he believed, Republican defectors aghast at the Goldwater seizure of their party far outweighed whites drawn to the Republican candidate on the racial issue.[15]

In 1965, in the wake of the huge Democratic electoral landslide of the previous November, Lubell issued a third edition of *The Future of American Politics*. The text remained untouched, but Lubell added a preface, an introduction dealing with the 1964 election, and occasional new footnotes to the text reflective of 1964. The additions were remarkable. *The Future of American Politics*, Lubell wrote, appeared to have gained "a new timeliness" in the light of the 1964 election, "providing a fuller and deeper explanation of the Goldwater debacle than" any reporting he had done over the course of the campaign. For the Roosevelt coalition, after years of deadlock, had now "reestablished" its majority, "releasing a new push of revolutionizing political change." A "new political epoch" had been ushered in. Lyndon Johnson's Great Society legislation was energized by essentially the same coalition that had elected and reelected Roosevelt; the Roosevelt-to-Johnson coalition was akin to a "young man grown to middle-age." Further, the 1964 victory "did more than restore the Roosevelt majority; it also enlarged the makeup of that coalition for the first time since 1936." Many areas of the country that had resisted the Democratic sweeps of the 1930s succumbed to the party in 1964. The taking of "so many hitherto Republican" outposts meant that future elections would be fought "on new battlefields, much deeper into once Republican territory than ever before." Only in the Deep South did the Roosevelt coalition lose ground; elsewhere among Roosevelt coalition groups economic appeals trumped racism. Lubell did add a caveat far more prescient than all his excitement. The persistence of "deep racial divisions," he cautioned, would push for a political outlet, especially "if in the years ahead Democratic loyalties are weakened by setbacks in economic and foreign policy."[16] The Democratic economic setback was over a decade away, but the foreign policy imbroglio was underway even as Lubell wrote.

The apparently reinforced Democratic majority of 1964, of course, quickly unraveled. From later perspectives the events of 1964 took on a drastically different appearance than that described by Lubell and others in the immediate aftermath. Already by 1966 careful analysts were noting the pickup in strength of the GOP and the fading of the Democrats' 1964 triumph. Democratic gains among northern Republicans now increasingly appeared fleeting, while Republican inroads in the South seemed more promising. Further, the conservative takeover of the GOP in 1964 was never wholly undone. Richard Nixon as the party's presidential nominee in 1968 was more nearly in the Goldwater mold than he had been as the party's choice in 1960. In that sense, 1964 constituted an intraparty realignment, that is, a shift in internal party power from a base among moderate Republicans of the Thomas Dewey type to the more conservative Republicans who had supported Goldwater's nomination in 1964. Lastly, from the perspective certainly of the 1980s, Paul David in 1963 seemed to have it right. Goldwater in defeat played a historical role comparable to that of Al Smith thirty-six years earlier: His electoral pattern foreshadowed later GOP triumphs. In that sense the contest of 1964 was hardly a realigning election altering and strengthening the Democratic majority. Rather, it could now be seen as a deviating election, a brief Democratic upsurge before the deluge, and one that created new southern opportunities for long-term Republican growth.[17]

The 1968 election, marked by Richard Nixon's narrow victory and also by George Wallace's anti–civil rights third-party showing, inaugurated several years of feverish speculation about the possibility of a pro-Republican realignment based on the ferment of the late 1960s and early 1970s. The concept of critical elections and realignment had by this time been thoroughly popularized and was now increasingly discussed not only among political scientists and analysts, but also among journalists and commentators generally. It had also reached political strategists and candidates and helped shape Richard Nixon's efforts to make the GOP the new majority party.[18] The 1968 election itself, the shrinkage in the Democratic vote between 1964 and 1968, and the rifts within the Democratic party over the Vietnam War and issues of race and civil rights all contributed to an upsurge in discussion of and a flurry of books and articles about the possibility, the coming, or even the arrival of a pro-Republican realignment.[19] To many observers the signs of impending realignment seemed everywhere: political turmoil, issues cutting across the economic divisions proceeding out of the 1930s, a strong third-party effort, and for those of a cyclical bent, the fact that thirty-six years had elapsed since 1932, the purported approximate timing of realignments traced back to the early nineteenth century. The huge landslide reelection of Nixon in 1972 appeared to bring the point home.[20] As David R. Segal put it even before the 1968 election, the "passionate" politics of the time seemed to approximate "the conditions suggested by V. O. Key in his discussion of critical elections."[21]

Much of the attention was focused on the white South via the Republican Party's "southern strategy." Originating in the Goldwater campaign, the southern strategy was adapted by Nixon to the conditions of the late 1960s and early 1970s. Overt opposition to civil rights was avoided, but efforts were made to show Republican empathy with the concerns of southern whites so as to encourage disaffection with the Democrats and movement toward the GOP.[22] The hope to turn southern white supporters of George Wallace in 1968 to Nixon appeared to pay off handsomely with the latter's sweep of the South in his 1972 reelection. Overwhelmingly, Wallace voters in the South in 1968 became Nixon voters four years later.[23] The Goldwater-to-Wallace-to-Nixon movement seemed to have realigned the South in presidential politics. The rub was the lack of follow-through as of the early 1970s at the congressional and other levels. Strong Democratic showings in the South in the 1970 election appeared to many analysts to belie the notion of a pervasive regional realignment, evidencing instead the party's persistence and durability amidst all the turmoil. And rather than a pro-Republican realignment, as such observers saw it, diehard segregationists were simply opportunistically supporting whatever candidate appeared to serve them best at each election, irrespective of party label: Goldwater in 1964, Wallace in 1968, Nixon in 1972. This was evidence not of Republican growth, but rather of ideological consistency paired with partisan instability.[24] Contrary analysts held, however, that whatever the limits to Republican growth, a regional realignment either had occurred or was occurring. To some degree the shift was seen as Democratic-to-Independent-to-Republican, marking a gradual, rather than an abrupt, partisan realignment. In any event, the movement toward the Republicans was here deemed too strong to be de-emphasized or explained away, although acknowledgments were made of the distinction to be made and potential tensions between the economic appeals to middle-class and business-minded whites set forth successfully as far back as 1952 and the appeal to whites on the racial grounds associated with the southern strategy.[25]

The South received much attention, but the ferment and the expectations of possible realignment proceeded nationally as well. The challenge to Democratic hegemony by what became known as the "social issue"—public reaction to war protesters, cultural upheaval, riots, and crime—brought forth party efforts to neutralize the negative impact on the Democrats and to stress instead the Democrats' traditional strength dating back to the 1930s on economic issues. Hence, Democrats were urged to adopt postures that would offset Republican onslaughts on the cluster of concerns dubbed the social issue and to stress the party's economic stands. On the issue of civil rights, which in some definitions overlapped or was included as part of the social issue, Democrats were urged to support efforts to improve the lot of African Americans within the context of efforts to better the lives of Americans as a whole. The 1968 Democratic nominee for president, Hubert Humphrey, lost to Nixon. But, he came close under extremely adverse conditions; he narrowed the gap from the huge margin that had existed after the summer party conventions; and he had considerable success in bringing white northerners attracted to George Wallace's candidacy on the social issue back to the Democrats on economic issues. Indeed, some initial analyses of the election in northern areas held that despite Humphrey's loss, the traditional appeal of the Democrats on economic issues essentially trumped the effort to use the social issue to offset and undermine that appeal.[26]

The goal of Nixon Republicans was of course exactly the opposite: to use the social issue as a device to cut across the decades-long Democratic economic advantage and to promote realignment along GOP lines. In the view of James Sundquist, one of the most authoritative analysts of the concept, realignments did "not automatically occur. A new issue, or set of issues, powerful enough to cause realignment" would have to arise.[27] Many Republicans believed that the social issue provided just that set of concerns. By exploiting white northern apprehensions, especially ethnic and working-class anxieties, about "permissiveness," the erosion of "traditional values," the perceived threat to homogeneous neighborhoods, riots, and crime, the GOP goal was to offset the traditional Democratic economic advantage by stressing perceived cultural threats. Where "liberalism" once suggested the minimum wage and social security, it would now be portrayed as soft on crime and a threat to revered traditions. Where the Democrats were traditionally seen as the party of the average person, they would now be portrayed as elitist snobs content to let northern white workers bear the brunt of racial adjustment. Overcoming the economic issue patterns so favorable to the Democrats, the GOP goal was to duplicate the perceived triumphs of the 1860s and 1930s: to create a new dominant set of issues and a newly dominant majority party via a critical election or series of critical elections. The years 1968 and 1972 would be the Republican 1932 and 1936; reaction to cultural upheaval—the social issue—would replace the issues of Great Depression– and New Deal–based economics; Nixon would be to FDR what Goldwater was to Al Smith.[28]

For all the talk of the social issue, the most salient aspect of it—although some considered it a separate matter—was race. Nixon avoided overt racism, but undertook to meld concerns over race into the social issue. And the Democratic Party was increasingly vulnerable as the issue of civil rights moved center stage. It had, after all, historically been the party of southern whites and northerners not noted for sympathy toward African-American aspirations. The 1930s created the anomaly of a Democratic Party with a southern white base founded essentially on tradition and a more decisively important northern base—including most African Americans—united fundamentally by economic concerns arising out of the Great Depression and New Deal. Race gave the opposition an issue that could go to the very heart of Democratic dominance. Not only did it have the obvious potential to peel away southern whites, but in the upheaval of the 1960s, it also had the really decisive potential to disunite the North—to draw away northern whites upset over what they viewed as black militancy, or aggressiveness. A central black/white cleavage in American politics could thus come only at the Democrats' expense.[29] The highly respected political journalist David Broder in 1972 saw in the "racial question" the one issue that seemed "to pack the emotional punch necessary for a party realignment." It had not come yet, he believed, but as long as the racial issue festered, there remained the possibility of a realignment "of a very ugly kind."[30] James Sundquist in 1973 separated the social issue from that of race; the importance of the former had lessened, he contended, while the latter continued to hold "explosive" realignment potential.[31]

The book that became the centerpiece of discussion of the social issue— indeed the book that brought the term to the fore—was *The Real Majority* by Richard Scammon and Ben Wattenberg. Scammon was a veteran electoral analyst; Wattenberg had worked in Lyndon Johnson's White House and saw in Washington Senator Henry (Scoop) Jackson a potential Democratic presidential nominee who could resolve the party's difficulties by emphasizing traditional economic issues, while neutralizing the explosive threat of the social issue. Interestingly, the authors were Democrats, concerned with advancing political analysis, but also anxious to help the party cope with the upheaval and perils of the time. Their basic advice to Democrats was to keep the GOP from seizing the social issue. Democrats could neutralize it by attacking crime and disorder and excess themselves and by stressing the continuing importance of traditionally advantageous economic issues. Democrats, taking the advice in 1970, it was subsequently argued, parried the Republican thrusts, whereas presidential nominee George McGovern in 1972, ignoring that advice, led the Democrats to unmitigated disaster.[32] While a book for Democrats, it was also regarded as a model by some Republicans, including President Nixon. If the book told Democrats what to counter, it told Republicans what to hurl at the partisan foe.[33] A quarter-century later, Wattenberg boasted that he had since been told by politicians of both parties that they had regarded the tome as a political "bible."[34]

Scammon and Wattenberg did not believe that the coming political era would necessarily feature a Republican realignment. Evidence that realignments appeared to occur every thirty-six years or so they regarded not as proof of a cyclical pattern, but rather as a "quaint historical fact." They did, however, believe that something fundamental was happening. Economic issues had been the Democrats' strength since the 1930s. Now the Democrats faced the "Social Issue." If Republicans could seize on the social issue to the Democrats' disadvantage, they warned, the nation could "well see Republican Presidents . . . for a generation." In times of great change and upheaval, "one big issue" impacted on the electorate, lasting even for decades, as in the 1890s and 1930s. Now the "Social Issue" threatened to "rupture" the Democrats' connection to average voters based on economic concerns. But the Democrats, the authors stressed, were not inevitably on the downswing. The 1968 labor vote for Humphrey "showed that the . . . Economic Issue, . . . effectively voiced, could blunt much of the appeal of the Social Issue." Except for the white South, "the voting results of 1968 were not terribly different from the voting results of 1944." The loss of the South was no minor matter, they acknowledged. Further, there was "an erosion outside the South even though the patterns outside the South held fast." In aquatic terms, the movement in the South—largely based on race—was of "tidal" proportions, whereas the social issue's impact on the North in 1968 remained a "ripple." It was up to the Democrats to keep the ripple from becoming a tide.[35]

Both at the time and since, evaluations varied as to the lasting impact of the social issue; the matter, however, depended at least in part on whether race was separated from or integrated with the social issue in terms of the analysis. The racial component gave the social issue much of its weight. Democrats could successfully place themselves on the popular side of the social issue in terms of such matters as crime and disorder. And they could, as had been the case for decades, stress economics. As of the early 1970s, despite the Mc-

Govern candidacy of 1972, Democratic strength often seemed to analysts to be holding up.[36] David Broder, who as a young man studied political science at the University of Chicago with Charles Merriam serving as "mentor" and V. O. Key providing the "text," was impressed by how firmly the economic issue held for the Democrats in the North in 1968 in the face of the social issue onslaught.[37] James Reichley, himself a progressive Republican, held in 1971 that the social issue had not in fact been very rewarding electorally for the GOP. The party's effort to forge realignment based on the social issue had left it "a long way from the broad national majority needed to begin a new political era."[38] James Sundquist, Brookings Institution scholar and author of a major 1973 study of realignment, was perhaps the most forceful and systematic skeptic of the social issue's lasting electoral import. The Democrats, he believed, had largely neutralized the issue, and therefore, it could not become "the basis for a major realignment of the party system." Indeed, he found "no persuasive evidence that the major crosscutting issues . . . of the last half of the 1960s had much effect on basic party strength." The upshot was an increase in various kinds of independent voting, rather than significant Republican conversion. Sundquist, as noted, however, separated race from the social issue as such, a major caveat.[39] From a later perspective, to be sure, the politics of the time seemed rather different, especially with race factored in. The elections of 1964 and 1968, two 1995 analysts argued, brought an end to the politics of "the late New Deal era," dependent as it was on economic issues. The election of 1968 inaugurated a "new issue context" and marked "the beginning of a new political era." Cultural issues trumped economic ones, for 1968 was a year for cultural issues "if ever there was one."[40]

Samuel Lubell remained in the thick of political analysis in the late 1960s and early 1970s and indeed had anticipated many of the newer trends. Sometimes, in rather ironic ways, the newer trends irked him, even when he had foretold them. As early as 1965, for example, Lubell, the pioneer student of ethnicity in politics, expressed chagrin over the current emphasis on ethnicity in political analysis. In a letter to historian Arthur Mann, commending Mann for his book on the 1933 election, which brought Fiorello La Guardia to the New York City mayoralty, Lubell declared that the stress on "ethnic politics" had become a matter of "public nose-holding." The use of computer analysis, he contended, played into this; since ethnicity was "so readily identifiable a characteristic," it got "put into the IBM machine, while other more important influences" were "lost sight of." The stress on ethnic politics, Lubell further opined, only encouraged "political Machiavellians . . . to think it . . . smart politics to treat the electorate as ethnic bundles."[41] Lubell's major contribution during this period was 1970's *The Hidden Crisis in American Politics*. With a title very similar to one discarded earlier for *The Future of American*

Politics, the new volume, as David Broder put it, served to bring Lubell's "theories up to date."[42] The new book was widely compared with Scammon and Wattenberg's *The Real Majority*—and with the work of the young Kevin Phillips, who some might have styled a "political Machiavellian" par excellence.[43] Lubell undertook to promote his latest effort in characteristically enthusiastic terms. To erstwhile employer and benefactor, Governor Nelson Rockefeller of New York, leader of moderate Republicans and a failed GOP presidential contender, he declared that *The Hidden Crisis in American Politics* undertook to do for "the political conflicts of this generation" what "*The Future of American Politics* did for the generation before."[44] To his friend Arthur Schlesinger, Jr., who had earlier publicly declared there to be "no more astute observer of political tendencies than Samuel Lubell," he expressed the hope that the new book would "do for the immediate years ahead what *The Future of American Politics* did eighteen years ago." And he requested of Schlesinger "a full-length review."[45] The forthcoming review, not too surprisingly, found Lubell "much more penetrating" than the currently "fashionable soothsayers" Scammon and Wattenberg.[46] Lubell's last book, harking back by way of title to his greatest triumph, was *The Future While It Happened*, published in 1973.

Lubell believed that the tensions that climaxed in the late 1960s had torn the Democratic Party apart, irrevocably unraveling the Roosevelt coalition.[47] This was most clearly evident in the white South. But it was apparent to a lesser degree in the North as well. The making of the Democratic majority in the 1930s had involved the suppression of cultural, ethnic, and racial conflicts in favor of a common sense of economic purpose among otherwise disparate groups. The rise of cultural conflict, the "social issue," and race above all, had undermined that decades-old economic-based coalition. At the national level, with George Wallace's inroads among northern ethnic workers, and at the municipal level, with the rise to prominence of mayoral candidates playing on the social issue, the politics of common economic purpose was increasingly giving way to the politics of visceral cultural and racial feelings.[48] In the urban North, Lubell contended, "racial conflict" was a "key force shaping the new Nixon coalition replacing the old Roosevelt coalition."[49] Nationally, it shifted more voters to Nixon in the 1972 election "than any other single issue."[50] It was "deliberately" used by Nixon to divide the country in order to build a new Republican majority.[51] In the white South, economic policies and beliefs were at issue as well in the shift toward the GOP, but to Lubell race was decisive. And as the South became increasingly important in the GOP, the role of moderate northeastern Republicanism declined.[52] "The President's southern strategy," Lubell reported to Rockefeller in 1970, was "working" via a coalition with "a narrow and excluding base."[53] Ironically, Lubell was so well equipped to understand the reactions of urban ethnic northerners that at least one reviewer of *The Hidden Crisis in American Politics* intimated that the author's "empathy for poor and middle-class whites" was not evident vis-à-vis African Americans, an intimation that Lubell indignantly denied.[54]

Lubell's essential conclusion about the politics of the late 1960s and the early 1970s was that neither party had an assured majority. The Democrats' Roosevelt coalition had cracked, but a solid new Republican majority had not coalesced. The most striking thing about recent elections—and here Lubell ventured back as far as the 1950s—was the tendency of the electorate to veer back and forth between parties, with landslides alternating with cliffhangers. Wild swings in good measure had replaced strong party loyalty among many voters. "Free-floating" voters had become more important as staunch partisans declined, making it harder to form lasting party alignments or to sustain a long-term majority party.[55] Given the "unstable and erratic" gyrations, he held, no recent election had "reflected a true balance of party strength."[56] Voting historically had been "very sluggish" and "slow moving"; as with religious affiliation, citizens did not easily "change their voting" patterns; voting flowed in the streams of tradition outlined in *The Future of American Politics*. Already in *The Revolt of the Moderates*, however, Lubell pointed to a loosening of party loyalties in the 1950s; now he believed it had all come to a head. There had been a "quickening" of voter movements; with the decline of "party tradition," voters were now "using both parties"; the country, he concluded in 1970, had "not had a normal party vote" in decades.[57] Thus, the creator of the concept of a normal majority party departed from the field with a view of American politics in a state of uncertainty and flux. Lubell had hoped to bring the lessons of all his decades of analysis together in a final book. "This corpus Lubell," he believed, "could prove of considerable value in these critical times."[58] But a severe stroke forced him into retirement for the remaining years of his life.

The upheaval of the late 1960s in retrospect inaugurated an era of American politics in which the names writ large were those of Richard Nixon and Ronald Reagan. However, this seemed far from preordained at the time. Indeed some analysts—and political strategists—projected a very different future from that proposed by those focused on the social issue and the impact of race. With roots in the 1950s, a much discussed scenario of the late 1960s and early 1970s stressed the critical forthcoming role of well-educated middle-class citizens generally and of the new generation of baby-boom voters in particular. The belief here was that young professionals were more inclined toward the Democratic Party and liberal politics than the old small-business-oriented middle class of times past. This group, it was held, would create a new dominant Democratic Party, replacing the more working-class-oriented Roosevelt coalition emanating from the 1930s. Further, in this analysis, such voters would over time prove more potent an electoral factor than those attracted to the GOP by the social issue and race.[59] Louis Harris in 1973, for example, held that those motivated by the social issue constituted a fading "vote of the past," while "the educated, affluent vote" heralded the future.[60] Gerald Pomper in 1975 saw in the "young generation . . . the quantitative possibility of another epochal change" in American politics. If there was "to be a new politics," he speculated, the "new voters" of 1972 would lead the way as "Democrats and liberals in the future."[61] Nor was this vision of a new politics based on education wholly limited to those oriented toward the Democratic Party. Within the GOP, the moderate Ripon Society and others urged fellow Republicans to forsake the southern strategy and the social issue in favor of an appeal to well-educated suburban professionals, warning that stressing the former risked alienating the latter.[62]

Numerous analysts set forth versions of a new politics amidst the tumult of the late 1960s and early 1970s, among them Arthur Schlesinger, Jr. Son of the distinguished historian and cyclical theorist of the same name, the younger Schlesinger, a writer of epochal works of history, had served in John F. Kennedy's White House. He actively supported Robert F. Kennedy's bid for the 1968 Democratic presidential nomination and aided George McGovern in the 1972 campaign. A student of the Roosevelt era, and hence also a chronicler of the origins of the Roosevelt coalition, Schlesinger foresaw a new era replacing that created in the 1930s, but a new era quite different from that which Richard Nixon was trying to shape. Writing in 1967, Schlesinger set forth the possibility of a "new liberal coalition." The New Deal coalition based on the economic issues and divisions of the 1930s, he held, had "fallen apart." New cultural issues were replacing the old economic ones. The GOP could prove the beneficiary, but so could the Democrats if they seized the chance.[63] Shortly after the 1968 election, Schlesinger speculated that the contest might "well go down as the last hurrah of the Old Politics of this period— as . . . the 1928 election . . . was the last hurrah of the Old Politics of the twenties."[64] In the midst of the 1972 campaign—not the best context for dispassionate analysis—the historian cum political activist saw American voters in a state of flux, with "women, the young, the suburbanites . . . on the move as forces in their own right." For those seeking analogies for the McGovern candidacy, he held, "the appropriate analogy would be not Goldwater in 1964 but Roosevelt in 1932." FDR "represented . . . the New Politics of 1932."[65] No one should be held intellectually to account for utterances made as a campaign partisan; nonetheless, Schlesinger did capture some of the sense of possibility of those seeking alternatives to Nixonian scenarios of the future of American politics.

Another such figure was Lanny Davis. An activist in Democratic politics at the time, Davis became well known in the 1990s as point man for Bill Clinton in the Whitewater controversy.[66] Writing shortly after the McGovern debacle, Davis produced *The Emerging Democratic Majority*—a title obviously playing upon Kevin Phillips's highly influential *The Emerging Republican Majority* of 1969. The 1972 presidential returns to the contrary notwithstanding, Davis, based on analysis of congressional and gubernatorial contests, foresaw "the emergence of a new Democratic majority coalition, combining the New Politics constituency" of well-educated suburbanites, some of them former Republicans, with traditional Roosevelt coalition minorities and workers. The "growth areas" of the electorate were not those attracted by the social issue, but rather college-educated professionals, and here Davis believed that the Democrats were poised to make major gains at the GOP's expense.[67] John G. Stewart, in *One Last Chance: The Democratic Party, 1974–76*, provided a similar analysis. Noting that the old Roosevelt coalition had been based on economic interests, Stewart held that "noneconomic issues" had now opened up "the potential today for Democrats to reach beyond the New Deal alignment to a broader constituency" cutting "across traditional economic lines."[68] Analysts like Schlesinger, Davis, and Stewart in a sense harkened back to the appeal of Adlai Stevenson to many young professionals of the 1950s and looked forward to the talk of "yuppies" in the 1980s and "soccer moms" in the 1990s. Perhaps the most fully developed analysis along these lines came in 1971 with Frederick Dutton's *Changing Sources of Power*.

Dutton was active in California politics in the 1950s, served in the Kennedy administration, and was on both Robert Kennedy's staff in the 1968 campaign and George McGovern's in 1972. Dutton's analysis was based on the assumption that the era of the Roosevelt coalition was over, that politics was now in a state of flux characterized by a growth of independent voters, and that the future was open to varied possibilities. The key to the Democrats' future, Dutton believed, lay above all in gaining support from the new and large emerging generation of better-educated voters. Blue-collar workers were in relative decline electorally, while well-educated white-collar workers were rising dramatically. Traditional economic issues were becoming less important; "psychological" ones—a search for well-being in more than material ways—were becoming more so. In the vanguard of this change were college-educated voters, with less-well-educated voters impacted by the social issue and race providing the main opposition. In Dutton's view the former tendency was more likely to grow and prevail over time, providing an opportunity for the Democrats to seize while the GOP was preoccupied with shorter-run gains emanating out of the upheaval of the 1960s. The GOP had certainly made advances in both the South and North at the Democrats' expense due to that upheaval,

Dutton acknowledged, but simultaneously Republican support was "eroding among those educational and economic groups which . . . historically provided its staunchest support." That support was weakening even as those groups were rapidly expanding. The Democrats, meanwhile, while losing votes among white southerners and blue-collar workers, were poised to score lasting gains from "the new generation and its growing upper-middle-class allies." Historically, Dutton concluded, demographic trends had shaped electoral patterns; "every major realignment in . . . political history" had featured "the coming of a large new group into the electorate."[69]

Among political scientists, no one stressed such themes more than Everett Carll Ladd. Ladd was as convinced as anyone that the nation "was passing through an extraordinary transition period in its electoral history," with "the old electoral order . . . turned on its ear." But while he was well aware of Republican stratagems involving the social issue and race, he did not believe they had the staying power of the forces enhancing the Democratic Party's hegemony. Indeed, he deemed it "hard to find evidence of a general realignment likely to culminate in Republican ascendancy." The Democrats, on the other hand, he was convinced, had rather successfully converted themselves from the party of workers coming out of the 1930s to a party with a real appeal to the well-educated, professional, middle-class voters who constituted the defining electoral element of the present era. The Democrats had remained the majority party in good part because they were no longer defined by the Roosevelt coalition; they were now effectively competing with the GOP for the professional middle class. Ladd anticipated "a continuation of Democratic ascendancy" given the party's new source of strength; it would likely remain the majority party, but with a coalition differing from that of the Democratic Party as shaped in the era of Roosevelt.[70] Andrew Greeley sharply dissented from analyses like Ladd's. Writing in 1974, he held that middle-class professionals had by and large remained strongly Republican. He noted that in 1972 "some very sophisticated political scientists of my acquaintance argued . . . that while McGovern was going to lose the election, he would play the role for the Democratic candidate in 1976 that Alfred Smith played for Franklin Roosevelt." The priest-scholar-novelist pointedly added that he had "not heard that argument recently."[71]

Angus Campbell critically scrutinized the notion that young voters would constitute the decisive force for the future of American politics, noting that every age group had wide variations within it, making the development of a "homogeneous" approach unlikely. "Economic, social, and geographical . . . heterogeneity," he contended, would undermine efforts toward a generationally based politics. He found "no instance in modern history in which a major political movement" had emerged out of "a particular age group."[72]

Michigan School analysts were among those most skeptical generally of the notion that the late 1960s and early 1970s had brought or would bring sharp and enduring change, although the flow of events was by no means without an impact upon them. Campbell himself did speculate in June 1964 that Barry Goldwater's nomination coupled with the explosive issue of civil rights might cause a major reshuffling of voters between the parties.[73] But the GOP's southern strategy, he admonished in March 1968, looking back on the Goldwater debacle of 1964, had made gains in the Deep South at the expense of losing almost the entire northern African-American vote; hence, gearing national strategy to the South was "very misguided" and likely to involve "fatal side effects."[74] Looking back on the 1972 election, Campbell held that the contest was one in which party loyalty was in a measure set aside in favor of candidate evaluation. Further, the traditional Democratic coalition, he believed, had become "seriously unhinged." The white South was in revolt at the presidential level and traditional northern elements of the coalition were at least somewhat disaffected. Conceivably, no future Democratic presidential nominee could put the coalition back together again.[75]

Philip E. Converse and Warren E. Miller, two of the authors of *The American Voter*, writing with others, critically analyzed the 1968 election the following year. The electoral change since 1964, they acknowledged, had been massive, yet party identifications had remained largely unchanged. Hence, they attributed the admittedly "remarkable changes in voting at the presidential level" to short-term forces.[76] Writing in 1972, Converse found "signs" that a realignment might be "imminent." He noted that "critical realignment" appeared to follow a roughly cyclical pattern in the past and he found it "extremely plausible to imagine that the loosening of partisanship in the current period" was a prelude to realignment now.[77] In 1975 Converse agreed that "many of the elements familiar from past realignments" were upon the scene; yet, he saw no decisive evidence that a realignment was in fact underway. The upheaval of recent times, he speculated, might fade without creating a partisan realignment in its wake.[78] The following year he attributed the decline in party identification to the "immediate events" of the time.[79] Warren E. Miller, writing with Arthur H. Miller in 1975, agreed that the 1968 and 1972 elections had features suggestive of a massive partisan realignment, including declining party loyalty and crosscutting issues. Yet he saw no decisive evidence that a realignment had actually occurred, except in the white South.[80] Writing in 1976, with Teresa E. Levitin, Miller held that the contest of 1968 was akin to that of 1956. The 1972 election, he contended, did not pivot on any fundamental factors conducive to realignment.[81] As late as 1996, Miller, in his coauthored *The New American Voter*, found it "remarkable that the Democratic party did not suffer more . . . in 1968 and 1972, but there was in fact little subsequent evidence of realignment outside the South." Hence, the Nixon era joined that of Eisenhower as a lost opportunity for the GOP.[82]

Analysis in general of the degree to which realignment had or had not proceeded clearly ebbed and flowed with the election returns. The failure of the Republicans to make inroads in the 1970 congressional elections, for example, resulted in proclamations that a GOP realignment was not underway.[83] Indeed, the burden of opinion throughout the first half of the 1970s was that no realignment had occurred or was clearly in evidence. Even in the wake of Nixon's landslide reelection victory of 1972, this judgment largely stood. After all, Republicans continued to fail to make significant gains below the presidential level. Congress remained strongly Democratic. Hence, it was easy to describe the 1972 election, like that of 1968—and indeed like those of 1952 and 1956—as deviating and due to special, short-term factors.[84] Even those impressed by the degree of change were more inclined to emphasize Democratic weaknesses than Republican strengths and to note the growth of independent voters—"dealignment," as it became known.[85] James Sundquist summed up this case. Powerful crosscutting issues had emerged out of the 1960s, he acknowledged, and those issues and the events related to them had eroded support for both parties. But, at most, as of the early 1970s the country was in a "prerealignment" stage. Millions of voters had been shaken loose from the parties; more and more voters had proclaimed themselves independent; but no significant national shift in partisan strength had occurred.[86]

From a historical perspective, scholars were more inclined to see the late 1960s and early 1970s in terms of decisive change, whether expressed in classic realignment terminology or not.[87] But the remainder of the 1970s only reinforced the belief that no realignment had occurred or was in the offing.[88] Indeed, the disastrous impact of the Watergate scandal on the Republicans, growing economic problems under the GOP watch, the big Democratic gains in the Congressional elections of 1974, topped off by Jimmy Carter's presidential victory and near sweep of the electoral vote of the southern states in 1976 all conspired to make talk of a GOP realignment appear downright foolish. As one scholar put it, "since Carter's victory the period 1964–72 has looked more like a deviating interlude than a realigning era." The power of crosscutting forces had evidently "been exaggerated . . . as . . . more cautious observers, notably Converse and Sundquist, had always suspected."[89] Insofar as significant change had occurred, it was widely held that change consisted of dealignment, rather than realignment. The old Roosevelt coalition indeed had frayed; there was a growth of independence among voters; politics continued in a state of flux. Many concluded that dealignment rendered future realignment improbable and that elections and voting would be less subject to party loyalty and more attuned to short-term forces, instability, and volatility.[90]

The state of the economy played a major role in mid-1970s analyses. The operative assumption of the discussion of potential realignment coming out of the 1960s was that the social issue, race, cultural cleavages—noneconomic concerns—might override the traditional Democratic advantage regarding the economy. Economic issues had been deemed the Democrats' strength since the 1930s. If the economy could remain the focus, or again become the focus, the general belief was that this would be to the Democrats' advantage and to the disadvantage of the GOP. The growth of inflation and the impact of a major recession under Republican presidents were credited in some good measure for Democratic gains in 1974 and for the Democratic retaking of the White House in 1976. It now appeared that the cultural tumult of the 1960s on which Republicans played had faded, that the issues of that time were now "passing," and that the Democrats were resurgent on the basis of their traditional economic appeal.[91] This easy assumption of a Democratic benefit from economic difficulty was of course blown asunder in 1980, and, to be sure, mid-1970s commentators saw continuing Democratic difficulties over the impact of race on the party's traditional voter base.[92] But there was considerable commentary that 1974 and 1976 marked a Democratic restoration after what was now seen as the aberration of the late 1960s and early 1970s. Even the South seemed back in play. Republicans appeared to be at their nadir.[93] Gerald Pomper speculated that the 1976 results provided a basis for the reconstitution of a dominant Democratic coalition. The contest of 1976, he suggested, might be a "critical election" marking "the renewed ascendancy of the Democratic party," and "the decline of the Republicans to a permanent minority."[94]

No analyst appeared more willing to consign the Republicans to oblivion during the late 1970s than Everett Carll Ladd. Writing in 1978, he conceded that the Democrats had their problems. Their liberal stances on cultural issues were not attractive to large portions of the electorate, contributing to weakness in presidential elections. Further, he agreed that the GOP had made impressive inroads in the South, adding, however, that the party was now much weaker in the Northeast than in times past. He noted that the Republicans had lost strength in their traditional middle-class base and held that their use of the social issue had not garnered major gains among "lower-middle-class" voters. And he saw only a dismal recent past and present for the GOP. The Republicans had suffered "erosion" in the 1960s and 1970s, had been "trending downward" for a decade and a half, and Watergate and subsequent electoral losses had "vanquished the party's hopes of a few years past." In a series of somewhat hyperbolic historical references, Ladd concluded that present day Republicans were "in a weaker position than any major party . . . since the Civil War," even "weaker . . . than the Democrats . . . around 1900." The Democrats had "become the established governing party to a degree unequaled . . . since the Jeffersonians," while the GOP suffered in the weakest position relative to a party rival "since the death-throes of the Federalists."[95] All this came but two years before Ronald Reagan's 1980 presidential victory and the GOP capture of the Senate. Ladd, like many others of the time, was reacting in part to the projections of the young GOP analyst Kevin P. Phillips, whose 1969 book proclaimed an "emerging republican majority." Phillips, a lawyer turned journalist, was something of a partisan latter-day Samuel Lubell, a very knowledgeable and insightful student from outside the academy. His reputation and influence, and that of his book, reflected the ups and downs of the late 1960s, the 1970s, and beyond.

Chapter Ten

Prophets of Transformation

The two most discussed political analysts of the late 1960s and early 1970s were Kevin P. Phillips and Walter Dean Burnham. Phillips's *The Emerging Republican Majority* of 1969 and Burnham's *Critical Elections and the Mainsprings of American Politics* of 1970 proved to be seminal works. Phillips was not an academic, while Burnham was, but there was considerable similarity between them. Each authored a book with great and lasting impact; each espoused a cyclical theory of realignment; each also pondered whether epochal changes were underway that called into question the continued viability of traditional realignment processes.

Kevin P. Phillips, an "enfant terrible" to at least one contemporary observer, was a product of New York City, born in Gotham in 1940 and raised in the Parkchester section of the Bronx as the son of an official with the New York State Liquor Authority. He was of Irish, English, and Scotch ethnic background, with a Catholic father and a Protestant mother; his own religion, he wryly noted, "was reading the Sunday papers." Growing up in the extraordinary ethnic, religious, and racial potpourri of the Bronx, with its close-knit neighborhoods and cultural traditions, Phillips, not closely identified with any single narrow group, could undertake to observe and study his surroundings as something of an outsider. He started to explore the ethnic dimensions of politics as a young teenager, helped along (like Louis Bean earlier) by the election-data compilations of the *World Almanac*. He attended the academically prestigious Bronx High School of Science and went on to Colgate University as a National Merit Scholar, where he wrote an honors thesis on ethnic- and religious-based voting patterns in the 1928 and 1960 elections. He then proceeded to Harvard Law School and graduated in 1964, viewing that aspect of his career as an entrée into politics. Phillips had served as a campaign volunteer for Bronx Republican Congressman Paul Fino as a teenager, and from 1964 to 1968 served as his administrative assistant. Phillips was credited with shaping Fino, heretofore a moderate Rockefeller Republican, into a politician focused on the social and cultural tensions arising from the upheaval of the time. As James Boyd, writing about Phillips in 1970, put it, the young administrative assistant turned his employer's congressional district, with its large Italian- and Irish-American constituency, "into a laboratory of ethnic politics." The Bronx, however, as Boyd wrote, "could offer only local vindication of a continental thesis." In 1968 Phillips went national as a member of the Nixon team, pausing in the midst of the campaign to marry Martha Eleanor Henderson, who would in time become a prominent Republican congressional staff member, with whom he had twin sons.[1] Phillips brought to national politics a deep knowledge of the demographic bases of electoral behavior, soon to be copiously displayed in his *The Emerging Republican Majority*. While immensely learned on the subject, Phillips, like Samuel Lubell before him, disdained the "neoalgebraic coefficents" of academic political scientists.[2] He also brought to the national scene what Boyd called a "bad-guy image . . . compounded by . . . a kind of grim satisfaction" in his portrayal of the ethnically and racially based "incorrigible meanness of the American voter."[3]

Throughout his career as an analyst, Phillips made much of antielitism in one form or another as a key component of electoral behavior and he was never loath to expound antielitist pronouncements himself, whether geared to ethnic snobbery, class pretension, or bureaucratic arrogance, in his championship of what he deemed hard-pressed and hard-working middle-class citizens.[4] His electoral analysis of the mid- and late 1960s, with roots in his Bronx experience, also built upon the Goldwater strategy of 1964 with its concentration on the South and West.[5] His emphasis on demographic and regional patterns of voting behavior, as conveyed in numerous maps in *The Emerging Republican Majority*, linked him to the Frederick Jackson Turner school of political history and analysis. Phillips also benefited from the work of V. O. Key.[6] But clearly his greatest intellectual debt, as noted at the time, was to Samuel Lubell.[7] Phillips himself referred to Lubell's *The Future of American Politics* as a "masterful analysis," and paid homage to Lubell's concepts and insights.[8] He used "The Future of American Politics" as a chapter title in *The Emerging Republican Majority* and also as the title of a later article.[9] One sly commentator noted, however, that Phillips did "not follow Lubell's practice of interviewing live voters," and indeed found "no evidence" that Phillips had "talked to any voters at all."[10] Lubell and Phillips above all shared a common emphasis on the role of ethnic and racial factors in American politics. Phillips became famous, to some infamous, for his emphasis on the role of group antagonism, even hatred, as a defining element in American politics. Lubell also wrote of "contrasts among different groups" as constituting a "prime tool of voting analysis," and how, "as often as not, Americans vote against rather than for something," illuminating "the underlying tensions and conflicts in our history."[11] Lubell, however, did not share Phillips's accepting attitude toward those tensions and conflicts, nor was he an explicit partisan advocate and activist. Given these differences, as well as their similarities, Phillips could aptly be termed "a right-wing version of Lubell."[12]

Cultural politics, Phillips believed, was increasingly replacing the economically based divisions that had been set in the 1930s.[13] The "secret" to American politics, he famously told Garry Wills, lay in "knowing who hates who."[14] The rise of ethnic consciousness in the late 1960s and 1970s provided grist for Phillips's mill. The notion of assimilation he dismissed as "the melting pot myth." The 1969 New York City mayoral election, with its cleavages "along religious, ethnic and cultural lines," constituted a "clear mockery of the whole assimilationist concept." The upsurge of regionalism and regional resentments provided further evidence of the power of cultural conflict and "political splintering."[15] Above all lay racial tension and conflict. Phillips denied that he was interested in stirring up racial discord for political advantage. He did not contend that it "should happen"; he held, merely, that it did happen: "We have always had these ethnic cleavages."[16] The movement of newly registered southern African-American voters into the Democratic Party, he predicted, would drive southern whites out in droves and into the GOP.[17] Nationally, Republicans would never "get more than 10 to 20 percent" of the African-American vote, and they did not "need any more than that."[18]

The initial draft of *The Emerging Republican Majority* was in place in 1967 and reflected Phillips's sense of political trends, his analysis of demographic shifts, and his acceptance of a cyclical theory of American political history, which suggested that a realignment was now again due.[19] Prior to publication, however, Phillips won a position on the Nixon team, working for campaign manager John Mitchell as an expert on voting patterns.[20] Joe McGinniss, in his satirical take on the Nixon campaign in *The Selling of the President 1968*, portrayed the twenty-seven-year-old Phillips as full of youthful self-confidence. Certain that a Republican majority was emerging, Phillips proclaimed, according to McGinniss, "it is really coming to pass. But no one sees it. No one knows." Sure of his own importance, he allegedly told McGinniss that any memorandum he wrote to headquarters got "to the top of the heap in five minutes." John Wayne, McGinniss quoted Phillips as saying, "might sound bad to people in New York, but he sounds great to the schmucks" the Republicans were trying to appeal to "down there along the Yahoo Belt."[21] Theodore H. White, in *The Making of the President 1968*, quoted Phillips at one point during the campaign, before Hubert Humphrey's surge made the contest a squeaker, suggesting that Nixon's victory could be "bigger than Johnson's . . . in 1964," taking every state in the three-way contest with Humphrey and George Wallace, except Massachusetts, Rhode Island, Alabama, and Mississippi.[22]

With the inauguration of the new administration in 1969, Phillips, trained as a lawyer after all, found himself in the Justice Department as an aide to Attorney General John Mitchell. Given the controversial nature of portions of *The Emerging Republican Majority*, however, his government position became untenable and he resigned in March 1970.[23] The book itself nonetheless gained a reputation as the "bible" of Nixon's strategy to create a lasting Republican majority, even as Nixon and his associates publicly distanced themselves from its perceived message.[24] Nixon declared in September 1969 that he had not read the book and that insofar as Phillips called for a nationally divisive strategy he disagreed.[25] Two months later the Republican National Chairman dismissed Phillips's ideas as the contributions of a "clerk."[26] John Mitchell, when asked about Phillips's notions, replied that he did not "have a practice of subscribing to the theories of my aides. It generally works the other way."[27] Still, some rank-and-file Republicans enthusiastically endorsed Phillips's message and that message also fit President Nixon's own political instincts.[28] *The Emerging Republican Majority*, after all, for all its genuine learning and scholarly apparatus, was also written as a strategy book by a conservative Republican for conservative Republicans. It was in fact enthusiastically read by Nixon during Christmas vacation 1969 and recommended by him to his political aides as a guide to campaign strategy, although one not to be publicly acknowledged.[29]

The Emerging Republican Majority in some degree was to the decade that followed what *The Future of American Politics* was to the 1950s: a book that set the terms of further debate. Just as the latter made Lubell's reputation, the new book made Phillips a national figure before age thirty. Phillips had given serious thought to calling the volume *The Emerging Conservative Majority*, a title that reflected his focus.[30] He dedicated the book "to the emerging Republican majority and its two principal architects: President Richard M. Nixon and Attorney General John N. Mitchell."[31] Phillips proceeded on the basis of a cyclical version of American political history, the idea that partisan realignments had occurred every thirty-two or thirty-six years. In that sense, the pattern of cyclical realignment eras could be traced schematically: 1828 to 1860, 1860 to 1896, 1896 to 1932, and 1932, Phillips believed, to 1968. Hence, the 1968 election was viewed as marking the coming of a new political era—a turning point in the gradual replacement of the New Deal coalition by the emerging Republican majority.[32] From this perspective, the Goldwater campaign of 1964, like that of Al Smith in 1928, heralded the future.[33] Similarly, as in other eras of realignment, a third-party effort, in this case George Wallace's in 1968, could well provide a way station for converters from one major party to the other—now Democrats to Republicans.[34] The central cause of the breakup of the New Deal coalition, Phillips believed, opening up the opportunity for a newly dominant Republicanism, was race. The current manifestation of the issue was replacing partisan patterns dating back to the Civil War era.[35] Ethnic and racial tensions had long been powerful influences on American politics and given this history, it was no surprise that reaction to the civil rights revolution "almost inevitably had to result in political realignment."[36] Phillips utilized changing demographic patterns in relation to secular realignment theory in addition to the concept of a critical election era. In the past, realignment had been based on major demographic change—such as the rise of the immigrant population of the cities in the case of Al Smith and Franklin Roosevelt. Now the Republican Party, as the vehicle of Yankees from the Northeast and from areas Yankees had spread across in earlier times, was ending. The party was now basing itself instead upon disaffected white southerners, the growing regions of the "sunbelt," including the Southwest and the California bonanza, and the lower-middle-class white refugees from the northern cities, often Catholic and ethnic by background. The movement of some old Yankee and Scandinavian Republicans into the Democratic Party amounted to little compared with movement in the other direction, Phillips insisted. Key to it all was the growing role of African Americans in the Democratic Party; as the African-American role grew larger, especially in the South with reenfranchisement added by civil rights legislation, the white exodus from the party would mount.[37]

The Emerging Republican Majority received a great deal of play when it appeared. Not too surprisingly, conservatives were unstinting in their praise. M. Stanton Evans called it "the most important political book" of the time, "a landmark of political analysis."[38] *National Review* contended that Phillips's conclusions were confirmed by the presidential elections of 1968 and 1972.[39] But fusillades were forthcoming from the ranks of critics. Many were taken aback by what they saw as Phillips's amoral, cavalier, and cynical exploitation of race.[40] Additionally, despite Nixon's 1972 landslide, the GOP had not made significant congressional gains; at that level, the elections of 1970 and 1972, even in the South, appeared to many wholly to contradict Phillips's thesis.[41] As one analyst put it, Phillips's arguments might have the "unique distinction of serving to explain a rather short interval in American political history—1968 to 1972."[42] In the fullness of time, however, those on the other side of the political fence joined in viewing *The Emerging Republican Majority* as a prophetic classic. Alan Ehrenhalt, for example, in 1991 called the book "astonishingly accurate in its predictions about presidential politics," whatever its shortcomings about congressional prospects.[43] The liberal Paul Starr in 1997 held that the book remained "the single most brilliant recent work of political forecasting." Much of the analysis still stood "up a quarter of a century later."[44] Another 1997 appraisal summed it up. In *The Emerging Republican Majority*, wrote Peter Brimelow and Ed Rubenstein, "Phillips boldly predicted a generation of Republican victories. . . . He has been triumphantly vindicated."[45]

Phillips himself, however, struggled at the time with the apparent failure of the Republican majority to emerge on schedule in the 1970s. During the 1972 campaign he noted with pride that the Nixon campaign was "basically following the strategy set forth in . . . *The Emerging Republican Majority*."[46] The 1972 presidential election results, he later suggested, "followed region for region, constituency for constituency, the outline presented in *The Emerging Republican Majority*."[47] But the Nixon team failed to consolidate its gains. And for the period in between and afterward, Phillips had little but scorn for his former associates' political strategy. The administration did not follow his strategy in 1970, he held; it opted, instead, for Scammon and Wattenberg's social issue and failed to make Republican gains. Partisan affiliations aside, others might see little difference between what Scammon and Wattenberg, on the one hand, and Kevin Phillips, on the other, considered salient in American politics circa 1970, but Phillips himself chose not to stress the similarities. The appeal of the social issue, he held, with perhaps a little pique, provided "shrill negativism" and "a superficial hodgepodge" and, thus, backfired.[48] Further, Phillips contended, the Republican appeal to average Americans was undercut by the prominence given to such "genteel" figures as George Bush, not to mention the Nixon White House's "admen, managers and . . . technocrats with little feel for the sweep of America."[49] And then came the debacle of Watergate, which in Phillips's view aborted the prospect of a full-scale GOP realignment.[50] The result was a two-tiered political arrangement, a tendency to elect GOP presidents while Democrats continued to control Congress. Ticket splitting and growing voter independence appeared to be eroding traditional longer-term political patterns.[51]

In the last half of the 1970s, acknowledging the impact on his thinking of Walter Dean Burnham, Phillips conceded that dealignment, rather than realignment, had likely become the new reality and that a classic realignment had been rendered improbable by the weakening of the party system.[52] Phillips and Burnham, journalist and academic, seemed over the course of the late 1970s to develop something of a mutual admiration society, citing and praising each other's work in their own. They shared, certainly, a tendency to see epochal goings-on in American politics. Burnham, to be sure, in 1969 saw "no evidence anywhere to support Kevin Phillips's hypothesis regarding an emergent Republican majority."[53] But in 1974 Burnham found in *The Emerging Republican Majority* an "admirable" study of ethnic, cultural, and regional patterns in American politics.[54] And Phillips for his part praised Burnham as "one of the most penetrating . . . political observers" in the nation.[55]

Walter Dean Burnham, born in Columbus, Ohio, in 1930, graduated from Johns Hopkins in 1951 and did his graduate work at Harvard, from which he received his doctorate in 1962. He held several junior academic positions before moving to Washington University in 1966. From 1971 to 1988 he was at the Massachusetts Institute of Technology, and thereafter at the University of Texas.[56] Burnham, most basically, built upon the work of his mentor V. O. Key. He also was impressed by the work of Samuel Lubell, who in 1957 had asked Burnham to serve as one of his assistants, a request Burnham declined because of the press of dissertation work.[57] E. E. Schattschneider, with his interest in amplifying realignment theory, provided a stimulus on which Burnham drew, as did the work of Angus Campbell and his associates. Indeed, Burnham spent a year at the SRC in Ann Arbor. Reaching further back, Burnham expressed his regard for the pioneering work of Harold Gosnell.[58] In 1955 Burnham published a compilation of election statistics, *Presidential Ballots, 1836–1892*, in which he also noted the realigning significance of the election of 1896.[59] In the early 1960s he set forth the notion that the understanding of American politics required the melding of a quantitatively and historically based behavioral approach with an appreciation of elements of American history that could not be reduced to quantitative status. Survey research, he added, often left out "the evolution . . . of voting behavior over time."[60] Following publication of *Critical Elections and the Mainsprings of American Politics* in 1970, Burnham quickly became recognized as the leading authority on the subject.[61] In effect, he became a second V. O. Key, or, as one writer put it, "the second founder of realignment theory."[62] Key himself, ever cautious and understated, did not quite foresee this second coming. Burnham, wrote Key in a 1959 letter, was certainly "more than a fact collector," as his analytical commentaries in *Presidential Ballots* demonstrated. However, on the basis of that book, Key doubted that Burnham "would rank in the top 5 or 6 per cent" of emerging scholars; instead he would be found "in the cluster of quite able men just under that category."[63]

Burnham, as a matter of intellectual temperament, characteristically was on the lookout for upheaval, rather than incremental change, in the unfolding of American politics, an inclination and focus he shared with Kevin Phillips. The "earthquake," as two scholars put it, was the "physical analogy" most "central" to Burnham's work on realignment.[64] This affinity for what some saw as the apocalyptic led to charges that Burnham's theses possessed "a grandeur that neither his data nor his precision of language" could support.[65] Burnham was himself aware of, and at times indeed stressed, the divide between scholars geared to upheaval and those more attuned to continuity. Drawing upon students of history, geology, and biology, Burnham clearly saw himself in the camp of those stressing seminal and explosive change.[66] This matter of intellectual temperament or style played into controversies in which

Burnham was a major actor, as in that over interpretations of *The American Voter* as the political tumult of the late 1960s and early 1970s impacted upon scholarly analysis. To charges by coauthor Philip Converse that Burnham had caricatured *The American Voter*, attributing to the book positions that the authors had not actually taken, Burnham responded that what counted was not only what the book actually said, but also what readers of the book over time believed it said. Thus, in assessing the book's impact, it was appropriate, Burnham held, to deal with the set of ideas triggered by *The American Voter*, as well as with the more precise ideas enunciated in the book itself. Burnham countered Converse's argument that scholarship advanced through the cumulative development of knowledge and understanding, with each new work building upon its predecessors, with the notion that scholarship advanced through a dialectical process, with each new work countering the arguments of predecessors, ending with a higher level of understanding reached through intellectual confrontation and combat.[67]

As a student of history as well as of politics, Burnham was quite aware of the salience of sectional, ethnic, and class cleavages in the history of American political configurations.[68] He also believed there was a central periodicity in American political history, which he fashioned into an essential element of his theory of realignment. Realignment, Burnham held, was not fortuitous, not a matter of chance occurrences. There was a cyclical pattern, a "uniform periodicity," a rhythm to the realignment process. To be sure, realignments were not cyclical in terms of an absolutely precise number of years between them; still, Burnham insisted, pointing to history in the form of the elections of 1800, 1828, 1860, 1896, and 1932, realignments occurred roughly every generation, every thirty-odd years. To be sure, again, they historically required an event or crisis of a detonating caliber; thus, the "precise timing" could not be foretold; still, such crisis eras also tended to be forthcoming roughly on schedule. Thus, Burnham fashioned a cyclical theory of realignment, developed most fully and systematically in *Critical Elections and the Mainsprings of American Politics*, published in the midst of immense speculation as to the prospects of imminent realignment.[69] Building upon the work of Schattschneider and Key, Burnham emphasized that realignment involved not just changes in voting patterns, but also in issues and public policy; indeed, in his view a vital characteristic of realignment lay in the emergence of new issues and public policies powerful enough to reconfigure institutions and to shape a historical era.[70] Most importantly, and arguably Burnham's most distinctively original contribution to realignment theory, he added an underlying endogenous element. That is, while agreeing that an exogenous or external detonator to realignment was necessary in the form of a crisis of massive proportions, Burnham held that the inherent periodicity of realignment was based on the endogenous factor of the separation-of-powers and checks-and-balances nature of America's governmental institutions. Burnham's essential point here was that the nature of the American constitutional and political system led to an accumulation of problems and grievances that its slow-moving, laborious, and tedious institutions were unable to resolve without the explosive upheaval of realignment. Thus, realignment under American constitutional and governmental conditions was necessary for the breakthroughs needed to deal with pressing social and economic problems.[71] It was "a periodically recurring phenomenon . . . centrally related to" the nature of the governmental and political system; its "explosive character" arose "from the underlying characteristics of the constitutional system."[72]

Burnham, like Lubell before, did not limit himself to developing a theory of realignment; he also undertook to apply his ideas to the politics of his own time. Like Kevin Phillips, his cyclical theory appeared to fit the upheaval of the 1960s perfectly, although Burnham, unlike Phillips, lacked what he called the latter's "thirst" for contemporary upheaval.[73] In an initial foray, Burnham speculated about the realigning potential of the 1964 election; later, he inclined toward the view that deemed 1964 merely "deviating."[74] He was much impressed by the 1966 election's strong GOP gains. Normally, he wrote, off-year elections were not earthshaking, but the 1966 results suggested that "something very like a revolution" was underway, with battles now taking place in a political context "entirely different" than that "which Samuel Lubell . . . immortalized and under which we all grew up." The economic and ethnic appeals of Democrats dating to the New Deal era now appeared out-of-date. Thus, opportunities were in place for moderate Republicans to appeal to the new generation of more educated "metropolitan" voters if the GOP could avoid the pitfalls of a replay of the disastrous Goldwater strategy of 1964. The election of 1966, he concluded, with words that seemed preposterously out-of-date shortly thereafter, constituted "the latest installment of the revolt of the moderates."[75] By 1968 and 1969, Burnham was focusing on a very different kind of political tumult, discerning an era characterized by "the most explosive and indigestible set of social dislocations . . . since the Civil War," dislocations "with racial antagonisms at their core."[76] It was with this sense that a new political era might be at hand that Burnham discussed current realignment prospects in his *Critical Elections and the Mainsprings of American Politics* of 1970.

Burnham's seminal book was replete with rumbles of upheaval. The New Deal system forged more than three decades before now appeared at its end; the third-party effort of George Wallace in 1968 was viewed in terms of the historic role of such parties as harbingers of realignment. The possibility existed for "a realignment of enormous magnitude."[77] Burnham played with the notion that the upheaval might lead to a Democratic Party housing increasing numbers of well-educated and affluent citizens, a reconstituted coalition of "the top and bottom" sustaining the Democrats as the majority. But he found such a conclusion "premature" at the very least.[78] He acknowledged that Kevin Phillips had "persuasively argued" the case for "an emergent Republican majority." However, Burnham considered it "doubtful" that a new majority would be Republican in a strictly partisan sense, although it could well be ideologically conservative, based on the "intensity of polarized cultural conflict . . . already a conspicuous part of the current American political scene," including the nationalization of racial conflict. Here the origins of any current realignment could be traced to the racially oriented GOP strategy of 1964.[79] Burnham's crystal ball as to the ultimate outcome was a good deal less clear than Phillips's. The 1960s, he held, appeared to be "profoundly transitional," but there remained an "ambiguity" as to the nature of the transition. Political coalitions were clearly in flux, but thus far there had been no "crystallizing" crisis, no "triggering event of scope and brutal force" powerful enough to create a massive electoral transformation. Despite the ongoing cultural conflicts, no "detonator" had "yet appeared on the scene." Indeed, while clearly "emergent social tension" had "volatilized the mass electorate," there was no "a priori certainty" that "a detonator guaranteeing realignment" would "be ignited."[80]

In the early 1970s Burnham continued to emphasize the importance of upheaval in current and recent American politics.[81] As the decade of the 1970s wore on, however, he undertook something of a zigzagging path. On the one hand, he saw a growth of conservatism in American politics, as evidenced, among other things, by the Democrats' nomination of Jimmy Carter in 1976. On the other hand, it appeared that no clear-cut partisan realignment was in progress; indeed the GOP sagged badly in the mid-1970s under the impact of the Watergate scandal and economic tribulations. Instead of realignment there was a growth of ticket splitting and divided government.[82] Here entered another key part of Burnham's thesis, one dating back to the 1960s and both separate from and intimately intertwined with his realignment theory: what he termed "electoral disaggregation" and others simplified to "dealignment." From the perspective of the late 1980s and early 1990s, and sometimes earlier, Burnham saw fit to combine the two concepts of disaggregation and realignment. What had occurred in the late 1960s and early 1970s, he was now sure, was indeed a realignment creating a new "system," the key elements of which were the weakening of partisan loyalties and the growth of ticket splitting, leading to extended periods of divided government with one electoral pattern determining control of the presidency and the other determining control of Congress.[83] But Burnham was not always sure of the connection between realignment and disaggregation, and in his expositions there was at the very least a tension between the two.

To Burnham, one of the basic features of modern American politics, dating back to the Progressive era and only temporarily offset by the partisan fires of the New Deal era, was the secular weakening of parties. As evidenced in recent politics, this included a weakening of party organization and a growing decline in party loyalty. The strong partisan identifications emphasized in *The American Voter*, Burnham held, represented only the characteristics of a given time frame and not an equally potent continuing characteristic. In his most extreme or hyperbolic mood, Burnham even speculated about the disappearance of parties. However, in the context of the era of upheaval of the 1960s and 1970s, a more limited version of his analysis seemed to fit the times. Party identification appeared down; swings between elections were pronounced; organized parties seemed weaker. This secular decline of party and partisan identification, Burnham held at times, went counter to the historic pattern of realignment. Realignment presupposed an era of stability against which an electoral explosion was directed. If there were no longer to be eras of relative stability, if there were no longer to be strong patterns of party identification to be realigned, then realignment itself would disappear. Or, as Burnham sometimes also put it, electoral disaggregation would constitute a realignment to end all realignments. Put together, Burnham acknowledged, realignment and disaggregation constituted "an analytical dilemma."[84] Other analysts noted the apparent conflict and incompatibility between Burnham's theory of realignment and his concept of secular electoral disaggregation.[85] Some critics were harsher. One held that Burnham's theory of electoral disaggregation left his equally signature theory of cyclical realignment "in substantial disarray."[86] Another declared that faced with the choice of whether the party system was entering a state of cyclical realignment or of secular dissolution, Burnham hedged "his bets" and gave "evidence for both."[87] The observation had merit and at times, as noted, Burnham suggested that disaggregation had rendered realignment "extinct," whereas on other occasions he held that disaggregation constituted the latest realignment.[88] But in any case, Burnham was certainly accurate in his general observation that the upheaval, which "convulsed American politics" from the mid-1960s to the early 1970s, had led "to a growing crisis of explanatory paradigms" within the community of scholars of electoral behavior.[89]

Chapter Eleven

The Onset of Revision

Analysts writing at the close of the 1970s and those looking back on the 1960s and 1970s often concluded that realignment—or what was styled "classic realignment"—had not occurred. They tended to agree that something significant transpired, but as the use of the term "classic realignment" suggested, they concluded that what had happened did not closely correspond to the model of realignment as it was developed in the 1950s and early 1960s.[1] For some writers the upshot was rejection of realignment theory, while others opted for revision or elaboration of the received version. Political historian Richard L. McCormick contended in 1982 that realignment theory was "in disarray," raising questions about the continued usefulness of the concept.[2] Political historian Allan J. Lichtman writing that same year went further. Realignment theory, he held, was in "decay" and now constituted an "impediment" to political understanding. Efforts to maintain the theory through revision only evidenced its loss of vitality. The time for devising new explanations was "long overdue."[3] Other critics were less wholesale in their rejection. Some were content to reject the cyclical addition to realignment theory. The failure of realignment to occur in the late 1960s and early 1970s, this notion ran, invalidated only the notion of cyclical periodicity and not necessarily of realignment theory per se. Nor were all realignments created equal. The New Deal pattern, which underlay the development of realignment theory, it was held, was sharper and more dramatic than that of 1896, just as the impact of the Great Depression and earlier of the Civil War were more far-reaching than the upheaval of either the 1890s or of the 1960s. For some this meant that realignment theory based on the New Deal case was not generally applicable, while others merely contended that note had to be made of differing versions of the realignment phenomenon and that a current or future realignment would not necessarily conform to past patterns.[4]

Just as the concept of party identification and the classification of elections set forth by the Michigan School in *The American Voter* crystallized realignment theory, the electoral developments of the late 1960s and early 1970s called into question the conclusions of that school and book. One of the most common criticisms of *The American Voter*, particularly stressed by Gerald Pomper, was that the book was "time-bound"; that is, it drew—some said its readers rather than authors drew—general conclusions as to the nature of voting behavior that were really characteristic only of the 1950s.[5] The upshot of this criticism was that the portrait of the American voter presented by the Michigan School lacked explanatory power in dealing with the more dynamic politics and volatile electorate of the 1960s, that the concept of a "normal vote" from which short-term deviations could be measured was of little utility in a period of overall flux, and that the Michigan election classification system could not incorporate the variety of changes characteristic of a period of frenetic, rather than static, politics.[6] Questioning was also directed at the core of the Michigan School analysis—the role of party identification. As early as 1966, political scientist John Kessel anticipated a major point of later analysts when he suggested that short-term factors might skew measurement of party identification. Since it was assumed to be stable and durable, party identification was the basic standard by which the Michigan School measured short-term deviations, and the notion that those deviations impacted voter declarations of party identification was obviously of central import.[7]

The most spirited debate of the late 1960s and early 1970s centered on the relative importance of party identification and what was termed "issue voting." Over the course of the period, it was often pointed out that surveys revealed a significant and continuing decline in party identification as a stable and widely held voter characteristic and as a determinant of voting patterns. Concomitantly, it was held, most forcefully by Gerald Pomper, that issue voting was of rising importance in explaining electoral behavior.[8] Drawing upon V. O. Key's *The Responsible Electorate*, Pomper argued that the issue-oriented politics, parties, and campaigns of the 1960s ignited a greater issue orientation, consciousness, and response among voters. This demonstrated the importance of what Pomper termed the "political environment" of voter behavior, which was undervalued, he contended, in the Michigan School's preoccupation with the individual voter. Rather than party identification shaping voters' issue stands, voters could turn to one party or the other because of issue preference. A closer relation between voter issue and party preference moved in the direction, Pomper believed, of the responsible party system featuring coherent policy positions and electoral mandates called for by E. E. Schattschneider decades earlier.[9] The relation between party identification and issue voting was itself, however, more complicated when viewed in an historical setting; it was also closely intertwined with the concept of realignment. From this perspective, the issue voting of the 1960s represented less a break with Michigan School analysis based on the 1950s than a reflection of a period of realignment. Such voting was congruent with the Michigan affirmation that party identifications were forged in eras characterized by fervently held positions on issues.[10] Thus, Pomper criticized the Michigan School for emphasizing party identification over issues.[11] But he was echoing the Michigan School's analysis in terms of its historical dimension when he held that issues sometimes operated as long-term influences in shaping party identification—that "the origins of party loyalty" could be found in the issue ferment of eras such as those of the Civil War and New Deal.[12]

The initial response of the Michigan School and its close supporters to the ferment of the 1960s was to hold fast to positions previously set forth and to interpret apparent changes in terms of short-run deviations from more stable norms. Thus, Angus Campbell, on the eve of the upheaval of 1968, could confidently assert that "the pattern of party commitment—the long-standing loyalties to political parties" would not likely "change appreciably" with the approach of a new election.[13] Nelson Polsby and Aaron Wildavsky, in the 1968 edition of their *Presidential Elections: Strategies of American Electoral Politics*, clung to the analysis set forth in *The American Voter*, stressing party identification over issues.[14] Phillip E. Converse and Warren E. Miller, writing with others in 1969, clearly judged the 1968 election by the standards of their *American Voter* of 1960. While there was a "truly massive" shift in the presidential vote between 1964 and 1968 due to short-term concerns, they wrote, "the frantic motion of the electorate" must be "juxtaposed against the serene stability of party identifications." While the presidential election deviated from what would have been expected from the distribution of party identifications, the congressional elections "handsomely reflected" party loyalties.[15] Hence, as Warren Miller put it several years later, 1968 constituted a "deviating election."[16] While this characterization wholly fit the original Michigan analysis, Miller later acknowledged that "the bedrock of party identification cracked" in 1968 in terms of the intensity of partisan allegiance, setting in motion a continuing pattern of growing independence.[17] And indeed, over time the Michiganders partially retreated and accommodated their analyses to changing realities and their critics' points. As far back as 1966, for example, in response to John Kessel's concerns about the mutability of party-identification responses, Philip Converse, pointing to the landslides of 1956 and 1964, agreed that "the distribution of party identification" did sway "slightly in response to national tides surrounding a given election." This effect did "in one sense" shift "party identification from an independent to a dependent variable," although voters involved were "not in the midst of some permanent conversion from one party to the other" and "the 'real' stability of party identification" was not at issue.[18] Several years later, Converse acknowledged a decline in party identification, attributing it in good measure to the emergence of a new generation of voters lacking strong partisan loyalties.[19] He agreed that issue voting was more important in periods of change than stability, while pointing out that "defections" over issues sometimes hardened into "conversions" in terms of identification.[20] Warren E. Miller in coauthored pieces on the 1972 election concluded that the presidential contest marked a low in the "predictive power" of party identification in voting decisions, combined with a growth of "issue polarization" and political independence. Issue attitudes appeared more important than party loyalty in determining voter preference.[21] Still, he correctly insisted, the Michigan approach had not made party and issue voting mutually exclusive; "dramatically cataclysmic . . . events, such as depressions and civil wars," shaped the political attitudes that led to enduring party loyalties. Thus, "from the earliest days of the Michigan studies of party identification," it was "apparent" that party identification could be disrupted by the powerful issues of eras of realignment.[22]

Gerald Pomper, writing in 1975, held that the changed electoral patterns dating to 1964 persisted into 1972, thus making 1964 no "aberrant event," but rather the starting point for "a new period of American politics."[23] The election of 1976 appeared to call this conclusion into question; it seemed to reflect party identification rather than issues, although some analysts were quick to admonish that one election should not be taken as a break with the trend toward political independence.[24] Political scientist Morris P. Fiorina, a critic of the Michigan version of party identification, acknowledged that following the "turbulence of the late 1960s and early 1970s," the 1976 election looked "more like the elections known to a generation of students who cut their teeth on *The American Voter*."[25] Bruce A. Campbell, a political scientist and son of Angus Campbell, contended that 1976 "deflated" the belief that voters were throwing aside party loyalty in favor of issue voting; voters merely were more inclined to vote on issues in elections in which issues were prominent, as in 1964, 1968, and 1972, and reverted to party loyalty when issues were less evident, as in the 1950s and 1976.[26] The Michiganders and their allies, to be sure, had engaged in strategic retreats prior to 1976, but they had never caved. When Gerald Pomper sent a letter in 1974 to the profession's flagship journal, *The American Political Science Review*, repeating his assertion that *The American Voter* conveyed "a tone of proclaiming general" as distinct from "time-specific truths," managing editor Nelson Polsby sent a copy to Philip Converse. Polsby noted that of course Converse had the right to reply, but the managing editor expressed the hope that Converse would find it in his "heart to let Gerry make an ass out of himself unaided." Converse thereupon declared himself "a sphinx."[27] The election of 1976 buoyed the Michigan School. In a 1978 analysis, based on surveys to 1976, Converse held that for all the acknowledged upheaval of the period from 1964 to 1972—the decline of party identification, the rise of issue voting—the patterns of the mid-1970s were remarkably similar to those of the 1950s as documented in *The American Voter*.[28] After a time of attack and revision, vindication appeared at hand.

Alternative efforts to make sense of the era of upheaval proceeded along several lines. One tack, taking a cue from the time and sharing similarities with Arthur M. Schlesinger's issue-oriented concept set forth in 1939, was to stress ideology as distinct from partisanship. Or, in a rewind to Kevin Phillips's ambivalence over whether to call his 1969 book *The Emerging Republican Majority* or *The Emerging Conservative Majority*, some held that what emerged after 1968 was not a partisan Republican era, but rather an ideologically conservative era.[29] A more distinctly political scientific challenger to the realignment-Michigan synthesis, with roots in V. O. Key's *The Responsible Electorate*, came via the theory of "retrospective voting," that is, the notion that voters passed retrospective judgments on the performance of the parties in government. This theory appeared to fit an era of declining party loyalty with voting seemingly geared to each election as an increasingly discrete event.[30] As developed most fully by Morris P. Fiorina, due homage was paid to V. O. Key's parentage of the theory, but a challenge was laid down to the Michigan School's concept of party identification as a deeply rooted and enduring characteristic of individual voters. Rather, Fiorina argued, party identification should be understood as a voter's "running balance sheet" evaluating the performance of the parties, more subject thereby to short-run alterations, while also providing citizens with a shortcut to decision making—in the last sense similar to the original Michigan party-identification concept itself.[31]

The most pervasively held alternative concept to come out of the period of upheaval and revision was that of dealignment. This view held that the decline of party identification and the growth of political independence had created an electorate without moorings; instead of a politics of continuity characterized by party loyalties and group traditions, politics was now geared more to the short run, to individual candidates and campaigns. In such a context of flux and instability, the very notion of realignment appeared outlandish to many: How could there be a realignment without an enduring alignment from which to realign?[32] It is not too hard to see how the frustrated expectations of realignment coming out of the elections of 1964 and 1968 could contribute to the dealignment concept. But the idea of dealignment was not used just as an alternative to realignment. It could also be viewed as itself constituting a realignment—albeit a realignment differing from those of the past because of its characteristic growth of political independence. From this standpoint, a re-alignment need not create a durable new majority, but may be characterized only by significant shifts in the nature of electoral support.[33] And there was yet a third version of dealignment, which held that it was a stage in the develop-ment of realignment, one, moreover, which recurred historically. As developed particularly by Paul Allen Beck, this variation posited the existence of an "electoral cycle" in the realignment process. The cycle consisted of periods of realignment, stability, and dealignment, the last stage presaging a new era of realignment. In Beck's formulation, the fervor of a realigning era gradually declined with the passage of time and with the emergence of a new generation for which the emotional issues of an earlier realigning era were but memories. This led to a stage of dealignment, awaiting a new exogenous shock that would usher in a new era of realignment. The era of upheaval of the late 1960s—with its ticket splitting, divided government, and confused agenda—was to Beck a classic case of the recurring dealignment phase of the cycle. In this concept, dealignment, rather than constituting a substitute for realignment—or the re-alignment itself—was seen as a phase in the cycle preceding the realignment breakthrough.[34]

The failure clearly to find in the 1964–1972 period either a critical election or series of critical elections contributed, by the late 1970s, to a de-emphasis on dramatic electoral change. Rather, a shift occurred toward the secular realign-ment notions of the scholar who also wrought the critical election concept: the ubiquitous V. O. Key. Writing in the wake of the failure of classic realignment to occur, scholars increasingly focused on gradual, rather than "critical," change, holding that the appeal of dramatic upheaval had obscured secular aspects of re-alignment actually underway in favor of a focus on a critical electoral realign-ment that had not transpired.[35] James Sundquist, whose *Dynamics of the Party System* was first published in 1973 and reissued in a new edition in 1983, wove together Key's critical elections and secular realignment strands in his analysis.[36] Sundquist was credited with providing an exception to the cataclysmic emphases of realignment scholars by the two political scientists who emerged as perhaps the most effective proponents of the importance of secular change: Edward G. Carmines and James A. Stimson.[37] Writing in 1980 and 1981, Carmines and Stimson posited the theory of "issue evolution," essentially an elaboration of Key's explicitly acknowledged concept of secular realignment. In the Carmines and Stimson view, a focus on critical elections obscured important, but gradual, changes that occurred over the course of decades as a result of the combined im-pact of generational replacement and the unfolding of new issues—race provid-ing their current foremost example. Significant changes in party coalitions oc-curred over time, akin to Darwinian evolution, rather than suddenly, as suggested by analogies to the cataclysms of physical science. These changes "of massive proportions" were no less significant because they evolved slowly, rather than in a dramatic fashion.[38]

A final response to the complexities of the politics of the mid- and late 1960s and early 1970s, as judged by the model of "classic realignment," was an expanded, more comprehensive, and more policy- and leadership-contingent version of realignment theory. As put by Bruce A. Campbell and Richard J. Trilling in the introduction to their coedited 1980 book on the subject, what was needed was "a full-blown," "integrated," "general theory of realignment" linking electoral decisions to public policy outcomes.[39] Building upon the earlier insights of Schattschneider, Key, and Burnham, many scholars of the late 1970s and the turn of the decade sought to extend the theory of realignment beyond voters, elections, and parties to issues of governance and public policy. Their essential conclusion was that critical election eras provided opportunities for major developments in public policy. A crisis resulting in electoral upheaval, a perceived mandate from the voters, the momentum of a decisive victory, and the likelihood of enhanced partisan majorities in government all provided the basis for far-reaching changes and innovations in public policy departing from a preceding era of stalemate or incremental change.[40] By the same token, an apparently critical election could lead to a new administration unable to resolve a crisis, ineffective in leadership—and thus a chance for realignment would be squandered and lost. Application to the aftermaths of 1964 and 1972 was all too apparent. Hence realignment did not automatically flow from cyclical electoral upheavals.[41] A great deal depended on effective leadership; if it was lacking, then the chance for realignment would disappear. What consolidated potential realignment was effective leadership in meeting a crisis and implementing policies deemed successful by the electorate. Realignment in that sense was actually a top-down accomplishment.[42] The stage was here set for the electoral upheaval of 1980 and the leadership and policy agenda of President Ronald Reagan.

Chapter Twelve

Grappling with Incongruity

The 1980 victory of Ronald Reagan, together with the GOP seizure of the Senate for the first time since Eisenhower's 1952 win, set in motion a decade of informed speculation about a pro-Republican realignment. Analysis was facilitated by the comprehensive survey database of the National Election Studies that absorbed, continued, and built upon the decades-old Michigan surveys at the end of the 1970s. The Michigan methodological and conceptual approach remained, however, and given the stress on party identification as revealed in public opinion surveys since the days of Angus Campbell, the ongoing decrease in Democratic Party identification and the mid-decade surge in Republican Party identification to some observers constituted final, definitive evidence that the long-awaited GOP realignment had become, or at least was becoming, a reality.[1] As a 1985 analyst put it, changes in party identification favorable to the GOP demonstrated that realignment was "no longer incipient, but upon us."[2] And just as the New Deal Democratic hegemony was linked to an agenda shaped by Franklin Roosevelt, the continued impact of the social issue of the 1960s and the disruptive impact of race on the New Deal Democratic coalition was viewed as having created a new dominant set of issues. That new agenda, combined with the economic traumas of the Carter years, went hand in hand with a clear realignment in the white South and erosion of Democratic support in the white North.[3] But while realignment theory received an encore of sorts, the 1980s simultaneously brought forth additional efforts at elaboration and reconfiguration. The failure of the 1980s, like the period from 1968–1972, to correspond to "classic realignment," that is, to realignment theory as it developed in the wake of the 1930s upheaval, led to further variations of (and caveats to) the basic concept. And proffered alternatives to realignment theory emerging out of the 1970s were interwoven with versions of the realignment idea itself, even as they continued as contrary explanations, as was the case with the realignment version of dealignment advanced, notably, by Paul Allen Beck. In its current application, dealignment in the 1970s could or would end in realignment in the 1980s if voters perceived that a newly installed party had been successful in dealing with the problems that had brought it to power.[4]

Realignment theory, as developed by Lubell and Key, had first been applied retrospectively to historical epochs. Efforts to apply it contemporaneously were inherently more tentative and perilous, as demonstrated by the aftermath of 1964 and of 1968–1972. Much the same was true of the 1980s, as analysts endeavored to balance attention-grabbing conclusions with self-protective qualifications. Thus, political scientist William Schneider, for example, believed that the current realignment combined the social-issue driven movement toward the GOP of 1968–1972 with the economically driven movement of 1980–1984, but that 1988 would tell the tale of its durability. Just as Republicans had long rationalized that the 1932–1944 string of Democratic victories was an aberration only to get their comeuppance in 1948, Schneider suggested that a GOP presidential victory in 1988 would demonstrate that "the same thing" had "happened in our time," and that realignment had stuck.[5] (Years later Schneider would dispense daily wisdom as CNN's "Inside Politics" maven.) Michael Barone, political journalist and major shaper of the biannual *Almanac of American Politics*, tended toward a dealignment explanation of current politics through most of the 1980s. But in the wake of 1988, he changed his tune. Drawing a parallel with continued Democratic successes coming out of the New Deal era, he held that after 1988 GOP presidential victories could no longer be considered aberrant or due to ephemeral factors. Writing of the "Democrats' problems" in 1991, he declared that for the first time in sixty years "the Democrats had no hope of winning" the next presidential election. Still, he concluded, "the most puzzling development of the 1980s" remained the GOP's failure to emerge as the clear "national majority party" across the boards.[6] Writing in 1986, three political scientists held that a 1988 GOP presidential victory would bring many of their brethren to the conclusion that a "pattern of electoral volatility" had been broken and "that Republican presidential dominance must be viewed as a realignment."[7] And in 1989 Gerald Pomper concluded that the 1988 result confirmed that a "'secular realignment' of American politics toward a Republican presidential majority" had occurred.[8] A problem for realignment theory, however, was that the GOP presidential victories had not brought partisan triumphs throughout. The Democrats won back the Senate in 1986 and continued their hold over the House of Representatives.

Nonetheless, some enthusiasts were unable to contain themselves after 1988, seeing current Republican presidential hegemony as comparable to that of the decades prior to 1932.[9] Except for the Watergate-inspired Carter interlude, wrote a 1985 analyst, the country would now be heading toward its twentieth consecutive year of Republican presidents—a period equal in length to Democratic presidential dominance under Roosevelt and Truman.[10] Another analyst that year held that the Republicans had now become "the majority or 'sun party' in presidential elections."[11] Writing in 1992, Earl Black and Merle Black exclaimed that in the wake of the 1960s, the GOP had "developed nothing less than its broadest base in history" in terms of presidential elections. The Democratic Party, meanwhile, had "been reduced to its weakest position in presidential politics since . . . the Civil War and Reconstruction," one that bore "a strong resemblance to the Republican party during the New Deal." Indeed, concluded the Blacks, the New Deal era stood out as the single exception to "the twentieth century . . . general rule" that the GOP "normally enjoyed a substantial advantage in presidential elections."[12] Still, leaving aside the obvious observation that this judgment was rendered shortly before the Democrats retook the White House, the more significant point to note is the common use of the term "presidential" before the terms "dominance" or "realignment." How could the Republicans be deemed the beneficiaries of a successful realignment when they only sporadically controlled the Senate and had not won the House of Representatives since the election of 1952? The lack of a clear majority party, divided partisan control of the national government, and a rough parity or balance of support between the major parties, all led to talk of a "presidential" realignment, or a "partial" realignment, or a realignment still "in progress," even as some analysts continued to hold that a dealignment, rather than a realignment, had taken hold and that short-term forces had replaced long-term factors in shaping electoral outcomes.[13] In any event, as a 1988 writer put it, "the ongoing rearrangement" did "not fit the realignment paradigm of political scientists" as originally constructed in the wake of the upheaval of the 1930s.[14]

Clearly, however, everyone agreed that something substantial had happened. A common view postulated a two-stage or piggyback electoral shift, uniting 1968–1972 with the 1980s and overriding the Watergate interruption. Just as 1988 confirmed 1980 and 1984, furthermore, the economic debacle of the Carter years provided the proverbial icing on the cake, or from a Democratic perspective, the last nail in the coffin, in relation to the social-issue-oriented GOP gains of 1968–1972. After all, as Scammon and Wattenberg and others had urged in the earlier period, the effective Democratic strategy would be to neutralize the social issue while stressing the economic issue: the long-held notion that the Democrats were the party of good times. In this analysis, to be sure, the cultural upheaval (including racial strife) arising out of the 1960s had weakened the Democrats. But the party had rebounded in 1974 and 1976 owing not only to Watergate, but also to the failure of the Republican administration to cope with the combined problems of inflation and recession or slow growth ("stagflation" in the parlance of the time). The crusher here was the comparable failure of President Carter to meet the central economic dilemmas of the decade effectively. Since Roosevelt the Democrats had drawn upon their reputation as successful macroeconomic managers; for all the upheaval of the 1960s, economic growth had been extraordinary and ongoing. Yet by 1980 the Democratic administration had squandered this positive partisan reputation. By 1984, with inflation down and an apparent boom underway, Reagan was handsomely rewarded by the electorate; and the continued perception of economic well-being, in addition to replays of the social issue, contributed to George Bush's victory in 1988. Contrary to the norm from the 1930s to the 1970s, 1980s public opinion surveys showed the GOP to be the more trusted guarantor of national economic prosperity and growth. Thus, loss of the economic issue—the Democrats' erstwhile strength—added to the social issue (itself linked to race) left the once dominant party almost wholly bereft of its traditional armor and weaponry. Had it not been for the economic failures of the Carter years, from this perspective, the GOP victories of 1968 and 1972 conceivably might have continued to be perceived as comparable to those of 1952 and 1956: deviating elections in an otherwise ongoing Democratic era.[15]

Two highly influential analysts resistant to the notion of national realignment in the wake of 1968–1972, James Sundquist and Warren E. Miller, were in a good degree converts in the 1980s. Sundquist, a midcentury Democratic Party operative before turning full-time scholar, continued, in the early 1980s as in the 1970s, to reject the notion that the social issue had led, or was leading, to a pro-Republican realignment. Nor in the early 1980s was he convinced that economic difficulties were leading to lasting GOP gains. But writing in 1985, Sundquist perceived a degree of realignment underway that, while "much less than in 1936," was "more than at any time in the half century since then." The "Reagan Revolution" had "brought about the greatest transformation in five decades," and its "realigning forces" were "still at work." The mid-decade state of the economy constituted the strongest force behind the impressive national gains in GOP party identification, Sundquist held, and now added to the previous and ongoing gains recorded in the white South. A large number of independents remained in the electorate, but the GOP had pulled into parity with the Democrats. The basic issue agenda arising out of the 1930s had not been displaced, but changed perceptions of the parties could have an impact comparable to that of new crosscutting issues. What remained in question, he concluded, was "the durability of the changes." If the "current trends" continued into 1988, it would "probably be justified" to declare "that a realignment—not one as decisive as that of the 1930s but one of a second order of magnitude—had occurred."[16] Miller, of

American Voter fame, was initially cautious in assessing realignment prospects in the wake of Reagan's 1980 victory. But following 1984, he was increasingly convinced that a nationwide change was underway. It was essentially based not on the cultural and racial upheaval arising out of the 1960s, nor on an ideological transformation among the citizenry, but rather on positive perceptions of the economic performance and leadership of the Reagan administration. Appropriately for a charter member of the Michigan School, the underlying persuasive ingredient for Miller was the closing gap between Democrats and Republicans in party identification, albeit admittedly a gap now linked to retrospective evaluations and one whose durability remained in question as of mid-decade. In 1990, however, Miller concluded that "between 1980 and 1988 . . . at least a limited version of the long-heralded partisan realignment took place." The "secular realignment" long underway in the white South was now joined by the "national realignment" of the Reagan era.[17]

Thomas Byrne Edsall, a journalist whose 1991 book *Chain Reaction* provided an overview of change since the 1960s, and Everett Carll Ladd, who spent much of the decade struggling with the realignment concept, were convinced that the 1980s had confirmed an era of historic transition. Edsall held that the cultural and racial upheaval of the 1960s, critically augmented by the economic traumas of the 1970s, had created a new balance of power of rough parity between the parties and a policy agenda favorable to the Republicans. In *Chain Reaction* he, together with his wife, Mary D. Edsall, provided the capstone to a generation of realignment speculation and discussion stretching from 1964 to 1988. A "new polarization of the electorate" had occurred, they held, one that had displaced "the traditional New Deal cleavages" in place "from 1932 to 1964." Race had been the critical 1960s factor breaking up the New Deal coalition, while the loss of the Democrats' economic issue in 1980 provided the coup de grace. The election of 1964 had started the process in motion, and that of 1968 "in many respects defined . . . American politics for the next twenty years." After the Watergate interlude came the debacle of 1980, followed by the Democrats' "political nadir."[18] The prolific and peripatetic Ladd was quite certain that something highly significant had happened since the 1960s, but he was not always sure that what happened should be termed a "realignment." Shortly before the 1980 election, Ladd was convinced that dealignment, rather than realignment, best accounted for recent changes. Following the 1980 election, he held that Reagan's victory best fit the "dealignment model." In 1985, however, Ladd veered toward the notion that the GOP had made significant gains. The white South's shift had become "nothing less than the net partisan conversion of an entire region." Nationally, the party was benefiting from positive evaluations of the Reagan administration's economic performance. The GOP had "closed the gap"

with the Democrats in party identification. "Something substantial" had occurred, even lacking a "majority party," and "realignment" was "a good word for
it." This "split personality" realignment, with a GOP hold on the presidency, but
Democratic strength elsewhere, was "proving . . . remarkably enduring."
Dealignment, he now held, was a "feature" of the "present realignment." The
1988 election, he concluded, "confirmed the latest of our country's great partisan realignments—this one having begun in the late 1960s." The Republicans,
he now believed, had built up strength "not seen since the first quarter of this
century," while the Democrats had lapsed into their historic position of weakness
in presidential elections, achieving since 1856 "a sustained presidential majority
only during the New Deal and under just one man—Roosevelt."[19]

Ladd's hopscotching reflected the basic 1980s conundrum: the difficulty in
applying realignment theory to the decade's puzzling electoral vagaries. This
conundrum led to increasingly variegated concepts of realignment, as well as
to growing questioning of the theory's continued validity. One effort at adaptation held that there had been a "policy" realignment under Reagan without—
or at least preceding—an electoral realignment, demonstrating that the role of
leadership had been hitherto theoretically underrated in favor of the stress on
the electorate.[20] An additional version contended that there had been no critical election in the current realignment, even as most presidential elections between 1964 and 1988 contributed significantly to the realigning process; lacking a single explosive factor such as the Civil War or the Great Depression, the
présent realignment was gradual and cumulative in nature.[21] Convinced that
Reagan's 1984 landslide victory confirmed the growth of just such a gradual
realignment, political scientist John Petrocik (like Ladd at this point) argued
that a coalition shift need not result in a new majority party to be considered
realigning; rough partisan parity could itself reflect realignment, given loss of
the longtime Democratic edge.[22] But while some analysts set forth notions of
elite, noncritical, or nonmajority realignment (not to mention qualifiers like
"partial," "incomplete," and "truncated"), others insisted that lacking enduring
partisan domination of both Congress and the presidency, there could be said
to be no realignment at all.[23] Apparent realignment had been rendered "hollow," it was argued, failing to pervade the electoral process due to the combined effects of dealignment and retrospective voting.[24] And the contention
was made that dealignment and retrospective voting had rendered realignment
theory itself hollow. In this view, the GOP victories of the Reagan–Bush years
simply showed that a dealigned electorate punished perceived failure and rewarded perceived success.[25]

The complexities of realignment theory in the 1980s were further illustrated by the overlapping, but distinct, paths taken by the two leading proponents of the concept in the late 1960s and early 1970s: Kevin Phillips and
Walter Dean Burnham.

Phillips, who was swept to fame as a prophet of GOP realignment in 1969 only to be disillusioned by the developments of the 1970s, had a take on the new decade that reflected both his distaste for the Republican regime of the 1980s and his loss of faith in realignment theory. Reagan's 1980 victory, in Phillips's view, resulted in an economically elitist administration dedicated to enriching the rich, rather than serving the middle class. It was geared by doctrinal faith to minimizing government's economic role, rather than developing the more positive government needed, as Phillips saw it, to advance America's economic interests in the global market. The coalition behind Reagan, based on popular support for cultural issues arising from the 1960s and distress over 1970s economic difficulties, was not congruent with the administration's elitist economic policy agenda. Reagan's policies also risked alienating well-educated GOP moderates. Phillips's early 1980s expectations, therefore, focused on continued flux, rather than on what he deemed the less likely prospect of a consolidated realignment. Upheaval indeed no longer portended realignment; presidential sweeps no longer assured congressional victories; GOP domination of the White House had not brought partisan domination overall. The notion of historical cycles of realignment that weighed so heavily in *The Emerging Republican Majority* analysis of 1969, Phillips believed, had likely played out. Watergate, he continued to maintain, had exploded what otherwise might have become a traditional realignment; further, the electoral patterns of Reagan's 1984 triumph closely paralleled Nixon's in 1972. Nonetheless, Phillips foresaw the likelihood of shorter cycles. In the mid-1980s he suggested that the conservative momentum dating back to Nixon had peaked and that Reagan Republicans were now overplaying their hand. Citing Arthur Schlesinger, Jr. and the theory of cyclical ideological change, Phillips speculated that support for a more positive governmental agenda might follow. The Democrats' presidential defeat in 1988 Phillips traced to their strategic ineptitude and George Bush's success in reviving cultural resentments dating to the 1960s. But a continued Republican hold, Phillips cautioned, was shaky—especially in the event of a faltering economy, that "old bugaboo" of the GOP.[26]

Phillips's fellow prophet of upheaval in the late 1960s and early 1970s, Walter Dean Burnham, continued as an authoritative 1980s analyst of change, albeit one who also continued to struggle with the relation between realignment theory and his concept of secular partisan decline. Burnham's initial response to the 1980 election was highly suggestive. Whatever the Democrats' continuing edge in party identification, he held, the Republicans had approached status as a "normal . . . majority" party in presidential elections and had taken over the Senate as well. Clearly, he believed, the 1980 rejection of the Democrats had been decisive. The GOP now held sway on the economic issue; major shifts in public policy were underway; and perceptions of Reagan administration successes could well lead to "something approximating . . . critical realignment." Still, Burnham cautioned, party decomposition remained; the crisis at hand lacked the proportions of the Civil War or Great Depression; and even with the 1984 Reagan landslide victory, the Republican hold did not extend to the House of Representatives. The 1986 election, Burnham contended, with the GOP loss of the Senate, gave "the idea of electoral realignment . . . a virtual coup de grace." An electoral, as distinct from an elite, policy realignment had "not happened." Dealignment and "split partisan outcomes at all levels of government" prevailed instead. Yet in the late 1980s, Burnham suggested that the changes since "1968–72" were "momentous enough to be described as a critical realignment." A traditional realignment had not occurred in that the GOP had failed to attain total partisan control of the national government. But a GOP hold on the presidency had been established. And a uniquely "antipartisan" realignment centered on policy rather than on the electorate in traditional partisan terms had occurred. In the early 1990s Burnham continued to profess and defend this version of realignment theory. It was cyclical and endogenous, as he had held from the beginning; its most recent manifestation via divided government arose out of the late 1960s and early 1970s; and as of 1991 the Democrats had "all but disappeared as a credible force in presidential elections."[27]

Patently, the lines between proponents of revised versions of realignment and those who maintained that realignment theory did not fit present reality were blurred and overlapping. And analysts went back and forth. Everett Carll Ladd, who had reason to know, held in 1985 that for twenty years political scientists had "stumbled and sloshed around" in the "conceptual swamp" they had created "called realignment." A basic reason for the confusion, he maintained, was that the realignment model was based on the peculiarities of the New Deal era.[28] In 1991 Ladd set forth to do battle with the realignment concept once again, holding that political scientists' attachment to the concept had "been mostly unfortunate" and that the failure of recent decades to conform to the model had made it "a bit silly" by 1972 and "ludicrous by the 1980s." The unique New Deal experience could not accurately be turned into a general electoral theory.[29] Others expressed similar views as to the nontransferability of the traditional realignment model or of its inapplicability to recent developments.[30] The question was whether realignment theory should be revised or jettisoned. Two proposed modifications suggested that the realignment concept had acquired assumed characteristics that were not existent at the creation. One was the criterion of party identification. To be sure, this was added early by way of Angus Campbell and the Michigan School. But as some 1980s analysts saw it, electoral returns were superior to party-identification data as reflections of realignment. Republicans had dominated presidential elections since 1968 even as party identification had changed only glacially. Yet governmental control was set by voters in elections rather than by respondents in surveys.[31] Arguably even more important was the association of realignment theory with cyclical patterns, a linkage that was not part of the original concept and yet was widely assumed to be an integral element of realignment theory. It, too, was early connected to realignment theory and became pervasive as anticipation mounted in the late 1960s and early 1970s that the cyclical moment for realignment had arrived. Yet if realignment was seen in largely exogenous terms—that is, propelled by crises outside the political system—the cyclical addendum could be viewed as so much excess baggage. There was no reason to assume that a Civil War or a Great Depression would arrive on a cyclical schedule.[32]

The most widely held alternatives to realignment theory in the 1980s were dealignment, retrospective voting, or an amalgam of the two, even as such explanations were also at times intertwined with that of realignment. Debate continued as to whether 1970s dealignment presaged realignment, as allegedly had occurred historically as part of a "realignment cycle," or whether dealignment was now a secular replacement and substitute for realignment.[33] Paul Allen Beck, himself the prime creator of the notion of a realignment cycle, also contended that dealignment called into question certain verities of realignment theory. Dealignment, he held in 1986, posed a "serious challenge to the role of partisanship assigned by the Michigan Model" since "the Michigan researchers did not foresee the possibility of partisan dealignment" as distinct from realigning and deviating elections.[34] Others believed that the very nature of dealignment precluded realignment. There could be no "standing decision," in the famous terminology of V. O. Key, for the increasing number of independent voters. Lacking deep and widespread party loyalty, ticket splitting and divided government were increasingly to be expected. The "catchword" was electoral "volatility," and the focus was on short-term forces, individual candidates, and the belief that to a great extent each election was episodic.[35] Dealignment also went hand in hand with the idea of retrospective voting. If underlying party loyalties had declined as a factor in voter decision making, then voters were freer to judge officeholders and administrations based on performance. To many analysts, the elections of the 1980s lent themselves ideally to retrospective voting. The voters punished the Democrats for their failures in 1980, and rewarded the Republicans in 1984 and 1988 for perceived success.[36] Retrospective voting was generally presented as an alternative to realignment theory, but the 1980s also brought forth suggestions that retrospective voting could underpin a realignment, even if a performance-based realignment would require theoretical revision as to how realignments occurred.[37]

Retrospective voting theory was further connected to the concept of party identification. For the authors of *The American Voter* and the vast array of political scientists they persuaded, party identification was the highly stable factor that guided the voter decision-making process as regards issues and candidates. If short-term factors drew party identifiers away from their "normal" voting tendency, "deviating" elections could occur. But it took a relatively rare "realigning" election for party loyalties to be widely uprooted and shifted. The newer concept of party identification, building in good measure on the retrospective voting concept, held that party identification was much more malleable than the Michigan School had supposed. In this view, party identification was more subject to short-term factors and therefore less an anchor or standard by which to judge realigning forces than had been believed. Rather, party identification was now increasingly perceived as a performance-based, cumulative tally among voters as to their judgments of the successes or failures of Republicans and Democrats in government. The process of conversion could be ongoing and continuous, rather than an infrequent consequence of wrenching realignment.[38] In reaction, *The American Voter* coauthor Philip E. Converse noted that some early critics of the Michigan party-identification concept had "scoffed at" it. It took years of data, Converse maintained, to demonstrate the distinction between an underlying psychological affinity for a party and actual voting behavior in a given election. The basic question was whether a deviation at the ballot box would then incline the voter away from his traditional party or whether the "homing tendency"—the pull of party loyalty—would more likely prevail given the deviating voter's continuing identification with that party as reported in surveys. Granting that both occurred, Converse held that the latter more often prevailed. Thus, while party identification was not "immutable," it was "durable."[39] Fellow Michigan veteran Warren E. Miller similarly stressed the impact of party identification on short-term factors even as he conceded that policy preference and retrospective judgments of partisan performance could influence party identification itself.[40]

The cyclical theory originated by Arthur M. Schlesinger and still vigorously advocated by, among others, his prolific historian and publicist son Arthur M. Schlesinger, Jr., provided another approach to political analysis in the 1980s. At a time when the national government tacked sharply conservative, the Schlesinger concept provided sustenance to those who hoped to shift directions that their day would come again. Predating realignment theory, which in good part was forged in reaction to cyclical interpretations, statements of Schlesingerian cyclical theory often were intertwined with the putative notion that realignment theory itself was cyclical. Arthur Schlesinger, Jr. himself referred to realignment as "an alternative cyclical interpretation of American political history," one that in his view had lost its relevance in an era of dealignment. Similarly, political historian Richard L. McCormick asserted that realignment theory accorded with Schlesinger's "own view of the cyclical course of American politics." Political scientist Samuel P. Huntington considered realignment and reform to be "closely intertwined" and suggested also that the realignment "process" was different from, but possibly related to, the "reform cycle" associated with the Schlesingers. (Huntington had his own concept of long cycles, highlighted by eras of "creedal passion," but he did not include the New Deal era, which engendered realignment theory, as well as a great burst of reform, among them.) Political scientist Andrew S. McFarland compared Schlesinger's concept with the realignment "cyclical theory" of politics created by "V. O. Key and . . . others," which was correct with respect to others. Further, he held, Schlesinger's theory revolved around changes in the political agenda, a notion that was indeed consistent with that aspect of realignment theory.[41] Certainly there was no paucity of proclamations by Schlesinger of a coming reform era. Thus, in 1980 he noted that the country was currently in the conservative "phase of the cycle," but that a swing to reform was "bound to come, and soon." In 1984 he expected a revival of the reform cycle "in the late 1980s or early 1990s." In 1986 he suggested that, as with the Civil War era, the intensity of 1960s reform had triggered an unusually long period of reaction and that a new reform era should begin around 1990. In 1987 he saw signs of cyclical change in the making and in 1991 he was sure that a new reform wave would appear by 1996.[42] Thus, the Schlesinger concept was applied flexibly, with dates of conservative and reform ascendancy open to rearrangement and subject to "novelties," facilitating evasion of the charge—faced by realignment theory in its cyclical manifestation—that the turn of the cycle had not come on schedule. The turn could be postponed.[43]

The Schlesingers' cyclical theory, however, like realignment theory, ran into difficulty in the 1980s due to factors beyond timing. Much as some 1980s political developments did not appear to square with elements of realignment theory, so, too, aspects of the Reagan era seem incongruent with the cyclical theory of reform and conservatism. In the Schlesinger formulation, reform was both activist and secularly dominant. Reform eras were periods of galvanizing energy and lasting impact; conservative eras were typically passive. Reform would give way to conservatism, but conservatism would not undo the basic advances of reform. Thus, as the Schesingers put it, the appropriate metaphor was a spiral—one scholar preferred a ratchet—in the sense that the advances of reform eras were cumulative. The Reagan administration seemed to call this formulation into question; its activism was manifest and its impact appeared to have long-run potential. As Arthur Schlesinger, Jr. allowed in 1986, the identification of "conservatism with the status quo" fit Coolidge and Eisenhower, but was dubious with regard to Reagan, who "was in his own way a reformer."[44] Suggestively, political scientists Erwin C. Hargrove and Michael Nelson altered their theory of "presidential policy cycles" during the Reagan era. "Empowering" elections, they had held, opened the way to presidencies of "reform" such as those of Woodrow Wilson, Franklin Roosevelt, and Lyndon Johnson. But in 1985 they changed their terminology: Presidencies of reform became "presidencies of accomplishment."[45] Nonetheless, there was a sense by the late 1980s that a long period of conservatism was bound soon to end. Journalist E. J. Dionne and historian Robert McElvaine both divined an underlying shift in the reform direction.[46] James Sundquist, the scholar of realignment, had also long adhered to a "cyclical or pendulum" theory of political issues and policy and believed in the 1980s that conservative ascendancy would give way to reform, just as reform had earlier predictably yielded to conservatism. A new "liberal ascendancy" could come "in the 1990s," he wrote in 1985, "but whether sooner or later, it will surely come at some time."[47]

The lack of cataclysmic transformation along New Deal lines underlay the continued impact during the 1980s of the emphasis on more gradual versions of electoral change. Evidenced here was the continuing influence of the secular realignment idea stemming from V. O. Key as distinct from his critical election concept. The changes dating to the 1960s, proponents held, could best be accounted for by incremental, continuous movement, rather than by quick, dramatic upheaval.[48] The single most influential extension and development of this approach was that of "issue evolution" advanced by Edward G. Carmines and James A. Stimson in a series of articles culminating in a 1989 book. Their ideas had an impact upon, among others, Thomas and Mary Edsall's analysis in *Chain Reaction*. A theory of realignment based on critical elections, they held, derived originally from the peculiarities of the New Deal transformation, overestimated the impact of brief periods of dramatic upheaval, while underestimating the cumulative impact of more gradual change. They, on the other hand, posited an "evolutionary model of partisan change . . . consistent with Key's notion of secular realignment." Carmines and Stimson, explicitly alluding also to the approaches of Schattschneider and Sundquist, stressed the impact of issues and ideology on electoral shifts. At times issues become so powerful and enduring, they held, combining "great salience and longevity" with electoral shifts, as "to define the party system." An "aging party alignment," such as that of the New Deal after a quarter-century, increasingly lacked emotional hold, as the period that gave birth to it receded and inheritance replaced experience. In such circumstances, a new dominant issue could emerge. "The struggle over race," reaching its greatest intensity at mid-decade in the 1960s, wrote Carmines and Stimson, "permanently rearranged the American party system." That period of intensity—what they labeled a "critical moment"—initiated a gradual reorientation of the electorate along different issue lines and accounted for the break in politics dating to that time.[49]

An additional secular idea was that of a political "order" or what in time became known as a "regime." Here the notion was not cyclical, nor was it realignment in the traditional sense. Rather, elaborating the idea that American history had been characterized by successive "party systems," it suggested that politics was characterized by sequential eras, each with its own particular logic, encompassing issues, ideology, public policies, electoral patterns, and institutional arrangements.[50] In a version developed by British political scientist Byron E. Shafer, this concept paralleled realignment theory in that it posited a point of discontinuity and a distinctive new time frame. It also shared a stress on issues with Carmines and Stimson, as well as with realignment theorists such as Schattschneider and Sundquist. In Shafer's formulation, the election of 1988 confirmed the existence of a new order dating back to the mid- and late 1960s. In Shafer's view the new political order had not been propelled by a "classical realignment"; rather, "a break without a realignment produced the modern electoral era." What emerged was not a realignment, but "a different type of electoral order" whose "moving force . . . was a new issue structure" and whose durability was evident after two decades. The notion of a new political order, Shafer tellingly argued, also trumped the dealignment explanation of post-1960s politics. Dealignment could not account for the pattern that did exist: a Democratic stranglehold on the House of Representatives coupled with Republican dominance of the presidency. Democratic strength was due to the continued support among the electorate, in Shafer's account, for governmental social programs. A Democratic House served as their guarantor. But GOP presidential ascendancy reflected public support for that party's positions on matters of cultural concern and foreign policy. An electorate with different majorities on different issue clusters thus resulted in a new political order characterized by divided government, one in place by the late 1980s—except for the Watergate "fluke" of Carter's presidency—for two decades.[51]

The most central 1980s thrust at revising realignment theory to meet political reality was that centered on the role of policy and leadership. Already underway via 1970s revisionism, the election of 1980 and the subsequent Reagan era further fueled this effort. Proponents of this rearranged view of realignment held that the standard version focused too heavily on the electorate. A rejection of a failed or unacceptable leader could lead to decisive victories by opponents, which in turn opened the way to major public policy initiatives not necessarily endorsed by the voters. Further, leadership ability, it was held, would determine whether or not the opportunity opened would proceed to realignment. In that sense, realignment was a two-way street. An election opened the possibility of realignment, but only successful leadership could exploit that possibility.[52] As two 1983 analysts put it, leadership decision making constituted "one of the important forces determining . . . partisan alignment." They thus countered the notion that partisan alignments were "largely dependent upon slow demographic changes or dramatic crises" in favor of a greater stress on the impact of political leadership on "partisan strength."[53] Applicability to Reagan's role was clear and George Bush's victory in 1988 appeared to solidify the GOP's "electoral lock" on the presidency shaped by his predecessor. Talk of a presidential realignment abounded. But obviously the Republicans had not become the majority party as traditionally defined. Thus, at decade's end, debate continued as to whether realignment theory remained useful in a revised version or whether it should be cast aside in favor of other modes of political analysis and explanation.

Chapter Thirteen

Divergent Scenarios

The 1990s began with widely divergent expectations. One view, in the wake of a third straight Republican presidential victory in 1988, was that of a GOP electoral lock on the presidency. A second focused on the possibility of a significant shift toward the Democrats. Leading the way for the second approach was Kevin P. Phillips, the now disillusioned prophet of the emerging Republican majority, but as always an analyst inclined to see epochal change in the offing. In *The Politics of Rich and Poor* (1990) and in related and subsequent efforts, Phillips once again set the stage for controversy, notoriety, and an effort at a prophetic second coming. As early as 1984 he agreed that "an era of activism" was "overdue," although he professed "mystery about just what forces" would "produce one."[1] By 1990 he had found his answer, one similar to, yet different from, that of 1969. The trigger would once again be middle-class resentment, but it would now be economic, rather than cultural, and would redound to the benefit of the Democrats rather than the GOP. With decay of the Republican presidential ascendancy dating to 1968, with resentment of the "Park Avenue–Palm Beach" Republicanism of George Bush, the Democratic Party once again had its chance. Republican dominance in the 1980s, in ways comparable to the 1920s and the Gilded Age of the late nineteenth century, Phillips contended, constituted a "capitalist heyday" with its upward redistribution of income and disregard for the needs and concerns of average citizens. As in the two earlier instances, Phillips suggested, resentment could lead in a cyclical fashion to a new era of reform—comparable to the Progressive era of the early twentieth century and to the New Deal. What was needed to detonate the growing resentment was an economic downturn. The recession of the early 1990s and the Democratic victory in 1992, Phillips believed, lent sustenance to this thesis.[2]

The Politics of Rich and Poor, like *The Emerging Republican Majority* more than two decades earlier, brought forth a torrent of often polarized commentary albeit with a partisan and ideological inversion. Phillips's new book was widely viewed as a blueprint for a new era of Democratic and reform ascendancy, all the more potent because its author was commonly identified as a conservative Republican analyst.[3] On the other side of the political divide came cries of betrayal and scorn. *The Politics of Rich and Poor*, it was countered (correctly), lacked the detailed demographic electoral analysis of *The Emerging Republican Majority*. Further, critics from the right contended, Phillips's record as a political prophet had not been nearly as impressive in the 1980s as in the Nixon era. Finally, the new Phillips was dismissed as "frantic," "carping," "whining," huffing and puffing, "trying to spread hatred of the rich."[4] More substantively, it was held that what the Democrats needed was not resentment based on income distribution, but rather a recession under GOP management; perhaps, suggested Garry Wills, only an "economic collapse on the scale of 1929" would do.[5] Phillips, of course, believed that a recession would help the political reversal he projected. Most critical was the question of whether economically fueled resentment could overcome the racially and culturally fueled resentment of the Democrats dating back to the 1960s. The very voters most susceptible to an economic and class appeal, it was noted, were also those most impacted by the racial and cultural upheaval that had benefited the GOP at the Democrats' expense.[6] This case was made most vigorously by Thomas Byrne Edsall, whose own *Chain Reaction* was scheduled for early release even as he reviewed *The Politics of Rich and Poor*. Edsall took note of Phillips's "remarkable political and intellectual journey," which had led the latter from the Nixon White House to advocacy of an "uprising against the . . . coalition that his own tactics helped to put in place." But Edsall suggested that Phillips's case reflected, of all things, naiveté, especially in the apparent belief that economic issues would "supersede questions of culture, ethnicity, and race." Phillips failed "to take into account the continuing power of race," the very ingredient he had emphasized "in his masterwork, *The Emerging Republic Majority*." Nor did Phillips in *The Politics of Rich and Poor* provide the analytical electoral underpinning that was the great strength of his 1969 opus. Racial divisions, Edsall concluded, continued to constitute "an enormous obstacle to a revival" of progressive reform. Only a recession would add plausibility to the new Phillips scenario.[7]

Phillips continued to espouse a cyclical notion of politics. But his cyclical notion was no longer systematically linked to realignment theory. Rather, as some commentators observed, it was similar to the Schlesingers' notion of alternating periods of conservatism and reform.[8] In early 1993 Phillips penned lines that could have come from an acolyte of the cyclical theory of reform. The economic conditions of the early 1990s, he held, had "provoked political turmoil unequaled" since 1933; and "not since Franklin Roosevelt" had "a president so boldly challenged the nation's financial and economic elites" as did Bill Clinton. The "battle to reverse . . . the 1980s" was "unlikely to be more than partially successful," Phillips allowed. The new president's "efforts could bog down." But they were "just beginning."[9] Phillips's *Arrogant Capital* of 1994 rehashed many of the ideas about American politics that he had set forth over the previous quarter-century.[10] At least one conservative critic saw the new book as "a frantic attempt to call back the big bet Phillips placed on Bill Clinton" in 1993.[11] Like Phillips, Arthur Schlesinger, Jr. also saw a new era of reform underway. In 1990 Schlesinger alluded to the belief of "the astute conservative analyst Kevin Phillips . . . that a new liberal phase" was approaching. In 1992 Schlesinger held that the tide was "plainly turning" in a "revulsion against the values and policies of the Reagan years." Following the 1992 election he declared "the epoch dominated by Reaganism . . . at an end" in keeping with the cyclical "rhythms of American politics."[12] Schlesinger, to be sure, applied his father's theory elastically, altering the historical and projected ends and beginnings of liberal and conservative eras.[13] Fellow historian Leo P. Ribuffo saw it rather differently in 1994. Perhaps, he suggested, great reform epochs were merely "historical aberrations rather than periodic turns in a Schlesingerian cycle of reform and reaction."[14] From a liberal reform perspective, certainly, the rosy scenarios of 1992 gave way to gloom in the wake of the election of 1994.

The magnitude of the rejection of George Bush's reelection bid in 1992 was sobering to those who had envisioned a continuing GOP lock on the presidency. The combined effect of recession and time, it seemed, had trumped the cultural issues dating to the 1960s.[15] To those who saw the 1992 election as affording a break with the Reaganite past, Clinton in 1993 had an opportunity to forge a new era of progressive reform and Democratic ascendancy. If he could push through a legislative package focused on health care, education, and training, the thinking ran, the Democrats could once again, as in the days of Roosevelt and Truman, reap the support of an American working and middle class that saw government as a benefactor. Or, if unable to make a huge breakthrough, Clinton, it was speculated, might at least push an agenda that would pave the way for a future era of reform achievement and Democratic electoral victory.[16] Others were far more dubious, however, viewing Bush's 1992 defeat as a retrospective judgment on the failure to deal with recession rather than an endorsement of Clinton's program. From this perspective, 1992 could be viewed merely as an outcome that deviated from the existent pattern, rather than as a break with either GOP electoral domination of the presidency or the dominance of the Republican agenda. The 1992 GOP defeat was here attributed to short-run factors rather than to any basic partisan or programmatic shift by the electorate. A recession obviously did not pack the same lasting punch as a Great Depression.[17] A third view split the difference. The early 1990s, in this view, witnessed the discrediting of the Reagan agenda just as the traditional Democratic agenda had been discredited in 1968 and 1980. The 1992 election put a minority Democratic president in the White House without expanding the Democrats' base of support among the electorate. It remained to be seen when and if either party could regain partisan or agenda hegemony.[18]

Walter Dean Burnham, in the 1990s the doyen of American electoral analysts, could be expected to provide an analysis of the import of each succeeding election. The election of 1992, he proclaimed, constituted "a landslide vote of no confidence" in the Reagan agenda. Reaganism was now on the "way to the same discard pile" to which traditional liberalism had been sent in 1980. This made "the 1992 election of far more than usual consequence. Rejections of this order of magnitude" had not occurred "very often over the course of American political history." But there was more. And more was less. While Reaganism had been repudiated, the "regime" that had replaced "the New Deal order" dated to 1968. The 1992 decision marked a repudiation of Reaganism, but it did not constitute realignment. In terms of basic voting patterns, not much had changed. Rather than any "radical" change, Burnham classified the 1992 shift—reaching back to Lubell for his phrasing—as "above all a revolt of the moderates," that is, of middle-class voters dissatisfied with the state of the economy. Hence 1992 was by no means 1932; indeed, the GOP even made modest congressional gains in 1992 in sharp contrast to the Republicans' across-the-board debacle of 1932. Further, the South's "secular realignment" toward the GOP continued apace. Thus, in Burnham's view, the 1992 outcome represented "remarkable continuity" with the basic patterns first laid down in 1968. The policies of the Reagan–Bush era were rejected, but the voting alignments of the post-1968 "electoral era" remained essentially in place. Thus, "the electoral regime set up in and after the critical realignment of the late 1960s" had "not yet run its course or been replaced by something basically different." The question remained whether President Clinton could successfully forge a new electoral and policy era or whether an "acceleration" of partisan "decay" would ensue.[19]

The 1994 election—with its huge Republican gains and GOP takeover of both houses of Congress for the first time in four decades—brought forth a plethora of speculation and interpretation in which realignment theory played a central and controversial role. To many analysts the 1994 contest was indeed a "critical election" signaling realignment. The change in partisan strength in

Congress was enormous; the shift between 1992 and 1994 appeared dramatic and decisive; prior GOP success in presidential elections was now equaled by success in congressional races; proof was in place of an intensified conservative ideological and programmatic hegemony.[20] Some of the pronouncements were extraordinary. Political scientist Gary C. Jacobson declared that the 1994 outcome had left the "Republicans in better shape than . . . at any time since the New Deal realignment."[21] Political journalists Dan Balz and Ronald Brownstein proclaimed 1994 "an upheaval reminiscent of the Democratic sweep of 1930 that foreshadowed the coming of Franklin Roosevelt and the New Deal."[22] Veteran political analysts David Broder and Haynes Johnson, reverting to an aquatic terminology long popular in electoral analysis, contended that the 1994 "Republican tide was strong and deep and historic—a tsunami . . . a huge wave" signaling "the most decisive shift in the role and direction of government since . . . Roosevelt and the New Deal."[23] Others preferred Samuel Lubell's astronomical "sun" and "moon" analogy. *Wall Street Journal* political journalist Paul Gigot wrote shortly after the 1994 election that Lubell's was now "the trendiest name in Republican circles." In the wake of 1994, Gigot reported, GOP analysts were now proclaiming "a new Lubellian universe" with the Republicans as "the sun" and the Democrats as "the moon" in terms of ideological and programmatic dominance.[24] Thomas Edsall similarly noted that Lubell had described "the Democratic Party as the energy-generating sun of American politics, and the Republican Party as the moon." Lubell's "sun-moon relationship" between the parties, Edsall declared, had now "been reversed."[25] Historian Ronald Radosh, using another concept developed by Lubell, declared that the Democrats were now the "minority party" and were "likely to remain" such if they did not collapse altogether.[26] And other determinative judgments were rendered. Michael Barone held that the 1994 election went "about as far as any election could" toward proving the invalidity of Schlesingerian cyclical theory.[27] The reaction against Clinton, political journalist Richard Reeves contended, indicated that the power of the cultural issues of the 1960s had not abated.[28]

But as strong as the GOP showing was in 1994, there remained uncertainty among analysts as to what it reflected and portended in terms of realignment theory itself. As some analysts framed it, the 1994 outcome could be seen as the culmination of a long realignment toward the GOP, or it could be seen as "phase one" of a new "'critical election' period."[29] There was widespread agreement that 1994 signaled the final breakthrough in the long Republican march toward ascendancy in the white South. GOP congressional strength in the region now approached earlier presidential strength. This had national implications, lessening Democratic strength overall.[30] Still, the volatility of the switch in sentiment between the 1992 and 1994 elections could also be seen as continued evidence of dealignment. There had been no "cataclysmic event" such as a Civil War or Great Depression prior to 1994 and such events were historically linked to past realignments.[31] No one grappled with such issues more than Walter Dean Burnham. Not too surprisingly, Burnham saw 1994 as an "earthquake," one of those "rare bursts of sweeping convulsive change" characteristic of American politics. The 1994 election "abruptly terminated" the electoral system of "normal" divided government in place since 1968; it was thus distinct from the "great realignment . . . of the 1960s." But in 1994, Burnham acknowledged, there was "no dog barking in the night," no "stress factor" such as recession or war. Nonetheless, "mass discontent with government—a dominant theme of American politics since the beginning of the decade"—lay behind the 1994 outcome. The divided government of 1995 was based on "electoral foundations" quite unlike those of "the classic 1969–93 version." The earlier version reflected the decline of partisanship; 1994 bore "many of the features of a partisan-centered event." True, Burnham allowed, 1994 was a bit early in terms of the usual historical cycle of thirty-plus years since the onset of the last realignment. Still, in Burnham's familiar endogenous analysis, the buildup of the tensions of the socioeconomic system in a constitutional order given to inertia and stasis had again broken through electorally. "Successive electoral and regime orders" were "not overthrown and replaced from nowhere," and this was what 1994 was "about."[32]

Other political analysts very much downplayed the significance of the 1994 election, viewing the electoral patterns as consistent with those in place since the late 1960s and attributing the result largely to short-term factors and therefore subject to reversal. The election of 1994 was not viewed as an endorsement of the conservative Republican agenda.[33] Rather, from this perspective, the 1994 result reflected voter discontent with the perceived state of the economy and with the Clinton administration. An economic recovery was underway, but many voters did not see it or felt that it had not positively impacted them. Moreover, the Clinton administration had believed that its health care initiative would cement middle-class support for its progressive agenda. The failure of the Democratic Congress to pass health care reform legislation was, according to this analysis, a central factor in the electorate's repudiation of the Democrats in 1994. Whether voters favored health care reform or not, the new Democratic administration could be viewed as incompetent and ineffective.[34] As bad as all this was from the Democrats' perspective, the short-term interpretation still provided a measure of hope. Viewing 1994 in realignment terms could augur a generation or more of GOP rule.[35] Seeing the event in more immediate terms suggested the possibility of successful readjustment and a quick comeback.

The easy reelection of President Clinton in 1996 appeared to lend support to the notion that the big GOP triumph in 1994 did not forecast a Republican surge across the boards. On the other hand, the GOP hold on Congress was affirmed. Indeed, Clinton essentially repeated the pattern of his 1992 win, while Republicans repeated the pattern of their 1994 congressional victory. Clinton had now twice broken the GOP domination of presidential elections, bringing erstwhile Democrats back to the party. Given his strength in the North, he would have won even had he not carried a single southern state.[36] But Republicans confirmed their congressional upsurge of 1994. There was no big Democratic rebound. The GOP gains in the South in particular now appeared solid and enduring, consolidating the secular trend to the Republicans.[37] As Walter Dean Burnham put it, except for the presidential contest, "the 1996 election was basically a reiteration of the 1994 outcome." It was, he contended, "a confirming event following a historically rare level of upheaval."[38] Michael Barone similarly stressed the "fundamental" importance of the continuing GOP hold on Congress; it indicated that Republicans represented "a potential majority coalition . . . in presidential as well as congressional contests."[39] Others were inclined to see short-run factors as more determinative of the 1996 election results. Clinton now benefited from voters' perceptions of positive economic conditions; the Republican Congress, as the election approached, dropped confrontation in favor of cooperation with the president on some of the latter's legislative priorities. Indeed, Clinton in 1996 did not repeat his 1992 call for a dynamic reform agenda, and the Republicans pulled back from their sharp-edged conservatism of 1994.[40] From a longer-term, historical perspective, the divided partisan result of 1996 could be viewed as consistent with the norm since 1968. The difference now was that the Democrats controlled the White House and the Republicans ran Congress. Neither could claim "majority-party" status in an era of rough partisan parity.[41]

If Democrats speculated that they were on a reform roll in 1993 only to see their hopes dashed in 1994, and if Republicans saw their conservative "revolution" of 1994 derailed in 1995 and 1996, the remainder of the decade was replete with talk of "moderation" and a move to the "center." Across the nation Democrats and Republicans seemed "to be racing for the center," wrote one analyst on the eve of the 1998 election.[42] But there were different concepts of moderation and different definitions of the nature and whereabouts of the center.[43] From one perspective, Clinton after the debacle of 1994 had skillfully and successfully positioned himself as a moderate in terms of avoiding the excesses of Republicanism, while remaining within the essential parameters established in a conservative era. Here Clinton was compared with the "me-too" Republicans of the 1940s and 1950s who accepted the reforms of the New Deal while promising to be more efficient in their administration. Clinton would smooth out the rough edges of Reaganism, rather than depart from it, much as Labour Party Prime Minister Tony Blair in Great Britain undertook to soften, rather than displace, the conservative legacy of Margaret

Thatcher.[44] On the other hand, it was widely pointed out that Republicans, while maintaining control of Congress in 1998, did so by the skin of their teeth and by moderating their stances and moving toward acceptance of at least a modicum of more positive government. The social and cultural issues so beneficial to the GOP since the 1960s appeared to have largely played out. Similarly, the disputed election of 2000, with its virtual tie in both the presidential and congressional races, could be viewed as a culmination of the political era inaugurated in 1968. It could simultaneously be seen as that era's ideological swan song as Republicans sidestepped 1960s-style social and cultural issues in favor of the more benign rhetoric of inclusion and "compassionate conservatism."[45]

In the politics of stasis of 2000, analysts saw an electoral balance between the parties reminiscent of the late nineteenth century, as well as an increasing degree of partisanship among voters. The even outcome appeared to discredit performance-based retrospective theory: Contrary to the theory's proponents, the boom's high tide did not win the Democrats a decisive endorsement by the electorate. The even balance itself appeared to reflect the cumulative realigning effect of electoral changes dating from the 1960s through the 1990s. Speculation focused on what might break apart the equilibrium and shift the advantage to one party or the other.[46] And nothing could stop speculative analysts from speculating. To the irrepressible Walter Dean Burnham, writing prior to the election, economic tribulations under Republican control could lead in the coming decade to a "political explosion" and a Democratic "progressive realignment."[47] To the wayward Kevin Phillips, the GOP return to power was comparable to the Democratic post-Watergate win of 1976; in each instance the party on the rise secularly saw its opponent "artificially restored." The GOP cycle he had "predicted more than 30 years ago . . . basically ended in 1992"; the 2000 endgame notwithstanding, underlying currents were running in the opposite direction, more so than at any time since 1964.[48] Visions of an "emerging Democratic majority" competed with projections of increasing Republican ascendancy.[49] Such analyses continued to draw—whether in terms of a critical "explosion" or of gradual evolution—on the battered but resilient contributions of realignment theory.

Chapter Fourteen

Realignment in Retrospect

Explanations of electoral change developed in the wake of the upheaval of the 1960s continued into the 1990s, most notably the ideas of dealignment and retrospective voting, often expressed in tandem.[1] This amalgam constituted the strongest challenge to realignment theory or to a secular concept of any kind, an "alternative" to the "realignment hypothesis" as Morris P. Fiorina put it. Further, the divided government of recent decades had become the norm, it was argued; due to dealignment and retrospective voting, across-the-board partisan victories such as those of the 1930s had been rendered highly unlikely. Divided government, indeed, over the course of the 1990s became something of an alternative concept in itself. Rather than realignment theory's notion of the voter's "standing decision" based on partisan affinity, some divided-government analysts contended that the phenomenon could be seen as reflective of the conscious decision of a small, but significant, number of voters to split their tickets. For policy or ideological reasons, such voters opted for one party for the presidency and the other for Congress. Here was an echo, revised and reconstituted, of V. O. Key's discerning "switchers" of *The Responsible Electorate*. Yet, unlike Key's switchers, who could often retrospectively punish failure and reward success in the context of one-party control of both executive and legislative branches, it was acknowledged that a norm of divided government at least somewhat impeded retrospective evaluation: Which party should be punished or rewarded when both had a share of power and responsibility? Moreover, critics maintained that few voters had the knowledge and sophistication to make so conscious a decision for divided government.[2]

Divided government could also be understood as a defining and continuing characteristic of the realignment dating to 1968–1972. And despite challenges, doubts, and internal divisions, realignment theory continued prominently into the 1990s, still influencing both analysis and strategy. It was, to be sure, widely acknowledged that realignments differed significantly; the New Deal's in particular was deemed exceptional in its transforming impact. Reflective of actual developments of recent decades, analysts were more inclined to think in terms of gradual, secular change than abrupt, dramatic upheaval.[3] Party identification based on voter surveys was often treated as malleable, subject to short-run forces, and therefore not a firm standard against which to measure realignment.[4] Still, veteran Michigander Warren E. Miller contended that the concept did isolate an "enduring" phenomenon and, thus, remained an essentially valid tool by which to separate long- and short-term factors in voter behavior.[5]

The continuance of realignment theory, however, came with a good dose of irony. By the 1990s analysts were as far from 1968 and 1972 as V. O. Key had been from 1928 and 1932 when he first set forth his theory of critical elections. Realignment theory—especially with its cyclical addition attuned to the idea that a new critical election era occurred every thirty or so years—had been applied endlessly to almost every successive presidential election from 1964 through 1988 with, at best, mixed results at the time. But over the course of the 1990s, looking back on what was now widely perceived as an era, analysts reached a degree of convergence and consensus by applying realignment theory to explain changes since 1968. Long-time realignment scholars, such as Warren E. Miller, Walter Dean Burnham, and Everett Carll Ladd, played significant roles in this regard, as did relative newcomers. Thus, what was employed at times as a theory with purported predictive power appeared by century's end to be most useful in the mode in which it began, as a concept to explain political history. Realignment theory, after all, always included the notion that only a time lapse would reveal if realignment had occurred. By the 1990s that time lapse was in place as applied to the electoral consequences and aftermath of the 1960s and with it came the benefit of historical perspective.

Heinz Eulau in 1996 characterized Warren E. Miller as "the major custodian of the evolving Michigan dispensation," and *The New American Voter* of 1996, coauthored by Miller with J. Merrill Shanks, was appropriately dedicated "to Angus Campbell, without whom none of this would have happened."[6] Miller and Shanks set out to explain "why . . . 1968 to 1988" should be "treated as a defining political 'period.'" Compared with the Civil War and the Great Depression, they believed, the "turmoil" of the era from Lyndon Johnson to George Bush "was more diffuse and chronologically dispersed but no less important as a watershed in national presidential politics." In their interpretive schema Miller and Shanks undertook to encompass the "secular realignment" of the white South toward Republicanism dating to the 1960s, the years of "so-called partisan dealignment" of the 1970s, and the nationwide changes of the

1980s. In their view the patterns of realignment of the 1960s and 1970s involved white southerners rather than white northerners, with the latter group
demonstrating movement toward the Republicans only after the election of
1980. But the "secular" movement "of massive proportions" by white southerners toward a Republican Party identity, "a virtual revolution," seemed "to
be evidence of a classic version of the realignment of partisanship." The decline in partisanship beginning in 1968 and continuing in the 1970s spawned,
Miller and Shanks wrote with Burnham in mind, a sometimes "hyperbolic"
and "frenetic discussion." But the "apparent dealignment" of the time was mis-
construed in their view. It was "limited in magnitude" largely to the new generation of voters and was due to the "immediate impact" of the tumultuous
"events of the late 1960s and early 1970s." Finally, the 1980s witnessed a
"limited national realignment," which reduced the Democrats' historic lead in
party identification to the benefit of the Republicans, although the chance of a
fuller breakthrough was lost during the Bush presidency.[7]

Miller, as had long been the case with Michiganders, viewed Walter Dean
Burnham in adversarial terms. But Burnham's basic take on the post-1968 era
as expressed in the 1990s was by no means wholly unlike Miller's. It also
managed, for example, to encompass dealignment within realignment, albeit
along different lines. Burnham had long veered between the notion that partisan decomposition was a secular trend that would negate future realignments
and the idea that it was an integral and defining part of the latest realignment.
In the 1990s he confirmed the latter conclusion, melding his latest observations into his continuing analysis. He was quite scornful of political analysts
(especially those who were also political historians) who stressed short-run
factors in accounting for electoral behavior. He added the updated notion of a
political "regime order" to his analytical lexicon and granted the need further
to augment "first-generation" realignment theory with accounts of elite activity and policy change. He reaffirmed his basic concept that realignments were
endogenous and historically cyclical, reflecting the tension between a dynamic
socioeconomic order and a straitjacketed constitutional system. Importantly,
however, he stressed that different historical realignments also differed in sub-
stance. Thus, he contended that the New Deal realignment "was in a class by
itself" and that "the historically concrete ways in which . . . bursts of . . .
change" manifested themselves differed "over time." Further, he held, realignments need not be "partisan events," but could involve "other reorgani-
zations of the political landscape." Partisan realignments might "have become
extinct," but this did not "mean that all possible types of . . . realignment" had
"ceased to exist." Notably, the "realignment of . . . 1966–72" was characterized by the lessening role of partisan attachments and organizations. Hence, in
"the strange case of the missing realignment of 1968," the realignment was

"not missing after all." It involved not the anticipated partisan upheaval, but rather an upheaval resulting from partisan decline, and its consequence was a new era of "normal" divided government.[8]

Everett Carll Ladd, who had at times battled with Burnham (and with himself) over the utility of realignment theory, settled into a position comparable to that of his erstwhile adversary as to the existence, nature, and meaning of the post-1968 political era. As Ladd saw it, "the sequence of elections that began in 1968" constituted a discrete historical epoch (although unlike Burnham he saw 1994 as a continuation of, rather than a break with, that epoch). Where realignment theory had gone wrong, he held, was with the Lubellian corollary that a new era required a changed majority party. This was based too rigidly on the New Deal model, which had "for decades . . . mesmerized" political analysts and made "realignment . . . virtually synonymous" with a new or altered majority coalition. But history demonstrated that "each of the country's . . . realignments followed its own course." Indeed, one of the distinctive elements of the period since the 1960s was the very lack of a pervasive majority party. Efforts to ascertain a new majority blocked "attention to other transformations . . . of comparable sweep and consequence," notably the dealignment and divided government that to Ladd characterized the post-1968 "realignment." Current patterns differed "from the New Deal's more than the latter differed from the preceding Republican era's"; indeed, in some respects the "major political realignment" of recent decades could be deemed "the single largest . . . shift" in American history. Ladd's revived use of the realignment concept and term, he now explained, related to "realignment as major transformation of the party and election system" as distinct from "realignment in the 'critical elections'" and "'sun' and 'moon' . . . New Deal" mode.[9]

Secular interpretive schemes set forth as alternatives to realignment theory often ended up looking very much like versions of realignment theory itself. One such example was that of a political "regime," an "order" stretching across an era and encompassing electoral behavior, ideological attachment, and public policy. Stephen Skowronek and Karen Orren, for example, critical of the "behaviorally oriented" realignment theorists for undervaluing the importance of institutions, sought a more inclusive concept. Focusing on the presidency, Skowronek discerned a "recurring establishment and disintegration of . . . political regimes" across time; but he provided only a limited revision of the usual realignment era dates and in his presidential typology, one might perceive at least a faint resemblance to realignment theory's electoral typology. He explicitly noted his indebtedness to Burnham's work on the "realignment synthesis"; and, indeed, two commentators saw in Skowronek's configuration a "cyclical view of American political development" akin to Burnham's.[10] Of particular note here was David Plotke's 1996 study of a New Deal "Democratic political order" shaped in the 1930s and 1940s and ending in the late 1960s and early 1970s. In Plotke's view, as in Lubell's decades earlier, the consolidation of the "Democratic political order," the dominance of the New Deal's Democratic Party, was evidenced by Truman's 1948 victory. As Lubell had argued at the time, Plotke now contended that "the main story of American politics in the late 1940s was Democratic persistence," that the "central" aspect of the late 1940s was confirmation of "the key political . . . shifts of the 1930s." Democratic voters in 1948 had acted "mainly out of political commitment to a new regime." In developing his concept of a "regime" or "order," Plotke undertook to critique the Michigan concept of party identification. What Democratic voters identified with, he held, was not the party, but the New Deal ideas, issues, policies, and programs linked to the party as part of a "broader political order." It was misleading of the Michigan School "to blur the distinction between identification with the regime and with the party, and then consider both attachments as 'partisan' in a narrower party sense." But it hardly seemed incompatible with the Michigan approach to hold that "many people voted for the Democratic Party as a way to approve crucial elements of recent Democratic administrations" and that support for the party reflected "support for the Democratic order."[11] After all, Angus Campbell and his associates were focused on a Democratic Party as it had emerged out of the realigning crucible of the 1930s. When they spoke of party, it came with the same essential associations that Plotke defined as an "order." Similarly, the notion of an "order" appeared to have many of the elements of Samuel Lubell's "sun," that is, of a politically and programmatically dominant majority party. It also appeared to echo E. E. Schattschneider's emphasis on the importance of issue agendas in party allegiance. Plotke further contended that while realignment theory remained "descriptively useful," it did "not come close to grasping the dynamic and powerful political action required to give potential electoral change an enduring political meaning." It very much downplayed "the role of active political leadership." It did not have the power of "a regime perspective in analyzing change in American politics."[12] But going back even to V. O. Key's efforts to integrate voting-behavior analysis into analyses of political and governmental processes and certainly proceeding into later efforts to incorporate elites and leadership into a more comprehensive realignment theory, it did not appear that Plotke added much that was not there before. The notion of a "regime" or "order" thus appeared to provide a new name for what was essentially a broadened realignment concept.

Much the same point may be made about Sean Q. Kelly's notion of "punctuated change" advanced in 1994. As Kelly saw it, realignment theory was "developed to explain and predict the operation" of a political system based on strong partisan ties and parties and constituted "a useful analytical paradigm" in that context. Realignment theory, however, Kelly contended, provided "little insight into" an "era of divided government." He suggested as a more encompassing "alternative to the realignment perspective" the "theory of punctuated change." But Kelly's concept of punctuated change appeared not all that different from realignment theory, especially from realignment theory as applied in the 1990s to the post-1968 era. American history, Kelly maintained, was marked by "political eras with well-defined electoral characteristics and policy agendas, punctuated by compressed periods of rapid transformation" leading to new eras, most recently that of divided government with its own "unique institutional and policy dynamics." Kelly agreed that realignment theory also suggested "a dimension of transformative political change," yet contended that it was the concept of punctuated change that removed "the blinders from . . . political analysts" geared to "a theory of realignment." Such was the case, Kelly continued, because realignment theory dictated "a search for repetition of historical patterns and regularities in timing," whereas the theory of punctuated change focused on developments that were "not necessarily replicable." Certainly realignment theory had been hampered by the added corollary of cyclical regularity, but equally certainly, realignment theory as applied to the era of divided government focused on its distinctions, indeed holding that the distinctions constituted the realignment. Kelly, however, tellingly pointed out that the divided government era had "a unique policy dynamic" in that it could not "provide a coherent agenda for policy change." In this respect the era of divided government departed from earlier eras of punctuated change—or realignment.[13] And Kelly's point drew into question Burnham's endogenous concept of realignment. If realignment manifested the tension between the nation's socioeconomic and governmental systems leading to periodic breakthroughs to address backlogged problems, what kind of breakthrough could an era of divided government, magnifying the constitutional separation of powers, be expected to provide?

Other efforts similarly displayed a degree of convergence between realignment theory and alternative secular explanations. Byron Shafer, for example, posited an era of divided government dating from the 1960s, as did the likes of Burnham and Ladd. Shafer viewed the 1990s switch to a Democratic president and a Republican Congress as merely a variation of the continuing pattern.[14] Alexander P. Lamis, alluding to what he styled the "'twenty-five years' realignment" from 1964–1965 to 1988–1989, held that the developers of the theory of "issue evolution" and others had basically just substantiated "years later" the essential point that Samuel Lubell had made in *The Hidden Crisis in American Politics* of 1970. Lubell, he wrote, in his discussion of the impact of racial conflict on the New Deal coalition had contemporaneously "captured the essence of what was happening."[15] Political journalists Dan Balz and Ronald Brownstein pointed out in 1996 what Lubell had noted both historically and as a characteristic of the 1950s, that there had been earlier eras of divided government, notably that of the late nineteenth century.[16] While most analysts dated the modern era of divided government from 1968, others pushed it back into the 1950s.[17] Ironically, the author of a recent study of the 1948 election—which provided the critical stimulus to the development of realignment theory—viewed the late 1940s as the beginning of the era of partisan decline. That, Harold I. Gullan concluded, and not Truman's victory, made "1948 a watershed in American political history."[18] A comprehensive recent analysis of the nature of modern electoral change, tracing it to the 1950s and encompassing both dealignment and realignment, was provided in 1996 by David G. Lawrence in *The Collapse of the Democratic Presidential Majority*. There had not been a "full-blown" or "classic realignment" after 1968, wrote Lawrence. The Democrats drastically declined as a force in presidential elections, yet they largely maintained their hold on Congress. Dealignment theory, however, failed to account for the realignment-like dominance of the GOP in presidential elections. In Lawrence's schema, two "minirealignments," one dating from the late 1940s and the other beginning in the late 1960s, resulted in a GOP advantage in presidential elections, while dealignment prevented that advantage from being translated into corresponding congressional gains.[19]

Richard G. Niemi and John H. Aldrich in 1996 held that rapid and enduring change "in a broad range of crucial political variables" constituted the most critical factor in moving from one "party system" to another. The "critical-election era in the 1960s," they contended, inaugurated a new party system. The "massive alterations" of the 1960s became the norms of the 1970s and 1980s. The process was "unlike previous realignments, but all such periods" were "in some ways unique," for "each new critical era" established "patterns . . . unlike the old," requiring "analysis and interpretation of their own." Yet they hedged as to usefulness of "realignment" as a term encompassing the essential features of what had happened. Elections that led to "a new party system" might "constitute a 'realignment,' in which the minority party" became "a majority" as in the 1930s. But changes could also "be realized as fundamental shifts in partisan institutional arrangements," and for this reason, they preferred "the more general term . . . 'critical era.'"[20] They thus appeared to equate realignment with changed majority-party status. But Niemi, writing with Herbert F. Weisberg in 1993, allowed for a somewhat different terminological take. It could be contended, Niemi and Weisberg observed, that "past realignments were not all the same," and hence, there was no reason to assume that a 1960s realignment would "mirror" that of the 1930s. Political analysts geared to look for a change in majority-party status as proof of realignment could thus fail to realize that the anticipated "realignment . . . had occurred" in different terms. From this perspective "dealignment . . . constituted a realignment."[21]

William G. Mayer in 1995 provided perhaps the clearest statement of the major relevant issues and of the tendency toward convergence. A "decisive, durable break" had occurred in the 1960s, he held, triggered by the upheaval of the time. To those who declared that what transpired was not a realignment because it differed too much from earlier patterns, Mayer answered that alternative terms such as "party system" and "electoral era" appeared to involve "little more than the old realignment idea, wrapped in new clothing." Realignment in this sense was "no sooner killed off than it" sprang "back to life." Further, Mayer added, the 1930s realignment pattern need not be taken as the standard for a new realignment, just as the New Deal realignment differed from earlier historical manifestations. In particular, the realignment arising out of the 1960s was characterized (and "stunted") by partisan decline. Still, "the changes of the 1960s did accord with many of the established features of electoral change in the American past" as illuminated by realignment theory. Thus, to Mayer's mind, realignment remained "a useful and valid concept." Much of the controversy over its utility hinged not on substantive disagreement about what had happened since the 1960s, but rather on "thorny and probably unresolvable definitional questions."[22] In that sense, there was concrete and theoretical, if not terminological, convergence in efforts to explain the nature of change since the 1960s.

Coda

The Future of Realignment Theory

Over the past quarter-century a number of obituaries have been written for re-alignment theory. By no means have these postmortems been without merit. They have pointed out a number of flaws and conundrums in the realignment concept as it developed over time. The use of party identification as the definitive means of judging the onset and pace of realignment, for example, led to endless puzzlement and confusion when Democratic Party identification remained dominant through the 1970s, even as Republicans won presidential contests in 1968, 1972, and 1980. But realignment theory in its original in-carnation was based on hard electoral data, rather than self-professed voter party identification. The Michigan School's contribution, it must be said, quickly became an integral part of the fully developed theory of realignment. In other respects, however, realignment theory's difficulties have often been additive and peripheral. Notable in this regard were efforts to fasten cycles to realignment theory, to provide the theory with endogenous underpinnings, and to use the theory for predictive purposes.

The process by which realignment theory became linked to cycles is replete with irony. Realignment theory was born in revolt against the theory of rela-tively short cycles developed especially by Louis Bean and the senior Arthur Schlesinger. Samuel Lubell, V. O. Key, and Angus Campbell all explicitly re-jected this version of cyclical theory as they constructed their secular alterna-tive. Key in particular struggled to transcend the cyclical theory he had earlier embraced, a cyclical theory that—in retrospect—had helped to prevent earlier theorists, notably Harold F. Gosnell, from making the breakthrough eventually forged. The election of 1948 provided the electoral underpinning for the intel-lectual breakthrough anticipated, but not realized earlier. The expected swing of the cycle or pendulum to the Republicans did not materialize. There was no President Thomas E. Dewey. The Democrats' triumph was now viewed as something more than a cult of personality around Franklin D. Roosevelt. Realignment theory ensued as a secular as opposed to a cyclical concept. But cyclical theory came in through the back door. Applying realignment theory to history, scholars lighted on 1800, 1828, 1860, 1896, and 1928 or 1932 as critical elections, and behold a cyclical pattern appeared. Critical elections every thirty or so years ushered in a new "party system" to characterize and dominate the political process. No wonder that as the concept spread, the hunt was on in 1964, 1968, and 1972 for the next critical election and swing of the realignment cycle. When the outcomes failed to satisfy all the criteria then deemed characteristic of realignment, it was also no wonder that disillusionment set in. But a cyclical schema was not part of realignment theory as originally designed.

Realignment theory as originally developed was also essentially exogenous. Lubell, Key, and Schattschneider, to be sure, were all much interested in connecting voting-behavior and electoral analysis to broader political and governmental patterns. Lubell as a free-wheeling journalist was just as comfortable discussing the policies of Presidents Roosevelt, Truman, and Eisenhower as he was interviewing voters for the anecdotal material that so enlivened his electoral analysis. Key was forever urging Angus Campbell and others to link voter-behavior analysis to the larger processes of politics and government. Schattschneider added the focus on issues and policy agendas in connection with his quest for a responsible party system. But none of them saw realignment theory in endogenous terms. Each viewed it in an exogenous framework. Electoral upheaval was triggered by external events, by crises—a Civil War, a Great Depression. Changes also flowed from demographic movements. It fell to Walter Dean Burnham to add a critical endogenous element to realignment theory. This was the idea that periodically—cyclically—throughout American history, electoral outbursts had occurred as a means of energizing a constitutionally straitjacketed government to deal with accumulated problems and grievances. There is no gainsaying that Burnham's endogenous notion was brilliant and insightful. But, like the cyclical element per se, it added a mechanistic element to realignment theory. Indeed, when applied in tandem with cyclical theory, it ran the risk of turning an illuminating idea into a deterministic impediment. It is one thing to see the constitutional system as making dynamic policy change difficult in the absence of an unquestioned electoral mandate; it is something else to posit that the constitutional system underlay the eruption of that mandate at regular cyclical intervals. Burnham himself kept looking for an exogenous "triggering" crisis to set off an electoral explosion, demonstrating that the endogenous element still needed an external stimulus.

Realignment theory further suffered when it was utilized as a predictive device. The theory began its career as an effort to explain the recent past. Samuel Lubell fastened on a catchy title with *The Future of American Politics*, but his real mission was to explain the origins and course of the Roosevelt coalition, while speculating about its present and prospective state. V. O. Key focused on decades-old contests as he developed his critical election concept. Realignment theory came originally with historical perspective and was based originally on the statistical data of past electoral results. But the concept proved to be too intriguing, suggestive, and indeed fascinating to be left to political historians and historically oriented political scientists. Especially as linked to cyclical theory, and particularly as it made its way into the realm of commentators and political strategists, realignment theory became the plaything of quadrennial contests. Hence, 1964 was thirty-six years after 1928; 1968 was thirty-six years after 1932. Was not a critical election due? Was not an electoral realignment to be expected? But who could say when a triggering element of sufficient magnitude might occur. Civil Wars did not recur cyclically. A Great Depression was not predictable in 1929. The turmoil of the 1960s was but dimly seen as the decade began. The hindsight available to Lubell and Key in looking back at the 1930s was obviously absent amidst the confusion of 1968 and 1972. In retrospect a realignment of sorts did begin at that time, but it was hardly the kind of realignment predicted. Nor did the association of party identification with realignment help in this regard. Elections were held at two- and four-year intervals. Surveys of voters to determine changes in party identification could be done virtually at will. The temptation of on-the-spot realignment analysis and speculation was irresistible.

Realignment theory has obviously been most credible and successful when applied retrospectively. As developed by Key, it postulated that only in the fullness of time would it be evident whether any given election was critical. The big win of Lyndon Johnson and the Democrats in 1964 at the time was indeed defined by some analysts as realigning. It was quickly overwhelmed and undone by the turmoil of the 1960s. Only after two decades and more did a consensus of sorts develop as to the nature and meaning of the political upheaval centered on the 1964–1972 period. Political prophecy and instant analysis are both tempting and unavoidable. But realignment theory by its very nature is longitudinal, and it takes historical time to make considered judgments as to just when a durable political disjuncture occurs and what its essential characteristics are. History by its very nature encompasses continuity and change. Realignment theory remains of value historically because it focuses upon and illuminates the recurrence of discontinuity and its unfolding, whether relatively abruptly or gradually, in the electoral process. But too rigid and mechanical a concept of realignment theory obscures the differing characteristics of different disjunctures and their ramifications over time, as has been increasingly recognized and acknowledged by scholars. Surely, in terms of the events from which Key originally proceeded, the disruptive force of the Civil War and of the Great Depression and New Deal were of a magnitude not evident elsewhere. The impacts of the 1890s and of the 1960s were great, but of a lesser magnitude. Nor should the commonality of realignments obscure historical differences. The Civil War realignment brought forth a whole new party; the New Deal reversed majority parties. The 1890s moved from partisan parity to GOP dominance, the 1960s from Democratic dominance to divided government. Successful administrations in the first three chronological instances may have consolidated realignment. Failed presidencies in the last instance, both Democratic and Republican, may have fed the disillusionment that fused realignment with dealignment. The Civil War era and the New Deal engendered bursts of seminal policy accomplishment. The 1890s ushered in the Progressive era, but that era's most significant burst of national reform accomplishment did not come until 1913–1916. The great policy accomplishments of the 1960s came at mid-decade, antedating the upheaval of 1968–1972.

Even as a rough gauge, historic realignment chronologies should make contemporary electoral analysts circumspect about too quick a judgment. Realignments historically have been engendered by an extended period of upheaval, not just a year or two. The upheaval of the Civil War lasted four years; add Reconstruction and it lasted a dozen more. The 1890s depression stretched from 1893 to 1897 and was preceded by years of agrarian unrest. The Great Depression was three years old when FDR defeated Hoover; the New Deal's politics of upheaval continued for another six years. The 1960s tumult climaxed in 1968, but could be dated from 1963–1965 and lasted into Nixon's first term. If one thinks in piggyback terms, the cultural ferment of the 1960s was followed by the economic traumas of the 1970s; Reagan's 1980 triumph had behind it seven years of stagflation dating to 1973. Thus, at the very least, contemporary analysts, if history is any guide, should not jump to conclusions based on evanescent events or a single election; at the very least, they should think in terms of years of difficulty and distress before contemplating realignment.

While the reach of realignment theory with its added components stretched too far and its exponents' ambitions proved too grandiose, there remains a central paradox: that of cyclical predictability. For realignment of a kind did indeed emerge out of the 1960s, even if it was not the realignment anticipated at the time and became fully clear only in long-term perspective. But it did come, so to speak, on schedule, following the 1860s, 1890s, and 1930s. Assuredly, this apparent regularity of intervals may be deemed, as is contended herein, fortuitous and coincidental. For those who think otherwise, however, and who note the interval since 1968–1972, a new era of realignment speculation beckoned at century's turn. Less cosmically, and more modestly, realignment theory remains useful as a concept, guide, and tool. It should not be treated as the key to the future; nor should it be viewed as a recipe or formula to be discarded if each ingredient or facet of each realigning era fails to fit an allotted slot. The tendency in recent decades to add further ingredients to meet new electoral twists and turns has only added to the confusion. To be sure, important aspects of early realignment theory also proved misleading when it came to the events of the late 1960s and their aftermath. Lubell had indeed seen earlier periods of rough partisan balance, but he had viewed them in terms of an interregnum, believing that realignment would bring a revived or new majority party. The rearrangements of 1968–1972 proved no interregnum or, in Michigan terms, deviation. Angus Campbell's stress on party loyalty as a benchmark of electoral behavior likewise was no guide to the upheaval that emerged out of the 1960s. Still, the kernel of realignment theory as set forth by Key—the focus on durable change in electoral patterns—did fit the new era. Realignment theory thus retains qualities essential to the retrospective analysis of American politics. This in turn assures realignment theory a continuing role in the future of American electoral study.

Notes

CHAPTER ONE

1. Clyde P. Weed, *The Nemesis of Reform: The Republican Party During the New Deal* (New York: Columbia University Press, 1994), 85; Harvey L. Schantz, "Sectionalism in Presidential Elections," in *American Presidential Elections: Process, Policy, and Political Change*, ed. Harvey L. Schantz (Albany: State University of New York Press, 1996), 93–94; Richard J. Jensen, "Historiography of American Political History," in *Encyclopedia of American Political History: Studies of the Principal Movements and Ideas*, ed. Jack P. Greene (New York: Charles Scribner's Sons, 1984), 6–7; Richard Jensen, "American Election Analysis: A Case History of Methodological Innovation and Diffusion," in *Politics and the Social Sciences*, ed. Seymour Martin Lipset (New York: Oxford University Press, 1969), 232, 234–35.

2. Gerald H. Gamm, *The Making of New Deal Democrats: Voting Behavior and Realignment in Boston, 1920–1940* (Chicago: The University of Chicago Press, 1989), 3, 8–10; Jensen, "Historiography of American Political History," 8; Charles A. Beard, *The American Party Battle* (New York: The Book League of America, 1928), 29.

3. Samuel J. Eldersveld, "Theory and Method in Voting Behavior Research," *The Journal of Politics* 13 (Feb. 1951): 70 n.1; Karl A. Lamb, "Plotting the Electorate's Course in Dangerous Waters," *The Political Science Reviewer* 2 (1972): 39 n.1; Albert Somit and Joseph Tanenhaus, *The Development of American Political Science: From Burgess to Behavioralism* (Boston: Allyn and Bacon, 1967), 71–72, 74; Seymour Martin Lipset, "The Political Animal: Genus Americana," *Public Opinion Quarterly* 23 (Winter 1959): 555.

4. Peter H. Rossi, "Four Landmarks in Voting Research," in *American Voting Behavior*, ed. Eugene Burdick and Arthur J. Brodbeck (Glencoe, Ill.: The Free Press, 1959), 10, 13–14, 437 n.9; Jean M. Converse, *Survey Research in the United States: Roots and Emergence, 1890–1960* (Berkeley: University of California Press, 1987), 70.

5. Lipset, "The Political Animal," 555.

6. Stuart A. Rice, *Farmers and Workers in American Politics* (New York: Columbia University Studies in History, Economics, and Public Law, 1924), 7; Stuart A. Rice, "Some Applications of Statistical Method to Political Research," *The American Political Science Review* 20 (May 1926): 313, 323–24; Stuart A. Rice, "The Historico-Statistical

Approach to Social Studies," 1, and Stuart A. Rice, "Statistical Studies of Social Attitudes and Public Opinion," 173, both in *Statistics in Social Studies*, ed. Stuart A. Rice (Philadelphia: University of Pennsylvania Press, 1930).

7. Rice, *Farmers and Workers in American Politics*, 17, 20, 23; Stuart A. Rice, "What Do the Different Party Labels Mean?" *Current History* 20 (Sept. 1924): 904.

8. "Appendix A: Harold D. Lasswell: A Biographical Memoir," in Gabriel A. Almond, *A Discipline Divided: Schools and Sects in Political Science* (Newbury Park, Calif.: Sage Publications, 1990), 291–92; Robert A. Dahl, "The Behavioral Approach in Political Science: Epitaph for a Monument to a Successful Protest," *The American Political Science Review* 55 (Dec. 1961): 763; Martin Bulmer, "Quantification and Chicago Social Science in the 1920s: A Neglected Tradition," *Journal of the History of the Behavioral Sciences* 17 (1981): 320–21; Dorothy Ross, *The Origins of American Social Science* (New York: Cambridge University Press, 1991), 395–96, 452; James Farr, "Remembering the Revolution: Behavioralism in American Political Science," in *Political Science in History: Research Programs and Political Traditions*, ed. James Farr et al. (New York: Cambridge University Press, 1995), 209–11; John G. Gunnell, "Continuity and Innovation in the History of Political Science: The Case of Charles Merriam," *Journal of the History of the Behavioral Sciences* 28 (April 1992): 135, 140.

9. Bulmer, "Quantification and Chicago Social Science in the 1920s," 313, 318–19, 322; Martin Bulmer, *The Chicago School of Sociology: Institutionalization, Diversity, and the Rise of Sociological Research* (Chicago: The University of Chicago Press, 1984), 164–65.

10. Harold F. Gosnell, "Statisticians and Political Scientists," *The American Political Science Review* 27 (June 1933): 392–93, 399, 403; Harold F. Gosnell, "Technique of Measurement," in *Chicago: An Experiment in Social Science Research*, ed. T. V. Smith and Leonard D. White (Chicago: The University of Chicago Press, 1929), 90, 112; Harold F. Gosnell, "Some Practical Applications of Psychology in Government," *American Journal of Sociology* 28 (May 1921): 735, 743.

11. Barry D. Karl, *Charles E. Merriam and the Study of Politics* (Chicago: The University of Chicago Press, 1974), 148; Somit and Tanenhaus, *Development of American Political Science*, 131; Charles Edward Merriam and Harold Foote Gosnell, *Non-Voting: Causes and Methods of Control* (Chicago: The University of Chicago Press, 1924), xiii; Philip E. Converse, "Public Opinion and Voting Behavior," in *Handbook of Political Science*, Vol. 4, *Nongovernmental Politics*, ed. Fred I. Greenstein and Nelson W. Polsby (Reading, Mass.: Addison-Wesley, 1975), 112; Angus Campbell and Homer C. Cooper, *Group Differences in Attitudes and Votes: A Study of the 1954 Congressional Election* (Ann Arbor: Survey Research Center/Institute for Social Research, University of Michigan, 1956), 1; Bulmer, *Chicago School of Sociology*, 169.

12. Merriam and Gosnell, *Non-Voting*, xi, 19, 22.

13. Harold F. Gosnell, *Machine Politics: Chicago Model* (Chicago: The University of Chicago Press, 1937), viii.

14. Converse, *Survey Research in the United States*, 84.

15. Joel H. Silbey, Allan G. Bogue, and William H. Flanigan, "Introduction," *The History of American Electoral Behavior*, ed. Joel H. Silbey, Allan G. Bogue, and William H. Flanigan (Princeton: Princeton University Press, 1978), 10–11; David A. Bositis, "Harold F. Gosnell (1896–)," in *Political Parties and Elections in the United States: An Encyclopedia,* Vol. I, ed. L. Sandy Maisel (New York: Garland Publishing, 1991), 441.

16. Herbert Tingsten, *Political Behavior: Studies in Election Statistics* (London: P. S. King and Son, 1937), 7, 9.

17. V. O. Key to Harry M. Scoble, Jan. 4, 1963, General Correspondence, 1963, A–Z, V. O. Key Papers, Harvard University Archives, Cambridge, Mass.

18. V. O. Key to Samuel Lubell, Jan. 26, 1956, General Correspondence, 1956, A–P, Key Papers.

19. Jensen, "American Election Analysis," 238, 243.

20. "David Truman [Interview]," in *Political Science in America: Oral Histories of a Discipline*, ed. Michael A. Baer, Malcolm E. Jewel, and Lee Sigelman (Lexington: The University Press of Kentucky, 1991), 137–38.

21. Silbey et al., "Introduction," in *History of American Electoral Behavior*, ed. Silbey et al., 11.

22. Paul F. Lazarsfeld, Bernard Berelson, and Hazel Gaudet, *The People's Choice: How the Voter Makes up His Mind in a Presidential Campaign*, Third Edition (New York: Columbia University Press, 1968), 1–2; Walter Berns, "Voting Studies," in *Essays on the Scientific Study of Politics*, ed. Herbert J. Storing (New York: Holt, Rinehart, and Winston, 1962), 4.

23. Eldersveld, "Theory and Method in Voting Behavior Research," 76–77.

24. Peter H. Odegard and E. Allen Helms, *American Politics: A Study in Political Dynamics* (New York: Harper and Brothers, 1938), x; Somit and Tanenhaus, *Development of American Political Science*, 132–33; Charles H. Titus and Joe Bain, "Voting in Tennessee, 1900–1932," *Social Forces* 14 (Dec. 1935): 273, 281, 285; Roscoe E. Martin, "The Municipal Electorate: A Case Study," *The Southwestern Social Science Quarterly* 14 (Dec. 1933): 236.

25. Max Visser, "The Psychology of Voting Action: On the Psychological Origins of Electoral Research, 1939–1964," *Journal of the History of the Behavioral Sciences* 30 (Jan. 1994): 43; Titus and Bain, "Voting in Tennessee," 285; Charles H. Titus, "Voting in California Cities, 1900–1925," *Political and Social Science Quarterly* 8 (1928): 385.

26. James K. Pollock and Samuel J. Eldersveld, *Michigan Politics in Transition: An Areal Study of Voting Trends in the Last Decade* (Ann Arbor: University of Michigan Press, 1942), 1, 3.

27. Dahl, "The Behavioral Approach to Political Science," 763; Bulmer, *Chicago School of Sociology*, xiii; Heinz Eulau, *Micro-Macro Dilemmas in Political Science: Personal Pathways Through Complexity* (Norman: University of Oklahoma Press, 1996), 79, 96; James Farr and Raymond Seidelman, "Introduction [to Part 2]," in *Discipline and History: Political Science in the United States*, ed. James Farr and Raymond Seidelman (Ann Arbor: University of Michigan Press, 1993), 108.

28. Donald Knoke, *Change and Continuity in American Politics: The Social Bases of Political Parties* (Baltimore: The Johns Hopkins University Press, 1976), 1; Hadley Cantril, "The Issue Behind the Issues," *New York Times Magazine*, Oct. 22, 1944, 8, 40; Claude E. Robinson, *Straw Votes: A Study of Political Prediction* (New York: Columbia University Press, 1932), 112–13, 173–74.

29. Stuart A. Rice, *Quantitative Methods in Politics* (New York: Alfred A. Knopf, 1928), 303, 305.

30. Roy V. Peel and Thomas C. Donnelly, *The 1928 Campaign: An Analysis* (New York: Richard R. Smith, 1931), viii, x.

CHAPTER TWO

1. William Starr Myers, "Looking Toward 1932," *The American Political Science Review* 25 (Nov. 1931): 925–26; Edgar E. Robinson, *The Evolution of American Political*

Parties: A Sketch of Party Development (New York: Harcourt, Brace and Company, 1924), 259, 300, 327, 340; Howard R. Bruce, *American Parties and Politics: History and Role of Political Parties in the United States* (New York: Henry Holt and Company, 1927), 118, 122, 130; Robert Stanley Rankin, "The Future of the Democratic Party," *The South Atlantic Quarterly* 28 (July 1929): 225; Edgar Eugene Robinson, "The Decline of the Democratic Party," *The American Journal of Sociology* 20 (Nov. 1914): 315–16; Frank R. Kent, *The Democratic Party: A History* (New York: The Century Company, 1928), 11, 506–7, 512; Robert C. Brooks, *Political Parties and Electoral Problems*, Third Edition (New York: Harper and Brothers, 1933), 114; Silas Bent, "Will the Democrats Follow the Whigs?" *Scribner's Magazine* 86 (Nov. 1929): 474; Frank Kent, *Political Behavior* (New York: William Morrow, 1928), 67–68.

2. Hugh L. Keenleyside, "The American Political Revolution of 1924," *Current History* 21 (March 1925): 839–40.

3. Memorandum from E[mil] Edward Hurja to Louis McH. Howe, Jan. 10, 1933, box 70, Emil Hurja Papers, Franklin D. Roosevelt Library (FDRL), Hyde Park, N.Y.

4. Clyde P. Weed, *The Nemesis of Reform: The Republican Party During the New Deal* (New York: Columbia University Press, 1994), 47, 85–86; Arthur Krock, *In the Nation: 1932–1966* (New York: McGraw-Hill, 1966), 24–25.

5. Elmo Roper, *You and Your Leaders* (New York: William Morrow, 1957), 110; John Harding, "The 1942 Congressional Elections," *The American Political Science Review* 38 (Feb. 1944): 41; Edward G. Benson and Evelyn Wicoff, "Voters Pick Their Party," *Public Opinion Quarterly* 8 (Summer 1944): 165–66; Raymond Clapper, *Watching the World* (New York: Whittlesey House, 1944), 180–81; Irwin Ross, *The Loneliest Campaign: The Truman Victory of 1948* (New York: The New American Library, 1968), 263.

6. Robert T. Bower, "Opinion Research and Historical Interpretation of Elections," *Public Opinion Quarterly* 12 (Fall 1948): 458–59; Charles Hickman Titus, *Voting Behavior in the United States: A Statistical Study* (Berkeley: University of California Press, 1935), 56, 59, 63; "Who Will Win?" *New Republic*, Oct. 7, 1940, 499; O. Douglas Weeks, "The Democratic Victory of 1932," *Arnold Foundation Studies in Public Affairs: Southern Methodist University* 1 (Winter 1933): 7.

7. Frank R. Kent, "The Great Game of Politics," *Baltimore Sun*, April 28, 1940, news clipping in box 15, V. O. Key Papers, John F. Kennedy Library, Boston, Mass.

8. Clapper, *Watching the World*, 180.

9. Peter H. Odegard and E. Allen Helms, *American Politics: A Study in Political Dynamics*, Second Edition (New York: Harper and Brothers, 1947), 565, 824.

10. A. Lawrence Lowell, "Oscillations in Politics," *Annals of the American Academy of Political and Social Science* 12 (July 1898): 70–74, 93; A. Lawrence Lowell, *The Government of England*, Vol. II (New York: The Macmillan Company, 1908), 101–2, 104, 105 n.1.

11. William Bennett Munro, *The Invisible Government* (New York: The MacMillan Company, 1928), 58–62, 79–84.

12. Weed, *Nemesis of Reform*, 85; Edgar Eugene Robinson, *They Voted for Roosevelt: The Presidential Vote, 1932–1944* (Stanford, Calif.: Stanford University Press, 1947; New York: Octagon Books, 1970), v, 8–9, 15, 21; Samuel J. Eldersveld, "The Influence of Metropolitan Party Pluralities in Presidential Elections Since 1920: A Study of Twelve Key Cities," *The American Political Science Review* 43 (Dec. 1949): 1189–90, 1195, 1202–3, 1206; Samuel P. Huntington, "A Revised Theory of American Party Politics," *The American Political Science Review* 44 (Sept. 1950): 677; Wilfred E. Binkley, *American Political*

Parties: Their Natural History, Second Edition (New York: Alfred A. Knopf, 1947), 385, 396; Edward H. Litchfield, *Voting Behavior in a Metropolitan Area* (Ann Arbor: University of Michigan Press, 1941), 1–2; Gerald W. Johnson, "This Strange Campaign," *New York Times Magazine*, July 9, 1944, 11.

13. Stuart A. Rice, *Farmers and Workers in American Politics* (New York: Columbia University Press, 1924), 25, 29; F. Stuart Chapin, "The Variability of the Popular Vote at Presidential Elections," *The American Journal of Sociology* 18 (Sept. 1912): 223, 240.

14. Charles Edward Merriam, *The American Party System: An Introduction to the Study of Political Parties in the United States* (New York: The MacMillan Company, 1922), 27–28, 30.

15. Bruce, *American Parties and Politics*, 148.

16. Kent, *The Democratic Party*, 513.

17. Delbert Clark, "The Parties Sound the Tocsins," *New York Times Magazine*, June 14, 1936, 1; Claude E. Robinson, "Analysis of the Straw Votes: The Roosevelt Tide Assayed," *New York Times*, Oct. 16, 1932, Section 8, 3; "Landslide," *New York Times*, Nov. 8, 1936, Section 8, 1; James A. Farley, *Behind the Ballots: The Personal History of a Politician* (New York: Harcourt, Brace and Company, 1938), 184, 187, 191, 289, 359.

18. Charles A. Beard and Mary R. Beard, *America in Midpassage*, Vol. I (New York: The MacMillan Company, 1939), 148–49, 336–37.

19. Ralph Fletcher and Mildred Fletcher, "Consistency in Party Voting from 1896–1932," *Social Forces* 15 (Dec. 1936): 282–83, 285.

20. "Suggested Outline for Book," enclosed in Stanley High, Memorandum for the President, April 18, 1936, Good Neighbor League Folder, Stanley High Papers, FDRL.

21. Roy V. Peel and Thomas C. Donnelly, *The 1928 Campaign: An Analysis* (New York: Richard R. Smith, 1931), 81, 83.

22. Roy V. Peel and Thomas C. Donnelly, *The 1932 Campaign: An Analysis* (New York: Farrar and Rinehart, 1935), 216–17, 220, 224.

23. W. E. Binkley to Peter H. Odegard, Nov. 30, 1942, box 1, Peter H. Odegard Papers, FDRL.

24. Binkley, *American Political Parties*, 355–56, 395, 397–401.

25. Gerald H. Gamm, *The Making of New Deal Democrats: Voter Behavior and Realignment in Boston, 1920–1940* (Chicago: The University of Chicago Press, 1989), 10.

26. James Kerr Pollock, *Voting Behavior: A Case Study* (Ann Arbor: University of Michigan Press, 1939).

27. James K. Pollock to Samuel J. Eldersveld, Aug. 15, 1942, and Sept. 12, 1942; Samuel J. Eldersveld to James K. Pollock, Sept. 2, 1942; April 25, 1944; June 18, 1944; Sept. 27, 1944; all in box 8, James K. Pollock Papers, Bentley Historical Library (BHL), University of Michigan, Ann Arbor, Mich.

28. James K. Pollock and Samuel J. Eldersveld, *Michigan Politics in Transition: An Areal Study of Voting Trends in the Last Decade* (Ann Arbor: University of Michigan Press, 1942), 2, 15, 28, 35, 43–45, 46 n.5, 63, 65–66.

29. James Reston, *Deadline: A Memoir* (New York: Random House, 1991), 261; James Reston, "Why Forecasts Erred," *New York Times*, Nov. 4, 1948, 28.

30. Austin Ranney to E. E. Schattschneider, Nov. 29, 1948, box 3, E. E. Schattschneider Papers, Olin Library, Wesleyan University, Middletown, Conn.

31. E. E. Schattschneider, "Wartime Political Behavior," c. 1945 ms., 3–4, 7, box 20, E. E. Schattschneider Files, Olin Library, Wesleyan University, Middletown, Conn.

32. "Objectives in Research Concerning the Present Status of Political Parties in the United States: A Preliminary Statement by Elmer E. Schattschneider," c. 1947 ms., 1, box 20, Schattschneider Files.

33. Schattschneider notes on the 1948 election, box 2, Schattschneider Files.

34. Schattschneider notes on Arthur Holcombe, c. 1951, box 2, Schattschneider Files.

CHAPTER THREE

1. "Holcombe, Arthur Norman," *Who Was Who in America*, Vol. VII, *1977–1981* (Chicago: Marquis Who's Who, 1981), 279; Arthur N. Holcombe to Clarence Lohman, June 4, 1937, Personal Correspondence, 1937, Arthur N. Holcombe Papers, Harvard University Archives (HUA), Cambridge, Mass.

2. "Emmette S. Redford [Interview]," 58, and "R. Taylor Cole [Interview]," 70–71, both in *Political Science in America: Oral Histories of a Discipline*, ed. Michael A. Baer, Malcolm E. Jewell, and Lee Sigelman (Lexington: The University Press of Kentucky, 1991).

3. Arthur N. Holcombe to Walter Lippmann, Jan. 31, 1936, Personal Correspondence, 1934–1936, I–Z, Holcombe Papers.

4. Arthur N. Holcombe to Nicholas Roosevelt, Nov. 30, 1936, Personal Correspondence, 1934–1936, I–Z, Holcombe Papers.

5. Arthur N. Holcombe to Henry S. Dennison, Feb. 28, 1934, Professional Correspondence, 1934, Holcombe Papers.

6. Rudolf Heberle, *Social Movements: An Introduction to Political Sociology* (New York: Appleton-Century-Crofts, 1951), 240.

7. Arthur N. Holcombe, *The Political Parties of To-Day: A Study in Republican and Democratic Politics* (New York: Harper and Brothers, 1924), 88–92, 236, 242, 304–6, 310, 348–49.

8. Holcombe, *The Political Parties of To-Day*, 127, 296, 368, 370, 377.

9. Arthur N. Holcombe, *The Middle Classes in American Politics* (Cambridge: Harvard University Press, 1940), 57, 114–15, 117–18; A. N. Holcombe, "The Changing Outlook for a Realignment of Parties," in *The American Political Scene*, Revised Edition, ed. Edward B. Logan (New York: Harper and Brothers, 1938), 283, 286, 288; A. N. Holcombe, *The New Party Politics* (New York: W. W. Norton, 1933), vii, 11, 111; A. N. Holcombe, "American Politics at the Crossroads," in *Facts and Factors in Economic History: Articles by Former Students of Edwin Francis Gay*, ed. Arthur H. Cole et al. (Cambridge: Harvard University Press, 1932), 551–52, 554–55; A. N. Holcombe, *Government in a Planned Democracy* (New York: W. W. Norton, 1935), vii.

10. Heinz Eulau, *Class and Party in the Eisenhower Years: Class Roles and Perspectives in the 1952 and 1956 Elections* (New York: The Free Press, 1962), 8–9; Arthur N. Holcombe to Alfred Bingham, Nov. 26, 1935, Personal Correspondence, 1934–1936, A–H, Holcombe Papers; Arthur N. Holcombe to Sigmund Neumann, Sept. 13, 1935, Personal Correspondence, 1934–1936, I–Z, Holcombe Papers; Arthur N. Holcombe to Yorke Allen, Jr., Oct. 7, 1937, Personal Correspondence, 1937, A–H, Holcombe Papers; Arthur N. Holcombe to Mrs. E. C. Durfee, Jan. 25, 1938, Personal Correspondence, 1938–1939, A–H, Holcombe Papers; Arthur N. Holcombe, *Why We Have Political Parties* (Chicago: The University of Chicago Press [Government Lecture Series No. 9, Delivered May 31, 1932]), 8–9.

11. Arthur N. Holcombe, "Trench Warfare," *The American Political Science Review* 25 (Nov. 1931): 919; Arthur Holcombe to Herbert C. Pell, Dec. 9, 1932, box 9, Herbert C. Pell Papers, Franklin D. Roosevelt Library (FDRL), Hyde Park, N.Y.

12. Arthur N. Holcombe to Edward A. Filene, Nov. 5, 1936, Holcombe Papers, Personal Correspondence, 1934–1936, A–H, Holcombe Papers; Arthur N. Holcombe to Herbert C. Pell, Oct. 17, 1936, and Arthur N. Holcombe to Charles West, Oct. 15, 1936, both in Personal Correspondence, 1934–1936, I–Z, Holcombe Papers.

13. Holcombe, "The Changing Outlook for a Realignment of Parties," 278.

14. Arthur N. Holcombe to Franklyn Waltman, March 8, 1939, Personal Correspondence, 1939, I–Z, Holcombe Papers; "Professor Holcombe Finds Republican Election Comeback Nothing but a 'Normal Political Phenomenon' at Mid-Term," *Harvard Crimson*, Nov. 21, 1938, news clipping in box 9, Pell Papers.

15. Holcombe, *Middle Classes in American Politics*, 69, 86, 241; Arthur N. Holcombe, "Present-day Characteristics of American Political Parties," in *The American Political Scene*, ed. Edward D. Logan (New York: Harper and Brothers, 1936), 4, 20.

16. Arthur N. Holcombe, "The Changing Outlook for a Realignment of Parties," *Public Opinion Quarterly* 10, no. 4 (1946): 455.

17. Arthur N. Holcombe, *Our More Perfect Union: From Eighteenth-Century Principles to Twentieth-Century Practice* (Cambridge: Harvard University Press, 1950), 87–88, 102, 106.

18. Robert D. Cross, "Schlesinger, Arthur Meier," in *Dictionary of American Biography: Supplement Seven, 1961–1965*, ed. John A. Garraty (New York: Charles Scribner's Sons, 1981), 675–76; Arthur M. Schlesinger, *In Retrospect: The History of a Historian* (New York: Harcourt, Brace, and World, 1963), 35, 43.

19. Arthur M. Schlesinger, *New Viewpoints in American History* (New York: The MacMillan Company, 1922), 107, 123, 274, 277.

20. Schlesinger, *In Retrospect*, 127.

21. Arthur M. Schlesinger to Edgar Lawrence Smith, Feb. 2, 1939, and Arthur M. Schlesinger to F. Lauriston Bullard, Jan. 24, 1940, both in box 14, Arthur M. Schlesinger Papers, HUA.

22. Arthur M. Schlesinger, "Tides of American Politics," *The Yale Review* 29 (Dec. 1939): 217, 219–24, 226, 229; Schlesinger, *In Retrospect*, 108.

23. Arthur M. Schlesinger to Alfred A. Knopf, Jan. 24, 1940, box 14, Schlesinger Papers; Schlesinger, *In Retrospect*, 108.

24. Schlesinger, "Tides of American Politics," 225–26.

25. Harold D. Lasswell to Arthur M. Schlesinger, April 6, 1940, box 15, Schlesinger Papers.

26. Schlesinger, "Tides of American Politics," 224; Arthur M. Schlesinger to Harold Laski, Feb. 18, 1946, box 20, Schlesinger Papers.

27. Arthur M. Schlesinger, Jr., "His Rendezvous with History," *New Republic*, April 15, 1946, 553.

28. Arthur M. Schlesinger to Charles D. Anderson, Sept. 8, 1948, box 21, Schlesinger Papers.

29. Hedley Donovan, "How to Be a Political Prophet," *Fortune* 46 (Sept. 1952): 96.

30. Arthur M. Schlesinger to Samuel Lubell, March 27, 1952, box 149, Samuel Lubell Papers, Dodd Research Center, University of Connecticut, Storrs, Conn.

31. Theodore Rosenof, "The Legend of Louis Bean: Political Prophecy and the 1948 Election," *The Historian* 62 (Fall 1999): 63, 65, 72.

32. Louis Bean to Frank W. McCulloch, Aug. 19, 1948, and Louis Bean to Henry Morgenthau, III, Oct. 24, 1950, both in box 37, Louis Bean Papers, FDRL.

33. Louis H. Bean, *Ballot Behavior: A Study of Presidential Elections* (Washington, D.C.: American Council on Public Affairs, 1940), 5–6, 11–12, 49, 56, 58, 62, 67, 71–72; Louis H. Bean, *How to Predict Elections* (New York: Alfred A. Knopf, 1948), 12, 14, 16–18, 50–51, 64, 68, 88, 93, 95, 99–100; Louis H. Bean, "Tides and Patterns in American Politics," *The American Political Science Review* 36 (August 1942): 637, 639–42, 646–47; Louis Bean, "The Tides of Politics," *New Republic*, Oct. 7, 1940, 469–70.

34. Bean, *Ballot Behavior*, 56, 60, 65; Bean, *How to Predict Elections*, 16–18, 88; Bean, "Tides and Patterns in American Politics," 640, 642; Bean, "Tides of Politics," 470.

35. Bean, *Ballot Behavior*, 6, 56, 60, 83; Bean, *How to Predict Elections*, 7–8, 27–28, 38–39; Bean, "Tides and Patterns in American Politics," 639, 642; Bean, "Tides of Politics," 470; Louis H. Bean, "What Republican Tide?" *New Republic*, May 1, 1944, 593–95; Louis Bean to Dorothy Thompson, Oct. 19, 1940, box 29, Bean Papers; Louis Bean to William Diamond, Jan. 15, 1945, box 37, Bean Papers.

36. Bean, *How to Predict Elections*, 30–32, 34; Louis H. Bean, "Quantitative Analysis of Political Behavior," abstract of a May 9, 1947 talk, box 42, Bean Papers.

37. Louis H. Bean, "The Republican 'Mandate' and '48," *New York Times Magazine*, Jan. 19, 1947, 16, 52; Bean, *How to Predict Elections*, 4, 8–9, 16–17, 20, 23, 27, 29–30, 34, 52.

38. Bean, *How to Predict Elections*, 36, 42, 44, 46, 57, 133, 146, 158–59, 162–65.

39. Louis Bean to Nathan Koenig, Sept. 24, 1947, to Oscar Chapman, July 22, 1948, and to the Secretary of Agriculture, July 9, 1948 and Oct. 21, 1948, all in box 33, Bean Papers; Louis Bean to Creekmore Fath, Sept. 22, 1948, box 37, Bean Papers.

40. Rosenof, "Legend of Louis Bean," 69–72.

41. Louis H. Bean, "Forecasting the 1950 Elections," *Harper's Magazine* 200 (April 1950): 68–69; Louis Bean to The Secretary [of Agriculture], March 16, 1950, box 33, Bean Papers.

42. Louis H. Bean, *The Mid-Term Battle* (Washington, D.C.: Cantillon Books, 1950), 17, 95.

43. Martin Bulmer, *The Chicago School of Sociology: Institutionalization, Diversity, and the Rise of Sociological Research* (Chicago: University of Chicago Press, 1984), 165; "Harold Gosnell Dies at 100; Political Methodology Expert," *Washington Post*, Jan. 11, 1997, C4.

44. Yearbook page copy in Harold F. Gosnell, "Autobiography," Chapter 4, 4–6, ms., box 4, Harold F. Gosnell Papers, Regenstein Library, University of Chicago, Chicago, Ill.

45. "Appendix B: Chicago Days," in Gabriel A. Almond, *A Discipline Divided: Schools and Sects in Political Science* (Newbury Park, Calif.: Sage Publications, 1990), 322; Mary Ann Dzuback, *Robert M. Hutchins: Portrait of an Educator* (Chicago: University of Chicago Press, 1991), 173, 186; Bulmer, *Chicago School of Sociology*, 204.

46. Harold F. Gosnell to Dean [Robert] Redfield, July 20, 1942, box 3, Gosnell Papers.

47. Harold F. Gosnell to Herman Kehrli, June 24, 1944, and July 21, 1944, box 2, Gosnell Papers.

48. Gosnell, "Autobiography," Chapter 6, 6–12.

49. "Harold Gosnell Dies at 100; Political Methodology Expert," *Washington Post*, C4.

50. "Appendix B: Chicago Days," in Almond, *A Discipline Divided*, 324; "Gabriel Almond [Interview]," in *Political Science in America*, ed. Baer et al., 125.

51. Hanes Walton, Jr., Leslie Burl McLemore, and C. Vernon Gray, "The Problem of Preconceived Perceptions in Black Urban Politics: The Harold F. Gosnell, James Q. Wilson Legacy," *National Political Science Review* 3 (1992): 219.

52. "Robert Martin [Interview]," in *Political Science in America*, ed. Baer et al., 159, 161–62.

53. "Gosnell, Political Parties and Public Opinion, Preliminary Examinations, Autumn Quarter, 1941," in box 3, Gosnell Papers.

54. Harold F. Gosnell and Norman N. Gill, "An Analysis of the 1932 Presidential Vote in Chicago," *The American Political Science Review* 29 (Dec. 1935): 967, 983; Harold F. Gosnell, *Why Europe Votes* (Chicago: The University of Chicago Press, 1930), 198; Harold F. Gosnell, "The Voter Resigns," *New Republic*, Oct. 21, 1925, 224; Harold F. Gosnell, "Voting," in *Encyclopedia of the Social Sciences*, Vol. 15, ed. Edwin R. A. Seligman (1934; New York: The MacMillan Company, 1937), 288; Harold F. Gosnell, *Boss Platt and His New York Machine: A Study of the Political Leadership of Thomas C. Platt, Theodore Roosevelt, and Others* (1924; New York: Russell and Russell, 1969), 352–53.

55. Harold F. Gosnell to Robert Redfield, March 10, 1936, and May 5, 1936, box 19, Gosnell Papers.

56. Gosnell and Gill, "An Analysis of the 1932 Presidential Vote in Chicago," 967.

57. Harold F. Gosnell, *Machine Politics: Chicago Model* (Chicago: The University of Chicago Press, 1937), 125.

58. "Gosnell Finds Fortune Poll Close, Thinks Election Death of Old GOP," unnamed newspaper clipping, Nov. 6, 1936, in box 3, Gosnell Papers.

59. Harold F. Gosnell and Morris H. Cohen, "Progressive Politics: Wisconsin an Example," *The American Political Science Review* 34 (Oct. 1940): 920.

60. Harold F. Gosnell and William G. Colman, "Political Trends in Industrial America: Pennsylvania an Example," *Public Opinion Quarterly* 4 (Sept. 1940): 475.

61. Harold F. Gosnell and Norman M. Pearson, "Relation of Economic and Social Conditions to Voting Behavior in Iowa, 1924–1936," *The Journal of Social Psychology* 13 (Feb. 1941): 18, 26–27.

62. Gosnell and Colman, "Political Trends in Industrial America: Pennsylvania an Example," 486.

63. Harold F. Gosnell, "The Future of the American Party System," in *The Future of Government in the United States*, ed. Leonard D. White (Chicago: The University of Chicago Press, 1942), 107–8; Harold F. Gosnell, *Grass Roots Politics: National Voting Behavior of Typical States* (Washington, D.C.: American Council on Public Affairs, 1942), 131–33.

64. Gosnell and Colman, "Political Trends in Industrial America: Pennsylvania an Example," 473–74, 480–82, 486; Gosnell, "The Future of the American Party System," 104; Gosnell and Pearson, "Relation of Economic and Social Conditions to Voting Behavior in Iowa, 1924–1936," 34; Gosnell, *Grass Roots Politics*, 129–32; Harold F. Gosnell, "The Negro Vote in Northern Cities," *National Municipal Review* 30 (May 1941): 278.

65. Harold F. Gosnell, ms. review of *Voting Behavior in a Metropolitan Area* by Edward H. Litchfield, July 31, 1941, in box 14, Gosnell Papers.

66. Charles Edward Merriam and Harold Foote Gosnell, *The American Party System: An Introduction to the Study of Political Parties in the United States*, Revised [Second] Edition (New York: The MacMillan Company, 1929), 197–200.

67. Charles Edward Merriam and Harold Foote Gosnell, *The American Party System: An Introduction to the Study of Political Parties in the United States*, Third Edition (New York: The MacMillan Company, 1940), vi, 15; Charles Edward Merriam and Harold Foote Gosnell, *The American Party System*, Fourth Edition (New York: The MacMillan Company, 1949), 37.

68. Gosnell and Gill, "An Analysis of the 1932 Presidential Vote in Chicago," 984.

69. Gosnell and Pearson, "Relation of Economic and Social Conditions to Voting Behavior in Iowa, 1924–1936," 25.

70. Harold F. Gosnell and Margaret J. Schmidt, "Factorial and Correlational Analysis of the 1934 Vote in Chicago," *Journal of the American Statistical Association* 31 (1936): 518; Gosnell, *Machine Politics*, 124–25, 187, 209.

71. Gosnell and Colman, "Political Trends in Industrial America: Pennsylvania an Example," 474; Gosnell and Cohen, "Progressive Politics: Wisconsin an Example," 920–21; Gosnell, "The Future of the American Party System," 109; Gosnell, *Grass Roots Politics*, 6–7, 9, 11, 18, 133–34, 160.

72. Gosnell notes marked "Not Used," c. late 1950s, box 3, Gosnell Papers; Gosnell, "Autobiography," Miscellaneous.

73. Harold F. Gosnell, *Truman's Crises: A Political Biography of Harry S. Truman* (Westport, Conn.: Greenwood Press, 1980), 318; Harold F. Gosnell, *Champion Campaigner: Franklin D. Roosevelt* (New York: MacMillan, 1952), 91–92, 172, 216, 218.

74. Gosnell notes marked "Not Used"; Harold F. Gosnell to Charles [last name not indicated], July 13, 1950; Harold F. Gosnell to Al [De Grazia], July 5, 1950; Harold F. Gosnell to Ben Arneson, July 5, 1950, all in box 1, Gosnell Papers.

75. Gosnell, "Autobiography," Chapter 13, 6–24, and Miscellaneous.

76. Gosnell notes marked "Not Used."

CHAPTER FOUR

1. "Lubell, Samuel," *Current Biography 1956* (New York: H. W. Wilson, 1956), 387–88; "Biography," *Saturday Evening Post*, Nov. 30, 1940, 6; Miles A. Pomper, "Lubell, Samuel," in *The Scribner Encyclopedia of American Lives*, Vol. II, *1986–1990*, ed. Kenneth T. Jackson (New York: Charles Scribner's Sons, 1999), 556.

2. "Lubell, Samuel," *Current Biography 1956*, 387–88; Bernard M. Baruch, *Baruch: The Public Years* (New York: Holt, Rinehart and Winston, 1960), 304; Jordan A. Schwarz, *The Speculator: Bernard M. Baruch in Washington, 1917–1965* (Chapel Hill: The University of North Carolina Press, 1981), 458, 470, 474, 549, 554–56; "Walter Winchell of New York," May 4, 1952, news clipping in box 122, Samuel Lubell Papers, Dodd Research Center, University of Connecticut, Storrs, Conn.

3. "Lubell, Samuel," *Current Biography 1956*, 388; The Editors, "About the Author," *Saturday Evening Post*, Jan. 10, 1953, 26; "The Doorbell Ringer," *Time*, Oct. 15, 1956, 84.

4. Samuel Lubell to Carin Struminger, March 21, 1960, box 148, Lubell Papers.

5. Samuel Lubell to Carroll Kirkpatrick, June 10, 1952, box 122, Lubell Papers; Samuel Lubell to Harry Gilburt, July 13, 1952, box 145, Lubell Papers.

6. Samuel Lubell to Evan Thomas, Nov. 21, 1955, box 122, Lubell Papers.

7. John Braeman to Mrs. Samuel Lubell, Oct. 20, 1967; Samuel Lubell to John Braeman, Dec. 1, 1967, both in box 146, Lubell Papers.

8. Samuel Lubell, "Post-Mortem: Who Elected Roosevelt?" *Saturday Evening Post,* Jan. 25, 1941, 9–10, 43, 94, 96.

9. Samuel Lubell, *The Future of American Politics* (New York: Harper and Brothers, 1952), 5; Samuel Lubell to Ramona Herdman, Nov. 9, 1952, box 122, Lubell Papers; Samuel Lubell to Henry Allen Moe, Oct. 14, 1949, box 147, Lubell Papers.

10. Samuel Lubell to Jack Fischer, May 27, 1952, box 122, Lubell Papers; John L. B. Williams to Samuel Lubell, Nov. 28, 1949, box 146, Lubell Papers.

11. Lubell, *Future of American Politics,* 269.

12. Samuel Lubell to Jack Fischer, Dec. 12, 1949, box 122, Lubell Papers.

13. Arthur Schlesinger, Jr., "What Makes Us Vote the Way We Do," *New York Times Book Review,* April 13, 1952, 1; Elmer E. Cornwell, Jr., "Introduction," in Henry Jones Ford, *The Rise and Growth of American Politics* (New York: Da Capo Press, 1967), ix; V. O. Key to John Hohenberg, Feb. 16, 1957, General Correspondence, 1957, A–P, V. O. Key Papers, Harvard University Archives, Cambridge, Mass.; Lubell, *Future of American Politics,* 7; Richard Hofstadter, "On Voting Behavior," *Progressive,* July 2, 1952, magazine clipping in box 122, Lubell Papers.

14. Samuel Lubell, *The Revolt of the Moderates* (New York: Harper and Brothers, 1956), 260; Samuel Lubell, *The Future While It Happened* (New York: W. W. Norton, 1973), 20; Arthur N. Holcombe, "Presidential Leadership and the Party System," *The Yale Review* 43 (March 1954): 329; Lubell, *Future of American Politics,* 6; Samuel Lubell, *When People Speak: Their Opinions, Their Feelings* (New York: Opinion Reporting Workshop/Graduate School of Journalism, Columbia University, Sept. 1960), 15–16; Lubell to Gilburt, July 13, 1952; Samuel Lubell to James Pope, Sept. 15, 1957, box 226, Lubell Papers.

15. Lubell, *Revolt of the Moderates,* 259–60; Lubell, *Future of American Politics,* 6–7; Lubell, *When People Speak,* 29; Samuel Lubell to Harry Gilburt, July 7, 1956, box 145, Lubell Papers; Lubell to Gilburt, July 13, 1952.

16. Samuel Lubell to John Howe, Jan. 11, 1953, box 149, Lubell Papers.

17. Samuel Lubell to Arthur M. Schlesinger, Jr., Jan. 29, 1949, box P-18, Arthur M. Schlesinger, Jr. Papers, John F. Kennedy Library, Boston, Mass.; Samuel Lubell to Book Review Editor, *Chicago Sun-Times,* May 13, 1956, box 122, Lubell Papers.

18. Lubell, *Revolt of the Moderates,* 260.

19. Richard Neustadt, review of *Revolt of the Moderates* by Samuel Lubell, *Political Science Quarterly* 71 (Sept. 1956): 450.

20. Oliver Garceau to Corinne Silverman, May 28, 1956, box 149, Lubell Papers.

21. "Symposium on the Work of Samuel Lubell," *PS: Political Science and Politics* 23 (June 1990): 185.

22. Lubell, *When People Speak,* 26.

23. Key to Hohenberg, Feb. 16, 1957.

24. Jack Gould, "WOR Says Sam Lubell Outcomputed Computers on Lodge's Victory," *New York Times,* March 12, 1964, 71; Samuel Lubell, "Polls in Voting Process," *New York Times,* June 19, 1964, 30.

25. Donovan Richardson, "From the Bookshelf," *Christian Science Monitor,* April 16, 1952, Section Two, 1.

26. Schlesinger, "What Makes Us Vote the Way We Do," 1; Arthur Schlesinger, Jr., "Political Insights," *Progressive* (June 1956), 37, magazine clipping in box 122, Lubell Papers.

27. Nathan Glazer, "Immigrant Groups in Politics," *Commentary* 14 (July 1952): 87.

28. Holcombe, "Presidential Leadership and the Party System," 329; Sidney Hyman, "The Era of the Middle Class," *Saturday Review*, April 14, 1956, 24.

29. Daniel Boorstin to Samuel Lubell, Nov. 30, 1953, box 122, Lubell Papers.

30. Seymour Martin Lipset to Samuel Lubell, July 6, 1956, box 122, Lubell Papers.

31. Peter Odegard quoted in Edward J. Tyler, Jr. to Samuel Lubell, Feb. 21, 1956, box 122, Lubell Papers.

32. Lubell, *Future of American Politics*, 2–3, 198–200.

33. Samuel Lubell to Lewis Gannett [1952, never sent], box 122, Lubell Papers.

34. Lubell, *Future of American Politics*, 27, 43–44, 48–51, 57.

35. Samuel Lubell to Harold Leventhal, Nov. 22, 1948, box 149, Lubell Papers.

36. Samuel Lubell to Miss Anderson, Dec. 19, 1948, box 149, Lubell Papers.

37. Samuel Lubell, "Who Really Elected Truman?" *Saturday Evening Post*, Jan. 22, 1949, 15–16, 61.

38. Lubell, *Future of American Politics*, 1, 3, 60, 134–35, 227.

39. Lubell, *Revolt of the Moderates*, 113, 175, 185; Lubell, *Future of American Politics*, 30–33, 50, 98, 255–56.

40. Bernard Sternsher, "The Emergence of the New Deal Party System: A Problem in Historical Analysis of Voter Behavior," *Journal of Interdisciplinary History* 6 (Summer 1975): 138; Jerome M. Clubb and Howard W. Allen, "The Cities and the Election of 1928: Partisan Realignment?" *The American Historical Review* 74 (April 1969): 1207–8; Lubell, *Future of American Politics*, 35.

41. Lubell, *Revolt of the Moderates*, 79.

42. Lubell, *Revolt of the Moderates*, 270–71.

43. Samuel Lubell to A. M. Schlesinger [Sr.], March 19, 1952, box 122, Lubell Papers.

44. Lubell, *Future of American Politics*, 28–29, 34, 82.

45. Samuel Lubell to Donald Murphy, Aug. 4, 1951, box 122, Lubell Papers.

46. Lubell, *Future of American Politics*, 29–31.

47. Lubell, *Revolt of the Moderates*, 224, 230, 271.

48. Lubell, *Revolt of the Moderates*, 232, 236; Lubell, *Future of American Politics*, 249.

49. Lubell, *Future of American Politics*, 4, 6.

50. Lubell to Gannett [1952].

51. Garceau to Silverman, May 28, 1956.

52. Lubell, *Revolt of the Moderates*, 108–9; Lubell, *Future of American Politics*, 200–201.

53. Lubell, *Future of American Politics*, 3, 200, 203–5.

54. Lubell to Schlesinger, March 19, 1952.

55. Gerald H. Gamm, *The Making of New Deal Democrats: Voting Behavior and Realignment in Boston, 1920–1940* (Chicago: The University of Chicago Press, 1989), 11; Jerome M. Clubb, William H. Flanigan, and Nancy H. Zingale, *Partisan Realignment: Voters, Parties, and Government in American History* (Beverly Hills: Sage Publications, 1980), 43; Richard L. McCormick, "The Realignment Synthesis in American History," *Journal of Interdisciplinary History* 13 (Summer 1982): 97 n.27.

56. "Symposium on the Work of Samuel Lubell," 185–86.

57. Allan J. Lichtman, *Prejudice and the Old Politics: The Presidential Election of 1928* (Chapel Hill: The University of North Carolina Press, 1979), 19.

58. Peter B. Natchez, "Images of Voting: The Social Psychologists," *Public Policy* 18 (Summer 1970): 569 n.48.

59. Arthur M. Schlesinger, Jr., *The Cycles of American History* (Boston: Houghton Mifflin, 1986), 34–35.

60. Glazer, "Immigrant Groups in Politics," 87.

61. V. O. Key to Raymond Walters, Jr., March 23, 1952, Book Review Correspondence, Key Papers.

62. V. O. Key, Jr., "Roosevelt's Changelings," *Saturday Review*, April 12, 1952, 31.

63. V. O. Key to Samuel Lubell, March 23, 1952, and March 24, 1952, both in General Correspondence, 1948–1952, H–R, Key Papers.

64. V. O. Key to Samuel Lubell, March 28, 1952, General Correspondence, 1948–1952, H–R, Key Papers.

65. V. O. Key, Jr., *A Primer of Statistics for Political Scientists* (New York: Thomas Y. Crowell Company, 1954), 65–66.

66. Samuel Lubell to V. O. Key, Jan. 25, 1956, General Correspondence, 1956, A–P, Key Papers.

67. V. O. Key to Samuel Lubell, Jan. 26, 1956, General Correspondence, 1956, A–P, Key Papers.

68. V. O. Key commentary on Lubell in response to Henry Allen Moe to V. O. Key, Nov. 2, 1953, both in General Correspondence, 1951–1954, A–M, Key Papers.

69. V. O. Key to Franklin A. Lindsay, Feb. 6, 1956, General Correspondence, 1956, A–P, Key Papers.

70. Key to Hohenberg, Feb. 16, 1957.

CHAPTER FIVE

1. Elmer E. Cornwell, Jr., "Key, Valdimer Orlando, Jr., " in *Dictionary of American Biography: Supplement Seven, 1961–1965*, ed. John A. Garraty (New York: Charles Scribner's Sons, 1981), 430–31; H. Douglas Price, "Key, V. O., Jr., " in *International Encyclopedia of the Social Sciences*, Vol. 8, ed. David L. Sills (New York: The MacMillan Company and The Free Press, 1968), 366–67; H. Douglas Price, "Key, V. O., Jr., " in *The Encyclopedia of Democracy*, Vol. 2, ed. Seymour Martin Lipset (Washington, D.C.: Congressional Quarterly, Inc., 1995), 706; "R. Taylor Cole [Interview]," in *Political Science in America: Oral Histories of a Discipline*, ed. Michael A. Baer, Malcolm E. Jewell, and Lee Sigelman (Lexington: The University Press of Kentucky, 1991), 71; Alexander Heard, "Introduction to the New Edition," in V. O. Key, Jr., *Southern Politics in State and Nation* (Knoxville: The University of Tennessee Press, 1984), xxiii, xxviii; Andrew MacMillan Lucker, "V. O. Key, Jr.: The Quintessential Political Scientist" (Ph.D. thesis: Case Western Reserve University, 1998), 6–11.

2. Cornwell, "Key, Valdimer Orlando, Jr., " 430; Price, "Key, V. O., Jr., " in *International Encyclopedia*, 366; Joel H. Silbey, Allan G. Bogue, and William H. Flanigan, "Introduction," in *The History of American Electoral Behavior*, ed. Joel H. Silbey, Allan G. Bogue, and William H. Flanigan (Princeton: Princeton University Press, 1978), 12; "Appendix B: Chicago Days," in Gabriel A. Almond, *A Discipline Divided: Schools and Sects in Political Science* (Newbury Park, Calif.: Sage Publications, 1990), 324–25; Heinz Eulau, "Political Behavior," in *International Encyclopedia*, Vol. 12, 204.

3. V. O. Key to Joseph A. Willits, Oct. 13, 1957, and V. O. Key, "Research in Political Science," Oct. 22, 1957 ms., 12–13, both in box 38, V. O. Key Papers, John F. Kennedy Library (JFKL), Boston, Mass.

4. "David Truman [Interview]," in *Political Science in America*, ed. Baer et al., 142.

5. Harold Gosnell to V. O. Key, Jan. 7, 1959, General Correspondence, Jan. 1, 1959–Sept. 1, 1959, A–Z, V. O. Key Papers, Harvard University Archives (HUA), Cambridge, Mass.

6. Heard, "Introduction to the New Edition," xxiii.

7. Cornwell, "Key, Valdimer Orlando, Jr., " 430; Samuel P. Hays to V. O. Key, July 8, 1960, General Correspondence, Sept. 2, 1959–1960, A–Z, Key Papers, HUA; "David Truman [Interview]," 148; Mellisa P. Collie, "V. O. Key, Jr. (1908–1963)," in *Political Parties and Elections in the United States: An Encyclopedia*, Vol. 1, ed. L. Sandy Maisel (New York: Garland Publishing, 1991), 544; William C. Havard, "V. O. Key, Jr.: A Brief Profile," in Key, *Southern Politics in State and Nation*, xxxiv.

8. Heinz Eulau, *Micro-Macro Dilemmas in Political Science: Personal Pathways Through Complexity* (Norman: University of Oklahoma Press, 1996), 422.

9. Heard, "Introduction to the New Edition," xxii.

10. Peter B. Natchez, *Images of Voting/Visions of Democracy* (New York: Basic Books, 1985), 270.

11. "David Truman [Interview]," 142.

12. "Austin Ranney [Interview]," in *Political Science in America*, ed. Baer et al., 221–22.

13. Heard, "Introduction to the New Edition." xxv; Havard, "V. O. Key, Jr.," xxx.

14. V. O. Key to Pendleton Herring, Sept. 9, 1952, General Correspondence, 1948–1952, H–R, Key Papers, HUA.

15. V. O. Key, ms. review of *Texas Presidential Politics in 1952* by O. Douglas Weeks, 3, in General Correspondence, 1951–1954, A–M, Key Papers, HUA.

16. Angus Campbell, review of *The Responsible Electorate* by V. O. Key, *The American Political Science Review* 60 (Dec. 1966): 1007.

17. James L. Sundquist, *Dynamics of the Party System: Alignment and Realignment of Political Parties in the United States*, Revised Edition (Washington, D.C.: The Brookings Institution, 1983), 12 n.30.

18. Havard, "V. O. Key, Jr.," xxviii.

19. Heard, "Introduction to the New Edition," xxii.

20. M. Brewster Smith to V. O. Key, Sept. 1, 1954, box 21, Key Papers, JFKL.

21. Walter Dean Burnham, "Critical Realignment: Dead or Alive?" in *The End of Realignment? Interpreting American Electoral Eras*, ed. Byron E. Shafer (Madison: The University of Wisconsin Press, 1991), 107–8.

22. E. E. Schattschneider to V. O. Key, June 14, 1948, box 29, Key Papers, JFKL.

23. "Toward a More Responsible Two-Party System: A Report of the Committee on Political Parties," *The American Political Science Review* 44 (Sept. 1950), Supplement: 82.

24. Gerald H. Gamm, *The Making of New Deal Democrats: Voting Behavior and Realignment in Boston, 1920–1940* (Chicago: The University of Chicago Press, 1989), 12; James W. Prothro, review of *Public Opinion and American Democracy* by V. O. Key, *The Journal of Politics* 24 (Nov. 1962): 789; Natchez, *Images of Voting*, 187.

25. V. O. Key to Benjamin H. Schoenfeld, April 2, 1953, General Correspondence, 1951–1954, N–Z, Key Papers, HUA.

26. V. O. Key, Jr., "Issues and Problems of Political Science Research: Paper Presented at the Fiftieth Anniversary Celebration of the Department of Political Science at The University of Michigan, April 8, 1960," unpaginated, copy in box 34, Key Papers, JFKL.

27. V. O. Key to Harry M. Scoble, Jan. 4, 1963, General Correspondence, 1963, A–Z, Key Papers, HUA.

28. V. O. Key, Jr., "The State of the Discipline," *The American Political Science Review* 52 (Dec. 1958): 964.

29. Walter Berns, "Voting Studies," in *Essays on the Scientific Study of Politics*, ed. Herbert J. Storing (New York: Holt, Rinehart, and Winston, 1962), 4–5; David Butler and Donald Stokes, *Political Change in Britain: The Evolution of Electoral Choice*, Second Edition (New York: St. Martin's Press, 1974), 10 n.1; Havard, "V. O. Key, Jr., " xxxiii.

30. Key, "Issues and Problems of Political Science Research," unpaginated.

31. David B. Truman to V. O. Key, Sept. 28, 1954, box 21, Key Papers, JFKL; Natchez, *Images of Voting*, 191.

32. J. Morgan Kousser, "History – Theory = ?" *Reviews in American History* 7 (June 1979): 159.

33. Havard, "V. O. Key, Jr.," xxxiii–xxxiv.

34. Heard, "Introduction to the New Edition," xxiv.

35. V. O. Key, Jr., "Roosevelt Wins Again," *Events* (Dec. 1940): 413–14.

36. V. O. Key, Jr., *Politics, Parties, and Pressure Groups* (New York: Thomas Y. Crowell Company, 1942), 270.

37. V. O. Key to R. C. Martin, May 8, 1947, box 29, Key Papers, JFKL.

38. V. O. Key, Jr., "If the Election Follows the Pattern," *New York Times Magazine*, Oct. 20, 1946, 8.

39. V. O. Key, Jr., *Politics, Parties, and Pressure Groups*, Second Edition (New York: Thomas Y. Crowell Company, 1947), 247, 267, 275–79.

40. V. O. Key, Jr., "Now That 1954 Is Here," *New Republic*, Nov. 23, 1953, 12–13; V. O. Key, Jr., *American State Politics: An Introduction* (New York: Alfred A. Knopf, 1956), 28–31.

41. V. O. Key to Roger W. Shugg, April 6, 1948, Correspondence with Individuals at Alfred A. Knopf, Inc., Key Papers, HUA.

42. V. O. Key to Roger Shugg, Nov. 6, 1948, Correspondence with Individuals at Alfred A. Knopf, Inc., Key Papers, HUA.

43. V. O. Key to Taylor Cole, Nov. 5, 1948, General Correspondence, 1948–1952, A–G, Key Papers, HUA.

44. V. O. Key to Leon Henderson, Nov. 8, 1948, General Correspondence, 1948–1952, H–R, Key Papers, HUA; V. O. Key to Angus Campbell, March 12, 1953, General Correspondence, 1951–1954, A–M, Key Papers, HUA; "David Truman [Interview]," 145.

45. V. O. Key to Malcolm Moos, March 4, 1950, Correspondence with Individuals at Alfred A. Knopf, Inc., Key Papers, HUA.

46. V. O. Key, Jr., "Will a Big Vote Help the Democrats?" *New Republic*, Oct. 6, 1952, 14.

47. V. O. Key, Jr., *Politics, Parties, and Pressure Groups*, Third Edition (New York: Thomas Y. Crowell Company, 1952), 184–85, 196, 200, 210 n.26, 594 n.23, 596 n.28.

48. V. O. Key, Jr., "The Future of the Democratic Party," *The Virginia Quarterly Review* 28 (Spring 1952): 161, 163–64, 167.

49. V. O. Key, Jr. and Frank Munger, "Social Determinism and Electoral Decision: The Case of Indiana," in *American Voting Behavior*, ed. Eugene Burdick and Arthur J. Broderick (Glencoe, Ill.: The Free Press, 1959), 458 n.23. "It should be noted for the record that this essay was completed essentially in its present form in June, 1953 [459 n.26]."

50. V. O. Key to Angus Campbell, Feb. 9, 1953, General Correspondence, 1951–1954, A–M, Key Papers, HUA.

51. Key, ms. review of *Texas Presidential Politics in 1952* by Weeks, 2.

52. V. O. Key, Jr., *A Primer of Statistics for Political Scientists* (New York: Thomas Y. Crowell Company, 1954), 36.

53. M. Brewster Smith to V. O. Key, Aug. 21, 1954, box 23, Key Papers, JFKL.

54. Robert Lane to V. O. Key, Aug. 17, 1954, box 23, Key Papers, JFKL.

55. V. O. Key to Robert Lane, Aug. 26, 1954, box 23, Key Papers, JFKL.

56. Oliver Garceau to V. O. Key, Aug. 20, 1954, box 23, Key Papers, JFKL.

57. V. O. Key to Oliver Garceau, Aug. 21, 1954, box 23, Key Papers, JFKL.

58. V. O. Key, Jr., "A Theory of Critical Elections," *The Journal of Politics* 17 (Feb. 1955): 3–4, 6, 8–9, 11–13, 16–18.

59. Key to Garceau, Aug. 21, 1954.

60. Gamm, *Making of New Deal Democrats*, 39–40; Samuel T. McSeveney, "No More 'Waiting for Godot': Comments on the Putative 'End of Realignment,'" in *End of Realignment?* ed. Shafer, 93; John Zvesper, "Party Realignment: A Past Without a Future?" in *Explaining American Politics: Issues and Interpretations*, ed. Robert Williams (New York: Routledge, 1990), 171–72.

61. Louis M. Seagull, "Secular Realignment: The Concept and Its Utility," in *Realignment in American Politics: Toward a Theory*, ed. Bruce A. Campbell and Richard J. Trilling (Austin: University of Texas Press, 1980), 69; William Schneider, "Realignment: The Eternal Question," *PS: Political Science and Politics* 13 (Summer 1982): 449; Paul Kleppner, *Continuity and Change in Electoral Politics, 1893–1928* (New York: Greenwood Press, 1987), 5; Philip Williams, "Review Article: Party Realignment in the United States and Britain," *British Journal of Political Science* 15, no. 1 (1984): 98.

62. V. O. Key, Jr., "Secular Realignment and the Party System," *The Journal of Politics* 21 (May 1959): 198–200.

63. V. O. Key, Jr., *Politics, Parties, and Pressure Groups*, Fourth Edition (New York: Thomas Y. Crowell Company, 1958), 185, 187, 213, 215–17, 577–78 n.11.

64. V. O. Key, Jr., *Politics, Parties, and Pressure Groups*, Fifth Edition (New York: Thomas Y. Crowell Company, 1964), 535.

65. V. O. Key, Jr. with the assistance of Milton C. Cummings, Jr., *The Responsible Electorate: Rationality in Presidential Voting, 1936–1960* (Cambridge: The Belknap Press of Harvard University Press, 1966), 30, 61–62.

66. Key, *Politics, Parties, and Pressure Groups*, Fourth Edition, 588–89.

67. Key, *Politics, Parties, and Pressure Groups*, Fifth Edition, 542.

68. V. O. Key, Jr., "The Erosion of Sectionalism," *The Virginia Quarterly Review* 31 (Spring 1955): 163–64; Key, *Politics, Parties, and Pressure Groups*, Second Edition, 150–51, 167; Key, "Research in Political Science," 22.

69. "David Truman [Interview]," 146; James M. Glaser, *Race, Campaign Politics, and the Realignment in the South* (New Haven: Yale University Press, 1996), 4; Jack Bass and Walter De Vries, *The Transformation of Southern Politics: Social Change and Political Consequence Since 1945* (New York: Basic Books, 1976), ix.

70. Heard, "Introduction to the New Edition," xxiii.

71. V. O. Key to R. C. Martin, Sept. 18, 1945, box 29, Key Papers, JFKL.

72. V. O. Key to R. C. Martin, April 12, 1946, box 29, Key Papers, JFKL.

73. Heard, "Introduction to the New Edition," xxiii–xxiv.

74. Schattschneider to Key, June 14, 1948.

75. E. E. Schattschneider to V. O. Key, Dec. 7, 1948, box 29, Key Papers, JFKL.

76. V. O. Key to E. E. Schattschneider, Dec. 9, 1948, box 29, Key Papers, JFKL.

77. V. O. Key, Jr., "New Voters in the Making," *Reporter*, Dec. 6, 1949, 9; V. O. Key, Jr., *Southern Politics in State and Nation* (1949; New York: Vintage Books, n. d.), 670–71, 674.

78. V. O. Key, Jr., "Solid South: Cracked or Broken?" *New Republic*, Dec. 1, 1952, 9–11.

79. Key to Campbell, March 12, 1953.

80. Key, "Erosion of Sectionalism," 164–66; V. O. Key to Herbert Pell, Nov. 17, 1955, box 23, Key Papers, JFKL.

81. V. O. Key to O. Douglas Weeks, Jan. 31, 1956, box 16, Key Papers, JFKL.

82. Earl Black and Merle Black, *Politics and Society in the South* (Cambridge: Harvard University Press, 1987), 64, 102, 245–46, 292–93; Earl Black and Merle Black, *The Vital South: How Presidents Are Elected* (Cambridge: Harvard University Press, 1992), 147, 149.

CHAPTER SIX

1. Claude Robinson, review of *Ballot Behavior* by Louis Bean, *The Annals of The American Academy of Political and Social Science* 214 (March 1941): 240; V. O. Key, Jr., "A Theory of Critical Elections," *The Journal of Politics* 17 (Feb. 1955): 9 n.7.

2. Philip E. Converse, Heinz Eulau, and Warren E. Miller, "The Study of Voting," in *Part II: Behavioral and Social Science Research: A National Resource*, ed. Robert McC. Adams, Neil J. Smelser, and Donald J. Treiman (Washington, D.C.: National Academy Press, 1982), 38; William L. Miller, *The Survey Method in the Social and Political Sciences: Achievements, Failures, Prospects* (New York: St. Martin's Press, 1983), 47; Frederick Mosteller et al., *The Pre-election Polls of 1948: Report to the Committee on Analysis of Pre-election Polls and Forecasts* (New York: Social Science Research Council, 1949), 14, 30, 35–41, 53, 277.

3. Max Visser, "The Psychology of Voting Action: On the Psychological Origins of Electoral Research, 1939–1964," *Journal of the History of the Behavioral Sciences* 30 (January 1994): 43; Laura Fermi, *Illustrious Immigrants: The Intellectual Migration from Europe, 1930–41*, Second Edition (Chicago: The University of Chicago Press, 1971), 334; Max Kaase and Hans-Dieter Klingemann, "The Cumbersome Way to Partisan Orientations in a 'New' Democracy: The Case of the Former GDR," in *Elections at Home and Abroad: Essays in Honor of Warren E. Miller*, ed. M. Kent Jennings and Thomas Mann (Ann Arbor: The University of Michigan Press, 1994), 123.

4. Jean M. Converse, *Survey Research in the United States: Roots and Emergence, 1890–1960* (Berkeley: University of California Press, 1987), 298–99, 301; Peter B. Natchez, *Images of Voting/Visions of Democracy* (New York: Basic Books, 1985), 248.

5. "The People's Choice," *Life*, Nov. 11, 1940, 96, magazine clipping in box 15, V. O. Key Papers, John F. Kennedy Library (JFKL), Boston, Mass.

6. "The People's Choice," *Life*, 95.

7. Paul Lazarsfeld, Bernard Berelson, and Hazel Gaudet, *The People's Choice: How the Voter Makes Up His Mind in a Presidential Campaign*, Third Edition (New York: Columbia University Press, 1968), 27.

8. Walter Berns, "Voting Studies," in *Essays on the Scientific Study of Politics*, ed. Herbert J. Storing (New York: Holt, Rinehart and Winston, 1962), 17–18, 34–35; Heinz Eulau,

"Electoral Survey Data and the Temporal Dimension," in *Elections at Home and Abroad*, ed. Jennings and Mann, 41; Natchez, *Images of Voting*, 79.

9. Russell J. Dalton and Martin P. Wattenberg, "The Not So Simple Act of Voting," in *Political Science: The State of the Discipline II*, ed. Ada W. Finifter (Washington, D.C.: The American Political Science Association, 1993), 196–97; Martin P. Wattenberg, *The Rise of Candidate-Centered Politics: Presidential Elections of the 1980s* (Cambridge: Harvard University Press, 1991), 14–15.

10. Adam Clymer, "50 Years Later, Pollsters Analyze Their Big Defeat," *New York Times*, May 18, 1998, A10.

11. Allen Barton, "Paul Lazarsfeld and the Invention of the University Institute for Applied Social Research," in *Organizing for Social Research*, ed. Burkart Holzner and Jiri Nehnevajsa (Cambridge: Schenkman Publishing, 1982), 63.

12. Paul Lazarsfeld, "Remarks on Article by V. O. Key," 3, ms. enclosed in Bernard Berelson to V. O. Key, Feb. 25, 1953, box 22, Key Papers, JFKL.

13. Berelson to Key, Feb. 25, 1953.

14. Lazarsfeld, "Remarks on Article by V. O. Key," 1–2.

15. Bernard R. Berelson, Paul F. Lazarsfeld, and William N. McPhee, *Voting: A Study of Opinion Formation in a Presidential Campaign* (Chicago: University of Chicago Press, 1954), 315–17.

16. Berelson to Key, Feb. 25, 1953.

17. Paul F. Lazarsfeld, "Preface to the Third Edition," in Lazarsfeld et al., *The People's Choice*, xi.

18. Paul F. Lazarsfeld to V. O. Key, March 16, 1962, box 7, Key Papers, JFKL.

19. Eulau, "Electoral Survey Data and the Temporal Dimension," 39; Natchez, *Images of Democracy*, 100; Miller, *The Survey Method in the Social and Political Sciences*, 124; Heinz Eulau, *Micro-Macro Dilemmas in Political Science: Personal Pathways Through Complexity* (Norman: University of Oklahoma Press, 1996), 137; John S. Dryzek, "Opinion Research and the Counter-Revolution in American Political Science," *Political Studies* 40 (Dec. 1992): 682.

20. Clyde H. Coombs, "Angus Campbell," in National Academy of Sciences, Vol. 56, *Biographical Memoirs* (Washington, D.C.: National Academy Press, 1987), 43–44; Angus Campbell, "Biographical Notes," enclosed in Angus Campbell to Elizabeth Hall, Nov. 27, 1967, box 9, Angus Campbell Papers, Bentley Historical Library (BHL), University of Michigan, Ann Arbor, Mich.; *University of Michigan News*, Dec. 15, 1980, 2–3, copy in box 1, Philip E. Converse Papers, BHL.

21. Eulau, *Micro-Macro Dilemmas in Political Science*, 430.

22. Angus Campbell to Filomena Darroch, Dec. 19, 1949, box 2, Campbell Papers.

23. Converse, *Survey Research in the United States*, 350; Theodore M. Newcomb as interviewed by Robert W. Avery, "The Institute of Social Research at the University of Michigan: A Personal Recollection of Its Origins and First Three Decades," in *Organizing for Social Research*, ed. Holzner and Nehnevajsa, 182–83.

24. Eulau, "Electoral Survey Data and the Temporal Dimension," 62.

25. Angus Campbell, "The Pre-election Polls of 1948," *International Journal of Opinion and Attitude Research* 4 (1950): 35–36.

26. Angus Campbell to E. E. Schattschneider, May 28, 1952, box 2, E. E. Schattschneider Papers, Olin Library, Wesleyan University, Middletown, Conn.

27. Angus Campbell to V. O. Key, Aug. 2, 1951, General Correspondence, 1948–1952, A–G, V. O. Key Papers, Harvard University Archives (HUA), Cambridge, Mass.

28. Converse, *Survey Research in the United States*, 363; Warren E. Miller, "An Organizational History of the Intellectual Origins of the American National Election Studies," *European Journal of Political Research* 25 (April 1994): 248; Angus Campbell, "The Passive Citizen," *Acta Sociologica* 6, no. 1 (1962): 10–11; Warren E. Miller, "The Socio-Economic Analysis of Political Behavior," *Midwest Journal of Political Science* 2 (August 1958): 241–42; Peter B. Natchez, "Images of Voting: The Social Psychologists," *Public Policy* 18 (Summer 1970): 559–60; Natchez, *Images of Voting*, 162.

29. Angus Campbell and Henry Valen, "Party Identification in Norway and the United States," *Public Opinion Quarterly* 25 (Winter 1961): 524–25; Stein Rokkan and Angus Campbell, "Citizen Participation in Political Life: Norway and the United States of America," *International Social Science Journal* 12 (Spring 1960): 84; Angus Campbell to Henry Valen, Sept. 29, 1960, box 2, Campbell Papers.

30. Kenneth Prewitt and Norman Nie, "Review Article: Election Studies of the Survey Research Center," *British Journal of Political Science* 1 (Oct. 1971): 481; Berns, "Voting Studies," 9, 21–22; Donald E. Stokes, "Voting," in *International Encyclopedia of the Social Sciences*, Vol. 16, ed. David L. Sills (New York: The Macmillan Company and The Free Press, 1968), 388; Angus Campbell, "A Foreward to *A Mandate from the People*," 1967 ms., 3, enclosed in Angus Campbell to Pertti Pesonen, Aug. 29, 1967, box 2, Campbell Papers.

31. Angus Campbell and Robert L. Kahn, *The People Elect a President* (Ann Arbor: Survey Research Center/Institute for Social Research, University of Michigan, 1952), 1.

32. Converse, *Survey Research in the United States*, 360–62; Eulau, *Micro-Macro Dilemmas in Political Science*, 428–29; Angus Campbell to Finn Havaleschka, Dec. 20, 1979, box 1, Campbell Papers.

33. Campbell and Kahn, *The People Elect a President*, 2.

34. Angus Campbell, Gerald Gurin, and Warren E. Miller, *The Voter Decides* (Evanston, Ill.: Row, Peterson and Company, 1954), 89.

35. Angus Campbell to Peter H. Rossi, May 7, 1956, box 9, Campbell Papers.

36. Angus Campbell to V. O. Key, Dec. 30, 1952, box 22, Key Papers, JFKL.

37. Donald E. Stokes, "Some Dynamic Elements of Contests for the Presidency," *The American Political Science Review* 60 (March 1966): 19 n.1; Campbell et al., *The Voter Decides*, 85; Miller, "The Socio-Economic Analysis of Political Behavior," 240–41; Warren E. Miller, "The Political Behavior of the Electorate," in *American Government Annual, 1960–1961*, ed. Earl Latham (New York: Holt, Rinehart and Winston, 1960), 48.

38. Angus Campbell et al. [not named], "Social Determinism and Political Preference," 1952 ms., 1, 4, enclosed in Campbell to Key, Dec. 30, 1952.

39. Angus Campbell and Homer C. Cooper, *Group Differences in Attitudes and Votes: A Study of the 1954 Congressional Election* (Ann Arbor: Survey Research Center/Institute for Social Research, University of Michigan, 1956), 36, 93, 95; George Belknap and Angus Campbell, "Political Party Identification and Attitudes Toward Foreign Policy," *Public Opinion Quarterly* 15 (Winter 1951–52): 617.

40. Philip E. Converse, *The Dynamics of Party Support: Cohort-Analyzing Party Identification* (Beverly Hills: Sage Publications, 1976), 7.

41. Belknap and Campbell, "Political Party Identification and Attitudes Toward Foreign Policy," 608, 617–19.

42. Campbell and Kahn, *The People Elect a President*, 2, 65.

43. Campbell et al., *The Voter Decides*, 176–77, 183–84.

Notes to pp. 70–74

44. "Warren E. Miller [Interview]," in *Political Science in America: Oral Histories of a Discipline*, ed. Michael A. Baer, Malcolm E. Jewell, and Lee Sigelman (Lexington: The University Press of Kentucky, 1991), 238.

45. Campbell and Cooper, *Group Differences in Attitudes and Votes*, 18, 61, 81.

46. Donald E. Stokes, Angus Campbell, and Warren E. Miller, "Components of Electoral Decision," *The American Political Science Review* 52 (June 1958): 368–69; Eulau, "Electoral Survey Data and the Temporal Dimension," 43, 45; Converse, *Survey Research in the United States*, 364; Miller, *The Survey Method in the Social and Political Sciences*, 110–11.

47. Stokes, "Some Dynamic Elements of Contests for the Presidency," 19.

48. David Butler and Donald Stokes, *Political Change in Britain: The Evolution of Electoral Choice*, Second Edition (New York: St. Martin's Press, 1974), 11–12.

49. Angus Campbell to Stein Rokkan, March 14, 1960, box 2, Campbell Papers; Angus Campbell, "Memorandum," Feb. 11, 1955, 4–5, box 5, Campbell Papers; Angus Campbell to Thomas B. Alexander, Dec. 3, 1962, box 10, Campbell Papers.

50. Eulau, *Micro-Macro Dilemmas in Political Science*, 135.

51. V. O. Key, Jr., *Politics, Parties, and Pressure Groups*, Second Edition (New York: Thomas Y. Crowell Company, 1947), 584.

52. Natchez, *Images of Voting*, 99, 270.

53. V. O. Key, Jr., "Foreword," in Campbell et al., *The Voter Decides*; V. O. Key to Angus Campbell, Aug. 14, 1959, Correspondence, Subject File, Key Papers, HUA.

54. V. O. Key to Charlotte Kohler, Nov. 18, 1955, box 23, Key Papers, JFKL.

55. V. O. Key to Louis Harris, May 20, 1959, General Correspondence, Jan. 1, 1959–Sept. 1, 1959, A–Z, Key Papers, HUA.

CHAPTER SEVEN

1. Donald E. Stokes, "Voting," in *International Encyclopedia of the Social Sciences*, Vol. 16, ed. David L. Sills (New York: The Macmillan Company and The Free Press, 1968), 389; Peter B. Natchez, *Images of Voting/Visions of Democracy* (New York: Basic Books, 1985), 79–80; V. O. Key, Jr., with the assistance of Milton C. Cummings, Jr., *The Responsible Electorate: Rationality in Presidential Voting, 1936–1960* (Cambridge: The Belknap Press of Harvard University Press, 1966), 70.

2. V. O. Key to Paul F. Lazarsfeld, Feb. 28, 1953, box 22, V. O. Key Papers, John F. Kennedy Library (JFKL), Boston, Mass.

3. V. O. Key to Bernard Berelson, Feb. 16, 1951, box 37, Key Papers, JFKL.

4. V. O. Key to Bernard Berelson, July 17, 1952, General Correspondence, 1948–1952, A–G, V. O. Key Papers, Harvard University Archives (HUA), Cambridge, Mass.

5. V. O. Key to Angus Campbell, April 8, 1952, General Correspondence, 1948–1952, A–G, Key Papers, HUA.

6. V. O. Key to Eleanor E. Maccoby, June 26, 1953, General Correspondence, 1951–1954, A–M, Key Papers, HUA.

7. V. O. Key to Samuel Lubell, Jan. 26, 1956, General Correspondence, 1956, A–P, Key Papers, HUA

8. V. O. Key to Kenneth W. Thompson, Jan. 2, 1958, General Correspondence 1957, Q–Z, Key Papers, HUA.

9. V. O. Key to Ralph W. Tyler, May 4, 1960, General Correspondence, Sept. 2, 1959–1960, A–Z, Key Papers, HUA.

10. V. O. Key to Harry M. Scoble, Jan. 4, 1963, General Correspondence, 1963, A–Z, Key Papers, HUA.

11. V. O. Key, Jr., and Frank Munger, "Social Determinism and Electoral Decision: The Case of Indiana," in *American Voting Behavior*, ed. Eugene Burdick and Arthur J. Brodbeck (Glencoe, Ill.: The Free Press, 1959), 281, 297; V. O. Key, Jr., "The Politically Relevant in Surveys," *Public Opinion Quarterly* 24 (Spring 1960): 55; Key to Berelson, July 17, 1952; V. O. Key, "Research in Political Science," Oct. 22, 1957 ms., 31–2, 39, in box 38, Key Papers, JFKL; V. O. Key, Jr., "Issues and Problems of Political Science Research: Paper Presented at the Fiftieth Anniversary Celebration of the Department of Political Science at The University of Michigan, April 8, 1960," unpaginated, copy in box 34, Key Papers, JFKL.

12. Warren E. Miller, "The Electorate's View of the Parties," in *The Parties Respond: Changes in the American Party System*, ed. L. Sandy Maisel (Boulder: Westview Press, 1990), 97; Warren E. Miller and J. Merrill Shanks, *The New American Voter* (Cambridge: Harvard University Press, 1996), 151–52.

13. Key to Campbell, April 8, 1952.

14. Warren E. Miller, "An Organizational History of the Intellectual Origins of the American National Election Studies," *European Journal of Political Research* 25 (April 1994), 252; Philip E. Converse to V. O. Key, July 23, 1959, box 2, Philip E. Converse Papers, Bentley Historical Library (BHL), University of Michigan, Ann Arbor, Mich.

15. Frederick F. Stephan to V. O. Key, Dec. 2, 1959, and V. O. Key to Frederick F. Stephan, Dec. 12, 1959, both in General Correspondence, Sept. 2, 1959–1960, A–Z, Key Papers, HUA.

16. Key, "The Politically Relevant in Surveys," 55, 57.

17. V. O. Key to Angus Campbell, July 28, 1960, General Correspondence, Sept. 2, 1959–1960, A–Z, Key Papers, HUA.

18. Key to Thompson, Jan. 2, 1958.

19. V. O. Key to George A. Graham, May 27, 1961, General Correspondence, 1961, A–Z, Key Papers, HUA.

20. V. O. Key to Warren E. Miller, March 21, 1961; Philip E. Converse to Harvey E. Mansfield, June 22, 1962; Harvey Mansfield to Philip E. Converse, Aug. 28, 1962; Philip E. Converse to V. O. Key, Aug. 29, 1962; V. O. Key to Philip E. Converse, Aug. 31, 1962; all in box 2, Converse Papers.

21. "12-Year Voter Study Indicates Democratic Victory in the Fall," *New York Times*, May 8, 1960, 51.

22. Angus Campbell to V. O. Key, July 25, 1960, General Correspondence, Sept. 2, 1959–1960, A–Z, Key Papers, HUA.

23. Walter Berns, "Voting Studies," in *Essays on the Scientific Study of Politics*, ed. Herbert J. Storing (New York: Holt, Rinehart and Winston, 1962), 62.

24. Donald Stokes to Angus Campbell, Philip Converse, and Warren Miller, Feb. 27, 1964, box 1, Angus Campbell Papers, BHL.

25. Herbert H. Hyman to Angus Campbell, Oct. 17, 1967, box 5, Campbell Papers.

26. Gerald M. Pomper, "The Impact of *The American Voter* on Political Science," *Political Science Quarterly* 93 (Winter 1978): 617.

27. M. Kent Jennings and Thomas E. Mann, "Warren Miller and the Study of Elections," in *Elections at Home and Abroad: Essays in Honor of Warren E. Miller*, ed. M. Kent Jennings and Thomas E. Mann (Ann Arbor: The University of Michigan Press, 1994), 4.

28. Pomper, "The Impact of *The American Voter* on Political Science," 618–19; Jean M. Converse, *Survey Research in the United States: Roots and Emergence, 1890–1960* (Berkeley: University of California Press, 1987), 366.

29. Angus Campbell et al., *The American Voter* (New York: John Wiley and Sons, 1960), 151, 153, 159, 381, 534, 555.

30. Soren Holmberg, "Party Identification Compared Across the Atlantic," in *Elections at Home and Abroad*, ed. Jennings and Mann, 113–14; Warren E. Miller, "The Cross-National Use of Party Identification as a Stimulus to Political Inquiry," in *Party Identification and Beyond: Representations of Voting and Party Competition*, ed. Ian Budge, Ivor Crewe, and Dennis Farlie (New York: John Wiley and Sons, 1976), 25; Angus Campbell, review of *The Responsible Electorate* by V. O. Key, Jr., *The American Political Science Review* 60 (Dec. 1966): 1008.

31. Campbell et al., *The American Voter*, 118, 292; David Butler and Donald Stokes, *Political Change in Britain: The Evolution of Electoral Choice*, Second Edition (New York: St. Martin's Press, 1974), 276; Donald E. Stokes and Warren E. Miller, "Party Government and the Saliency of Congress," *Public Opinion Quarterly* 26 (Winter 1962): 535; Warren Miller, "The Political Behavior of the Electorate," in *American Government Annual, 1960–1961*, ed. Earl Latham (New York: Holt, Rinehart and Winston, 1960), 52, 56.

32. Norman H. Nie, Sidney Verba, and John R. Petrocik, *The Changing American Voter* (Cambridge: Harvard University Press, 1976), 45, 96, 192–93; Stokes, "Voting," 393; Miller, "The Cross-National Use of Party Identification as a Stimulus to Political Inquiry," 24.

33. Campbell et al., *The American Voter*, 65, 120, 151; Philip E. Converse and Gregory B. Markus, "Recent Evidence on the Stability of Party Identification: The New Michigan Election Study Panel," in *Realignment in American Politics: Toward a Theory*, ed. Bruce A. Campbell and Richard J. Trilling (Austin: University of Texas Press, 1980), 140; Philip E. Converse, Angus Campbell, Warren E. Miller, and Donald E. Stokes, "Stability and Change in 1960: A Reinstating Election," *The American Political Science Review* 55 (June 1961): 273–74, 279–80; Angus Campbell et al., *Elections and the Political Order* (New York: John Wiley and Sons, 1966), 7; Angus Campbell, "Surge and Decline: A Study of Electoral Change," in Campbell et al., *Elections and the Political Order*, 45; Donald E. Stokes, "Party Loyalty and the Likelihood of Deviating Elections," *The Journal of Politics* 24 (Nov. 1962): 689–90; Angus Campbell to V. O. Key, March 9, 1961, General Correspondence, 1961, A–Z, Key Papers, HUA; Angus Campbell to V. O. Key, June 9, 1955, box 8, Campbell Papers.

34. Angus Campbell, "Voters and Elections: Past and Present," *The Journal of Politics* 26 (Nov. 1964): 754–56.

35. Campbell et al., *The American Voter*, 535.

36. Campbell et al., *The American Voter*, 89.

37. Campbell et al., *The American Voter*, 554–55.

38. W. Phillips Shively, "The Nature of Party Identification: A Review of Recent Developments," in *The Electorate Reconsidered*, ed. John C. Pierce and John L. Sullivan (Beverly Hills: Sage Publications, 1980), 219–20; Natchez, *Images of Voting*, 268; William G. Mayer, "Changes in Elections and the Party System: 1992 in Historical Perspective," in *The New American Politics: Reflections on Political Change and the Clinton Administration*, ed. Bryan D. Jones (Boulder: Westview Press, 1995), 23.

39. Campbell et al., *The American Voter*, 531.

40. David G. Lawrence, *The Collapse of the Democratic Majority: Realignment, Dealignment, and Electoral Change from Franklin Roosevelt to Bill Clinton* (Boulder:

Westview Press, 1996), 15; Miller, "An Organizational History of the Intellectual Origins of the American National Election Studies," 252; J. Clark Archer and Peter J. Taylor, *Section and Party: A Political Geography of American Presidential Elections from Andrew Jackson to Ronald Reagan* (New York: Research Studies Press, 1981), 7, 10, 18–19; Philip E. Converse to V. O. Key, Feb. 26, 1963, box 2, Converse Papers.

41. Heinz Eulau, review of *The American Voter* by Angus Campbell et al., *The American Political Science Review* 54 (Dec. 1960): 993.

42. Philip E.Converse, Heinz Eulau, and Warren E. Miller, "The Study of Voting," in *Part II: Behavioral and Social Science Research: A National Resource*, ed. Robert McC. Adams, Neil J. Smelser, and Donald J. Treiman (Washington, D.C.: National Academy Press, 1982), 46–47.

43. "Schattschneider, Elmer Eric," *Who Was Who in America*, Vol. 5, *1969—1973* (Chicago: Marquis Who's Who, 1973), 638.

44. Heinz Eulau, *Micro-Macro Dilemmas in Political Science: Personal Pathways Through Complexity* (Norman: University of Oklahoma Press, 1996), 367–68.

45. "Austin Ranney [Interview]," in *Political Science in America: Oral Histories of a Discipline*, ed. Michael A. Baer, Malcolm E. Jewel, and Lee Sigelman (Lexington: The University Press of Kentucky, 1991), 218–19.

46. E. E. Schattschneider, *Politics, Pressures and the Tariff: A Study of Free Private Enterprise in Pressure Politics, as Shown in the 1929–1930 Revision of the Tariff* (New York: Prentice Hall, 1935), 5, 7.

47. E. E. Schattschneider, "1954: The Ike Party Fights to Live," *New Republic*, Feb. 23, 1953, 15–17; E. E. Schattschneider, *The Semisovereign People: A Realist's View of Democracy in America* (New York: Holt, Rinehart and Winston, 1960), 11, 21, 78, 86, 89–90, 93; E. E. Schattschneider, "United States: The Functional Approach to Party Government," in *Modern Political Parties: Approaches to Comparative Politics*, ed. Sigmund Neumann (Chicago: The University of Chicago Press, 1956), 201, 203, 206, 208–9.

48. David Adamany, "The Political Science of E. E. Schattschneider: A Review Essay," *The American Political Science Review* 66 (Dec. 1972): 1329, 1331; James L. Sundquist, *Dynamics of the Party System: Alignment and Realignment of Political Parties in the United States*, Revised Edition (Washington, D.C.: The Brookings Institution, 1983), 12–14; Schattschneider, *The Semisovereign People*, 88–89; E. E. Schattschneider to V. O. Key, Dec. 7, 1948, box 29, Key Papers, JFKL.

49. E. E. Schattschneider to V. O. Key, Oct. 12, 1948, box 29, Key Papers, JFKL.

50. "Toward a More Responsible Two-Party System: A Report of the Committee on Political Parties," *The American Political Science Review* 44 (Sept. 1950), Supplement: viii, 1, 10, 15–16; "Objectives in Research Concerning the Present Status of Political Parties in the United States: A Preliminary Statement by Elmer E. Schattschneider," c. 1947 ms., 2, in box 20, E. E. Schattschneider Files, Olin Library, Wesleyan University, Middletown, Conn.

51. Schattschneider notes on Arthur Holcombe, c. 1951, box 2, Schattschneider Files.

52. "Objectives in Research Concerning the Present Status of Political Parties in the United States: A Preliminary Statement by E. E. Schattschneider," 2–3; E. E. Schattschneider, "Some Suggestions for Regional Political Research," c. 1947 ms., 2, in box 20, Schattschneider Files.

53. E. E. Schattschneider to Adlai E. Stevenson, Nov. 9, 1952, box 3, E. E. Schattschneider Papers, Olin Library, Wesleyan University, Middletown, Conn.

54. "Toward a More Responsible Two-Party System: A Report of the Committee on Political Parties," *The American Political Science Review*, 13.

55. V. O. Key, Jr., *Public Opinion and American Democracy* (New York: Alfred A. Knopf, 1961), 432–34, 442–43, 456, 458, 460–61, 473.

56. Key, *The Responsible Electorate*, 52–53, 55 n.11, 58–59, 61, 63, 75, 91, 104, 150–51.

57. Pomper, "The Impact of *The American Voter* on Political Science," 618; A. J. Mackelprang, Bernard Grofman, and N. Keith Thomas, "Electoral Change and Stability: Some New Perspectives," *American Politics Quarterly* 3 (July 1975): 317; Sheldon Kamieniecki, *Party Identification, Political Behavior, and the American Electorate* (Westport, Conn.: Greenwood Press, 1985), 186; Natchez, *Images of Democracy*, 203.

58. Campbell, review of *The Responsible Electorate* by V. O. Key, Jr., 1008.

59. Philip E. Converse, review of *The Responsible Electorate* by V. O. Key, Jr., *Political Science Quarterly* 81 (Dec. 1966): 633.

60. Milton Cummings to Philip E. Converse, Jan. 13, 1967, box 1, Converse Papers.

61. Key, *The Responsible Electorate*, 148.

62. Allan J. Lichtman, "The End of Realignment Theory? Toward a New Research Program for American Political History," *Historical Methods* 15 (Fall 1982): 171; Peter H. Argersinger and John W. Jeffries, "American Electoral History: Party Systems and Voting Behavior," in *Research in Micropolitics: Voting Behavior*, ed. Samuel Long (Greenwich, Conn.: JAI Press, 1986), 3; Lawrence, *The Collapse of the Democratic Majority*, 3; Carl A. Sheingold, "Social Networks and Voting: The Resurrection of a Research Agenda," *American Sociological Review* 38 (Dec. 1973): 716.

63. William Nisbet Chambers, "Party Development and the American Mainstream," in *The American Party Systems*, ed. William Nisbet Chambers and Walter Dean Burnham, Revised Edition (New York: Oxford University Press, 1975), 29–30; Joel H. Silbey and Samuel T. McSeveney, "The Historical Structure of American Popular Voting Behavior," in *Voters, Parties, and Elections: Quantitative Essays in the History of American Popular Voting Behavior*, ed. Joel H. Silbey and Samuel T. McSeveney (Lexington, Mass.: Xerox College Publishing, 1972), 2–3; Thomas P. Jahnige, "Critical Elections and Social Change: Towards a Dynamic Explanation of National Party Competition in the United States," *Polity* 3 (Summer 1971): 498.

64. Paul T. David, "The Changing Party Pattern," *The Antioch Review* 16 (Sept. 1956): 333–35.

65. Avery Leiserson, *Parties and Politics: An Institutional and Behavioral Approach* (New York: Alfred A. Knopf, 1958), 166, 284.

CHAPTER EIGHT

1. Arthur Krock, *In the Nation, 1932–1966* (New York: McGraw-Hill, 1966), 139–40.

2. Hedley Donovan, "How to be a Political Prophet," *Fortune* 46 (Sept. 1952): 194.

3. Clinton Rossiter, *Parties and Politics in America* (Ithaca: Cornell University Press, 1960), 167; Sidney Hyman, "The Great X Factor—The Silent Vote," *New York Times Magazine*, Oct. 30, 1960, 90, 92; Charles A. H. Thomson and Frances M. Shattuck, *The 1956 Presidential Campaign* (Washington, D.C.: The Brookings Institution, 1960), 351.

4. William H. Whyte, *The Organization Man* (New York: Simon and Schuster, 1956; Garden City, New York: Doubleday and Company, n. d.), 331–32.

5. Louis Harris, *Is There a Republican Majority? Political Trends, 1952–1956* (New York: Harper and Brothers, 1954), 9–10, 19–21, 39, 44, 177, 187, 196–200, 213.

6. Paul T. David, "Comparative State Politics and the Problem of Party Realignment," in Stephen K. Bailey et al., *Research Frontiers in Politics and Government* (Washington, D.C.: The Brookings Institution, 1955), 191, 199–200; Donald S. Strong, "The Presidential Election in the South, 1952," *The Journal of Politics* 17 (Aug. 1955): 382, 389.

7. Theodore H. White, *The Making of the President 1960* (New York: Atheneum, 1961), 352, 359–60.

8. Thomson and Shattuck, *The 1956 Presidential Campaign*, 347; Eugene H. Roseboom, *A History of Presidential Elections* (New York: Macmillan, 1957), 541–42; Richard M. Scammon, "The Road to 1960," in *American Government Annual, 1960–1961*, ed. Earl Latham (New York: Holt, Rinehart and Winston, 1960), 28.

9. Davis R. B. Ross, "The Democratic Party, 1945–1960," in *History of U.S. Political Parties*, Vol. IV, *1945–1972*, ed. Arthur M. Schlesinger, Jr. (New York: Chelsea House Publishers, 1973), 2707; Herbert B. Asher, *Presidential Elections and American Politics: Voters, Candidates, and Campaigns Since 1952* (Homewood, Ill.: The Dorsey Press, 1976), 158; Louis Harris and Associates, "A Brief Analysis of the 1960 Presidential Election," Nov. 21, 1960 ms., 14, in box 8, Richard M. Scammon Papers, John F. Kennedy Library (JFKL), Boston, Mass.

10. James Reston, "Washington," *New York Times*, Nov. 4, 1960, 32; Arthur M. Schlesinger, *In Retrospect: The History of a Historian* (New York: Harcourt, Brace, and World, 1963), 190–91.

11. E. E. Schattschneider to Adlai E. Stevenson, Nov. 9, 1952, box 3, E. E. Schattschneider Papers, Olin Library, Wesleyan University, Middletown, Conn.

12. E. E. Schattschneider, *The Semisovereign People: A Realist's View of Democracy in America* (New York: Holt, Rinehart and Winston, 1960), 90–93; E. E. Schattschneider, "United States: The Functional Approach to Party Government," in *Modern Political Parties: Approaches to Comparative Politics*, ed. Sigmund Neumann (Chicago: The University of Chicago Press, 1956), 209–11.

13. Angus Campbell, "The Case of the Missing Democrats," *New Republic*, July 2, 1956, 14.

14. Angus Campbell, Gerald Gurin, and Warren E. Miller, *The Voter Decides* (Evanston, Ill.: Row, Peterson and Company, 1954), 176–77; Angus Campbell and Homer C. Cooper, *Group Differences in Attitudes and Votes: A Study of the 1954 Congressional Election* (Ann Arbor: Survey Research Center/Institute for Social Research, University of Michigan, 1956), 61.

15. "12–Year Voter Study Indicates Democratic Victory in the Fall," *New York Times*, May 8, 1960, 51.

16. Angus Campbell et al., *The American Voter* (New York: John Wiley and Sons, 1960), 11.

17. V. O. Key, Jr., "The 'Moral Victory' of the Republicans," *New Republic*, Dec. 6, 1954, 9.

18. V. O. Key, Jr., "Eisenhower's Coalition Government," *New Republic*, April 30, 1956, 19; V. O. Key, Jr., "Two Political Parties in 1960?" *New Republic*, Dec. 3, 1956, 14–15.

19. V. O. Key, Jr., *Public Opinion and American Democracy* (New York: Alfred A. Knopf, 1961), 477–78.

20. V. O. Key, Jr., with the assistance of Milton C. Cummings, Jr., *The Responsible Electorate: Rationality in Presidential Voting, 1932–1960* (Cambridge: The Belknap Press of Harvard University Press, 1966), 71.

21. Samuel Lubell to Evan Thomas, April 21, 1954, box 122, Samuel Lubell Papers, Dodd Research Center, University of Connecticut, Storrs, Conn.

22. Samuel Lubell to Book Review Editor, *Chicago Sun-Times*, May 13, 1956, box 122, Lubell Papers.

23. V. O. Key to Samuel Lubell, April 14, 1956, box 149, Lubell Papers.

24. Samuel Lubell, *The Revolt of the Moderates* (New York: Harper and Brothers, 1956), 17, 38, 40, 105, 119–20, 165, 261–62; Samuel Lubell, "Who Elected Eisenhower?" *Saturday Evening Post*, Jan. 10, 1953, 78; Samuel Lubell, "How Taft Did It," *Saturday Evening Post*, Feb. 10, 1951, 144, 147–48; Samuel Lubell, *The Future of American Politics* (New York: Harper and Brothers, 1952), 1, 226, 261; Samuel Lubell to Editor, *America Magazine,* April 24, 1952, and Samuel Lubell to Jack Fischer, Dec. 12, 1949, both in box 122, Lubell Papers; Samuel Lubell to Harry Gilburt, July 7, 1956, box 145, Lubell Papers.

25. Oliver Garceau to Corinne Silverman, May 28, 1956 box 149, Lubell Papers.

26. Samuel Lubell, "Preface to the Second Edition," in Samuel Lubell, *The Future of American Politics*, Second Edition (Garden City, New York: Doubleday and Company, 1956), viii; Lubell, *Revolt of the Moderates*, 5–6, 18, 108–9, 115, 117–18, 165, 210–11, 224; Samuel Lubell, "Can Eisenhower Be Re-Elected?" *Saturday Evening Post*, Feb. 12, 1955, 79–80; Lubell, *Future of American Politics* [1952], 236–37, 260–61; Lubell to Editor, *America Magazine*, April 24, 1952; Samuel Lubell to Lewis Gannett [1952, never sent], box 122, Lubell Papers; Samuel Lubell to Lester Markel, Aug. 16, 1957, box 226, Lubell Papers.

27. Lubell, "Who Elected Eisenhower?" 26–27, 78.

28. Lubell, *Revolt of the Moderates*, 108–9; Samuel Lubell, "Can the GOP Win Without Ike?" *Saturday Evening Post*, Jan. 26, 1957, 30, 74–76; Lubell, "Can Eisenhower Be Re-Elected?" 26, 79–80; Samuel Lubell, "Are the Republicans Through?" *Saturday Evening Post*, Feb. 14, 1959, 27, 59; Samuel Lubell, "The Key State of Michigan," *Saturday Evening Post*, Oct. 27, 1956, 112, 114.

29. Lubell, *Revolt of the Moderates*, 232; Lubell, *Future of American Politics* [1952], 260–61.

30. Lubell, *Revolt of the Moderates*, 271; Lubell, *Future of American Politics* [1952], 216.

31. Lubell, "Who Elected Eisenhower?" 78; Lubell, *Future of American Politics* [1952], 202, 226.

32. Lubell to Gilburt, July 7, 1956.

33. Lubell, *Future of American Politics* [1952], 202.

34. Lubell, *Future of American Politics* [1952], 57–61; Lubell to Fischer, Dec. 12, 1949.

35. Lubell, *Revolt of the Moderates*, 18, 114–15, 117–18; Lubell, "Who Elected Eisenhower?" 78; Lubell, "Can Eisenhower Be Re-elected?" 79; Lubell, "How Taft Did It," 148; Samuel Lubell, review of *The Voter Decides* by Angus Campbell [et al.] and *Is There a Republican Majority?* by Louis Harris, 1954 ms., 3, in box 123, Lubell Papers.

36. Lubell, *Revolt of the Moderates*, 101–2, 104, 107; Lubell, "Who Elected Eisenhower?" 27; Samuel Lubell, "Who Will Take California?" *Saturday Evening Post*, Oct. 20, 1956, 121.

37. Lubell, "Can the GOP Win Without Ike?" 76; Lubell, "Are the Republicans Through?" 27, 59, 61; Lubell, "Who Will Take California?" 121.

38. Lubell, *Revolt of the Moderates*, 104.

39. Lubell, "Can the GOP Win Without Ike?" 76.

40. Lubell, "Are the Republicans Through?" 61.

41. Lubell, *Future of American Politics* [1952], 260.

42. Samuel Lubell to Leonard Weinberg, Nov. 22, 1961, box 148, Lubell Papers.

43. Samuel Lubell, "Has Truman Lost the South?" *Look*, Oct. 24, 1950, 129, 132, 134, 138.

44. Samuel Lubell, *When People Speak: Their Opinions, Their Feelings* (New York: Opinion Reporting Workshop/Graduate School of Journalism, Columbia University, Sept. 1960), 20; Samuel Lubell to Harry Gilburt, July 13, 1952, box 145, Lubell Papers.

45. Samuel Lubell, "The Future of the Negro Vote in the United States," *The Journal of Negro Education* 26 (Summer 1957): 411.

46. Lubell to Fischer, Dec. 12, 1949.

47. Thomas J. Sugrue, "Crabgrass-Roots Politics: Race, Rights, and the Reaction Against Liberalism in the Urban North, 1940–1964," 551–52, 578, and Gary Gerstle, "Race and the Myth of the Liberal Consensus," 582, both in *The Journal of American History* 82 (Sept. 1995).

48. Lubell, "Who Will Take California?" 121–22; Lubell, *Future of American Politics* [1952], 93–94, 98; Lubell, "The Future of the Negro Vote in the United States," 409.

49. Lubell, *Future of American Politics* [1952], 95–96.

50. Lubell, "The Future of the Negro Vote in the United States," 416–17.

51. Samuel Lubell to Elaine Weiss, Jan. 10, 1960, box 148, Lubell Papers.

52. Samuel Lubell, "Personalities vs. Issues," in *The Great Debates*, ed. Sidney Kraus (Bloomington: Indiana University Press, 1962), 152.

53. "Politics," *Time*, Nov. 8, 1963, 25.

CHAPTER NINE

1. Sidney M. Milkis, *The President and the Parties: The Transformation of the American Party System Since the New Deal* (New York: Oxford University Press, 1993), 176–77; Dan T. Carter, *The Politics of Rage: George Wallace, the Origins of the New Conservatism, and the Transformation of American Politics* (New York: Simon and Schuster, 1995), 211–12; Robert D. Novak, *The Agony of the GOP 1964* (New York: MacMillan, 1965), 92, 175, 192, 194; Theodore H. White, *The Making of the President 1964* (New York: Atheneum, 1965), 117, 281.

2. Charles Sellers, "The Equilibrium Cycle in Two-Party Politics," *Public Opinion Quarterly* 29 (Spring 1965): 37–38.

3. Roger D. Masters, "Realignment on the Right," *Reporter*, Nov. 7, 1963, 23.

4. Paul T. David, "Party Realignment," *Reporter*, Dec. 5, 1963, 8.

5. John Allswang to Samuel Lubell, Oct. 12, 1964, box 146, Samuel Lubell Papers, Dodd Research Center, University of Connecticut, Storrs, Conn.

6. Paul Tillett, "The National Conventions," in *The National Election of 1964*, ed. Milton C. Cummings, Jr. (Washington, D.C.: The Brookings Institution, 1966), 40–41.

7. Nelson W. Polsby, "Strategic Considerations," in *The National Election of 1964*, ed. Cummings, 83, 105, 107–8; Nelson W. Polsby and Aaron B. Wildavsky, *Presidential Elections: Strategies of American Electoral Politics*, Second Edition (New York: Charles Scribner's Sons, 1968), 202–3, 208, 210–11.

8. Gerald M. Pomper, *Elections in America: Control and Influence in Democratic Politics* (New York: Dodd, Mead and Company, 1968), 119–22.

9. Gerald M. Pomper with Susan S. Lederman, *Elections in America: Control and Influence in Democratic Politics*, Second Edition (New York: Longman, 1980), 98–99.

10. Angus Campbell, "Interpreting the Presidential Victory," in *The National Election of 1964*, ed. Cummings, 276–81.

11. Samuel Lubell, *White and Black: Test of a Nation* (New York: Harper and Row, 1964), 9, 47, 64, 127–28.

12. Samuel Lubell to Harry Gilburt, n. d. [late 1963 but prior to the Kennedy assassination], box 145, Lubell Papers.

13. Samuel Lubell to Jim Freeman, Dec. 2, 1963, box 145, Lubell Papers.

14. Samuel Lubell to Walker Stone, June 22, 1964 [never sent], box 148, Lubell Papers.

15. E. N. Kenworthy, "Democrats Fear Losses in South," *New York Times*, Aug. 4, 1964, 1, 14; "Voter Shifts Found to Favor Johnson," *New York Times*, Aug. 18, 1964, 18.

16. Samuel Lubell, *The Future of American Politics*, Third Edition (New York: Harper and Row, 1965), vii–viii, x, 1–5, 15–17, 23 n.1, 121 n.10, 239 n.7.

17. Mary C. Brennan, *Turning Right in the Sixties: The Conservative Capture of the GOP* (Chapel Hill: The University of North Carolina Press, 1995), 80–81, 134; John H. Kessel, *The Goldwater Coalition: Republican Strategies in 1964* (Indianapolis: Bobbs-Merrill, 1968), 307; William H. Flanigan and Nancy H. Zingale, "Summarizing Quantitative Data," in *Analyzing Electoral History: A Guide to the Study of American Voter Behavior*, ed. Jerome M. Clubb, William H. Flanigan, and Nancy H. Zingale (Beverly Hills: Sage Publications, 1981), 223, 226; Robert Alan Goldberg, *Barry Goldwater* (New Haven: Yale University Press, 1995), 208, 237; Edward G. Carmines and Robert Huckfeldt, "Party Politics in the Wake of the Voting Rights Act," in *Controversies in Minority Voting: The Voting Rights Act in Perspective*, ed. Bernard Grofman and Chandler Davidson (Washington, D.C.: The Brookings Institution, 1992), 124–25, 130–31; Jerome L. Himmelstein, *To the Right: The Transformation of American Conservatism* (Berkeley: University of California Press, 1990), 69.

18. Timothy A. Byrnes, "Issues, Elections, and Political Change: The Case of Abortion," in *Do Elections Matter?* Third Edition, ed. Benjamin Ginsberg and Alan Stone (Armonk, N.Y.: M. E. Sharpe, 1996), 111–12; Morris Janowitz, *The Last Half-Century: Societal Change and Politics in America* (Chicago: The University of Chicago Press, 1978), 491–92; Max Frankel, "Nixon So Far: Trend Is Mixed," *New York Times*, July 13, 1969, 54; Theodore H. White, *The Making of the President 1972* (New York: Atheneum, 1973), 299–300; Philip Frymer and John David Skrentny, "Coalition-Building and the Politics of Electoral Capture During the Nixon Administration: African Americans, Labor, Latinos," *Studies in American Political Development* 12 (Spring 1998): 131, 136.

19. Everett Ladd, Jr., Charles Hadley, and Lauriston King, "A New Political Alignment?" *The Public Interest*, no. 23 (Spring 1971): 46; Dan T. Carter, *From George Wallace to Newt Gingrich: Race in the Conservative Counterrevolution, 1963–1994* (Baton Rouge: Louisiana State University Press, 1996), 39–40; David S. Broder, *The Party's Over: The Failure of Politics in America* (New York: Harper and Row, 1972), 192–3; James L. Sundquist, *Dynamics of the Party System: Alignment and Realignment of Political Parties in the United States* (Washington, D.C.: The Brookings Institution, 1973), 1–2.

20. Philip E. Converse and Gregory B. Markus, "Recent Evidence on the Stability of Party Identification: The New Michigan Election Study Panel," in *Realignment in Ameri-*

can Politics: Toward a Theory, ed. Bruce A. Campbell and Richard J. Trilling (Austin: University of Texas Press, 1980), 149; Ivor Crewe, "Prospects for Party Realignment: An Anglo-American Comparison," *Comparative Politics* 12 (July 1980): 379–80; David G. Lawrence, *The Collapse of the Democratic Presidential Majority: Realignment, Dealignment, and Electoral Change from Franklin Roosevelt to Bill Clinton* (Boulder: Westview Press, 1996), 20, 169; Broder, *The Party's Over*, 190–92, 201, 212.

21. David R. Segal, "Partisan Realignment in the United States: The Lesson of the 1964 Election," *Public Opinion Quarterly* 32 (Fall 1968): 443–44.

22. Numan V. Bartley and Hugh D. Graham, *Southern Politics and the Second Reconstruction* (Baltimore: The Johns Hopkins University Press, 1975), 186–87; A. James Reichley, "That Elusive Political Majority," *Fortune* 84 (March 1971): 72; Joseph A. Aistrup, *The Southern Strategy Revisited: Republican Top-Down Advancement in the South* (Lexington: The University Press of Kentucky, 1996), 42.

23. Carter, *Politics of Rage*, 369; Bartley and Graham, *Southern Politics and the Second Reconstruction*, 172–73; E. M. Schreiber, "'Where the Ducks Are': Southern Strategy Versus Fourth Party," *Public Opinion Quarterly* 35 (Summer 1971): 167; Dewey W. Grantham, *The Life and Death of the Solid South: A Political History* (Lexington: The University Press of Kentucky, 1988), 180; Jack Bass and Walter De Vries, *The Transformation of Southern Politics: Social Change and Political Consequence Since 1945* (New York: Basic Books, 1976), 403.

24. Broder, *The Party's Over*, 198–99; William C. Havard, "From Past to Future: An Overview of Southern Politics," in *The Changing Politics of the South*, ed. William C. Havard (Baton Rouge: Louisiana State University Press, 1972), 719, 721–22, 729; Sundquist, *Dynamics of the Party System*, 259–61; Reg Murphy and Hal Gulliver, *The Southern Strategy* (New York: Charles Scribner's Sons, 1971), 244, 249, 264–65, 269–70; Donald S. Strong, "Further Reflections on Southern Politics," *The Journal of Politics* 33 (May 1971): 254–55; George Brown Tindall, *The Disruption of the Solid South* (Athens: University of Georgia Press, 1972), 46; Andrew M. Greeley, *Building Coalitions: American Politics in the 1970s* (New York: New Viewpoints, 1974), 132.

25. Bartley and Graham, *Southern Politics and the Second Reconstruction*, 196; Arthur H. Miller and Warren E. Miller, "Issues, Candidates and Partisan Divisions in the 1972 American Presidential Election," *British Journal of Political Science* 5 (Oct. 1975): 426; Schreiber, "'Where the Ducks Are,'" 159–61, 164–67; Louis M. Seagull, *Southern Republicanism* (New York: John Wiley and Sons, 1975), v, 53; Monroe Lee Billington, *The Political South in the Twentieth Century* (New York: Charles Scribner's Sons, 1975), 181, 183.

26. John G. Stewart, *One Last Chance: The Democratic Party, 1974–76* (New York: Praeger, 1974), 121–22; Gerald M. Pomper, *Voters' Choice: Varieties of American Electoral Behavior* (New York: Dodd, Mead, 1975), 137–38; Frank J. Munger, "New York," II 75, and Abraham Miller, "Illinois," II 159, both in *Explaining the Vote: Presidential Choices in the Nation and the States, 1968. Part II: Presidential Choices in Individual States*, ed. David M. Kovenock et al. (Chapel Hill: Institute for Research in Social Science, 1973).

27. Sundquist, *Dynamics of the Party System*, 283.

28. E. J. Dionne, Jr., *Why Americans Hate Politics* (New York: Simon and Schuster, 1991), 12, 79–80, 89, 109; Norman H. Nie, Sidney Verba, and John R. Petrocik, *The Changing American Voter* (Cambridge: Harvard University Press, 1976), 11; Karl A. Lamb, "Plotting the Electorate's Course in Dangerous Waters," *The Political Science Reviewer* 2 (1972): 61; Reichley, "That Elusive Political Majority," 72; Richard W. Boyd,

"Popular Control of Public Policy: A Normal Vote Analysis of the 1968 Election," *The American Political Science Review* 66 (June 1972): 434.

29. Dionne, *Why Americans Hate Politics*, 78; Everett Carll Ladd, Jr., "The Fabric of Contemporary American Electoral Politics," in Everett Carl Ladd, Jr. and Seymour Martin Lipset, *Academics, Politics, and the 1972 Election* (Washington, D.C.: American Enterprise Institute for Public Policy Research, 1973), 47; Ladd et al., "A New Political Realignment?" 56, 59, 62–63; Carter, *Politics of Rage*, 347–50; Richard J. Trilling, "Party Image and Electoral Behavior," in *American Electoral Behavior: Change and Stability*, ed. Samuel A. Kirkpatrick (New York: Sage Publications, 1976), 82, 100.

30. Broder, *The Party's Over*, 203–4.

31. Sundquist, *Dynamics of the Party System*, 355, 357.

32. Sundquist, *Dynamics of the Party System*, 330; William C. Berman, *America's Right Turn: From Nixon to Bush* (Baltimore: The Johns Hopkins University Press, 1994), 171; Ronald Radosh, *Divided They Fell: The Demise of the Democratic Party, 1964–1996* (New York: The Free Press, 1996), 155; Lamb, "Plotting the Electorate's Course in Dangerous Waters," 42, 52.

33. Dionne, *Why Americans Hate Politics*, 199–200; Byrnes, "Issues, Elections, and Political Change," 112–13; John Leonard, "Books of the Times," *New York Times*, Sept. 25, 1970, 41; David W. Reinhard, *The Republican Right Since 1945* (Lexington: The University Press of Kentucky, 1983), 221.

34. Ben J. Wattenberg, *Values Matter Most: How Republicans or Democrats or a Third Party Can Win and Renew the American Way of Life* (New York: The Free Press, 1995), 12.

35. Richard M. Scammon and Ben J. Wattenberg, *The Real Majority* (New York: Coward-McCann, 1970), 20, 22, 30, 32, 63, 80–81, 174–76, 180–82, 184, 194, 211, 290.

36. Carter, *Politics of Rage*, 377–78; Pomper, *Voters' Choice*, 153–54, 161.

37. Broder, *The Party's Over*, 83, 180.

38. Reichley, "That Elusive Political Majority," 147, 150.

39. Sundquist, *Dynamics of the Party System*, 330–31, 337, 353, 355.

40. Byron E. Shafer and William J. M. Claggett, *The Two Majorities: The Issue Context of Modern American Politics* (Baltimore: The Johns Hopkins University Press, 1995), 175, 186, 189.

41. Samuel Lubell to Arthur Mann, Sept. 23, 1965, box 148, Lubell Papers.

42. Broder, *The Party's Over*, 193.

43. Elliott Abrams, "Winning Elections," *Commentary* 56 (Sept. 1973): 78.

44. Samuel Lubell to Nelson Rockefeller, June 20, 1970, box 128, Lubell Papers; Cary Reich, *The Life of Nelson A. Rockefeller: Worlds to Conquer, 1908–1958* (New York: Doubleday, 1996), 451–52.

45. Samuel Lubell to Arthur Schlesinger, Jr., May 9, 1970, box 128, and Samuel Lubell to Arthur Schlesinger, Jr., Aug. 25, 1970, box 147, both in Lubell Papers; Arthur Schlesinger, Jr., "The 1968 Election: An Historical Perspective," *Vital Speeches of the Day*, Dec. 15, 1968, 151.

46. Arthur Schlesinger, Jr., "The City Politic: Scammon and Wattenberg vs. Lubell," *New York*, Dec. 7, 1970, 8, 10.

47. Samuel Lubell, *The Hidden Crisis in American Politics* (New York: W. W. Norton, 1970), 278; "WMAL-TV 7 Program Transcript," July 12, 1970, 9–10, copy in box 128, Lubell Papers.

48. Lubell, *Hidden Crisis in American Politics*, 29, 87, 243; Samuel Lubell, *The Future While It Happened* (New York: W. W. Norton, 1973), 66, 90, 146–47; "Lubell Says Study of '69 Voting Here Shows Racial Trend," *New York Times*, July 13, 1970, 17.

49. Samuel Lubell, "The Hidden Crisis in American Politics," *Public Opinion Quarterly* 34 (Fall 1970): 463.

50. Lubell, *Future While It Happened*, 13.

51. "WMAL-TV 7 Program Transcript," July 12, 1970, 10.

52. Lubell, *Hidden Crisis in American Politics*, 30, 34, 68, 269, 271–72; Lubell, *Future While It Happened*, 43.

53. Lubell to Rockefeller, June 20, 1970.

54. Ronnie Dugger, "The Hidden Crisis in American Politics," *New York Times Book Review*, Aug. 16, 1970, 3; Samuel Lubell, "American Politics," *New York Times Book Review*, Sept. 27, 1970, 40.

55. Lubell, *Hidden Crisis in American Politics*, 22, 32, 41, 46, 48, 243, 247, 282.

56. Lubell, *Future While It Happened*, 44.

57. "WMAL-TV 7 Program Transcript," 5–6.

58. Samuel Lubell to David Riesman, July 22, 1973, box 144, Lubell Papers.

59. Theodore H. White, *The Making of the President 1968* (New York: Atheneum, 1969), 399–400; William H. Flanigan, *Political Behavior of the American Electorate*, Second Edition (Boston: Allyn and Bacon, 1972), 48; Michael W. Miles, *The Odyssey of the American Right* (New York: Oxford University Press, 1980), 301.

60. Louis Harris, *The Anguish of Change* (New York: W. W. Norton, 1973), 273–74.

61. Pomper, *Voters' Choice*, 91, 94, 113.

62. Nicol C. Rae, *The Decline and Fall of the Liberal Republicans from 1952 to the Present* (New York: Oxford University Press, 1989), 81, 102; Andrew Hacker, "Is There a New Republican Majority?" *Commentary* 48 (Nov. 1969): 66; Reichley, "That Elusive Majority," 72.

63. Arthur Schlesinger, Jr., "The New Liberal Coalition," *The Progressive* (April 1967): 15–17.

64. Schlesinger, "The 1968 Election," 151–52.

65. Arthur Schlesinger, Jr., "How McGovern Will Win," *New York Times Magazine*, July 30, 1972, 34.

66. Francis X. Clines, "For the President's Defender, a Task That Never Ends: Keeping 'The Beast' at Bay," *New York Times*, April 27, 1997, 22; Herbert S. Parmet, *The Democrats: The Years After FDR* (New York: Oxford University Press, 1977), 296.

67. Lanny J. Davis, *The Emerging Democratic Majority: Lessons and Legacies from the New Politics* (New York: Stein and Day, 1974), 172, 212.

68. Stewart, *One Last Chance*, 94, 139–40.

69. Frederick G. Dutton, *Changing Sources of Power: American Politics in the 1970s* (New York: McGraw-Hill, 1971), xi–xiii, 4–5, 12–13, 21, 25, 40, 54, 59–60, 63–64, 93–95, 108–9, 113–14, 119, 142–43, 151–52, 158–60, 187–89, 219–23, 225–29, 231–39, 256–57, 265.

70. Ladd et al., "A New Political Alignment?" 46–7, 55, 62–63; Everett Carll Ladd, Jr., *American Political Parties: Social Change and Political Response* (New York: W. W. Norton, 1970), 303–5; Ladd, "The Fabric of Contemporary American Electoral Politics," 33, 39.

71. Greeley, *Building Coalitions*, 12–13 n.2, 195–96.

72. Angus Campbell, "Politics Through the Life Cycle," *The Gerontologist* 11 (Summer 1971): 117.

73. Anthony Ripley, "Barry Race Could Upset Vote Patterns, Prof Says," *Detroit News*, June 14, 1964, news clipping in box 2, Angus Campbell Papers, Bentley Historical Library (BHL), University of Michigan, Ann Arbor, Mich.

74. Campbell speech transcript, Wisconsin State University–Whitewater, March 25–26, 1968, unpaginated, box 10, Campbell Papers.

75. Angus Campbell, "On from Nixon's Victory: 1 — The Democrats' Future," *New Society*, Jan. 25, 1973, 173–75.

76. Philip E. Converse et al., "Continuity and Change in American Politics: Parties and Issues in the 1968 Election," *The American Political Science Review* 63 (Dec. 1969): 1084–85.

77. Philip E. Converse, "Change in the American Electorate," in *The Human Meaning of Social Change*, ed. Angus Campbell and Philip E. Converse (New York: Russell Sage Foundation, 1972), 302, 321.

78. Philip E. Converse, "Public Opinion and Voting Behavior," in *Handbook of Political Science*, Vol. 4, *Nongovernmental Politics*, ed. Fred I. Greenstein and Nelson W. Polsby (Reading, Mass.: Addison-Wesley, 1975), 145, 147.

79. Philip E. Converse, *The Dynamics of Party Support: Cohort-Analyzing Party Identification* (Beverly Hills: Sage Publications, 1976), 69, 72.

80. Miller and Miller, "Issues, Candidates and Partisan Divisions in the 1972 American Presidential Election," 394, 424, 426, 433–34.

81. Warren E. Miller and Teresa E. Levitin, *Leadership and Change: The New Politics and the American Electorate* (Cambridge: Winthrop Publishers, 1976), 1, 10.

82. Warren E. Miller and J. Merrill Shanks, *The New American Voter* (Cambridge: Harvard University Press, 1996), 168.

83. William E. Porter, review of *The Hidden Crisis in American Politics* by Samuel Lubell, *Public Opinion Quarterly* 35 (Spring 1971): 153; Ladd et al., "A New Political Alignment?" 46–47; Jack Newfield and Jeff Greenfield, *A Populist Manifesto: The Making of a New Majority* (New York: Praeger, 1972), 209–10; Reichley, "That Elusive Majority," 69, 72; Nelson W. Polsby and Aaron B. Wildavsky, *Presidential Elections: Strategies of American Electoral Politics*, Third Edition (New York: Charles Scribner's Sons, 1971), 177–78.

84. Broder, *The Party's Over*, xxiv, 1, 212; Flanigan, *Political Behavior of the American Electorate*, Second Edition, 126; Hugh A. Bone and Austin Ranney, *Politics and Voters*, Fourth Edition (New York: McGraw-Hill, 1976), 37, 53–54; Greeley, *Building Coalitions*, 183 n.7.

85. William L. Shade, *Social Change and the Electoral Process* (Gainesville: University of Florida Press, 1973), 43; The Ripon Society and Clifford W. Brown, Jr., *Jaws of Victory: The Game-Plan Politics of 1972, the Crisis of the Republican Party, and the Future of the Constitution* (Boston: Little, Brown, 1974), 157; Vermont Royster, "American Politics: 1932–1972," *The American Scholar* 42 (Spring 1973): 205–11, 214.

86. Sundquist, *Dynamics of the Party System*, 332, 340, 343, 345, 347, 350, 353, 358, 365.

87. Rae, *Decline and Fall of the Liberal Republicans*, 217; Theodore J. Lowi, *The End of the Republican Era* (Norman: University of Oklahoma Press, 1995), 79; Lewis L. Gould, *1968: The Election That Changed America* (Chicago: Ivan R. Dee, 1993), viii, 3, 164, 166; Carter, *From George Wallace to Newt Gingrich*, 53–54; William G. Mayer, "Mass Partisanship, 1946–1994," in Byron E. Shafer et al., *Partisan Approaches to Postwar American Politics* (New York: Chatham House, 1998), 214.

88. Louis M. Seagull, "Secular Realignment: The Concept and Its Utility," in *Realignment in American Politics*, ed. Campbell and Trilling, 72; David Knoke, *Change and Continuity in American Politics: The Social Bases of Political Parties* (Baltimore: The Johns Hopkins University Press, 1976), 129–30, 152–53; Richard L. Rubin, *Party Dynamics: The Democratic Coalition and the Politics of Change* (New York: Columbia University Press, 1976), 177.

89. Crewe, "Prospects for Party Realignment," 381.

90. Crewe, "Prospects for Party Realignment," 396–97; Seagull, "Secular Realignment," 72; Bruce A. Campbell, "Realignment, Party Decomposition, and Issue Voting," in *Realignment in American Politics*, ed. Campbell and Trilling, 82; Paul Kleppner, "Critical Realignments and Electoral Systems," in Paul Kleppner et al., *The Evolution of American Electoral Systems* (Westport, Conn.: Greenwood Press, 1981), 17, 24; Nie et al., *Changing American Voter*, 289, 346–48; Pomper, *Voters' Choice*, 39–40; Rubin, *Party Dynamics*, 178.

91. Richard J. Trilling, "Party Image and Partisan Change," in *The Future of Political Parties*, ed. Louis Maisel and Paul M. Sacks (Beverly Hills: Sage Publications, 1975), 95; Nie et al., *Changing American Voter*, 290; Knoke, *Change and Continuity in American Politics*, 130, 153, 160; Herbert B. Asher, *Presidential Elections and American Politics: Voters, Candidates, and Campaigns Since 1952* (Homewood, Ill.: The Dorsey Press, 1976), 132, 189.

92. Asher, *Presidential Elections and American Politics*, 305; Rubin, *Party Dynamics*, 177.

93. Lewis L. Gould, "A Life in the Republican Party," *Reviews in American History* 4 (March 1976): 105; William J. Keefe, *Parties, Politics, and Public Policy in America*, Second Edition (Hinsdale, Ill.: The Dryden Press, 1976), 109–10; Nelson W. Polsby and Aaron Wildavsky, *Presidential Elections: Strategies of American Electoral Politics*, Fourth Edition (New York: Charles Scribner's Sons, 1976), 164; Asher, *Presidential Elections and American Politics*, 180, 189; Wilson Carey McWilliams, "The Meaning of the Election," in *The Election of 1976: Reports and Interpretations*, ed. Marlene M. Pomper (New York: David McKay Company, 1977), 148–49, 151; Parmet, *Democrats*, 309; Aistrup, *Southern Strategy Revisted*, 39.

94. Pomper, *Elections in America*, 98–99, 102; Gerald M. Pomper, "The Presidential Election," in *The Election of 1976*, ed. Pomper, 78–79, 81–82.

95. Everett Carll Ladd, Jr., *Where Have All the Voters Gone? The Fracturing of America's Political Parties* (New York: W. W. Norton, 1978), xxii, 1–3, 5, 9–11, 13, 24, 27–28, 37–38, 43–44.

CHAPTER TEN

1. "Phillips, Kevin," *Current Biography Yearbook 1994* (New York: H. W. Wilson, 1994), 445, 448; James Boyd, "Nixon's Southern Strategy — 'It's All in the Charts,'" *New York Times Magazine*, May 17, 1970, 105–7; Richard Harris, *Justice: The Crisis of Law, Order, and Freedom in America* (New York: E. P. Dutton, 1970), 125.

2. Kevin Phillips, "Busting the Media Trusts," *Harper's* 255 (July 1977): 24.

3. Boyd, "Nixon's Southern Strategy," 106.

4. Lee W. Huebner, "The Republican Party, 1952–1972," in *History of U.S. Political Parties*, Vol. IV, *1945–1972*, ed. Arthur M. Schlesinger, Jr. (New York: Chelsea House Publishers, 1973), 3042; Garry Wills, *Nixon Agonistes: The Crisis of the Self-Made Man* (Boston: Houghton Mifflin, 1970), 265–66; Harris, *Justice*, 123–24.

5. George Brown Tindall, *The Disruption of the Solid South* (Athens: University of Georgia Press, 1972), 62; Jerome L. Himmelstein, *To the Right: The Transformation of American Conservatism* (Berkeley: University of California Press, 1990), 69, 71.

6. Douglas Price, "'Critical Elections' and Party History: A Critical View," *Polity* 4 (1971): 238; Karl A. Lamb, "Plotting the Electorate's Course in Dangerous Waters," *The Political Science Reviewer* 2 (1972): 46; Richard J. Jensen, "Historiography of American Political History," in *Encyclopedia of American Political History: Studies of the Principal Movements and Ideas*, ed. Jack P. Greene (New York: Charles Scribner's Sons, 1984), 7; J. Clark Archer, "Macrogeographical Versus Microgeographical Cleavages in American Presidential Elections: 1940–1984," *Political Geography Quarterly* 7 (April 1988): 112.

7. Price, "'Critical Elections' and Party History," 237–38.

8. Kevin P. Phillips, *The Emerging Republican Majority* (New Rochelle, N.Y.: Arlington House, 1969), 262, 353, 375; Kevin P. Phillips, *Mediacracy: American Parties and Politics in the Communications Age* (Garden City, N.Y.: Doubleday, 1975), x.

9. Phillips, *Emerging Republican Majority*, 461; Kevin Phillips, "The Future of American Politics," *National Review*, Dec. 22, 1972, 1396.

10. Lamb, "Plotting the Electorate's Course in Dangerous Waters," 46–47.

11. Samuel Lubell, *The Revolt of the Moderates* (New York: Harper and Brothers, 1956), 260.

12. Price, "'Critical Elections' and Party History," 238.

13. Phillips, *Mediacracy*, 59, 68–69; Kevin Phillips, "How Nixon Will Win," *New York Times Magazine*, Aug. 6, 1972, 9.

14. Wills, *Nixon Agonistes*, 265.

15. Kevin P. Phillips, "The Last Frontier?" *Newsweek*, July 10, 1972, 34; Kevin Phillips, "The Balkanization of America," *Harper's* 256 (May 1978): 37–38.

16. Quoted in "Republicans," *Time*, Aug. 1, 1969, 17.

17. Wills, *Nixon Agonistes*, 267.

18. Quoted in Boyd, "Nixon's Southern Strategy," 106.

19. "Phillips, Kevin," *Current Biography*, 445; Kevin P. Phillips, *Post-Conservative America: People, Politics and Ideology in a Time of Crisis* (New York: Random House, 1982), 54–55; Phillips, *Mediacracy*, 9–12; Phillips, *Emerging Republican Majority*, 21.

20. "Phillips, Kevin," *Current Biography*, 445; Wills, *Nixon Agonistes*, 264.

21. Joe McGinniss, *The Selling of the President 1968* (New York: Trident Press, 1969), 123–25.

22. Theodore H. White, *The Making of the President 1968* (New York: Atheneum, 1969), 330–31.

23. "Phillips, Kevin," *Current Biography*, 445–46.

24. Warren Weaver, Jr., "The Emerging Republican Majority," *New York Times Book Review*, Sept. 21, 1969, 3; Tom Wicker, "In the Nation: One Way to Bring Us Together," *New York Times*, Nov. 11, 1969, Section 4, E13; James M. Naughton, "President Backs a 'Middle Course' on Desegregation," *New York Times*, Sept. 27, 1969, 15.

25. Naughton, "President Backs a 'Middle Course' on Desegregation," 15.

26. Bill Kovach, "Morton Rejects Stress on South," *New York Times*, Nov. 22, 1969, 24.

27. Quoted in Harris, *Justice*, 125.

28. Michael Kazin, *The Populist Persusasion: An American History* (New York: Basic Books, 1995), 251; Wills, *Nixon Agonistes*, 269; James M. Naughton, "GOP Group Boos Keynote Speaker," *New York Times*, Oct. 3, 1970, 12.

29. Dan T. Carter, *From George Wallace to Newt Gingrich: Race in the Conservative Counterrevolution, 1963–1994* (Baton Rouge: Louisiana State University Press, 1996), 42, 44; Dan T. Carter, *The Politics of Rage: George Wallace, the Origins of the New Conservatism, and the Transformation of American Politics* (New York: Simon and Schuster, 1995), 379–80; Dean J. Kotlowski, "Nixon's Southern Strategy Revisited," *Journal of Policy History* 10, no. 2 (1998): 211.

30. Phillips, *Post-Conservative America*, 53.

31. Phillips, *Emerging Republican Majority*, 6.

32. Phillips, *Emerging Republican Majority*, 21–23, 25, 36–37, 207.

33. Phillips, *Emerging Republican Majority*, 57, 77, 348, 440.

34. Phillips, *Emerging Republican Majority*, 140, 266, 270, 286.

35. Phillips, *Emerging Republican Majority*, 39, 250, 290.

36. Phillips, *Emerging Republican Majority*, 22, 470.

37. Phillips, *Emerging Republican Majority*, 38–39, 42, 100–103, 111, 151, 168, 184, 232, 286–87, 317, 354–55, 410–11, 423–24, 437, 440–41, 445–46, 460, 464, 468–71, 474.

38. M. Stanton Evans, "Road Map to the Future," *National Review*, Sept. 9, 1969, 913.

39. "Realignment Politics," *National Review*, Feb. 28, 1975, 201.

40. Weaver, "The Emerging Republican Majority," 3; Lamb, "Plotting the Electorate's Course in Dangerous Waters," 51; John Herbers, "President Opens the White House to Negro Elected Officials Assembled in Capital for Conference," *New York Times*, Sept. 12, 1969, 22; Tully Plesser, "Charting the GOP's Future," *New York Times Magazine*, June 7, 1970, 80.

41. John G. Stewart, *One Last Chance: The Democratic Party, 1974–76* (New York: Praeger, 1974), 95; Frederick G. Dutton, *Changing Sources of Power: American Politics in the 1970s* (New York: McGraw-Hill, 1971), xiv; David S. Broder, *The Party's Over: The Failure of Politics in America* (New York: Harper and Row, 1972), 198; James Sundquist, *Dynamics of the Party System: Alignment and Realignment of Political Parties in the United States* (Washington, D.C.: The Brookings Institution, 1973), 364; Tindall, *Disruption of the Solid South*, 3, 5; David W. Reinhard, *The Republican Right Since 1945* (Lexington: The University Press of Kentucky, 1983), 221–22.

42. Plesser, "Charting the GOP's Future," 80.

43. Alan Ehrenhalt, *The United States of Ambition: Politicians, Power, and the Pursuit of Office* (New York: Times Books, 1991), 285.

44. Paul Starr, "An Emerging Democratic Majority," *The American Prospect*, no. 35 (Nov.-Dec. 1997): 19.

45. Peter Brimelow and Ed Rubenstein, "Electing a New People," *National Review*, June 16, 1997, 32.

46. Phillips, "How Nixon Will Win," 36.

47. Phillips, *Post-Conservative America*, 56.

48. Phillips, *Mediacracy*, vii–ix, 51, 61; Kevin Phillips, "Will Agnew Dump Himself?" *New York Times Magazine*, Nov. 14, 1971, 118–19.

49. Phillips, "The Last Frontier?" 34; Kevin P. Phillips, "A Reagan-Wallace Ticket," *Newsweek*, May 19, 1975, 13.

50. Phillips, *Post-Conservative America*, xviii, 28; Phillips, "The Future of American Politics," 1398.

51. Phillips, *Mediacracy*, 2, 130, 136, 145–47, 149.

52. Phillips, *Mediacracy*, ix, 137; Kevin Phillips, "An American Parliament," *Harper's* 261 (Nov. 1980): 14, 19–21.

53. Walter Dean Burnham, "The End of American Party Politics," *Trans-Action* 7 (Dec. 1969): 20.

54. Walter Dean Burnham, "The United States: The Politics of Heterogeneity," in *Electoral Behavior: A Comparative Handbook*, ed. Richard Rose (New York: The Free Press, 1974), 655.

55. Phillips, *Mediacracy*, 137.

56. "Burnham, Walter Dean," *Who's Who in America*, Vol. I, *1996* (New Providence, N.J.: Reed Reference Publishing, 1996), 581.

57. Walter Dean Burnham, *Critical Elections and the Mainsprings of American Politics* (New York: W. W. Norton, 1970), 140; Samuel Lubell to V. O. Key, April 27, 1957, General Correspondence, 1957, A–P, V. O. Key Papers, Harvard University Archives, Cambridge, Mass.; Walter Dean Burnham to Samuel Lubell, June 19, 1957, box 146, Samuel Lubell Papers, Dodd Research Center, University of Connecticut, Storrs, Conn.

58. Paul Allen Beck, "Micropolitics in Macro Perspective: The Political History of Walter Dean Burnham," *Social Science History* 10 (Fall 1986): 227–28; Walter Dean Burnham and John Sprague, "Additive and Multiplicative Models of the Voting Universe: The Case of Pennsylvania: 1960–1968," *The American Political Science Review* 64 (June 1970): 471 n.1; Warren E. Miller, "Research Life As a Collection of Intersecting Probability Distributions," in *Crossroads of Social Science: The ICPSR 25th Anniversary Volume*, ed. Heinz Eulau (New York: Agathon Press, 1989), 153; Philip E. Converse to Eugene Skolnikoff, Feb. 5, 1971, box 3, Philip E. Converse Papers, Bentley Historical Library (BHL), University of Michigan, Ann Arbor, Mich.

59. Walter Dean Burnham, *Presidential Ballots, 1836–1892* (Baltimore: The Johns Hopkins Press, 1955), xvii–xviii, 156.

60. Walter Dean Burnham, "The Alabama Senatorial Election of 1962: Return of Inter-Party Competition," *The Journal of Politics* 26 (Nov. 1964): 822; Walter Dean Burnham to Pendleton Herring, April 22, 1962, General Correspondence, 1962, A–Z, Key Papers.

61. Beck, "Micropolitics in Macro Perspective," 228; Richard L. McCormick, "The Realignment Synthesis in American History," *Journal of Interdisciplinary History* 13 (Summer 1982): 86; David G. Lawrence, *The Collapse of the Democratic Presidential Majority: Realignment, Dealignment, and Electoral Change from Franklin Roosevelt to Bill Clinton* (Boulder: Westview Press, 1996), 15.

62. Philip Williams, "Review Article: Party Realignment in the United States and Britain," *British Journal of Political Science* 15, no. 1 (1984): 104.

63. V. O. Key to Clinton Rossiter, March 16, 1959, General Correspondence, Jan. 1, 1959–Sept. 1, 1959, A–Z, Key Papers.

64. Edward G. Carmines and James A. Stimson, *Issue Evolution: Race and the Transformation of American Politics* (Princeton: Princeton University Press, 1989), 17 n.3.

65. Richard W. Boyd, review of *Critical Elections and the Mainsprings of American Politics* by Walter Dean Burnham, *Midwest Journal of Political Science* 15 (Aug. 1971): 597.

66. Walter Dean Burnham, "Critical Realignment: Dead or Alive?" in *The End of Realignment? Interpreting American Electoral Eras*, ed. Byron E. Shafer (Madison: The University of Wisconsin Press, 1991), 105; Walter Dean Burnham, "Realignment Lives: The 1994 Earthquake and Its Implications," in *The Clinton Presidency: First Appraisals*, ed. Colin Campbell and Bert A. Rockman (Chatham, N.J.: Chatham House, 1996), 372; Walter Dean Burnham to Samuel Lubell, Aug. 22, 1974, box 144, Lubell Papers.

67. Philip E. Converse to William E. Bicker, Dec. 12, 1973; Philip E. Converse to Nelson Polsby, March 9, 1973; Walter Dean Burnham to Philip E. Converse, March 12, 1973;

Philip E. Converse to Walter Dean Burnham, June 22, 1973, all in box 3, Converse Papers; Walter Dean Burnham to Philip E. Converse, July 2, 1973; Walter Dean Burnham, "Reply," 1973 ms., 1–3; Philip E. Converse to Walter Dean Burnham, Aug. 8, 1973, all in box 4, Converse Papers.

68. Walter Dean Burnham, "Party Systems and the Political Process," in *The American Party Systems*, Revised Edition, ed. William Nisbet Chambers and Walter Dean Burnham (New York: Oxford University Press, 1975), 283; Burnham, *Critical Elections and the Mainsprings of American Politics*, 13; Burnham, "The United States: The Politics of Heterogeneity," 654–56.

69. Burnham, "Party Systems and the Political Process," 288; Burnham, "Critical Realignment: Dead or Alive?" 108; Burnham, *Critical Elections and the Mainsprings of American Politics*, 1, 8, 17–18, 26–28, 170–71; McCormick, "The Realignment Synthesis in American History," 89–90; Lee Benson, Joel H. Silbey, and Phyllis F. Field, "Toward a Theory of Stability and Change in American Voting Patterns: New York State, 1792–1970," in *The History of American Electoral Behavior*, ed. Joel H. Silbey, Allan G. Bogue, and William H. Flanigan (Princeton: Princeton University Press, 1978), 79–80, 102.

70. Burnham, *Critical Elections and the Mainsprings of American Politics*, 2, 9–10, 184–85; McCormick, "The Realignment Synthesis in American History," 90; Walter Dean Burnham, Jerome M. Clubb, and William H. Flanigan, "Partisan Realignment: A Systemic Perspective," in *History of American Electoral Behavior*, ed. Silbey et al., 70–71.

71. Burnham, *Critical Elections and the Mainsprings of American Politics*, 27, 135–37, 181–83; Walter Dean Burnham, "Parties and Political Modernization," in *Political Parties and the Modern State*, ed. Richard L. McCormick (New Brunswick: Rutgers University Press, 1984), 115; Burnham, "The Alabama Senatorial Election of 1962," 824; Allan G. Bogue, Jerome M. Clubb, and William H. Flanigan, "The New Political History," *American Behavioral Scientist* 21 (Nov.–Dec. 1977): 208.

72. Burnham, "The End of American Party Politics," 22; Walter Dean Burnham, "The Constitution, Capitalism, and the Need for Rationalized Regulation," in *How Capitalistic Is the Constitution?* ed. Robert A. Goldwin and William A. Schambra (Washington, D.C.: American Enterprise Institute for Public Policy Research, 1982), 88.

73. Walter Dean Burnham, "Revitalization and Decay: Looking Toward the Third Century of American Politics," *The Journal of Politics* 38 (August 1976): 147; Lamb, "Plotting the Electorate's Course in Dangerous Waters," 61.

74. Walter Dean Burnham, "American Voting Behavior and the 1964 Election," *Midwest Journal of Political Science* 12 (Feb. 1968): 6; Burnham and Sprague, "Additive and Multiplicative Models of the Voting Universe," 478.

75. Walter Dean Burnham, "Death of the New Deal," *Commonweal*, Dec. 9, 1966, 284–87.

76. Walter Dean Burnham, "Election 1968—The Abortive Landslide," *Trans-Action* 6 (Dec. 1968): 22; Burnham, "The End of American Party Politics," 19–20.

77. Burnham, *Critical Elections and the Mainsprings of American Politics*, 27, 29, 91–93, 135.

78. Burnham, *Critical Elections and the Mainsprings of American Politics*, 158–59, 165.

79. Burnham, *Critical Elections and the Mainsprings of American Politics*, 118, 141–43, 166.

80. Burnham, *Critical Elections and the Mainsprings of American Politics*, 168–73, 191–93.

81. Walter Dean Burnham, "What Started the Landslide," *The National Observer*, Nov. 18, 1972, 30; Burnham, "Reply," 5.

82. Walter Dean Burnham, "American Politics in the 1980s," *Dissent* 27 (Spring 1980): 149; Walter Dean Burnham, "The 1976 Election: Has the Crisis Been Adjourned?" in *American Politics and Public Policy*, ed. Walter Dean Burnham and Martha Wagner Weinberg (Cambridge: The MIT Press, 1978), 4, 7–9; Burnham, "The United States: The Politics of Heterogeneity," 668, 716, 720; Walter Dean Burnham, "Insulation and Responsiveness in Congressional Elections," *Political Science Quarterly* 90 (Fall 1975): 411–12; Walter Dean Burnham, "Jimmy Carter and the Democratic Crisis," *New Republic*, July 3 and 10, 1976, 17.

83. Walter Dean Burnham, "The Politics of Repudiation 1992: Edging Toward Upheaval," *The American Prospect*, no. 12 (Winter 1993): 23–24; Burnham, "Critical Realignment: Dead or Alive?" 107; Walter Dean Burnham, "The Turnout Problem," in *Elections American Style*, ed. A. James Reichley (Washington, D.C.: The Brookings Institution, 1987), 123.

84. Burnham, "Critical Realignment: Dead or Alive," 106; Burnham, *Critical Elections and the Mainsprings of American Politics*, 5–6, 91–92, 120, 132–33, 172–75, 191–92; Burnham, "Revitalization and Decay: Looking Toward the Third Century of American Politics," 149, 168–69; Burnham, "The United States: The Politics of Heterogeneity," 716; Burnham, "Insulation and Responsiveness in Congressional Elections," 411; Burnham, "Jimmy Carter and the Democratic Crisis," 18.

85. James F. Ward, "Toward a Sixth Party System? Partisanship and Political Development," *The Western Political Quarterly* 26 (Sept. 1973): 391; Louis M. Seagull, *Southern Republicanism* (New York: John Wiley and Sons, 1975), 154–55.

86. Price, "'Critical Elections' and Party History," 241.

87. Boyd, review of *Critical Elections and the Mainsprings of American Politics* by Walter Dean Burnham, 596.

88. Walter Dean Burnham, "American Politics in the 1970s: Beyond Party?" in *The Future of Political Parties*, ed. Louis Maisel and Paul M. Sacks (Beverly Hills: Sage Publications, 1975), 238–39, 246, 258; Burnham, "Realignment Lives: The 1994 Earthquake and Its Implications," 371, 394; Burnham, "The United States: The Politics of Heterogeneity," 716, 720; Walter Dean Burnham, "Elections as Democratic Institutions," in *Elections in America*, ed. Kay Lehman Schlozman (Boston: Allen and Unwin, 1987), 43.

89. Walter Dean Burnham, "The Appearance and Disappearance of the American Voter," in *Electoral Participation: A Comparative Analysis*, ed. Richard Rose (Beverly Hills: Sage Publications, 1980), 36–37, 64–65.

CHAPTER ELEVEN

1. Samuel T. McSeveney, "No More 'Waiting for Godot': Comments on the Putative 'End of Realignment,'" in *The End of Realignment? Interpreting American Electoral Eras*, ed. Byron E. Shafer (Madison: The University of Wisconsin Press, 1991), 94–95; Louis M. Seagull, "Secular Realignment: The Concept and Its Utility," in *Realignment in American Politics: Toward a Theory*, ed. Bruce A. Campbell and Richard J. Trilling (Austin: University of Texas Press, 1980), 69, 72; Paul Kleppner, "Critical Realignments and Electoral Systems," in Paul Kleppner et al., *The Evolution of American Electoral Systems*

(Westport, Conn.: Greenwood Press, 1981), 11–12, 17; John E. Chubb, "Systems Analysis and Partisan Realignment," *Social Science History* 2 (Winter 1978): 145; Ivor Crewe, "Prospects for Party Realignment: An Anglo-American Comparison," *Comparative Politics* 12 (July 1980): 381; David G. Lawrence, *The Collapse of the Democratic Presidential Majority: Realignment, Dealignment, and Electoral Change from Franklin Roosevelt to Bill Clinton* (Boulder: Westview Press, 1996), xiii, 169–70.

2. Richard L. McCormick, "The Realignment Synthesis in American History," *Journal of Interdisciplinary History* 13 (Summer 1982): 94, 100, 103.

3. Allan J. Lichtman, "The End of Realignment Theory? Toward a New Research Program for American Political History," *Historical Methods* 15 (Fall 1982): 170–71, 186–87.

4. Carl D. Tubbesing, "Predicting the Past: Realigning Elections and Redistributive Policies," *Polity* 7 (Summer 1975): 501–3; Everett Carll Ladd, Jr. with Charles D. Hadley, *Transformations of the Party System: Political Coalitions from the New Deal to the 1970s*, Second Edition (New York: W. W. Norton, 1978), 375–76; Allan J. Lichtman, *Prejudice and the Old Politics: The Presidential Election of 1928* (Chapel Hill: The University of North Carolina Press, 1979), 244; Eric R. A. N. Smith, *The Unchanging American Voter* (Berkeley: University of California Press, 1989), 221–22.

5. Norman H. Nie, Sidney Verba, and John R. Petrocik, *The Changing American Voter* (Cambridge: Harvard University Press), 8, 43; Gerald M. Pomper, "The Impact of *The American Voter* on Political Science," *Political Science Quarterly* 93 (Winter 1978): 625; Gerald M. Pomper, *Voters' Choice: Varieties of American Electoral Behavior* (New York: Dodd, Mead, 1975), 11–12, 187; Gerald M. Pomper, "From Confusion to Clarity: Issues and American Voters," *The American Political Science Review* 66 (June 1972): 416, 427; Norman Nie to Philip Converse, Nov. 10, 1975, and Sidney Verba to Converse, Nov. 26, 1975, both in box 4, Philip E. Converse Papers, Bentley Historical Library (BHL), University of Michigan, Ann Arbor, Mich.

6. Chubb, "Systems Analysis and Partisan Realignment," 166; Richard M. Merelman, "Electoral Instability and the American Party System," *The Journal of Politics* 32 (Feb. 1970): 117, 119; William H. Flanigan and Nancy H. Zingale, "The Measurement of Electoral Change," *Political Methodology* 1 (Summer 1974): 51–52, 71; A. J. Mackelprang, Bernard Grofman, and N. Keith Thomas, "Electoral Change and Stability: Some New Perspectives," *American Politics Quarterly* 3 (July 1975): 318, 332; Herbert B. Asher, *Presidential Elections and American Politics: Voters, Candidates, and Campaigns Since 1952* (Homewood, Ill.: The Dorsey Press, 1976), 42; Gerald M. Pomper, "Impacts on the Political System," in *American Electoral Behavior: Change and Stability*, ed. Samuel A. Kirkpatrick (New York: Sage Publications, 1976), 138–39.

7. John H. Kessel, *The Goldwater Coalition: Republican Strategies in 1964* (Indianapolis: Bobbs-Merrill, 1968), 295–96 n.28, 303; John H. Kessel to Philip E. Converse, March 1, 1966, and March 11, 1966, both in box 3, Converse Papers.

8. Nie et al., *Changing American Voter*, 46–47, 96, 193; Gerald M. Pomper with Susan S. Lederman, *Elections in America: Control and Influence in Democratic Politics*, Second Edition (New York, Longman, 1980), 67, 71; Pomper, *Voters' Choice*, 11, 19; W. Phillips Shively, "The Nature of Party Identification: A Review of Recent Developments," in *The Electorate Reconsidered*, ed. John C. Pierce and John L. Sullivan (Beverly Hills: Sage Publications, 1980), 220–21.

9. Pomper, *Voters' Choice*, 162–63; Pomper, "From Confusion to Clarity," 416, 421, 423, 426–28; Gerald M. Pomper, "Toward a More Responsible Two-Party System? What, Again?" *The Journal of Politics* 33 (Nov. 1971): 924–25.

10. Nie et al., *Changing American Voter*, 192; [Ian Budge, Ivor Crewe, and Dennis Farlie], "Introduction: Party Identification and Beyond," in *Party Identification and Beyond: Representations of Voting and Party Competition*, ed. Ian Budge, Ivor Crewe, and Dennis Farlie (New York: John Wiley and Sons, 1976), 7; Richard W. Boyd, "Popular Control of Public Policy: A Normal Vote Analysis of the 1968 Election" *The American Political Science Review* 66 (June 1972): 446.

11. Gerald M. Pomper, "Rejoinder to 'Comments' by Richard A. Brody and Benjamin I. Page and John H. Kessel," *The American Political Science Review* 66 (June 1972): 466–67; Pomper, "Toward a More Responsible Two-Party System?" 924.

12. Pomper, *Elections in America*, 72–73; Pomper, "Rejoinder," 467.

13. Angus Campbell, "Civil Rights and the Vote for President," *Psychology Today* 1 (Feb. 1968): 70.

14. Nelson W. Polsby and Aaron B. Wildavsky, *Presidential Elections: Strategies of American Electoral Politics*, Second Edition (New York: Charles Scribner's Sons, 1968), 9, 13, 16.

15. Philip E. Converse et al., "Continuity and Change in American Politics: Parties and Issues in the 1968 Election," *The American Political Science Review* 63 (Dec. 1969): 1084–85.

16. Warren E. Miller and Teresa E. Levitin, *Leadership and Change: The New Politics and the American Electorate* (Cambridge: Winthrop Publishers, 1976), 9–10.

17. Warren E. Miller, "The Electorate's View of the Parties," in *The Parties Respond: Changes in the American Party System*, ed. L. Sandy Maisel (Boulder: Westview Press, 1990), 98.

18. Philip E. Converse to John Kessel, March 4, 1966, box 3, Converse Papers.

19. Philip E. Converse, "The Erosion of Party Fidelity," in *Controversies in American Voting Behavior*, ed. Richard G. Niemi and Herbert F. Weisberg (San Francisco: W. H. Freeman, 1976), 436–38.

20. Philip E. Converse, "Public Opinion and Voting Behavior," in *Handbook of Political Science*, Vol. 4, *Nongovernmental Politics*, ed. Fred I. Greenstein and Nelson W. Polsby (Reading, Mass.: Addison-Wesley, 1975), 134–35.

21. Arthur H. Miller, Warren E. Miller, Alden S. Raine, amd Thad A. Brown, "A Majority Party in Disarray: Policy Polarization in the 1972 Election," in *Controversies in American Voting Behavior*, ed, Niemi and Weisberg, 190, 192; Arthur H. Miller and Warren E. Miller, "Issues, Candidates, and Partisan Divisions in the 1972 American Presidential Election," *British Journal of Political Science* 5 (Oct. 1975): 422–23.

22. Warren E. Miller, "The Cross-National Use of Party Identification as a Stimulus to Political Inquiry," in *Party Identification and Beyond*, ed. Budge et al., 28–29.

23. Pomper, *Voters' Choice*, 207.

24. Arthur H. Miller, "Partisanship Reinstated? A Comparison of the 1972 and 1976 U.S. Presidential Elections," *British Journal of Political Science* 8 (April 1978): 130–31, 152; John R. Petrocik, "Contextual Sources of Voting Behavior: The Changeable American Voter," in *Electorate Reconsidered*, ed. Pierce and Sullivan, 268, 276–77.

25. Morris P. Fiorina, *Retrospective Voting in American National Elections* (New Haven: Yale University Press, 1981), 167–68.

26. Bruce A. Campbell, *The American Electorate: Attitudes and Action* (New York: Holt, Rinehart and Winston, 1979), 265.

27. Gerald M. Pomper to Nelson Polsby, Oct. 29, 1974; Polsby to Philip Converse, Nov. 6, 1974; Converse to Polsby, Nov. 18, 1974, all in box 4, Converse Papers.

28. Philip E. Converse and Gregory Markus, "What the Rocks Are Like: The New CPS Election Study Panel," Feb. 1978 ms., First Draft, 3–10, 14, 19, box 1, Converse Papers.

29. Nicol C. Rae, *The Decline and Fall of the Liberal Republicans: From 1952 to the Present* (New York: Oxford University Press, 1989), 217; Theodore J. Lowi, *The End of the Republican Era* (Norman: University of Oklahoma Press, 1995), xi, 79; Byron E. Shafer and William J. M. Claggett, *The Two Majorities: The Issue Context of Modern American Politics* (Baltimore: The Johns Hopkins University Press, 1995), 175, 186, 189, 192.

30. Everett Carll Ladd, "The Brittle Mandate: Electoral Dealignment and the 1980 Presidential Election," *Political Science Quarterly* 86 (Spring 1981): 24–25; Pomper, *Elections in America*, 75; Pomper, *Voters' Choice*, 146.

31. Lichtman, "End of Realignment Theory?" 183; Fiorina, *Retrospective Voting*, ix–x, 6–9; Morris P. Fiorina, "Economic Retrospective Voting in American Presidential Elections," *American Journal of Political Science* 22 (May 1978): 429; Morris P. Fiorina, "An Outline for a Model of Party Choice," *American Journal of Political Science* 21 (August 1977): 617–18.

32. Richard Jensen, "The Last Party System," in Kleppner et al., *Evolution of American Electoral Systems*, 232–33; Ladd, "Brittle Mandate," 3, 24; Paul Allen Beck, "Partisan Dealignment in the Postwar South," *The American Political Science Review* 71 (June 1977): 480, 495; Nie et al., *Changing American Voter*, 346–48; Everett Carll Ladd, Jr., "The Fabric of Contemporary American Electoral Politics," in Everett Carll Ladd, Jr. and Seymour Martin Lipset, *Academics, Politics, and the 1972 Election* (Washington, D.C.: American Enterprise Institute for Public Policy Research, 1973), 52; The Ripon Society and Clifford W. Brown, Jr., *Jaws of Victory: The Game-Plan Politics of 1972, the Crisis of the Republican Party, and the Future of the Constitution* (Boston: Little, Brown, 1974), 187, 196; Daniel J. Gans, "Persistence of Party Success in American Presidential Elections," *Journal of Interdisciplinary History* 16 (Winter 1986): 223.

33. Richard G. Niemi and Herbert F. Weisberg, "Is the Party Balance Shifting?" in *Controversies in American Voting Behavior*, ed. Niemi and Weisberg, 363; John R. Petrocik, *Party Coalitions: Realignment and the Decline of the New Deal Party System* (Chicago: The University of Chicago Press, 1981), 8, 11, 21–22, 158; Martin P. Wattenberg, "Dealignment in the American Electorate," in *Parties and Politics in American History: A Reader*, ed. L. Sandy Maisel and William G. Shade (New York: Garland Publishing, 1994), 226; Lawrence, *Collapse of the Democratic Majority*, xiii, 170; Ladd, "Fabric of Contemporary American Electoral Politics," 41, 51.

34. Jerome M. Clubb, William H. Flanigan, and Nancy H. Zingale, *Partisan Realignment: Voters, Parties, and Government in American History* (Beverly Hills: Sage Publications, 1980), 120, 122, 138; Paul Allen Beck, "The Electoral Cycle and Patterns of American Politics," *British Journal of Political Science* 9 (April 1979): 129–32, 135–38, 141, 149, 151, 154–55; Lichtman, "End of Realignment Theory?" 177; Paul Allen Beck, "A Socialization Theory of Partisan Realignment," in *Controversies in American Voting Behavior*, ed. Niemi and Weisberg, 403, 406, 409, 411; Philip Williams, "Review Article: Party Realignment in the United States and Britain," *British Journal of Political Science* 15, no. 1 (1984): 105.

35. Bruce A. Campbell and Richard J. Trilling, "Toward a Theory of Realignment: An Introduction," 6, 12, and Lawrence G. McMichael and Richard J. Trilling, "The Structure and Meaning of Critical Realignment: The Case of Pennsylvania, 1928–1932," 25–26, both in *Realignment in American Politics*, ed. Campbell and Trilling; Seagull, "Secular Realignment," 69, 71, 73–74; Pomper, *Elections in America*, 103; Williams, "Review Article," 100, 102–3.

36. James L. Sundquist, *Dynamics of the Party System: Alignment and Realignment of Political Parties in the United States*, Revised Edition (Washington, D.C.: The Brookings Institution, 1983), 11–12.

37. Edward G. Carmines and James A. Stimson, *Issue Evolution: Race and the Transformation of American Politics* (Princeton: Princeton University Press, 1989), 193 n.2.

38. Edward G. Carmines and James A. Stimson, "Issue Evolution, Population Replacement, and Normal Partisan Change," *The American Political Science Review* 75 (March 1981): 107–10, 114–17; Edward G. Carmines and James A. Stimson, "The Racial Reorientation of American Politics," in *Electorate Reconsidered*, ed. Pierce and Sullivan, 199, 201–2, 209.

39. Bruce A. Campbell and Richard J. Trilling, "Preface," in *Realignment in American Politics*, ed. Campbell and Trilling, ix–x; Campbell and Trilling, "Toward a Theory of Realignment," 10–11.

40. Clubb et al., *Partisan Realignment*, 156; Beck, "Electoral Cycles and Patterns of American Politics," 149, 154; McMichael and Trilling, "Structure and Meaning of Critical Realignment," 49; David W. Brady, "Elections, Congress, and Public Policy Changes: 1886–1960," 199–201, and Susan B. Hansen, "Partisan Realignment and Tax Policy: 1789–1976," 291–92, both in *Realignment in American Politics*, ed. Campbell and Trilling; Benjamin Ginsberg, "Elections and Public Policy," *The American Political Science Review* 70 (March 1976): 41, 48–49; Daniel Elazar, "The Generational Rhythm of American Politics," *American Politics Quarterly* 6 (Jan. 1978): 81, 85–86.

41. Sundquist, *Dynamics of the Party System*, 46–47; Chubb, "Systems Analysis and Partisan Realignment," 145, 148; C. Anthony Broh and Mark S. Levine, "Patterns of Party Competition," *American Politics Quarterly* 6 (July 1978): 372–73.

42. Allan J. Lichtman, "Critical Election Theory and the Reality of American Presidential Politics, 1916–40," *The American Historical Review* 81 (April 1976): 343, 346; Clubb et al., *Partisan Realignment*, 32, 293–94; McCormick, "Realignment Synthesis in American History," 97–99; Lichtman, "End of Realignment Theory?" 180; Pomper, *Elections in America*, 99.

CHAPTER TWELVE

1. "The Origins of NES," http://www.umich.edu/~nes/overview/origins.htm (July 24, 2002); Helmut Norpoth, "Under Way and Here to Stay: Party Realignment in the 1980s?" *Public Opinion Quarterly* 51 (Fall 1987): 387; Herbert F. Weisberg and David C. Kimball, "Attitudinal Correlates of the 1992 Presidential Vote: Party Identification and Beyond," in *Democracy's Feast: Elections in America*, ed. Herbert F. Weisberg (Chatham, N.J.: Chatham House, 1995), 75; Paul Allen Beck, "Incomplete Realignment: The Reagan Legacy for Parties and Elections," in *The Reagan Legacy: Promise and Performance*, ed. Charles O. Jones (Chatham, N.J.: Chatham House, 1988), 155–56.

2. Laurily K. Epstein, "The Changing Structure of Party Identification," *PS: Political Science and Politics* 18 (Winter 1985): 48, 51–52.

3. Ellis Sandoz and Cecil V. Crabb, Jr., "Conclusion: Electoral and Policy Realignment or Aberration?" in *A Tide of Discontent: The 1980 Elections and Their Meaning*, ed. Ellis Sandoz and Cecil V. Crabb, Jr. (Washington, D.C.: Congressional Quarterly Press, 1981), 194; A. James Reichley, "Religion and Political Realignment," *The Brookings Review* 3

(Fall 1984): 35; Robert Huckfeldt and Carol Weitzel Kohfeld, *Race and the Decline of Class in American Politics* (Urbana: University of Illinois Press, 1989), 39–41, 132, 149, 156; William A. Galston, "The Future of the Democratic Party," *The Brookings Review* 3 (Winter 1985): 16, 19–20; Edward G. Carmines and Harold W. Stanley, "The Transformation of the New Deal Party System: Social Groups, Political Ideology, and Changing Partisanship Among Northern Whites, 1972–1988," *Political Behavior* 14, no. 3 (1992): 213–14, 219; Earl Black and Merle Black, *The Vital South: How Presidents Are Elected* (Cambridge: Harvard University Press, 1992), 10, 169, 366.

4. Paul Allen Beck, "The Dealignment Era in America," in *Electoral Change in Advanced Industrial Democracies: Realignment or Dealignment?* ed. Russell J. Dalton, Scott C. Flanagan, and Paul Allen Beck (Princeton: Princeton University Press, 1984), 241, 264–65; Beck, "Incomplete Realignment," 165, 168–69; John R. Petrocik, "Realignment: New Party Coalitions and the Nationalization of the South," *Journal of Politics* 49 (May 1987): 350 n.2; John R. Petrocik, "Realignment: The South, New Party Coalitions and the Elections of 1984 and 1986," in *Where's the Party? An Assessment of Changes in Party Loyalty and Party Coalitions in the 1980s*, ed. Warren E. Miller and John R. Petrocik (Washington, D.C.: Center for National Policy, 1987), 31, 33, 54; William H. Flanigan and Nancy H. Zingale, *Political Behavior of the American Electorate*, Fifth Edition (Boston: Allyn and Bacon, 1983), 30, 34, 36, 58, 60.

5. William Schneider, "Realignment: The Eternal Question," *PS: Political Science and Politics* 13 (Summer 1982): 451; William Schneider, "Half a Realignment," *New Republic*, Dec. 3, 1984, 21–22; William Schneider, "The November 6 Vote for President: What Did it Mean?" in *The American Elections of 1984*, ed. Austin Ranney (Durham: Duke University Press, 1985), 205–6, 239–40, 242, 244; William Schneider, "The Political Legacy of the Reagan Years," in *The Reagan Legacy*, ed. Sidney Blumenthal and Thomas Byrne Edsall (New York: Pantheon Books, 1988), 63, 67–68.

6. Michael Barone and Grant Ujifusa, *The Almanac of American Politics 1984* (Washington, D.C.: National Journal, 1983), xxix; Michael Barone and Grant Ujifusa, *The Almanac of American Politics 1988* (Washington, D.C.: National Journal, 1987), xlii–xliii; Michael Barone and Grant Ujifusa, *The Almanac of American Politics 1990* (Washington, D.C.: National Journal, 1989), xxvi–xxvii; Michael Barone and Grant Ujifusa, *The Almanac of American Politics 1992* (Washington, D.C.: National Journal, 1991), xxxii–xxxiv; Michael Barone, *Our Country: The Shaping of America from Roosevelt to Reagan* (New York: The Free Press, 1990), 669.

7. Paul R. Abramson, John H. Aldrich, and David W. Rohde, *Change and Continuity in the 1984 Elections* (Washington, D.C.: Congressional Quarterly Press, 1986), 75.

8. Gerald M. Pomper, "The Presidential Election," in *The Election of 1988: Reports and Interpretations*, ed. Gerald M. Pomper (Chatham, N.J.: Chatham House), 147.

9. Sandoz and Crabb, "Conclusion: Electoral and Policy Realignment or Aberration?" 194.

10. Galston, "The Future of the Democratic Party," 17.

11. Steven J. Rosenstone, "Explaining the 1984 Presidential Election," *The Brookings Review* 3 (Winter 1985), 28.

12. Black and Black, *Vital South*, 12, 57, 72.

13. Paul R. Abramson, John H. Aldrich, and David W. Rohde, *Change and Continuity in the 1980 Elections* (Washington, D.C.: Congressional Quarterly Press, 1982), 6; Abramson et al., *Change and Continuity in the 1984 Elections*, 6, 10.

14. John Kenneth White, *The New Politics of Old Values* (Hanover, N.H.: University Press of New England, 1988), 77.

15. William Schneider, "Democrats and Republicans, Liberals and Conservatives," 227, and Patrick H. Caddell, "The Democratic Strategy and Its Electoral Consequences," 272, 295, 300–301, both in *Party Coalitions in the 1980s*, ed. Seymour Martin Lipset (San Francisco: Institute for Contemporary Studies, 1981); E. J. Dionne, *Why Americans Hate Politics* (New York: Simon and Schuster, 1991), 141, 243; Gary Orren and E. J. Dionne, "The Next New Deal," *Working Papers for a New Society* 8 (May–June 1981): 26, 29; Pippa Norris, "The 1988 American Elections: Long, Medium and Short-Term Explanations," *The Political Quarterly* 60 (April–June 1989): 205, 214, 221; William C. Berman, *America's Right Turn: From Nixon to Bush* (Baltimore: The Johns Hopkins University Press, 1994), 4, 24, 43, 136; David G. Lawrence, *The Collapse of the Democratic Presidential Majority: Realignment, Dealignment, and Electoral Change from Franklin Roosevelt to Bill Clinton* (Boulder: Westview Press, 1996), 132; Steven M. Gillon, *The Democrats' Dilemma: Walter F. Mondale and the Liberal Legacy* (New York: Columbia University Press, 1992), 282; Rosenstone, "Explaining the 1984 Presidential Election," 28–30; Douglas A. Hibbs, Jr., "President Reagan's Mandate from the 1980 Elections: A Shift to the Right?" *American Politics Quarterly* 10 (Oct. 1982), 407, 417.

16. James L. Sundquist, "Whither the American Party System?—Revisited," *Political Science Quarterly* 98 (Winter 1983–84): 575, 591; James L. Sundquist, "The 1984 Election: How Much Realignment?" *The Brookings Review* 3 (Winter 1985): 9, 11–12, 15; James L. Sundquist and Richard M. Scammon, "The 1980 Election: Profile and Historical Perspective," in *Tide of Discontent*, ed. Sandoz and Crabb, 24–26, 34, 42; Thomas E. Cavanagh and James L. Sundquist, "The New Two-Party System," in *The New Direction in American Politics*, ed. John E. Chubb and Paul E. Peterson (Washington, D.C.: The Brookings Institution, 1985), 34, 37, 42–43, 51, 54, 59, 67; James L. Sundquist, *Dynamics of the Party System: Alignment and Realignment of Political Parties in the United States*, Revised Edition (Washington, D.C.: The Brookings Institution, 1983), 413, 420, 425, 437, 440, 444.

17. Warren E. Miller, "The Electorate's View of the Parties," in *The Parties Respond: Changes in the American Party System*, ed. L. Sandy Maisel (Boulder: Westview Press, 1990), 99–100, 108, 110–12; Warren E. Miller, "Party Identification, Realignment, and Party Voting: Back to the Basics," *The American Political Science Review* 85 (June 1991): 561–62, 564, 566; J. Merrill Shanks and Warren E. Miller, "Partisanship, Policy and Performance: The Reagan Legacy in the 1988 Election," *British Journal of Political Science* 21 (April 1991): 130–32, 138–45, 150–51, 172, 184, 193, 195–97; Warren E. Miller and J. Merrill Shanks, *The New American Voter* (Cambridge: Harvard University Press, 1996), 145, 166, 169; Warren E. Miller, "The Election of 1984 and the Future of American Politics," in *Elections in America*, ed. Kay Lehman Schlozman (Boston: Allen and Unwin, 1987), 293, 304, 309; Warren E. Miller, "Party Identification and Political Belief Systems: Changes in Partisanship in the United States, 1980–84," *Electoral Studies* 5, no. 2 (1986): 101–3, 105, 107, 114, 116–19; Warren E. Miller, "A New Context for Presidential Politics: The Reagan Legacy," *Political Behavior* 9, no. 2 (1987): 96, 100, 106.

18. Thomas Byrne Edsall, "The Changing Shape of Power: A Realignment in Public Policy," in *The Rise and Fall of the New Deal Order, 1930–1980*, ed. Steve Fraser and Gary Gerstle (Princeton: Princeton University Press, 1989), 269–70, 275, 285–86, 289; Thomas Byrne Edsall, *The New Politics of Inequality* (New York: W. W. Norton, 1984), 39, 66, 208; Thomas Byrne Edsall, "The Reagan Legacy," in *Reagan Legacy*, ed. Blu-

menthal and Edsall, 15, 21; Thomas Byrne Edsall with Mary D. Edsall, *Chain Reaction: The Impact of Race, Rights, and Taxes on American Politics* (New York: W. W. Norton, 1991), 3, 5, 7, 10, 17, 21–22, 24, 27–28, 34–37, 39, 44, 47, 49, 58–59, 74, 79, 97–99, 101, 103–5, 129, 134–37, 142, 155, 158–59, 172–73, 196–98.

19. Everett Carll Ladd, "The 1988 Elections: Continuation of the Post–New Deal System," *Political Science Quarterly* 104 (Spring 1989): 1, 3–4, 7–8, 18; Everett Carll Ladd, "On Mandates, Realignments, and the 1984 Presidential Election," *Political Science Quarterly* 100 (Spring 1985): 7–8, 12, 22, 24; Everett Carll Ladd, "The Brittle Mandate Extended: An In-Depth Examination of the Voters' 1982 Verdict," *Public Affairs Review* 4 (1983): 23–25, 36; Everett Carll Ladd, "The GOP Upsets the Balance of Parties," *Wall Street Journal*, April 8, 1985, 16; Everett C. Ladd, "Realignment? No, Dealignment? Yes," *Public Opinion* 3 (Oct.–Nov. 1980): 13–15, 54–55; Everett Carll Ladd, "As the Realignment Turns: A Drama in Many Acts," *Public Opinion* 7 (Dec. 1984–Jan. 1985): 4–7; Everett Carll Ladd, *Where Have All the Voters Gone? The Fracturing of America's Political Parties*, Second Edition (New York: W. W. Norton, 1982), xii–xiii; Everett Carll Ladd, *The Ladd Report #3: Alignment and Realignment: Where Are All the Voters Going?* (New York: W. W. Norton, 1986), 2, 24, 26; Everett Carll Ladd, "The 1980 Presidential Election: In Search of Its Meaning," *Public Affairs Review* 2 (1981): 5, 20, 23; Everett Carll Ladd, "The Democrats and the Presidency," *Christian Science Monitor*, July 7, 1989, 18; Everett Carll Ladd, "The '80s Generation Went Republican," *Christian Science Monitor*, Oct. 13, 1989, 18; Everett Carll Ladd, "The National Election," *Public Opinion* 11 (Nov.–Dec. 1988): 2, 60.

20. Thomas Ferguson and Joel Rogers, *Right Turn: The Decline of the Democrats and the Future of American Politics* (New York: Hill and Wang, 1986), 11–12; Howard J. Gold, *Hollow Mandates: American Public Opinion and the Conservative Shift* (Boulder: Westview Press, 1992), 2; Adam Clymer, "Academics Debate Changes in Party Loyalty," *New York Times*, Sept. 7, 1981, A7; John E. Chubb and Paul E. Peterson, "Realignment and Institutionalization," in *New Direction in American Politics*, ed. Chubb and Peterson, 1, 3–4, 8–9, 21–22, 24–25, 30; John E. Chubb, "Realignment, Institutionalization, and the 1986 Elections," in *The Reagan Revolution?* ed. B. B. Kymlicka and Jean V. Matthews (Chicago: The Dorsey Press, 1988), 111–12, 120.

21. Petrocik, "Realignment: New Party Coalitions and the Nationalization of the South," 368, 373; Petrocik, " Realignment: The South, New Party Coalitions and the Elections of 1984 and 1986," 33, 49, 54; Morris P. Fiorina, "The Reagan Years: Turning to the Right or Groping Toward the Middle?" in *The Resurgence of Conservatism in Anglo-American Democracies*, ed. Barry Cooper, Allan Kornberg, and William Mishler (Durham: Duke University Press, 1988), 431, 433; John G. Geer, "The Electorate's Partisan Evaluations: Evidence of a Continuing Democratic Edge," *Public Opinion Quarterly* 55 (Summer 1991): 229.

22. John R. Petrocik and Frederick T. Steeper, "Realignment and 1984: New Coalitions and New Majorities?" *Election Politics* 2 (Winter 1984–85): 5–6; Petrocik, "Realignment: New Party Coalitions and the Nationalization of the South," 373; Petrocik, "Realignment: The South, New Party Coalitions and the Elections of 1984 and 1986," 49, 54.

23. David G. Lawrence and Richard Fleisher, "Puzzles and Confusions: Political Realignment in the 1980s," *Political Science Quarterly* 102 (Spring 1987): 87–90; David W. Brady, *Critical Elections and Congressional Policy Making* (Stanford: Stanford University Press, 1988), 165–66, 177; Beck, "Incomplete Realignment," 166–71.

24. Morris P. Fiorina, "The Electorate in the Voting Booth," in *Parties Respond*, ed. Maisel, 116, 130; David W. Brady and Patricia A. Hurley, "The Prospects for Contemporary Partisan Realignment," *PS: Political Science and Politics* 18 (Winter 1985): 68; Martin P. Wattenberg, "The Hollow Realignment: Partisan Change in a Candidate-Centered Era," *Public Opinion Quarterly* 51 (Spring 1987): 58–59, 67, 69, 72–73.

25. Gold, *Hollow Mandates*, 133–35, 138, 140, 146–47, 149–50; Jerome L. Himmelstein, *To the Right: The Transformation of American Conservatism* (Berkeley: University of California Press, 1990), 165–66.

26. Kevin Phillips, *Boiling Point: Republicans, Democrats, and the Decline of Middle-Class Prosperity* (New York: Random House, 1993), 32–34; Kevin P. Phillips, *Post-Conservative America: People, Politics and Ideology in a Time of Crisis* (New York: Random House, 1982), xiii–xviii, xxi, 16–18, 26, 53–55, 60, 123–24, 147, 214, 220–24, 227–28; "The Election and After [a symposium]," *New York Review of Books*, Aug. 16, 1984, 35; Kevin Phillips, "A Democrat in the White House?" *New York Times Book Review*, Aug. 9, 1987, 10; Kevin Phillips, "The Inept Campaign," *New York Review of Books*, Dec. 22, 1988, 16, 18; "A Conversation With Kevin Phillips: 'Frustrated Middle Class' Will Shake Up Politics," *U.S. News and World Report*, Oct. 11, 1982, 41; Kevin Phillips, "The Postconservative Era," *Newsweek*, Nov. 15, 1982, 46; E. J. Dionne, Jr., "High Tide for Conservatives, But Some Fear What Follows," *New York Times*, Oct. 13, 1987, A1, A33; Kevin Phillips, "A Campaign That Was Destined for the Gutter," *New York Times*, Sept. 12, 1988, A21; Kevin Phillips, "Hubris on the Right," *New York Times Magazine*, May 12, 1985, 48, 50, 57, 60, 63; Kevin P. Phillips, "A New GOP Majority?" *New York Times*, April 19, 1984, A19; Kevin Phillips, "Suddenly, Bush Has Reasons to Fear '92," *New York Times*, Oct. 10, 1990, A23; Kevin Phillips, "Post-Conservative America," *New York Review of Books*, May 13, 1982, 27, 29, 31.

27. Walter Dean Burnham, "The Ascendancy of the Right," *Dissent* 30 (Fall 1983): 434; Walter Dean Burnham, "Critical Realignment: Dead or Alive?" in *The End of Realignment? Interpreting American Electoral Eras*, ed. Byron E. Shafer (Madison: The University of Wisconsin Press, 1991), 101–2, 106–7, 110, 113, 115–16, 125–27, 135; Walter Dean Burnham, "The 1980 Earthquake: Realignment, Reaction, or What?" in *The Hidden Election: Politics and Economics in the 1980 Presidential Campaign*, ed. Thomas Ferguson and Joel Rogers (New York: Pantheon Books, 1981), 100, 110, 117, 127; Walter Dean Burnham, "Foreword," in Martin P. Wattenberg, *The Decline of American Political Parties, 1952–1980* (Cambridge: Harvard University Press, 1984), ix–xi; Walter Dean Burnham, *The Current Crisis in American Politics* (New York: Oxford University Press, 1982), 269, 280–81, 285, 289, 306–7, 311–12; "The Election and After [a symposium]," *New York Review of Books*, 33; Walter Dean Burnham, "The Turnout Problem," in *Elections American Style*, ed. A. James Reichley (Washington, D.C.: The Brookings Institution, 1987), 123; Walter Dean Burnham, "The Reagan Heritage," in *The Election of 1988*, ed. Pomper, 3, 14, 16, 20–21, 25–27; Walter Dean Burnham, "Elections As Democratic Institutions," in *Elections in America*, ed. Schlozman, 45, 54–55; Walter Dean Burnham, "The Eclipse of the Democratic Party," *Democracy* 2 (July 1982): 7–9; Walter Dean Burnham, "A Continuing Political Gridlock," *Wall Street Journal*, June 24, 1985, 18; Walter Dean Burnham, "Elections Dash GOP Dreams of Realignment," *Wall Street Journal*, Nov. 26, 1986, 20; Walter Dean Burnham, review of *The Rise of Candidate-Centered Politics* by Martin P. Wattenberg, *The American Political Science Review* 86 (June 1992): 550; Walter Dean Burnham, "Me-First Politics," *The Wilson Quarterly* 15 (Summer 1991): 90.

28. Ladd, "On Mandates, Realignments, and the 1984 Presidential Election," 10–11; Ladd, "As the Realignment Turns: A Drama in Many Acts," 4.

29. Everett Carll Ladd, "Like Waiting for Godot: The Uselessness of 'Realignment' for Understanding Change in Contemporary American Politics," in *End of Realignment?* ed. Shafer, 25, 27, 29, 31.

30. Joel H. Silbey, "Beyond Realignment and Realignment Theory: American Political Eras, 1789–1989," 3–4; Byron E. Shafer, "The Notion of an Electoral Order: The Structure of Electoral Politics at the Accession of George Bush," 37, 40–41, 62–63; Samuel T. McSeveney, "No More 'Waiting for Godot': Comments on the Putative 'End of Realignment,'" 95, all in *End of Realignment?* ed. Shafer; Lawrence and Fleisher, "Puzzles and Confusions: Political Realignment in the 1980s," 92; David W. Brady, "A Reevaluation of Realignments in American Politics: Evidence from the House of Representatives," *The American Political Science Review* 79 (March 1985): 37–40, 42; David W. Brady, *Critical Elections and Congressional Policy Making* (Stanford: Stanford University Press, 1988), 95, 99, 102, 136, 164.

31. Robert Erikson, Thomas D. Lancaster, and David W. Romero, "Group Components of the Presidential Vote, 1952–1984," *Journal of Politics* 51 (May 1989): 338; James E. Campbell, "Sources of the New Deal Realignment: The Contributions of Conversion and Mobilization to Partisan Change," *The Western Political Quarterly* 38 (Sept. 1985): 367 n.16.

32. Paul Kleppner, *Continuity and Change in Electoral Politics, 1893–1928* (New York: Greenwood Press, 1987), 14–15; Philip Williams, "Review Article: Party Realignment in the United States and Britain," *British Journal of Political Science* 15, no. 1 (1984): 100.

33. Russell J. Dalton, Paul Allen Beck, and Scott C. Flanagan, "Electoral Change in Advanced Industrial Democracies," 14, and Russell J. Dalton, Scott C. Flanagan, and Paul Allen Beck, "Political Forces and Partisan Change," 454, 460–1, both in *Electoral Change in Advanced Industrial Democracies*, ed. Dalton et al; Williams, "Review Article," 115; John Zvesper, "Party Realignment: A Past Without a Future?" in *Explaining American Politics: Issues and Interpretations*, ed. Robert Williams (New York: Routledge, 1990), 181; Lawrence Le Duc, "Partisan Change and Dealignment in Canada, Great Britain, and the United States," *Comparative Politics* 17 (July 1985): 379.

34. Paul Allen Beck, "Choice, Context, and Consequence: Beaten and Unbeaten Paths Toward a Science of Electoral Behavior," in *Political Science: The Science of Politics*, ed. Herbert F. Weisberg (New York: Agathon Press, 1986), 255, 267–68.

35. Martin P. Wattenberg and Arthur H. Miller, "Decay in Regional Party Coalitions: 1952–1980," in *Party Coalitions*, ed. Lipset, 367; Beck, "The Dealignment Era in America," 263–66; Wattenberg, *Decline of American Political Parties*, 23, 25, 130–31; Sundquist and Scammon, "The 1980 Election: Profile and Historical Perspective," 40–42.

36. Martin P. Wattenberg, *The Rise of Candidate-Centered Politics: Presidential Elections of the 1980s* (Cambridge: Harvard University Press, 1991), 4, 9, 21–22, 29–30, 92; Fiorina, "The Reagan Years: Turning to the Right or Groping Toward the Middle?" 452–53; Abramson et al., *Change and Continuity in the 1980 Elections*, 49.

37. Arthur Miller and Brad Lockerbie, "The United States of America," in Mark N. Franklin et al., *Electoral Change: Responses to Evolving Social and Attitudinal Structures in Western Countries* (New York: Cambridge University Press, 1992), 379–80.

38. Sheldon Kamieniecki, *Party Identification, Political Behavior, and the American Electorate* (Westport, Conn.: Greenwood Press, 1985), 147–48, 166; Clymer, "Academics

Debate Changes in Party Loyalty," A7; Charles H. Franklin and John E. Jackson, "The Dynamics of Party Identification," *The American Political Science Review* 77 (Dec. 1983): 957–59, 968–69; Michael B. MacKuen, Robert S. Erikson, and James A. Stimson, "Macropartisanship," *The American Political Science Review* 83 (Dec. 1989): 1125–26, 1130, 1138; John R. Petrocik, "An Expected Party Vote: New Data for an Old Concept," *American Journal of Political Science* 33 (Feb. 1989): 45; Richard A. Brody and Lawrence S. Rothenberg, "The Instability of Partisanship: An Analysis of the 1980 Presidential Election," *British Journal of Political Science* 14 (Oct. 1988): 445–46, 464–65; Richard G. Niemi and M. Kent Jennings, "Issues and Inheritance in the Formation of Party Identification," *American Journal of Political Science* 35 (Nov. 1991): 970, 986.

39. Philip E. Converse and Roy Pierce, "Partisanship and the Party System," *Political Behavior* 14, no. 3 (1992): 239–40; Philip E. Converse and Roy Pierce, "Measuring Partisanship," *Political Methodology* 11 (1985): 145–47.

40. Warren E. Miller, "Party Identification," in *Political Parties and Elections in the United States*, Vol 2, ed. L. Sandy Maisel (New York: Garland Publishing, 1991), 752; J. Merrill Shanks and Warren E. Miller, "Policy Direction and Performance Evaluation: Complementary Explanations of the Reagan Elections," *British Journal of Political Science* 20 (April 1990): 154, 175, 187, 192–94, 230.

41. Arthur M. Schlesinger, Jr., *The Cycles of American History* (Boston: Hougton Mifflin, 1986), 34–36; Samuel P. Huntington, *American Politics: The Promise of Disharmony* (Cambridge, Mass.: Harvard University Press, 1981), 112–13, 147–48, and passim; Richard L. McCormick, "Introduction," in *Political Parties and the Modern State*, ed. Richard L. McCormick (New Brunswick: Rutgers University Press, 1984), 8; Andrew S. McFarland, "Interest Groups and Political Time: Cycles in America," *British Journal of Political Science* 21 (July 1991): 258–60, 276.

42. Arthur Schlesinger, Jr., "Is Liberalism Dead?" *New York Times Magazine*, March 30, 1980, 73; "The Election and After [a symposium]," *New York Review of Books*, 36; Schlesinger, *Cycles of American History*, 24, 45, 47; Arthur Schlesinger, Jr., "America's Political Cycle Turns Again," *Wall Street Journal*, Dec.10, 1987, 28; "The Tide Is Turning: A New Political Cycle in the 1990s [Interview with Arthur M. Schlesinger, Jr.]," *Challenge* 34 (Nov.–Dec. 1991): 9–11, 14.

43. David Resnick and Norman C. Thomas, "Cycling Through American Politics," *Polity* 23 (Fall 1990): 18; Schlesinger, *Cycles of American History*, 30–31; John J. Broesamle, *Reform and Reaction in Twentieth Century American Politics* (New York: Greenwood Press, 1990), 1–2, 87, 460; Stephen P. Depoe, *Arthur M. Schlesinger, Jr., and the Ideological History of American Liberalism* (Tuscaloosa: The University of Alabama Press, 1994), 21, 27, 111–13.

44. Schlesinger, *Cycles of American History*, 24–25, 46–47; Broesamle, *Reform and Reaction in Twentieth Century American Politics*, 93, 448.

45. Erwin C. Hargrove and Michael Nelson, "Presidents, Ideas, and the Search for a Stable Majority," in *Tide of Discontent*, ed. Sandoz and Crabb, 52–53; Edwin C. Hargrove and Michael Nelson, "The Presidency: Reagan and the Cycle of Politics and Policy," in *The Elections of 1984*, ed. Michael Nelson (Washington, D.C.: Congressional Quarterly Press, 1985), 190–91, 194.

46. Dionne, *Why Americans Hate Politics*, 283, 294–95, 298, 312, 316; E. J. Dionne, "Let Democrats Be Democrats," *New York Times Book Review*, Nov. 15, 1987, 9; Robert S. McElvaine, *The End of the Conservative Era: Liberalism After Reagan* (New York: Arbor House, 1987), ix, 4, 8–10.

47. James L. Sundquist, *Politics and Policy: The Eisenhower, Kennedy, and Johnson Years* (Washington, D.C.: The Brookings Institution, 1968), 496–97, 506, 536; James L. Sundquist, "Has America Lost Its Social Conscience—And How Will It Get It Back?" *Political Science Quarterly* 101, no. 4 (1986): 527, 529–30; Sundquist, "The 1984 Election: How Much Realignment?" 15; Sundquist and Scammon, "The 1980 Election: Profile and Historical Perspective," 40; Cavanagh and Sundquist, "The New Two-Party System," 66.

48. Petrocik, "Realignment: New Party Coalitions and the Nationalization of the South," 353 n.7; Huckfeldt and Kohlfeld, *Race and the Decline of Class in American Politics*, 102–3; John G. Geer, "Critical Realignments and the Public Opinion Poll," *Journal of Politics* 53 (May 1991): 434–35, 450; Thad A. Brown, *Migration and Politics: The Impact of Population Mobility on American Voting Behavior* (Chapel Hill: The University of North Carolina Press, 1988), 154–55; Ladd, *Ladd Report #3*, 9–10; Michael Lyons, "GOP Realignment Isn't Dead Yet," *Wall Street Journal*, Feb. 4, 1987, 30; MacKuen et al., "Macropartisanship," 1139.

49. Edward G. Carmines and James A. Stimson, "The Dynamics of Issue Evolution: The United States," in *Electoral Change in Advanced Industrial Democracies*, ed. Dalton et al., 135, 139, 141, 151–52; Edward G. Carmines, John P. McIver, and James A. Stimson, "Unrealized Partisanship: A Theory of Dealignment," *The Journal of Politics* 49 (May 1987): 380–81; Edward G. Carmines and James A. Stimson, *Issue Evolution: Race and the Transformation of American Politics* (Princeton: Princeton University Press, 1989), xiii, 20–22, 157, 160; Edward G. Carmines and James A. Stimson, "On the Structure and Sequence of Issue Evolution," *The American Political Science Review* 80 (Sept. 1986): 901–2, 915; Alan I. Abramowitz, "Issue Evolution Reconsidered: Racial Attitudes and Partisanship in the U.S. Electorate," *American Journal of Political Science* 38 (Feb. 1994): 1–2.

50. Gary Gerstle and Steve Fraser, "Introduction," in *Rise and Fall of the New Deal Order*, ed. Fraser and Gerstle, ix–xi.

51. Shafer, "The Notion of an Electoral Order: The Structure of Electoral Politics at the Accession of George Bush," 64–65; Byron E. Shafer, "The Election of 1988 and the Structure of American Politics: Thoughts on Interpreting an Electoral Order," *Electoral Studies* 8 (April 1989): 5–7, 9,11–12, 19.

52. Patricia A. Hurley, "Partisan Representation and the Failure of Realignment in the 1980s," *American Journal of Political Science* 33 (Feb. 1989): 241; Zvesper, "Party Realignment: A Past Without a Future?" 173; Chubb, "Realignment, Institutionalization, and the 1986 Elections," 112, 120; William G. Mayer, *The Changing American Mind: How and Why American Public Opinion Changed between 1960 and 1988* (Ann Arbor: The University of Michigan Press, 1992), 17–18.

53. Franklin and Jackson, "The Dynamics of Party Identification," 969–70.

CHAPTER THIRTEEN

1. "The Election and After [a symposium]," *New York Review of Books*, Aug. 16, 1984, 36.

2. Kevin Phillips, *The Politics of Rich and Poor: Wealth and the American Electorate in the Reagan Aftermath* (New York: Random House, 1990), x–xi, xix–xx, xxii–xxiii, 33, 54–55, 101, 155, 185, 201, 208–9, 215, 221; Kevin Phillips, *Boiling Point: Republicans, Democrats, and the Decline of Middle Class Prosperity* (New York: Random House, 1993), xi–xii, 26, 32–34, 56–57, 59, 63, 71, 247; "Middle-class warfare [interview with

Kevin Phillips]," *U.S. News and World Report*, June 25, 1990, 52; Kevin Phillips, "The Bush Blueprint Bombs," *Newsweek*, Nov. 19, 1990, 40–41; "In His Words: Analyst Kevin Phillips Saw the Republican Majority Coming; Now He's Pronouncing Its Epitaph," *People Weekly*, Nov. 5, 1990, 147, 150.

3. Ben J. Wattenberg, *Values Matter Most: How Republicans or Democrats or a Third Party Can Win and Renew the American Way of Life* (New York: The Free Press, 1995), 76–77; Tom Mathews, "Picking up the Pieces," *Newsweek*, July 23, 1990, 19; Christopher Lehmann-Haupt, "A Vision Beyond the New Gilded Age," *New York Times*, June 21, 1990, C21; Eric Alterman, "A Pop(ulist) Quiz," *New York Times*, July 25, 1990, A19; Everett Carll Ladd, "A Polemic With Potholes," *Christian Science Monitor*, July 23, 1990, 13; David Brock, "Anti-Reagan Sophistry," *Wall Street Journal*, June 14, 1990, A12.

4. Mark Cunningham, "Kevin Phillips: Left Out," *National Review*, Aug. 6, 1990, 36; Michael Novak, "A Hanging Judge," *Forbes*, Aug. 6, 1990, 73; George Szamuely, "Kevin Phillips Turns the Screws on Conservatives," *The American Spectator* 23 (Sept. 1990): 12–13.

5. James Q. Wilson, "Malaise II," *Commentary* 90 (Oct. 1990): 56; Garry Wills, "The Politics of Grievance," *New York Review of Books*, July 19, 1990, 3.

6. Michael Waldman, "Swing Time," *The Nation*, Aug. 13 and 20, 1990, 176; Joe Klein, "A Republican Looks Back in Anger," *Boston Globe*, June 17, 1990, B45.

7. Thomas Byrne Edsall, "The Hidden Role of Race," *New Republic*, July 30 and Aug. 6, 1990, 35–40.

8. Kirk Scharfenberg, "Populism in the Age of Celebrity," *The Atlantic* 265 (June 1990), 117; Priscilla Painton, "Is a Populist Revolt at Hand?" *Time*, June 25, 1990, 69; Dennis H. Wrong, "In the U.S., the Have-Nots Have Less," *New York Times Book Review*, June 24, 1990, 26.

9. Kevin Phillips, "Down and Out," *New York Times Magazine*, Jan. 10, 1993, 32–33; Kevin Phillips, "Counterpoint: Finally, a President Does the Right Thing," *Wall Street Journal*, Feb. 18, 1993, A19.

10. Kevin Phillips, *Arrogant Capital: Washington, Wall Street, and the Frustration of American Politics* (Boston: Little, Brown, 1994), xiii–xv, 10, 12–17, 29, 65, 92, 167–68, 175.

11. David Frum, "The Prophet of Resentment," *National Review*, April 3, 1995, 60.

12. Arthur M. Schlesinger, Jr., "The Liberal Opportunity," *The American Prospect*, no. 1 (Spring 1990): 11; Arthur Schlesinger, Jr., "Afterword," in *Democrats and the American Idea: A Bicentennial Appraisal*, ed. Peter B. Kovler (Washington, D.C.: Center for National Policy Press, 1992), 363; Arthur M. Schlesinger, Jr., "The Turn of the Cycle," *New Yorker*, Nov. 16, 1992, 46, 53.

13. Stephen P. Depoe, *Arthur M. Schlesinger, Jr., and the Ideological History of American Liberalism* (Tuscaloosa: The University of Alabama Press, 1994), 130, 134.

14. Leo P. Ribuffo, "Why Is There So Much Conservatism in the United States and Why Do So Few Historians Know Anything About It?" *The American Historical Review* 99 (April 1994): 449.

15. E. J. Dionne, Jr., *They Only Look Dead: Why Progressives Will Dominate the Next Political Era* (New York: Simon and Schuster, 1996), 67, 76; Jack W. Germond and Jules Witcover, *Mad as Hell: Revolt at the Ballot Box, 1992* (New York: Warner Books, 1993), 511–12.

16. Nicholas Lerman, "Hope Against History," *New Republic*, March 13, 1995, 33; Dionne, *They Only Look Dead*, 93, 119, 146–50, 181–82, 279; Michael Nelson, "The Presidency: Clinton and the Cycle of Politics and Policy," in *The Elections of 1992*, ed. Michael Nelson (Washingon, D.C.: CQ Press, 1993), 128, 145, 149; Haynes Johnson and

David S. Broder, *The System: The American Way of Politics at the Breaking Point* (Boston: Little, Brown, 1996), 11, 155, 234; George Stephanopoulos, *All Too Human: A Political Education* (Boston: Little, Brown, 1999), 198, 201.

17. Everett Carll Ladd, "The 1992 Vote for President Clinton: Another Brittle Mandate?" *Political Science Quarterly* 108 (Spring 1993): 1–2; Bert A. Rockman, "Leadership Style and the Clinton Presidency," in *The Clinton Presidency: First Appraisals*, ed. Colin Campbell and Bert A. Rockman (Chatham, N.J.: Chatham House, 1996), 331–32, 351; Michael Barone and Grant Ujifusa, "Postwar Politics," in Michael Barone and Grant Ujifusa, *The Almanac of American Politics 1994* (Washington, D.C.: National Journal, 1993), xxv–xxvi, xxx–xxxi; David G. Lawrence, *The Collapse of the Democratic Presidential Majority: Realignment, Dealignment, and Electoral Change from Franklin Roosevelt to Bill Clinton* (Boulder: Westview Press, 1996), 8–10; Anthony J. Corrado, "The 1992 Presidential Election: A Time for Change?" in *The Parties Respond: Changes in American Parties and Campaigns*, Second Edition, ed. L. Sandy Maisel (Boulder: Westview Press, 1994), 231; David R. Mayhew, "U.S. Policy Waves in Comparative Perspective," in *New Perspectives on American Politics*, ed. Lawrence C. Dodd and Calvin Jillson (Washington, D.C.: CQ Press, 1994), 336; Michael Minkenberg, "The End of Conservatism? Public Opinion and the American Electorate in the 1990s," in *The American Impasse: U.S. Domestic and Foreign Policy after the Cold War*, ed. Michael Minkenberg and Herbert Dittgen (Pittsburgh: The University of Pittsburgh Press, 1996), 147–48.

18. Stanley B. Greenberg, *Middle Class Dreams: The Politics and Power of the New American Majority* (New York: Times Books, 1995), 54, 58, 121, 297; Gwen Ifill, "Democrats Get a New Chairman, and a Warning," *New York Times*, Jan. 22, 1993, A13.

19. Walter Dean Burnham, "The Politics of Repudiation 1992: Edging Toward Upheaval," *The American Prospect*, no. 12 (Winter 1993): 22, 25, 30–33; Walter Dean Burnham, "The Legacy of George Bush: Travails of an Understudy," in *The Election of 1992: Reports and Interpretations*, ed. Gerald M. Pomper (Chatham, N.J.: Chatham House, 1993), 1–2, 15.

20. Adam Clymer, "Theorists Look at '94 Voting: Was It a Major or Minor Trend?" *New York Times*, Sept. 4, 1995, 8; Johnson and Broder, *System*, 562; Colin A. Campbell and Bert A. Rockman, "Introduction," in *Clinton Presidency*, ed. Campbell and Rockman, 11–12; John H. Aldrich and Richard G. Niemi, "The Sixth American Party System: Electoral Change, 1952–1992," in *Broken Contract? Changing Relationships Between Americans and Their Government*, ed. Stephen C. Craig (Boulder: Westview Press, 1996), 105; James E. Campbell, review of *Midterm: The Elections of 1994 in Context*, edited by Philip A. Klinkner, *Political Science Quarterly* 112 (Winter 1997–98): 699; Alfred J. Tuchfarber et al., "The Republican Tidal Wave of 1994: Testing Hypotheses About Realignment, Restructuring, and Rebellion," 694, and Andrew E. Busch, "Political Science and the 1994 Elections: An Exploratory Essay," 710, both in *PS: Political Science and Politics* 28 (Dec. 1995).

21. Gary C. Jacobson, "The 1994 House Elections in Perspective," *Political Science Quarterly* 111 (Summer 1996): 221.

22. Dan Balz and Ronald Brownstein, *Storming the Gates: Protest Politics and the Republican Revival* (Boston: Little, Brown, 1996), 55.

23. Johnson and Broder, *System*, 552.

24. Paul A. Gigot, "Potomac Watch: Beltway Gets Vertigo as Sun, Moon Shift," *Wall Street Journal*, Dec. 9, 1994, A16.

25. Thomas B. Edsall, "The Cultural Revolution of 1994: Newt Gingrich, the Republican Party, and the Third Great Awakening," in Byron E. Shafer et al., *Present Discontents: American Politics in the Very Late Twentieth Century* (Chatham, N.J.: Chatham House, 1997), 136.

26. Ronald Radosh, *Divided They Fell: The Demise of the Democratic Party, 1964–1996* (New York: The Free Press, 1996), ix–x, 234.

27. Michael Barone et al., "Introduction," in Michael Barone et al., *The Almanac of American Politics 1995* (Washington, D.C.: National Journal, 1994), xxiii–xxiv.

28. Richard Reeves, *Running in Place: How Bill Clinton Disappointed America* (Kansas City: Andrews and McMeel, 1996), 76, 78.

29. Tuchfarber et al., "The Republican Tidal Wave of 1994," 691, 694; William G. Mayer, "Changes in Elections and the Party System: 1992 in Historical Perspective," in *The New American Politics: Reflections on Political Change and the Clinton Administration*, ed. Bryan D. Jones (Boulder: Westview Press, 1995), 47–48.

30. Dionne, *They Only Look Dead*, 80; Marjorie Randon Hershey, "The Congressional Elections," in Gerald M. Pomper et al., *The Election of 1996: Reports and Interpretations* (Chatham, N.J.: Chatham House, 1997), 219; Paul Frymer, "The 1994 Electoral Aftershock: Dealignment or Realignment in the South," in *Midterm: The Elections of 1994 in Context*, ed. Philip A. Klinkner (Boulder: Westview Press, 1996), 111–12; David W. Brady et al., "The Perils of Presidential Support: How the Republicans Took the House in the 1994 Midterm Elections," *Political Behavior* 18 (Dec. 1996): 346, 362; Peter Applebome, *Dixie Rising: How the South Is Shaping American Values, Politics, and Culture* (San Diego: Harcourt Brace, 1996), 7, 94, 108; Byron E. Shafer, "The Mid-Term Election of 1994: Upheaval in Search of a Framework," in *The Republican Takeover of Congress*, ed. Dean McSweeney and John E. Owens (New York: St. Martin's Press, 1998), 17.

31. Stanley, "The Parties, the President, and the 1994 Midterm Elections," 197; Frymer, "The Electoral Aftershock," 99; Alan I. Abramowitz and Kyle L. Saunders, "Ideological Realignment in the U.S. Electorate," *The Journal of Politics* 60 (Aug. 1998): 635.

32. Walter Dean Burnham, "Drift or Mandate?" *The American Prospect*, no. 27 (July–August 1996): 43–44, 46; Walter Dean Burnham, "Realignment Lives: The 1994 Earthquake and Its Implications," in *Clinton Presidency*, ed. Campbell and Rockman, 363, 367, 369–71, 373–75.

33. Clymer, "Theorists Look at '94 Voting," 8; Dionne, *They Only Look Dead*, 66; Everett Carll Ladd, "1994 Vote: Against the Backdrop of Continuing Realignment," in *America at the Polls 1994*, ed. Everett Carll Ladd (Storrs, Conn.: Roper Center, 1995), 19–20, 22; E. J. Dionne, Jr., "Back From the Dead: Neoprogressivism in the '90s," *The American Prospect*, no. 28 (Sept.–Oct. 1996), 26–27; Wilson Carey McWilliams, *The Politics of Disappointment: American Elections, 1976–94* (Chatham, N.J.: Chatham House, 1995), 196–97; David R. Mayhew, "Innovative Midterm Elections," in *Midterm*, ed. Klinkner, 169.

34. Greenberg, *Middle Class Dreams*, 263; Dionne, *They Only Look Dead*, 14, 82, 88–89, 147, 176; Stanley, "The Parties, the President, and the 1994 Midterm Elections," 193–95; Wilson Carey McWilliams, "The Meaning of the Election," in Pomper et al., *Election of 1996*, 243; Ruy A. Teixeira, "Economics of the 1994 Election and U.S. Politics Today," *Challenge* 39 (Jan.–Feb.1996): 27–29; Clyde Wilcox, *The Latest American Revolution? The 1994 Elections and Their Implications for Governance* (New York: St. Martin's Press, 1995), 9, 83; Philip A. Klinkner, "Court and Country in American Politics: The Democratic Party and the 1994 Election," in *Midterm*, ed. Klinkner, 71; James W. Ceaser and Andrew W. Busch, *Losing to Win: The 1996 Elections and American Politics* (Lanham, Md.: Rowman and Littlefield, 1997), 34–35.

35. Campbell and Rockman, "Introduction," 12; A. James Reichley, "Get Ready for 60 Years of GOP Rule," *Wall Street Journal*, Dec. 5, 1994, A14.

36. Theda Skocpol and Stanley B. Greenberg, "A Politics for Our Time," in *The New Majority: Toward a Popular Progressive Politics*, ed. Stanley B. Greenberg and Theda Skocpol (New Haven: Yale University Press, 1997), 5; Robert W. Speel, *Changing Patterns of Voting in the Northern United States: Electoral Realignment, 1952–1996* (University Park, Penn.: The Pennsylvania State University Press, 1998), 203–4; Ceaser and Busch, *Losing to Win*, 158.

37. Paul Starr, "The Clinton Presidency, Take Three," *The American Prospect*, no. 30 (Feb. 1997), 7; Hershey, "The Congressional Elections," 227; McWilliams, "The Meaning of the Election," 258; Speel, *Changing Patterns of Voting in the Northern United States*, 195.

38. Walter Dean Burnham, "Bill Clinton: Riding the Tiger," in Pomper et al., *Election of 1996*, 7–8.

39. Michael Barone et al., "Introduction," in Michael Barone et al., *The Almanac of American Politics 1998* (Washington, D.C.: National Journal, 1997), 22, 37.

40. Robin Toner, "Coming Home from the Revolution," *New York Times*, Nov. 10, 1996, E1; Scott Keeter, "Public Opinion and the Election," 120, and McWilliams, "The Meaning of the Election," 251, both in Pomper et al., *Election of 1996*; Byron E. Shafer, "The Partisan Legacy: Are There Any New Democrats? (And by the Way, Was There a Republican Revolution?)," in *Clinton Legacy*, ed. Campbell and Rockman, 25–27.

41. Everett Carll Ladd, "1996 Vote: The 'No Majority' Realignment Continues," *Political Science Quarterly* 112 (Spring 1997): 2–3, 10; Paul R. Abramson, John H. Aldrich, and David W. Rhode, *Change and Continuity in the 1996 and 1998 Elections* (Washington, D.C.: CQ Press, 1999), 282; Shafer, "The Partisan Legacy," 28–29.

42. Nicholas Lemann, "The New American Consensus," *New York Times Magazine*, Nov. 1, 1998, 38.

43. Adam Nagourney, "A Party So Happy It Could Burst," *New York Times*, Nov. 15, 1998, section 4, 3.

44. R. W. Apple, Jr., "Talking Like a Front-Runner," *New York Times*, Jan. 24, 1996, A12; Alison Mitchell, "President and Allies Hail 'Milestone,'" *New York Times*, Aug. 6, 1997, A14; Michael Lind, *Up from Conservatism: Why the Right Is Wrong for America* (New York: The Free Press, 1996), 236; David Sanders, "The New Electoral Battleground," in Anthony King et al., *New Labour Triumphs: Britain at the Polls* (Chatham, N.J.: Chatham House, 1998), 210; Ceaser and Busch, *Losing to Win*, 171; Alexander P. Lamis, "Southern Politics in the 1990s," in *Southern Politics in the 1990s*, ed. Alexander P. Lamis (Baton Rouge: Louisiana State University Press, 1999), 402.

45. Todd S. Purdam, "Facets of Clinton," *New York Times Magazine*, May 19, 1996, 36–37, 77–78; Richard L. Berke, "Fulfilling '92's Promise, Capturing a '96 Issue," *New York Times*, Aug. 1, 1996, A25; Gail Collins, "Why Newt Gingrich Is in Deep, Deep Trouble," *New York Times*, Nov. 6, 1998, A32; John B. Judis, "The Hunted," *New Republic*, April 17 and 24, 2000, 34; Richard Norton Smith, "Rockefeller Republicans, in All but Name," *New York Times*, July 16, 2000, Section 4, WK15; Alison Mitchell, "Trying to Escape the Purgatory of Parity," *New York Times*, Nov. 26, 2000, Section 4, WK3; Arthur Paulson, *Realignment and Party Renewal: Understanding American Electoral Politics at the Turn of the Twenty-First Century* (Westport, Conn.: Praeger, 2000), xi, xv, 173, 180; E. J. Dionne, Jr., "The Clinton Enigma: Seeking Consensus, Breeding Discord," in Gerald M. Pomper et al., *The Election of 2000: Reports and Interpretations* (New York: Chatham House, 2001), 5–7.

46. Michael Barone, "The 49% Nation," in Michael Barone and Richard E. Cohen with Charles E. Cook, Jr., *The Almanac of American Politics 2002* (Washington, D.C.: National Journal, 2001), 21–22; Daniel Wirls, "Voting Behavior: The Balance of Power in American Politics," 93, 106, and Gary C. Jacobson, "Congress: Elections and Stalemate," 188, both in *The Elections of 2000*, ed. Michael Nelson (Washington, D.C.: CQ Press, 2001); James W. Ceaser and Andrew E. Busch, *The Perfect Tie: The True Story of the 2000 Presidential Election* (Lanham, Md.: Rowman and Littlefield, 2001), 3–4, 6, 25, 166; Adam Clymer, "And the Winner Is Gore, If They Got the Math Right," *New York Times*, Sept. 4, 2000, A15; Ruy Teixeira and Joel Rogers, *America's Forgotten Majority: Why the White Working Class Still Matters* (New York: Basic Books, 2000), 136–37, 172–73; Earl Black and Merle Black, *The Rise of Southern Republicans* (Cambridge: The Belknap Press of Harvard University Press, 2002), 4, 25, 36, 205.

47. Walter Dean Burnham, "Whole Lotta Shakin' Goin' On," *Nation*, April 17, 2000, 11–15.

48. Kevin Phillips, "His Fraudulency the Second?" *American Prospect*, Jan. 29, 2001, 22–25.

49. John B. Judis and Ruy Teixeira, "Majority Rules," *New Republic*, Aug. 5 and 12, 2002, 18–23.

CHAPTER FOURTEEN

1. Donald E. Stokes and John J. Di Iulio, Jr., "The Setting: Valence Politics in Modern Elections," in *The Elections of 1992*, ed. Michael Nelson (Washington, D.C.: CQ Press, 1993), 6; David Sanders, "The New Electoral Battleground," in Anthony King et al., *New Labour Triumphs: Britain at the Polls* (Chatham, N.J.: Chatham House, 1998), 221–22; Allan J. Lichtman, *The Keys to the White House, 1996: A Surefire Guide to Predicting the Next President* (Lanham, Md.: Madison Books, 1996), 1, 9–10; Larry J. Sabato, "The November Vote: A Status Quo Election," in *Toward the Millenium: The Elections of 1996*, ed. Larry J. Sabato (Boston: Allyn and Bacon, 1997), 159–60.

2. Morris P. Fiorina, "Professionalism, Realignment, and Representation," *The American Political Science Review* 91 (March 1997): 156–57; David W. Brady, "The Causes and Consequences of Divided Government: Toward a New Theory of American Politics?" *The American Political Science Review* 87 (March 1993): 189–94; Gary C. Jacobson, "The Persistence of Democratic House Majorities," 76, 78, 81, and Morris P. Fiorina, "Divided Government in the States," 179, both in *The Politics of Divided Government*, ed. Gary W. Cox and Samuel Kernell (Boulder: Westview Press, 1991); Lee Sigelman, Paul J. Wahlbeck, and Emmett H. Buell, Jr., "Vote Choice and the Preference for Divided Government: Lessons of 1992," *American Journal of Political Science* 41 (July 1997): 879–81; Franco Mattei and John S. Howes, "Competing Explanations of Split-Ticket Voting in American National Elections," *American Politics Quarterly* 28 (July 2000): 379–85; Gary C. Jacobson, *The Electoral Origins of Divided Government: Competition in U.S. House Elections, 1946–1988* (Boulder: Westview Press, 1990), xv, 3, 105–6, 119–20, 133.

3. Peter F. Nardulli, "The Concept of a Critical Realignment, Electoral Behavior, and Political Change," *The American Political Science Review* 89 (March 1995): 12–15; Harold W. Stanley and Richard G. Niemi, "Partisanship and Group Support Over Time,"

in *Controversies in Voting Behavior*, ed. Richard G. Niemi and Herbert F. Weisberg (Washington, D.C.: CQ Press, 1993), 366; Robert W. Speel, *Changing Patterns of Voting in the Northern United States: Electoral Realignment, 1952–1996* (University Park, Penn.: The Pennsylvania State University Press, 1998), 2–5, 7, 11, 62, 65, 92, 97, 161, 201, 203; Alan I. Abramowitz and Kyle L. Saunders, "Ideological Realignment in the U.S. Electorate," *The Journal of Politics* 60 (Aug. 1998): 648.

4. Peter F. Nardulli, "A Normal Vote Approach to Electoral Change: Presidential Elections, 1828–1984," *Political Behavior* 16 (Dec. 1994): 498; William G. Mayer, "Mass Partisanship, 1946–1996," in Byron E. Shafer et al., *Partisan Approaches to Postwar American Politics* (New York: Chatham House, 1998), 190.

5. Warren E. Miller and J. Merrill Shanks, *The New American Voter* (Cambridge: Harvard University Press, 1996), 117, 119, 130, 149, 184, 387, 495, 506, 512.

6. Heinz Eulau, *Micro-Macro Dilemmas in Political Science: Personal Pathways Through Complexity* (Norman: University of Oklahoma Press, 1996), 139; Miller and Shanks, *The New American Voter*, v.

7. Miller and Shanks, *New American Voter*, 34–35, 46–47, 119, 139–40, 142–43, 149–50, 153–55, 157–61, 163, 184.

8. Walter Dean Burnham, "Realignment Lives: The 1994 Earthquake and Its Implications," in *The Clinton Presidency: First Appraisals*, ed. Colin Campbell and Bert A. Rockman (Chatham, N.J.: Chatham House, 1996), 371; Walter Dean Burnham, "Pattern Recognition and 'Doing' Political History: Art, Science, or Bootless Enterprise," in *The Dynamics of American Politics: Approaches and Interpretations*, ed. Lawrence C. Dodd and Calvin Jillson (Boulder: Westview Press, 1994), 62, 72, 74, 79; Walter Dean Burnham, "The Legacy of George Bush: Travails of an Understudy," in *The Election of 1992: Reports and Interpretations*, ed. Gerald M. Pomper (Chatham, N.J.: Chatham House, 1993), 21–22; Walter Dean Burnham, review of *The Thirteen Keys to the Presidency* by Allan J. Lichtman and Ken DeCell, *The Journal of Interdisciplinary History* 22 (Sept. 1991): 153; Walter Dean Burnham, review of *The Politics Presidents Make* by Stephen Skowronek, *The American Political Science Review* 88 (June 1994), 486.

9. Everett Carll Ladd, "1996 Vote: The 'No Majority' Realignment Continues," *Political Science Quarterly* 112 (Spring 1997): 13–14, 16–17, 23; Everett Carll Ladd, "The 1994 Congressional Elections: The Postindustrial Realignment Continues," *Political Science Quarterly* 110 (Spring 1995): 1–3; Everett Carll Ladd, review of *Changing Patterns of Voting in the Northern United States* by Robert W. Speel, *Political Science Quarterly* 114 (Summer 1999): 315–16.

10. Karen Orren and Stephen Skowronek, "Regimes and Regime Building in American Government: A Review of Literature on the 1940s," *Political Science Quarterly* 113 (Winter 1998–99): 690, 695; Karen Orren and Stephen Skowronek, "Beyond the Iconography of Order: Notes for a 'New Institutionalism,'" in *The Dynamics of American Politics*, ed. Dodd and Jillson, 313–14, 316; Karen Orren and Stephen Skowronek, "Order and Time in Institutional Study: A Brief for the Historical Approach," in *Political Science in History: Research Programs and Political Traditions*, ed. James Farr et al. (New York: Cambridge University Press, 1995), 303; Stephen Skowronek, "The Setting: Change and Continuity in the Politics of Leadership," in *The Elections of 2000*, ed. Michael Nelson (Washington, D.C.: CQ Press, 2001), 4; Stephen Skowronek, *The Politics Presidents Make: Leadership from John Adams to Bill Clinton* (Cambridge: The Belknap Press of Harvard University

Press, 1997), xii, 6–8, 469; Sidney Milkis and Jerome M. Mileur, "Introduction: The New Deal, Then and Now," in *The New Deal and the Triumph of Liberalism*, ed. Sidney Milkis and Jerome M. Mileur (Amherst, Mass.: The University of Massachusetts Press, 2002), 6.

11. David Plotke, *Building a Democratic Political Order: Reshaping American Liberalism in the 1930s and 1940s* (New York: Cambridge University Press, 1996), vii, 71–72, 189–92, 216–17, 219.

12. Poltke, *Building a Democratic Political Order*, 355–56, 372.

13. Sean Q. Kelly, "Punctuated Change and the Era of Divided Government," in *New Perspectives on American Politics*, ed. Lawrence C. Dodd and Calvin Jillson (Washington, D.C.: CQ Press, 1994), 162–63, 165–66, 178.

14. Byron E. Shafer, "The Mid-Term Election of 1994: Upheaval in Search of a Framework," in *The Republican Takeover of Congress*, ed. Dean McSweeney and John E. Owens (New York: St. Martin's Press, 1998), 20–22, 27–28.

15. Alexander P. Lamis, "Southern Politics in the 1990s," in *Southern Politics in the 1990s*, ed. Alexander P. Lamis (Baton Rouge: Louisiana State University Press, 1999), 401, 455.

16. Dan Balz and Ronald Brownstein, *Storming the Gates: Protest Politics and the Republican Revival* (Boston: Little, Brown, 1996), 363–64.

17. G. Calvin Mackenzie, *The Irony of Reform: Roots of American Political Disenchantment* (Boulder: Westview Press, 1996), 39–40.

18. Harold I. Gullan, *The Upset That Wasn't: Harry S. Truman and the Crucial Election of 1948* (Chicago: Ivan R. Dee, 1998), 212–14.

19. David G. Lawrence, *The Collapse of the Democratic Presidential Majority: Realignment, Dealignment, and Electoral Change from Franklin Roosevelt to Bill Clinton* (Boulder: Westview Press, 1996), 5–8, 11–12, 30, 171.

20. John H. Aldrich and Richard G. Niemi, "The Sixth American Party System: Electoral Change, 1952–1992," in *Broken Contract? Changing Relationships Between Americans and Their Government*, ed. Stephen C. Craig (Boulder: Westview Press, 1996), 88, 100–101, 104–5, 107.

21. [Richard G. Niemi and Herbert F. Weisberg], "Dealignment and Realignment in the Current Period," in *Controversies in Voting Behavior*, ed. Richard G. Niemi and Herbert F. Weisberg (Washington, D.C.: CQ Press, 1993), 326–27.

22. William G. Mayer, "Changes in Elections and the Party System: 1992 in Historical Perspective," in *The New American Politics: Reflections on Political Change and the Clinton Administration*, ed. Bryan D. Jones (Boulder: Westview Press, 1995), 26–29, 49.

Index

About the Author

Theodore Rosenof was born in Newark, New Jersey, in 1943 and has been an avowed "political junkie" since the 1952 Eisenhower–Stevenson campaign. He graduated from Rutgers University in 1965 and received his doctorate from the University of Wisconsin in 1970. After a period of research positions in Wisconsin and teaching posts in Texas he joined the faculty of Mercy College, New York, in 1979 where he is now a professor of History. In addition to articles and reviews, Rosenof is the author of three previous books: *Dogma, Depression, and the New Deal*; *Patterns of Political Economy in America*; and *Economics in the Long Run*.